Microprocessor and Microcomputer Data Digest

Microprocessor and Microcomputer Data Digest

by W. H. Buchsbaum, Sc.D.
and
Gina Weissenberg, M.E.E.

Reston Publishing Company, Inc.
A Prentice-Hall Company
Reston, Virginia

Library of Congress Cataloging in Publication Data

Buchsbaum, Walter H.

Microprocessor and microcomputer data digest.

1. Microprocessors—Handbooks, manuals, etc.
2. Microprocessors—Catalogs. I. Weisenberg, Gina. II. Title.
TK7895.M5B83 1983 621.3819'58 82-21620
ISBN 0-8359-4381-X

A Prentice-Hall Company
Reston, Virginia 22090

10 9 8 7 6 5 4 3 2

Printed in the United States of America

Interior designed by Dan McCauley

TABLE OF CONTENTS

ACKNOWLEDGMENTS

This book would not have been possible without the cooperation and assistance of all microprocessor and microcomputer IC manufacturers. Their technical publications staffs provided complete catalog data as well as advance technical data sheets which enabled us to bring you a completely up-to-date *Data Digest*.

We want to express our special appreciation to those manufacturers who granted us permission to reproduce specific logic or block diagrams, or the pertinent portions of the appendix. These companies are listed alphabetically below:

Advanced Micro Devices, Inc.
American Microsystems, Inc.
Commodore Business Machines, Inc.
Data General Corp.
Fairchild Camera & Instrument Corp.
General Instrument Corp.
Harris Semiconductor
Hitachi America, Ltd.
Intel Corporation
Motorola Inc.
National Semiconductor Corp.
NEC Electronics USA, Inc.
Oki Semiconductor, Inc.
RCA Solid State Div.
Rockwell International
Sanyo Semiconductor Inc.
Signetics Corporation
Texas Instruments Incorporated
Western Digital Corporation
Zilog

ABOUT THIS BOOK

The continuing growth of the microprocessor field and the many varieties already in use make it extremely difficult to keep a full set of technical data for each type number. Anyone involved in the maintenance, repair, troubleshooting, kit building, experimenting and electronics education field is bound to run into microprocessors at some time or other, because these key integrated circuits (ICs) are now used in anything from a TV receiver, an electronic game or toy, or a microwave oven to the dashboard of an automobile and a supermarket cash register. The detailed technical data for a particular microprocessor is essential only to the engineer involved in the original design of the device in which that IC is used. All other electronics personnel really need only a selected portion of the fullscale technical data sheets.

This book provides all of the essential technical data for each microprocessor IC that is currently listed as an off-the-shelf, "standard" item. This does not include those special ICs made only on a custom order and not listed in the manufacturer's manuals. This book does include microcomputers, considered a microprocessor which contains all of the other "on-board" functions to make it a complete computer. We also include slice microprocessors, ICs that contain only a portion of a complete central processing unit (CPU) and that require additional ICs to perform as a CPU. A new version, the microcontroller, is basically a CPU microprocessor, which has only a limited range of function. These ICs are also included in this book.

To enable even those readers not familiar with microprocessors to use the technical data provided in this book, the first chapter covers the fundamentals of microprocessors, explains the functions by means of detailed block diagrams and describes all of the classifications and categories. The use of auxiliary ICs, such as special interface ICs, random access memory (RAM) ICs and various controllers is discussed briefly. All of the key electrical parameters are defined and the principles of the "IN-CIRCUIT QUICK-TEST" are explained.

Each of the different categories of microprocessors is covered in numerical sequence, allowing the reader to look up any microprocessor IC and find all necessary information on two opposing pages. Each IC entry contains a pin connection diagram, a description of each pin connection and a brief functional description of that particular microprocessor, together with any references to similar ICs and special features. A functional block diagram is included to illustrate the IC's operation. The unique feature, however, is the "IN-CIRCUIT QUICK-TEST." This information enables the reader to test the IC in the actual circuit, with a minimum of test equipment. We present tests for two levels of confidence, wherever practical. The first "IN-CIRCUIT QUICK-TEST" provides a 75% confidence level that the test will show whether the IC is defective or not. The second test, usually more complex, provides a 90% confidence level. This information is not available in any manufacturer's manual, but offers the reader of this book the great advantage of being able to troubleshoot microprocessors without unsoldering leads or removing a complex and costly IC from the printed circuit board.

Troubleshooting electronic equipment that contains microprocessors can be quite difficult. With the *Microprocessor Data Digest* much of the difficulty is removed and anyone with a basic knowledge of electronics can use this book along with his test equipment to save time and unneccessary replacement ICs. A single repair job more than pays for the price of this book and once the reader has used it he will never want to start on a microprocessor troubleshooting job without his copy of *Microprocessor Data Digest* on the bench.

W. H. Buchsbaum, Sc.D.
G. Weissenberg, M.E.E.

HOW TO USE THIS BOOK

As its title indicates, this book is a digest of the technical data supplied by the manufacturers for their various types of microprocessor integrated circuits. The tab arrangement at the edge tells you immediately that there are four classes of microprocessors: *Slice Microprocessors (μP), Central Processing Units (CPU), Microcomputers (μC)* and *Microcontrollers (μController).* An explanation and detailed description of these four classes is contained in Chapter 1, but for now we can define the Slice μP as an integrated circuit (IC) that contains less than a full CPU IC would. The CPU itself is the "original" μP, an IC that contains all of the elements and can function as central processing unit in a computer. A microcomputer (μC) is defined as a CPU plus both a random access memory (RAM) and a read-only memory (ROM), on a single IC, capable of performing actual computer functions. The μController is really a μC that is limited to perform controlling functions, but cannot really act as computer. There is no "standard" industry-wide definition for these four classes, but the majority of manufacturer's technical manuals and catalogs uses these definitions.

Each of the four classes is arranged according to the "size" of the microprocessors in it. Size means the number of binary bits that the device can operate on simultaneously. As explained in Chapter One, μPs are designed to handle 4,8,16, and 32 bits in parallel and are therefore referred to as "4-bit Slice μP," "8-bit CPU," "16-bit μC," or "4-bit μController." Within each sub-class (bit-size), the microprocessors are listed in numerical sequence.

The number assigned to a particular μP often appears arbitrary, particularly when a "family" or a series of μPs is considered. Usually a manufacturer designs a new μP for a particular application. If that IC is successful and finds other applications, a series of variations is developed. Typical of this is the use of letters, added to the original design number which indicate, for example, an industrial version (I), a military version (M), a low power version, a higher clock speed version, etc. Different manufacturers use different letter symbols, or, to make matters more confusing, they even introduce different type numbers.

In many instances a series is indicated by the first two or three numbers, with the remainder denoting variations of the basic μP design. In the 6500 series, for example, the basic 8-bit CPU (6500) is available with 1.0 MHz clock speed. The "A" version accepts up to 2.0 MHz clock signals. There are also the 6502, 6503, 6504, 6505, 6506, 6507, 6512, and 6513, each available in the 1.0 MHz or the 2.0 MHz ("A") version. All of these μPs are software compatible, but vary in their input/output capabilities and have different packages and pin configurations. All are listed, in numerical order, after the description and block diagram of the 6500, which is the "original" 8-bit CPU of this series.

Most μP ICs are made by more than one manufacturer and the manufacturer listed on the title page for each μP is either the one who originated this particular device or the one who supplied us with technical data first. We have, in almost every instance, been able to list other manufacturers making the same device, but occasionally the "second source" has not been announced at the time we went to press. In addition to the actual type number, there are letters preceding the number which indicate the manufacturer's own coding. The 6800 8-bit CPU is listed as MC 6800 if bought from Motorola, F 6800 from Fairchild, S 6800 from AMI, HD 6800 from Hitachi, and MBM 6800 from Fujitsu. To avoid confusion, we have omitted these manufacturers designations on the margin labels and on the illustrations. To look up a μP by type, simply omit any letters preceding the type number and scan through the numerical listing in the table of contents.

Each μP type is introduced by a brief description that covers its essential features. Next there is a list of every signal or voltage with a brief description and an indication whether it is an input (I) or output (O). This list corresponds to the pin configuration diagram appearing on the same page. As standard practice, all pin configurations are shown as viewed from the top of the IC, and the key slot which is between the lowest and highest pin numbers as well as the dot identifying the number one pin are included. A few manufacturers do not provide the dot identifyer, but all include the slot.

Special features of each μP as well as notes and other manufacturers who make the same μP are included in the specific data digest. The block diagram illustrates how the various features and functions are implemented. Unfortunately, there are great variations in the way different manufacturers show these features. Some provide very detailed diagrams while others rely on the reader's technical knowledge to fill in a fairly general block diagram. We have tried to select the most detailed diagrams available in each case.

Probably the most unique and useful feature of this book is the IN-CIRCUIT QUICK-TEST section provided for each μP. It gives the reader a means to test the μP without disconnecting anything, without disturbing the operation of any part of the device in which the μP works, and it can be done with standard test equipment. A good voltmeter and an oscilloscope that can handle the clock signal of the μP under test are necessary. For the 75% confidence level tests any oscilloscope used for color TV servicing (4 to 5 MHz) will be satisfactory. In order to perform the 90% confidence level tests a dual trace oscilloscope is really necessary, but it is possible, though time consuming, to use a single trace oscilloscope and record the first signal on the screen with a grease pencil and then compare that tracing with the signal that would appear on the second trace.

The principle behind the IN-CIRCUIT QUICK-TEST is that first one determines that the correct DC voltages appear, and then considers certain key signals. For the 75% confidence level tests it is necessary to "see" the clock signal. As described in Chapter One, all of the μP functions depend on the clock signal. If that signal cannot be seen on the oscilloscope, the μP cannot be considered to function properly. The next test involves an output signal that is a submultiple of the clock signal. If the μP has a functioning clock and at least one output signal, it indicates that at least some key portions in the μP must be operating. An output signal that is the result of a number of internal operations, such as a "data ready", "valid address enable," or "start fetch cycle" signal is usually used.

The 90% confidence level is obtained by adding two more tests to those that must have been passed for the 75% confidence level. For these two tests output signals that are synchronized with the clock are usually used. By observing them on a dual trace oscilloscope it is possible to ensure that their amplitudes are essentially the same, and that rise and fall times are also alike. Logic signal amplitudes and timing characteristics are usually standardized for a particular μP. When all of these tests are performed correctly there is at least 90% certainty that the μP is operating correctly.

Replacing defective μPs usually requires an exact replacement. In a few instances it is possible to use a variation of the same type as replacement and this is indicated at the end of the IN-CIRCUIT QUICK-TEST section. Microcomputers include a ROM and when replacing a defective μC it is essential that the replacement contains the same information in its ROM. This usually means that it is necessary to obtain the replacement μC from the manufacturer of the device in which the μC is used, rather than from the μC manufacturer. The same applies to μControllers.

ICs are generally quite reliable and the likelihood of a defect in the μP is relatively small. Before attempting to test the μP, be sure that the defect is not in some other portion of device in which the μP is used. Capacitors, resistors, connectors, and the printed circuit board itself are more likely trouble sources than the μP. For a detailed guide to troubleshooting electronic devices we refer the reader to *Tested Electronics Troubleshooting Methods*, 2nd Edition, Prentice-Hall, '83, by W. H. Buchsbaum.

SUMMARY

Tabs indicate microprocessor slice (μP), central processing units (CPU), microcomputers (μC), and microcontrollers (μController). Within each tab section μPs are listed by "bit size" and within each "bit size" they are listed numerically.

To find a function and "bit size"—an 8-bit μC, for example—use the table of contents to find the page where that sub-class starts.

If you are looking for a particular μP by number, look it up in the numerical listing which is included in the table of contents.

If more information than is contained on the pages describing that μP is needed, try the appendix. Appendix A contains a list of all μP manufacturers, including phone number and the address of their main office. Appendix B contains dimensioned drawings of all standard DIPs (dual in-line package). Appendix C contains electrical characteristics for eight IC technologies as exemplified by typical μPs. This includes TTL, CMOS, HMOS, NMOS, PMOS, P^2MOS, I^2L and I^3L integrated circuits.

Before suspecting a defective μP, try troubleshooting the components and circuits associated with it. Then, if you are certain that the external circuitry is not defective, apply the IN-CIRCUIT QUICK-TEST method to determine if the μP is the source of the trouble.

CHAPTER 1

MICROPROCESSOR FUNDAMENTALS

In the area of electronics and computers, the word "microprocessor" has become the popular buzz word and an expression for everything that is new, small, powerful, and magical. This book contains the essential technical data needed by anyone working with microprocessors and in this chapter we cover some of the terminology, operations, and functions of this electronic miracle.

The term microprocessor is usually applied to any kind of integrated circuit (IC) that performs the key functions of a central processing unit, the center of the action in any computer. Microprocessors (μP), however, are available in a variety of versions, each incorporating specific features or attributes and, in some cases, the word microprocessor is incorrectly applied to what is, in effect, a microcomputer (μC).

The vast majority of μPs are either central processing units (CPU), or complete μC. Variations are the microprocessor slice, sometimes called slice-processor and the microcontroller (μ Controller). The microprocessor slice, as the name implies, provides only some of the microprocessor functions on a single IC. It usually requires several such microprocessor slices, together with auxilliary circuits, to make up a single CPU. Microprocessor slice arrangements are useful for special applications where high-speed performance of some of the elements of the CPU is more important than the smallest size possible when all functions are contained on a single IC. A typical example is the case where a high-speed arithmetic logic unit (ALU) is used together with ordinary speed operating functions in the CPU. For such applications it may be worthwhile to employ several microprocessor slices ICs, instead of a single microprocessor IC.

Microcontrollers are usually special purpose microcomputers which are preprogrammed to perform specific control tasks. These devices usually lack the flexibility of performing arithmetic and other functions as directed by a variety of programs but are solely designed to control some other electronic circuits and devices according to single, predetermined programs.

A microcomputer (μC) is generally defined as a single IC which contains a CPU, a read-only memory (ROM), a random-access memory (RAM), and all the interconnecting bus and port facilities that would make up a small, limited capacity computer. There are some microprocessors which can be used either as a CPU or a μC. These devices usually have a ROM and sometimes also a RAM and can be programmed to function either as a self-contained μC or as a very flexible, powerful CPU. In this book, any IC that contains both ROM and RAM, will be classified as a microcomputer (μC). If a microprocessor contains only a ROM, or only a RAM, it will be classified as a CPU since that will be its most frequent application.

For those who are not familiar with computers, CPUs, ROMs, and RAMs, basic block diagrams and brief operational descriptions are included in this chapter. Individual textbooks could be written on all of these topics, but in the space available here, only the fundamental concepts of each of these essential computer elements is included.

HOW A COMPUTER WORKS

The computer block diagram of Fig. 1-1 shows the essential elements that apply to any kind of computer, whether it be a small personal computer or a large main frame occupying an entire room. The main difference between the various computer sizes will be the number of keyboards, TV displays, disk, memory, and other peripherals connected to the CPU. This, of course, will require a different size and speed CPU, but the essential functions of each of the elements shown in the block diagram of Fig. 1 are always the same.

The CPU acts as the command center, the brain, of the entire system. It receives instructions from the human operator through the keyboard and provides information to the human operator on the TV display. The information that goes in and out of the CPU is generally divided into two categories: the program and the data. The program is in the form of coded instructions which tell the computer what functions to perform, while the data is the information on which the computer is asked to operate. The instruction "ADD" is part of the program, but the numbers that we want the computer to add, are considered data.

In Fig. 1-1, we have shown a separate IC memory and a disk which also serves as memory. The main difference between the two is that, while the IC memory operates faster than the disk, its contents are lost when power is turned off, while the magnetic information on the disk remains available until it is deliberately erased. In most systems, the IC memory is used as temporary storage and information from the disk is loaded into the

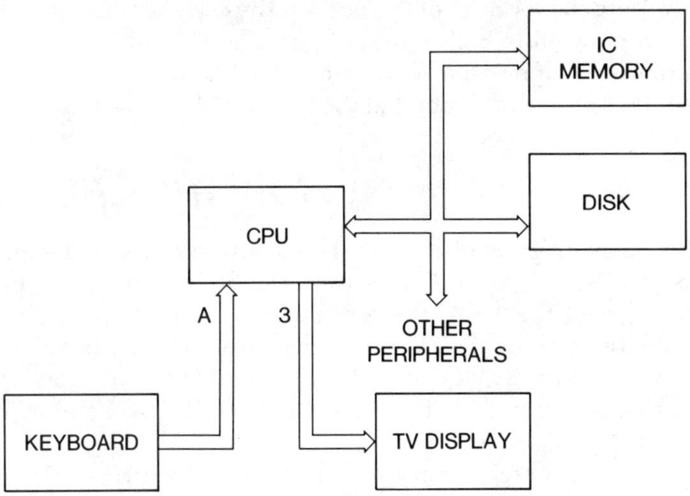

Computer Block Diagram
Fig. 1-1

IC memory so that the CPU can work with the data at relatively high speed.

Other peripherals that are usually part of a computer system, are additional disks, magnetic tape, punched papertape, and, of course, printers which change the computer coded information into the alphanumerics familiar to the human operator. Computer systems are usually designed for a certain number of keyboard and TV displays (generally called CRT terminals), a specific complement of disk drives, IC memories, tape decks, and other peripherals. Whatever the configuration, the CPU is the conductor of this digital orchestra and it alone determines when each functional block in the system performs its assigned task.

Later in this chapter we discuss the bus structure and its operation in detail, but it is worth briefly noting that there are two basically different types of bus structures. As illustrated in Fig. 1-1, connections from the keyboard to the CPU and from the CPU to the TV display are each a uni-directional bus. Signals travel in one well defined direction. The bus connecting the CPU to the IC memory, the disk and other peripherals, is a bidirectional structure and permits the transmission of signals in both directions. A bus is actually just a set of parallel conductors that provides a path for electronic signals.

In normal operation, the information from the disk will reach the IC memory by first going through the CPU. There is a special feature called Direct Memory Access (DMA), available in many computers, that permits portions of the memory to be accessed directly either by the TV display or by a printer. The points marked A, B, and C at the periphery of the CPU block, indicate the location of the ports at these points. The port at point A is an input port while B is an output port and C is an input/output (I/O) port because its signals go both into the CPU and out from it. Further details of these topics are found at the end of the next section.

How the CPU Works

The CPU block diagram of Fig. 1-2 shows only the essential elements that comprise a CPU. As you will note from the block diagrams appearing on the data pages of this book, the configuration of these essential elements varies greatly between different microprocessor CPUs. In some of them, certain functions are expanded, duplicated, and triplicated, but all of them have at least one of each of functions shown in Fig. 1-2 and explained in the following paragraphs.

Information enters from the outside world via the I/O ports. Note that two arrows go from the I/O ports to two functions in the CPU. One arrow carries instructions to the instruction register (IR). This information contains the program instruction on which the control unit will act and

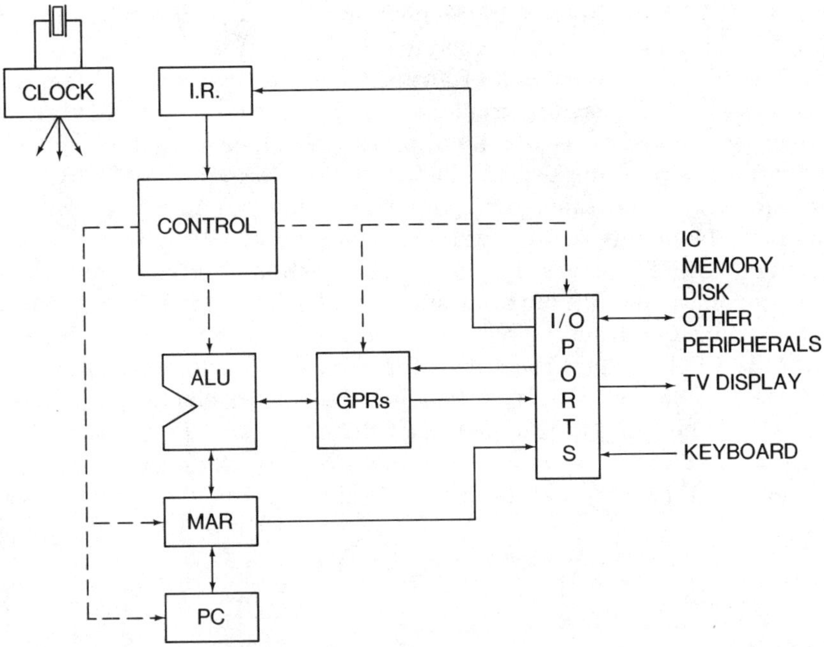

CPU Block Diagram
Fig. 1-2

which will decide what function the CPU will perform next. The data that will be used in this function enters from the I/O ports to the block labelled GPRs (General Purpose Registers). The GPRs are used for temporary storage of data.

Two arrows go from functional blocks to the I/O ports. One of these arrows goes from the GPRs where the output data are temporarily stored. The second path comes from the Memory Address Register (MAR) which sends out the memory address for the next program instruction or data. Once an instruction is stored in the IR, it is decoded and acted upon in the control section. The dotted lines going from the control section to the other elements indicate that signals from the control section determine the function and timing of these other elements. The ALU is the function block that performs both arithmetic and logical functions on the data. Note that the ALU is connected by a double-ended arrow to the GPRs and to the MAR. In general, data go from the GPRs to the ALU where they are manipulated according to the program instructions under the supervision of the control section. If two numbers are to be added, they will go from the GPR to the ALU and their sum will be returned to the GPR for storage in the memory or for display on the TV screen. At the same time, the MAR will furnish the correct memory address for the data that come from the

GPR. The MAR will also supply the next program instructions by indicating the memory location where it is stored.

One of the key elements of any CPU is the program counter (PC) which is updated for each instruction and provides temporary storage for the instruction number. When the program indicates a jump to an entirely different instruction number, the PC will be set through the MAR to that new number. At the same time, this new number will be sent to the memory to fetch the desired program instruction, which will then be entered into the IR. If there is no "jump" instruction, each subsequent step of the program will cause the program counter to be incremented by one, a function controlled from the control section.

Many CPUs contain the circuit for generating a clock signal within the same IC. An external crystal or other resonant element is usually required to determine the frequency of this clock. In a few of the CPUs described in this book, there is no internal clock but clock signals must be supplied from an external source. In either event, clock signals are

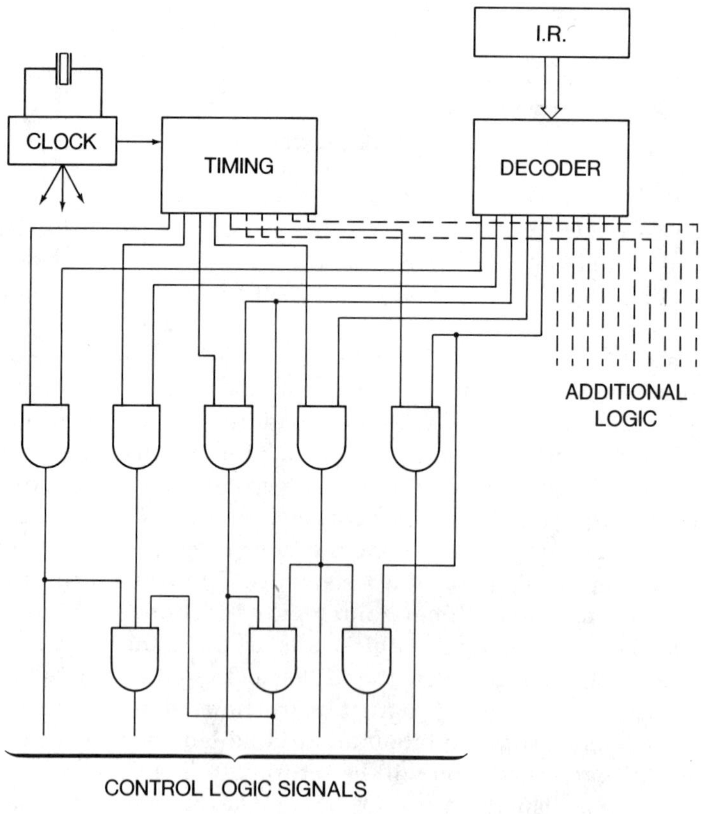

Control Section Logic Diagram
Fig. 1-3

distributed to all of the elements of the CPU and their timing is determined by the control section.

CPU control sections generally consist of a fairly complex array of logic elements, usually gates and inverters, which convert the program instruction in the instruction register (IR) into a series of timed control signals which then activate the other functional elements in the CPU. Fig. 1-3 shows only a few of these gates to illustrate the function of the control section. The information from the IR is first decoded. If the IR is eight bits long, the decoder will have to decode this 8-bit (one byte) wide information into one of 256 possible signals. This means that a CPU with an 8-bit IR, can accept up to 256 separate program instructions. The size of the IR will also determine the size of the control section and all of the registers, counters, etc., within the CPU.

Each of the 256 decoded instructions results in a number of control signals which are applied to various CPU elements only during a particular time slot. These time periods are provided by the timing circuit, an elaborate system of dividers and gates which are synchronized to the squarewave clock signal. While the actual operation of the timing and control signals can be quite complex, Fig. 1-4 shows five basic signals frequently encountered in CPUs. The square wave clock signal is the highest frequency and is counted down to provide proper gates to shift

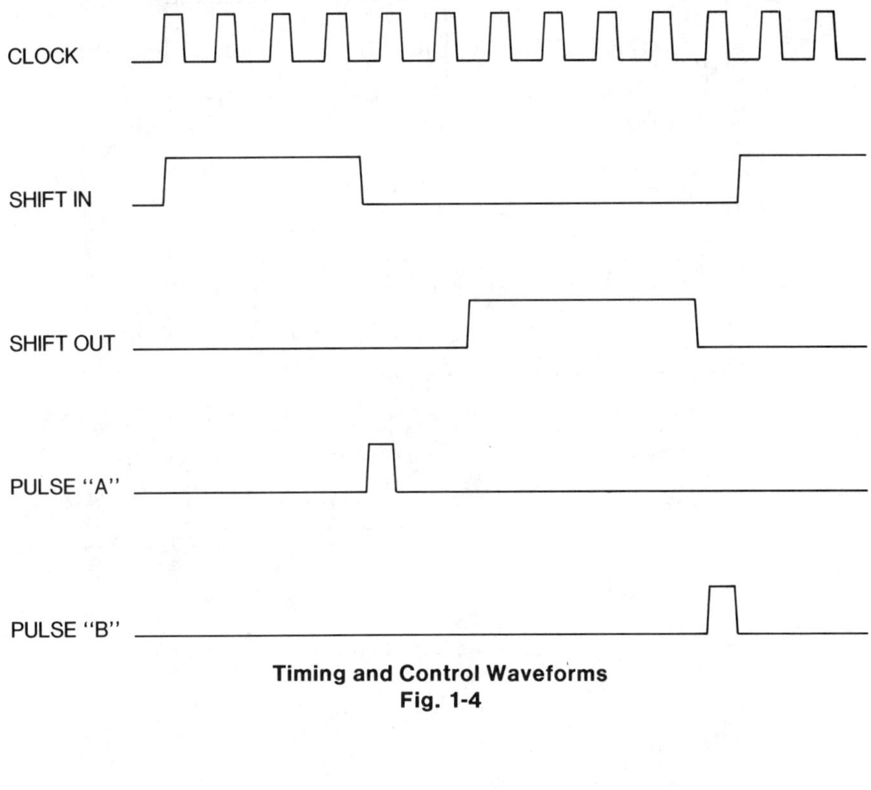

Timing and Control Waveforms
Fig. 1-4

information in and out of a particular functional block. In this example, there is a time period of approximately two clock pulses, after the information is shifted in and before it is again shifted out of some particular register, possibly in a GPR section. If a certain event occurs after the data is shifted in, pulse A will enable certain action. After the information is shifted out, pulse B will occur to initiate another action somewhere else. Detailed manufacturer's instructions usually include timing and control waveforms for all essential parts of the CPU.

The ALU functions are illustrated in Fig. 1-5. Only three functions are shown in this simple version of an ALU. The adder can perform all four

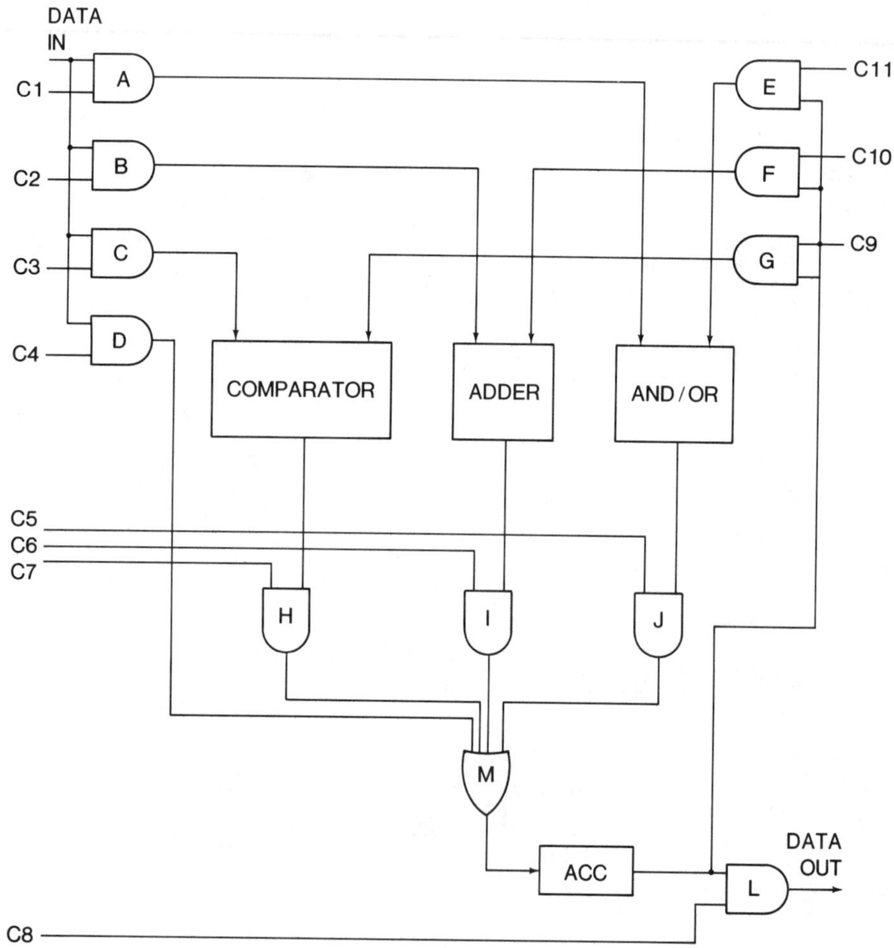

ALU Logic Diagram
Fig. 1-5

arithmetic functions, addition, subtraction, multiplication, and division, by using binary arithmetic. The comparator determines whether two binary numbers are equal or which one is the larger or smaller one. The AND/OR function provides the elementary binary logic based on Boolean algebra. In the CPU block diagram of Fig. 1-2, we show that the ALU has a data-in/data-out connection with a GPR and with the MAR. The data input of the ALU logic diagram is in the upper left hand corner and the data output in the lower right-hand corner.

The ALU logic diagram of Fig. 1-5 is a good example of how control signals from the control section, applied at various times, and at various points, determine the operation of a particular logic block.

Note that the data input is controlled by the four AND circuits A, B, C, and D. Each of these logic gates is controlled by the control signals, C1 through C4, which are generated in the control section of the CPU. In this manner the control section determines whether the data going into the ALU will be applied to the comparator, the adder, or to the AND/OR section. The fourth choice is to apply the data directly via the 4-input OR gate M to the accumulator (ACC). In a similar way, AND gates E, F, and G are controlled by signals C9, C10, and C11 to determine where the output

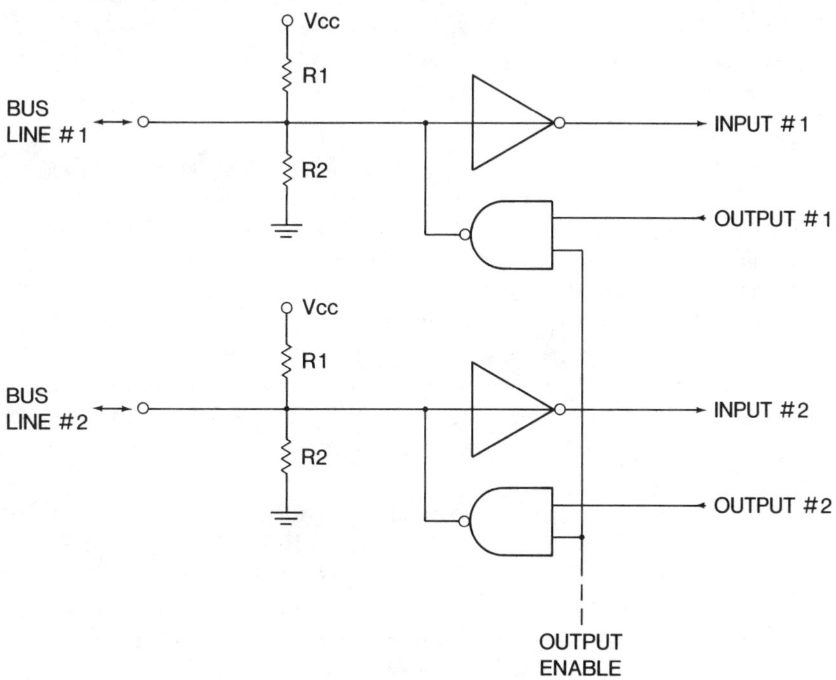

I/O Port Logic Diagram
Fig. 1-6

of the accumulator goes. The remaining control lines and gates determine the outputs of the comparator, adder, AND/OR section, and the accumulator itself.

Many different circuit arrangements are used to implement the input and output (I/O) functions at the port. Fig. 1-6 shows the logic diagram of a bi-directional (I/O) port. Only the bus interface circuitry is shown here, but in almost all I/O ports additional logic circuitry is required to synchronize the interchange of data. In essence, however, each bus line is terminated in a resistive voltage divider, R1, R2, in Fig. 1-6.

When signals originating at some other port reach the inverting amplifier, the output of that stage will be an inverted signal. The control section determines whether or not the input signal will be accepted.

In a similar fashion, the output enable signal, originating at the control section of the CPU, will enable outputs 1, 2, etc. to go through the NAND gate and on to the bus line. Different control systems, such as hand-shaking or synchronized transmission, are used in different computer systems but the key functions of the I/O port logic are the same for any bi-directional port.

Depending on the type of microprocessor and its application, a fairly large number of I/O or only I, or only O ports, may be assigned to a particular IC. In some CPUs the ALU functions will be emphasized and several separate ALUs may be included. In other CPUs, the I/O ports are more important.

How the ROM Works

The ROM is a device in which the desired information is entered at the time the IC is manufactured. Early ROMs used diode matrixes in which some diodes, like fuses, were open-circuit, while other diodes acted in the normal fashion. The resulting pattern of "O" and "1" constituted the information. The ROMs we use today generally consist of individual transistor circuits which make up the memory matrix. In many ways a punched papertape can be considered a ROM, because the information entered by punching the hole pattern in the tape can be read many times, but cannot be altered.

ROMs usually store information that does not change in the course of the computer's operation. Typical of the kind of information that is stored in the ROM would be the fundamental instructions to operate the CPU. In more elaborate computers, the "operating system" and the conversion from BASIC to machine language, might be contained in the ROM. In μC the ROM program is determined by the operational requirements. If a μC is used to operate a microwave oven, for example, all of the instructions and control functions will be stored in the ROM.

The block diagram of a simple ROM IC is shown in Fig. 1-7.

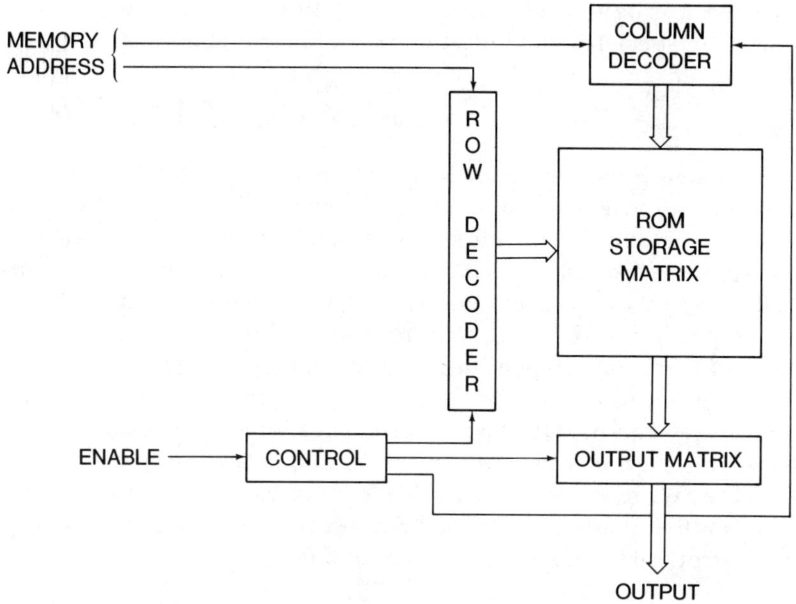

ROM Block Diagram
Fig. 1-7

Whenever information is read-out, the storage matrix is addressed through the column and the row decoders. The information stored in the ROM is then presented, one line at a time, at the output matrix and from there it goes to the bus. The IC's control section activates the row and column decoders and, after a suitable time interval, the output matrix, to generate the output. Timing and clock signals to move address and data are not shown here. More elaborate ROM arrangements are used in many ICs but all of the basic functions shown in Fig. 1-7 must be provided.

While the basic ROM is programmable only at the time of manufacture, different versions are now available which can be programmed and reprogrammed by the user. Some ICs are available in which the desired information can be entered by means of high voltage or high current signals, but, once the ROM is filled this way, it cannot be altered. This so-called PROM (Programmable-Read-Only Memory) is available in different versions, some of which permit erasing all of the PROM's content by exposure to ultra-violet light and then, after a brief time period, the ROM can be programmed again by relatively high voltage or high current signals. Still another variety is the EPROM (Electrically Programmable-Read-Only Memory) in which electrical signals are used instead of the ultra-violet light to erase the information. A ROM version that is halfway between the read-only and the random access memory is the EAROM (Electrically Alterable Read-Only Memory) in which the information stored need not be entirely erased but portions of it can be altered by application of special signal pulses on selected terminals.

HOW THE RAM WORKS

While the name, Random-Access Memory, only indicates the way in which information is retrieved and stored, practically all RAMs are ICs which provide either static or dynamic storage of information. Fig. 1-8 shows the block diagram of a simple static RAM. As in Fig. 1-7, the memory address is entered into row and column decoders. The decoder output enables the addressed portion of the RAM storage matrix which contains, in essence, an array of flip-flops. Depending on the control settings, read or write (R/W), and the presence of an "enable" signal, the information that has been addressed can be either written-in or read-out. The "enable section" turns either the write or the read section on, but data must be present at the input to the "write section" if these data are to be entered at this selected address. Omitted in both Fig. 1-7 and Fig. 1-8 are the timing or clock signals which control the in and out movement of data.

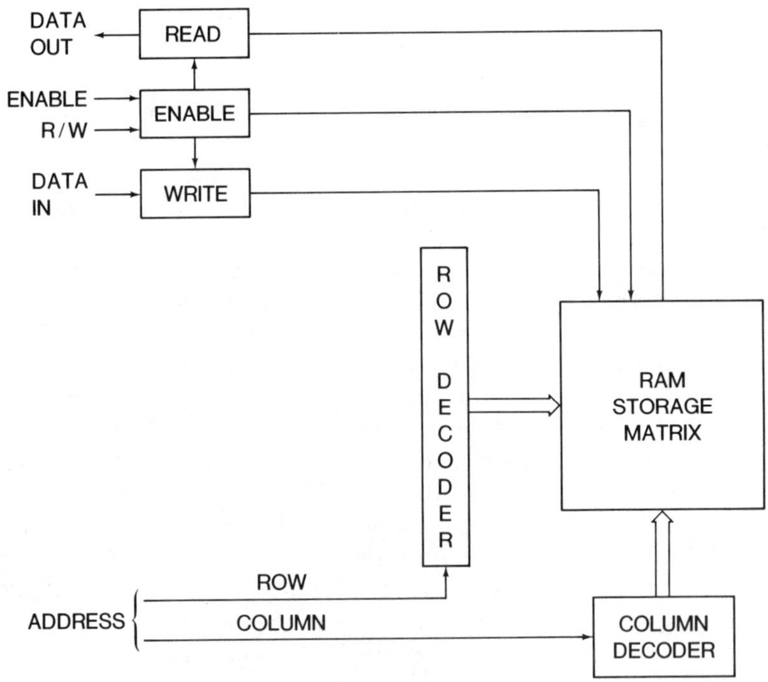

Static RAM Block Diagram
Fig. 1-8

As mentioned above, Fig. 1-8 shows a static RAM which is somewhat different from the dynamic RAM. The static RAM must have one flip-flop for every bit of information and, once entered, that bit of information remains in that particular flip-flop. In the dynamic RAM, the information is constantly moving. Originally, dynamic RAMs consisted of long shift registers with the output connected back to the input. The advantage of the dynamic RAM is that, instead of a two-transistor flip-flop, a single transistor stage with a small capacitance can be used to store the bit temporarily. The information must be continuously shifted from one stage to the next in order to keep these small capacitors charged and discharged. In today's dynamic RAM ICs it is possible to provide a larger number of stages and therefore store a larger number of bits than in a comparable size static RAM. The provision of special "refresh" circuits which generate pulses periodically to shift the information through, is a slight disadvantage in designing dynamic RAM ICs but the economy of size is sufficient to warrant the special circuitry.

Most of the μCs that contain RAMs usually provide only a relatively small amount of storage and that is in the form of a static rather than a dynamic memory. Single ICs which can store up to 64k bits are available and are usually connected into larger memory matrixes on a PC board. This is the type of memory referred to in Fig. 1-1 as IC memory.

Complete computers contain additional ICs to control certain peripherals, such as floppy disks, printers, communications terminals, etc. Single IC CPUs and μCs however, are invariably composed of the basic building blocks described in this chapter. Sometimes more than one ALU is used in the CPU. Sometimes the RAM or ROM in a microcomputer is smaller or larger, but they all function essentially in the way described here.

CHAPTER 2

4-BIT SLICE

AM 2901/2901A/2901B/2901C (AMD)

MICROPROCESSOR.4-BIT SLICE[1]

This device is designed as a high-speed cascadable element intended for use in CPU's, peripheral controllers, programmable microprocessors. It consists of a 16-word by 4-bit two-port RAM, a high-speed ALU, and the

[1]Note: The same microprocessor is manufactured by: FAIRCHILD-F2901A; MOTOROLA-MC2901A; NATIONAL-IDM2901A/A-1; NEC Micro-μPB2901.

associated shifting, decoding and multiplexing circuitry. The nine-bit microinstruction word is organized into three groups of three bits each and selects the ALU source operands, the ALU function, and the ALU destination register. The microprocessor is cascadable with full-look-ahead or with ripple-carry.

The AM2901A is a plug-in replacement for the AM2901, but is 25% faster than the AM2901.

The AM2901B is a plug-in replacement for the AM2901 or the AM2901A, but is 25% faster than the AM2901A and 50% faster than the AM2901.

The AM2901C is a plug-in replacement for the AM2901, AM2901A, AM2901B, only the switching speeds are changed because this device is the fastest version of the popular AM2901, having 25–30% speed improvement on the critical paths versus the AM2901B.

PIN NAME	DESCRIPTION	TYPE
A0–A3	Address Lines	I
B0–B3	Address Lines	I
I0–I8	Instruction Control Lines	I
Q3, Q0	Shift Line (MSB, LSB) Q Register	Bidirectional
RAM3, RAM0	Register stack (MSB, LSB)	Bidirectional
D0–D3	Direct Data Inputs	I
Y0–Y3	Data Outputs	O
$\overline{OE}$	Output Enable	O
$\overline{G}$	Carry Generate	O
$\overline{P}$	Carry Propagate	O
OVR	Overflow	O
F = O	Open Collector Output	O
F3	The MS ALU Output Bit	O
C_n	Carry-in	I
C_{n+4}	Carry-out	O
CP	Clock	I
V_{cc}	Power Supply	
GND	Ground	

Special Features

- Two-address architecture: independent simultaneous access to two working registers saves machine cycles.
- Eight-function ALU: Performs addition, two subtraction operations, and five logic functions on two source operands.
- Flexible data source selection: ALU data is selected from five source ports for a total of 203 source operand pairs for every ALU function.

- Left/right shift independent of ALU: Add and shift operations take only one cycle.
- Four status flags: Carry, overflow, zero, and negative.
- Expandable: For longer word lengths connect any number of AM2901's.
- Microprogrammable: Three groups of three bits each for source operand, ALU function, and destination control.

IN-CIRCUIT QUICK-TESTS

For 75% Confidence Level:

1. Volt-ohmmeter Measurements: The PC board ground should be connected directly to pin 30 on DIP and pin 27 on Flatpack. Power supply voltage of no less than 4.5 volts DC and no more than 5.5 volts DC should be measured at pin 10 on DIP and pin 6 on flatpack.
2. Oscilloscope Measurements: Clock signals with a frequency of 5.0 MHz to 16.0 MHz should appear at pin 15 on DIP and pin 11 on

Pin Configuration

Dip Version

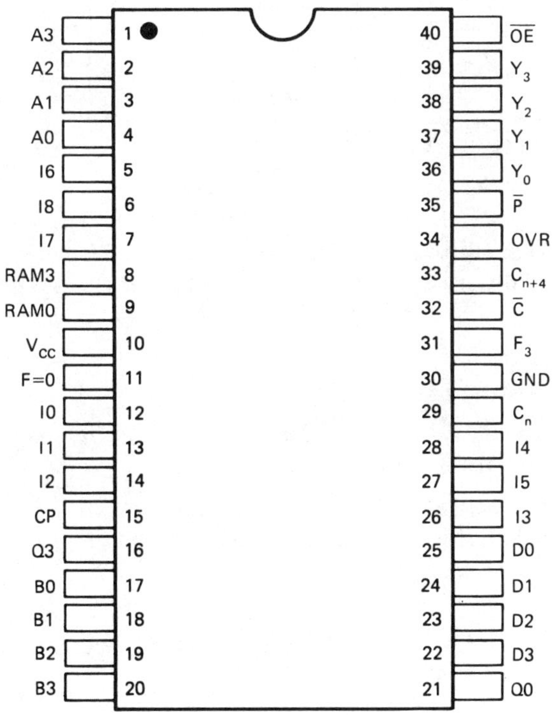

Pin Configuration

Flatpack Version

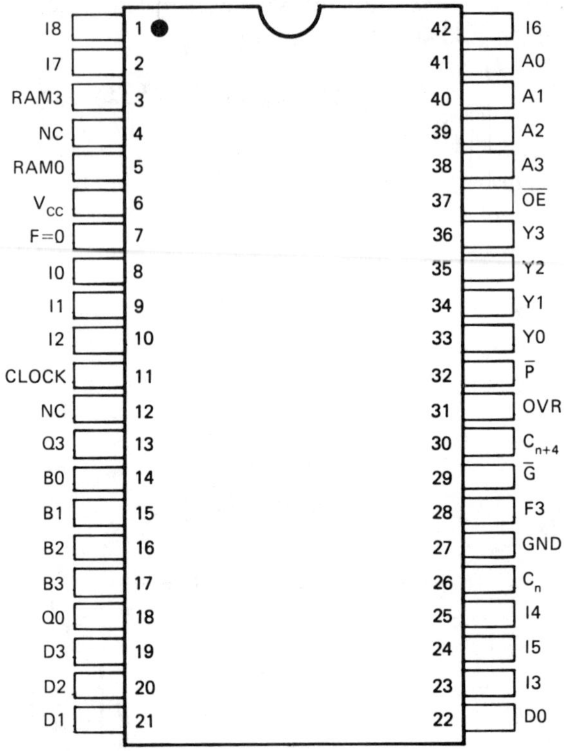

flatpack with an amplitude of 2.4 to 5.5 volts peak. Also check the signal on pin 21 on DIP and 18 on flatpack. This should be a pulse train, synchronized to the clock and related to shift lines for the RAM.

For 90% Confidence Level:

All of the measurements made for the 75% confidence level must be correct. Add the following:

Monitor the clock on pin 15 or 11 respectively, in conjunction with the OG signal on the oscilloscope. The OE signal on pin 40 on DIP and pin 37 on flatpack is related to the OUTPUT ENABLE operation of this IC.

EXACT REPLACEMENT PREFERRED—See introduction paragraph for phys-in replacement possibilities.

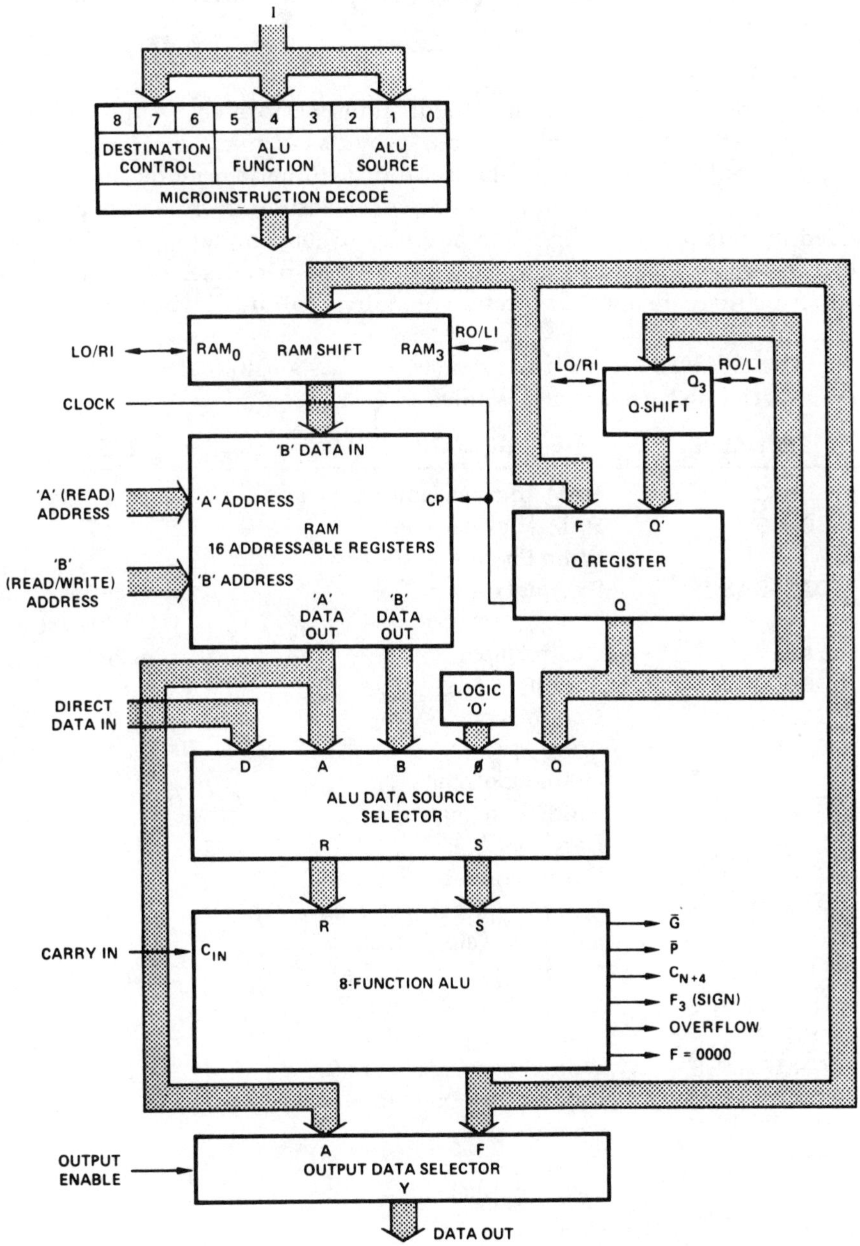

Courtesy Advanced Micro Devices, Inc.

Block Diagram—2901, 4-Bit Slice μP
Fig. 2-1

AM 2903/29203 (AMD) MICROPROCESSOR, 4-BIT SLICE[2]

This is a device that performs all functions performed by the industry standard AM2901 and, in addition, provides a number of significant enhancements that are especially useful in arithmetic-oriented processors. Infinitely expandable memory and 3-port, 3-address architecture are provided by this microprocessor. In addition to its complete arithmetic and logic instruction set, the AM2903 provides a special set of instructions which facilitate the implementation of multiplication, division, normalization, etc.

The AM29203 is a similar device, but has additional I/O capability, more special instructions and is at least 30% faster.

PIN NAME	DESCRIPTION	TYPE
A0–A3	RAM Address Input	I
B0–B3	RAM Address Input	I
$\overline{WE}$	Write Enable	I
DA0–DA3	External Data	I (2903) I/O (29203)
$\overline{EA}$	Control Input	I
DB0–DB3	External Data	I/O
$\overline{OE_B}$	Control Input	I
C_n	Carry-in	I
I0–I8	Instruction Inputs	I
$\overline{IEN}$	Instruction Enable	I
C_{n+4}	Carry-out	O
$\overline{G}$/N	Carry Generate/Sign	O
$\overline{P}$/OVR	Carry Propagate/Overflow	O
Z	Indicates outputs low	I/O
SIO_0, SIO_3	Serial Shift (ALU shifter)	I/O
QIO_0, QIO_3	Serial Shift (Q shifter)	I/O
$\overline{LSS}$	Least Significant Slice	I
$\overline{WRITE}/\overline{MSS}$	Write/Most Significant Slice	I/O
Y_0–Y_3	Data Inputs/Outputs	I/O
$\overline{OE_Y}$	Control	I
CP	Clock	I
V_{cc}	Power Supply	
GND	Ground	

[2]Note: The same microprocessor is manufactured by: FAIRCHILD–F2903; MOTOROLA–MC2903; NATIONAL–IDM2903.

PIN CONFIGURATION

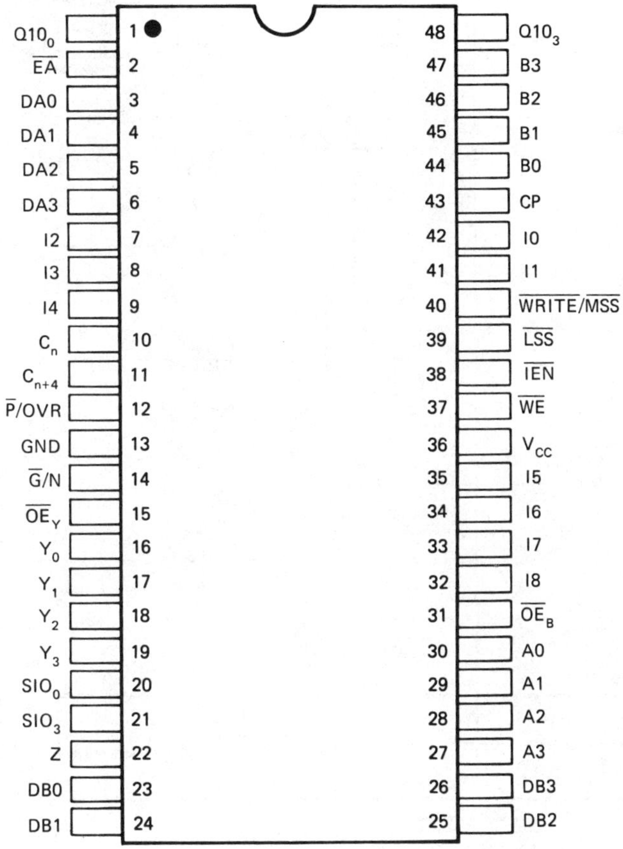

Special Features

- Expandable Register File: Like AM2901, AM2903/AM29203 contains 16 internal working registers arranged in a two-address architecture but the AM2903/AM29203 includes the necessary "hooks" to expand the register file externally to any number of registers.
- Built-in Multiplication Logic: The needed gates to performing multiplication are contained on-chip.
- Built-in Division Logic: It contains all logic and interconnects for execution of a non-restoring, multiple-length division with correction of the quotient.
- Built-in Normalization Logic: It can simultaneously shift the Q Register and count in a working register.

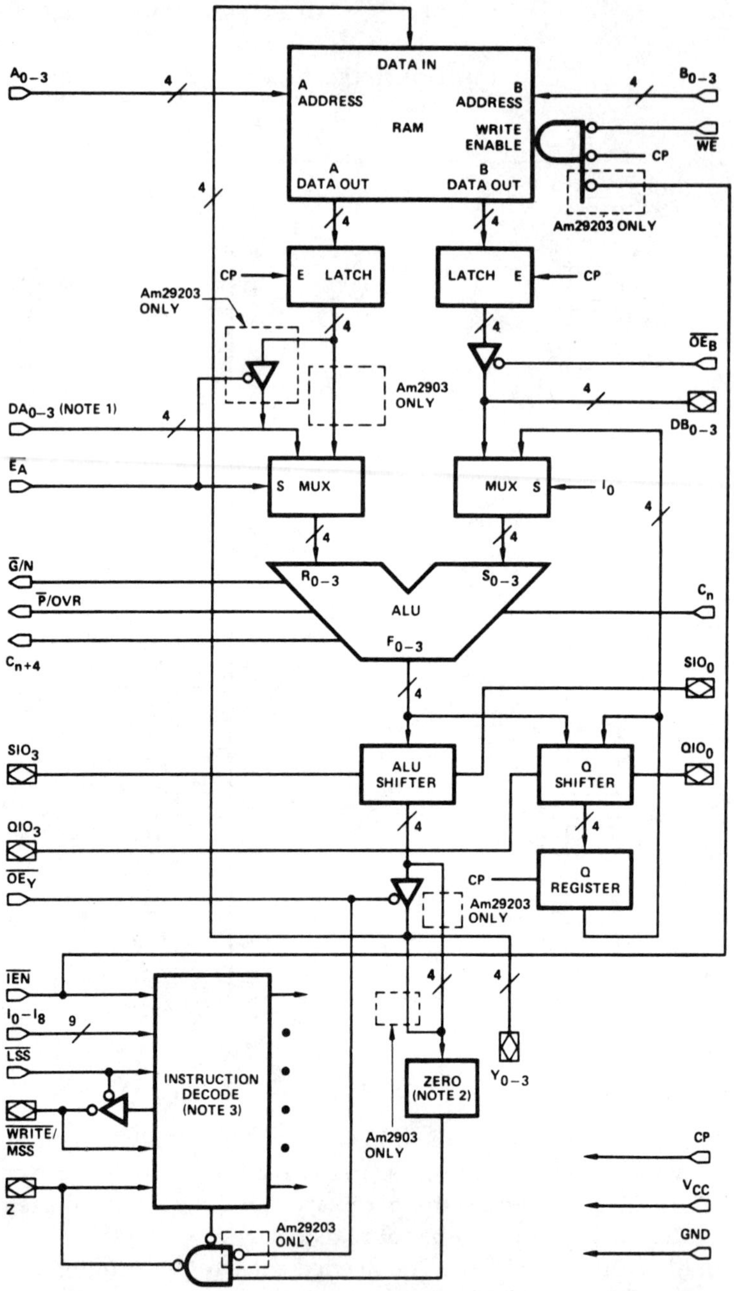

Courtesy Advanced Micro Devices, Inc.

Notes: 1. $DA_{0\text{-}3}$ is input only on Am2903, but is I/O port on Am29203.
2. On Am2903, zero logic is connected to Y, after the $\overline{OE}_Y$ buffer.
3. On Am2903, $\overline{IEN}$ controls $\overline{WRITE}$. On Am29203 $\overline{WRITE}$ is not affected by $\overline{IEN}$.

Block Diagram—2903, 4-Bit Slice μP
Fig. 2-2

- Built-in Parity Generation Circuitry: It can supply parity across the entire ALU output for use in error detection.
- Built-in Sign Extension Circuitry: It provides the capability to extend the sign at any slice boundary.
- For the AM29203 only: Automatic BCD add and subtract and conversion between binary and BCD.
- Zero detection and register writing performed on a single byte rather than the whole word.
- Two Bidirectional Data Lines.

The AM2903A is a pin-for-pin replacement for the original version of the AM2903. Only the switching speed has changed. The design objective is for the AM2903A to be at least 30% faster than the original AM2903 on critical paths.

IN-CIRCUIT QUICK-TESTS

FOR 75% CONFIDENCE LEVEL:

1. Volt-ohmmeter Measurements: The PC board ground should be connected directly to pin 13. Power supply voltage of no less than 4.5 volts DC and no more than 5.5 volts DC should be measured from pin 36 to ground.
2. Oscilloscope Measurements: Clock signals with a frequency of 10.0 μHz to 16.0 μHz should appear at pin 43 with an amplitude of 2.4 to 5.5 volts peak. Also check the signal on pin 31. This should be a pulse train, synchronized to the clock and enabling the RAM operation.

FOR 90% CONFIDENCE LEVEL:

All of the measurements made for the 75% confidence level must be correct. Add the following:

Monitor the clock on pin 43 in conjunction with the WE signal on the oscilloscope. The WE signal on pin 37 is related to the WRITE ENABLE operation of this IC.

EXACT REPLACEMENT PREFERRED—See plug-in compatibility in introductory paragraph.

MC 10800 (MOTOROLA) 4-BIT SLICE

This device performs logic and arithmetic functions. Each part is four bits wide and is "sliced" parallel to the data flow. It is fully expandable to larger word length by connecting circuits in parallel and features three input/output data ports for system flexibility.

PIN NAME	DESCRIPTION	TYPE
A0-A3	Data Bus A	I
ØB0-ØB3	Output Bus	I/O
IB0-IB3	Input Bus	I/O
ASO-AS	Y Input Mux-Select	I
AS4	Increment/Decrement by Z Select	I
AS5, AS6	Output Bus Control and A Input Mux Select	I
AS10	Add/Substract Select	I
AS11	Binary/BCD Select	I
AS12	Arithmetic/Logic Mode Select	I
C_{in}	Carry-In	I
C_{out}	Carry-Out	O
PG	Group Propagate	O
GG	Group Generate	O
OF	Overflow	O
PC	Parity of Carries	O
PR	Parity of Result	O
ZD	Zero Detect	O
AS7	Shift Network-Source Select	I
AS13, AS14	Shift Network-Function Select	I
R4, R-1	Shift Network MSB, LSB	I/O
AS9, AS15	Accumulator Mux and Input Bus Control Select	I
AS8	Input Bus Driver-Enable	I
CLK	Accumulator-Clock	I
AS16 (LC)	Output Bus Latch	I
V_{EE}	-5.2V power supply	
V_{TT}	-2.0V power supply	
V_{CC}, V_{CCO}	Ground	

Special Features

- ALU provides: Full binary and BCD Arithmetic; A and Ø input data words treated equally; All logic functions; Internal look-ahead carry with propagate and generate outputs.
- Internal shift network—Left and Right logic shift; Sign protect for arithmetic shift.
- Master-slave accumulator for temporary storage.
- All necessary status outputs: overflow, zero detect, carry out and sign bit.
- Parity outputs for binary operations.
- Full masking of Ø bus to A bus is provided in the latch/mask network.

PIN CONFIGURATION

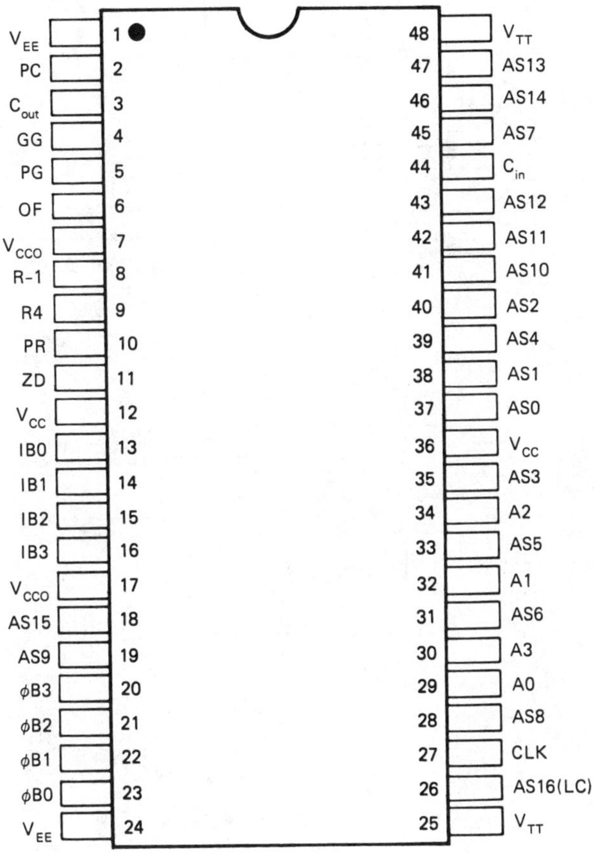

IN-CIRCUIT QUICK-TESTS

FOR 75% CONFIDENCE LEVEL:

1. Volt-ohmmeter Measurements: The PC board ground should be connected directly to pins 7, 12, 17 and 36. Power supply voltage of no less than −4.7 volts DC and no more than −5.7 volts DC should be measured from pins 1 and 24 to ground. Between −1.9 and −2.2 volts DC should be measured at pins 25 and 48.
2. Oscilloscope Measurements: Clock signals with a frequency of 5.0 MHz to 15.0 MHz should appear at pin 27 with an amplitude of −2.0 to −5.0 volts peak. Also check the signal on pin 8. This

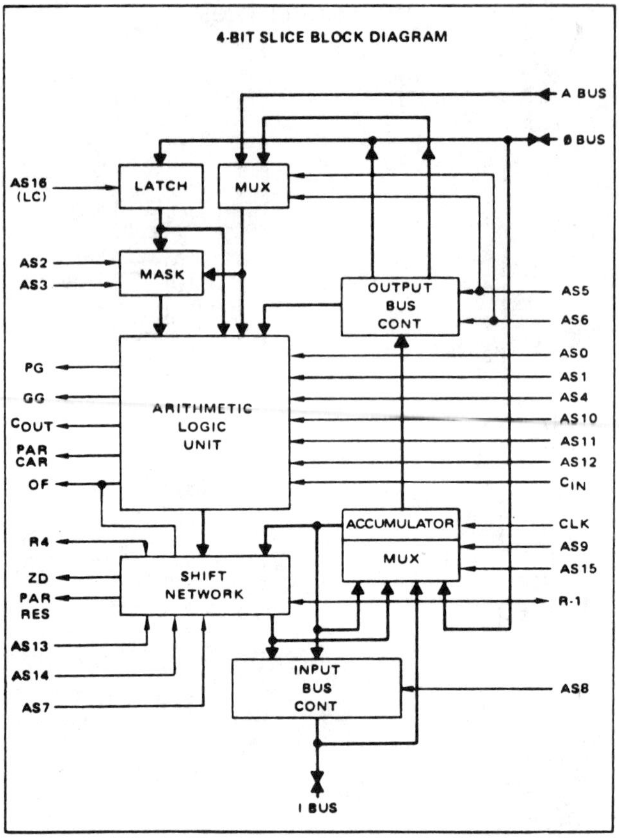

Courtesy Motorola, Inc.

Block Diagram — 10800, 4-Bit Slice μP
Fig. 2-3

should be a pulse train, synchronized to the clock and related to the I/O shift lines.

FOR 90% CONFIDENCE LEVEL:

All of the measurements made for the 75% confidence level must be correct. Add the following:

Monitor the clock on pin 27 in conjunction with the PR signal on the oscilloscope. The PR signal on pin 10 is related to the parity of the result.

EXACT REPLACEMENT ESSENTIAL.

CHAPTER 3

4-BIT CPU

PPS-4/2 (ROCKWELL) 4-BIT CPU

This device uses the same instruction set as the PPS-4 CPU (obsolete) but includes the clock generator function within the CPU circuit. It automatically floats all output lines when power is turned on. Functionally, there are no other differences between the PPS-4 and the PPS-4/2 CPU's. However, the PPS-4/2 CPU also has the capability of directly driving low-power light-emitting diode (LED) display segments. Fluorescent displays can also be driven if the system includes the appropriate power supply for the higher voltage display.

PIN NAME	DESCRIPTION	TYPE
A/B1-A/B12	Address Bus	0
I/D1-I/D8	Instruction Data Bus	I/O
DIA1-DIA4	Data Input A	I
DIO1-DIO4	Data Output A or Data Input B	I/O
DO1-DO4	Data Output A	O
W/IO	Write I/O	O
CLKA, CLK$\overline{\text{B}}$	Clock	I/O
XTALO, XTAL1	Crystal	I
SPO		O
PO	Power On	I
VCLK	Oscillator Power Supply	
V_{DD}	Power Supply	
V_{SS}	Ground	

Pin Configuration

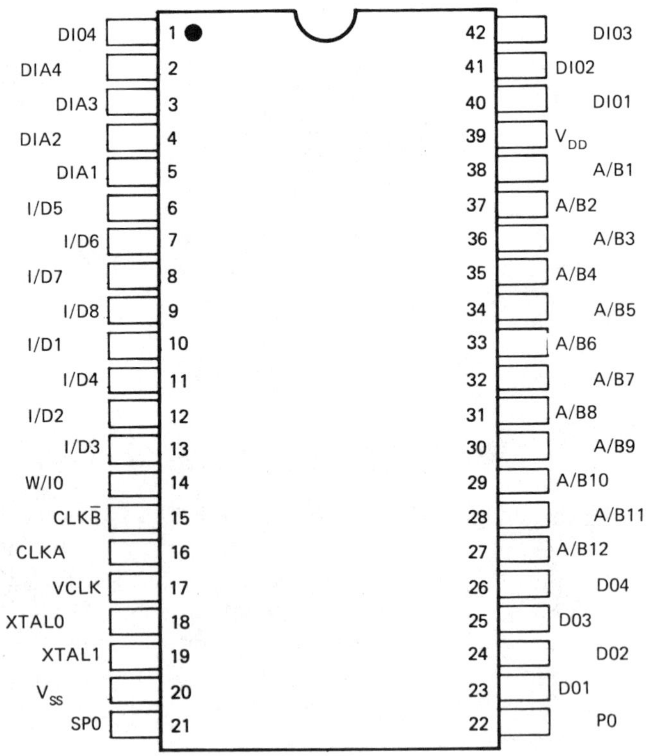

Special Features

- Expanded I/O using discrete I/O Commands.
- PPS-4 Bus System compatibility.
- 4 microsecond cycle time.
- 100 pf Bus Drive capability.

IN-CIRCUIT QUICK-TESTS

For 75% Confidence Level:

1. Volt-ohmmeter Measurements: The PC board ground should be connected directly to pin 20. Power supply voltage of no less than −18 volts DC and no more than −16 volts DC should be measured from pin 39 to ground.
2. Oscilloscope Measurements: Clock signals with a frequency of

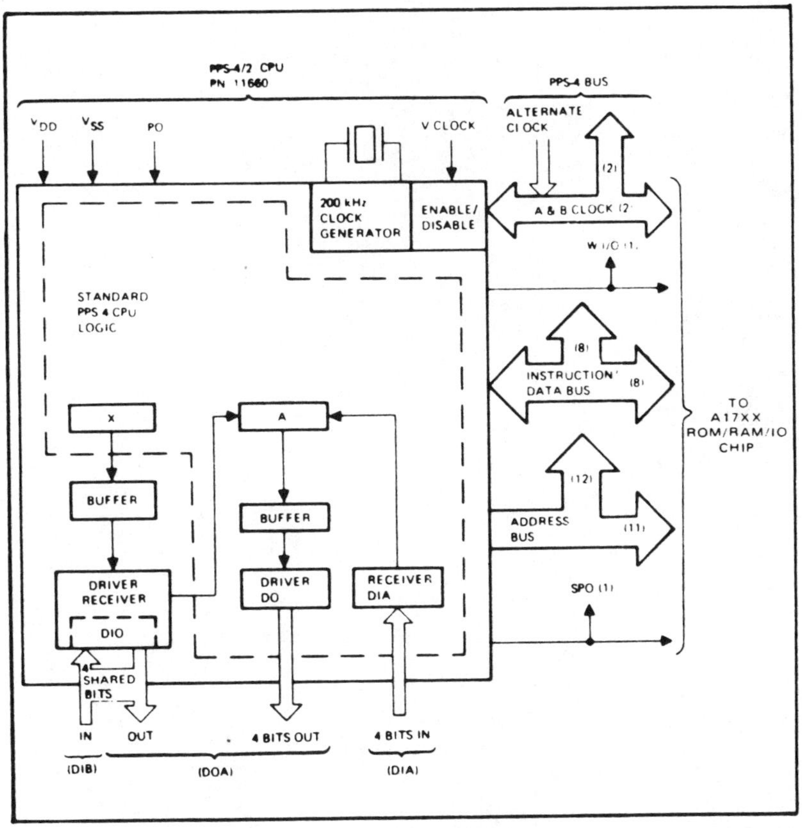

Courtesy Rockwell International.

Block Diagram—PPS 4/2, 4-Bit CPU
Fig. 3-1

100 kHz to 250 kHz should appear at pins 18 and 19 with an amplitude of −10 to −17.8 volts peak. Also check the signal on pins 15 and 16. This should be a pulse train, synchronized to the clock.

For 90% Confidence Level:

All of the measurements made for the 75% confidence level must be correct. Add the following:

Monitor the clock on pins 18 and 19 in conjunction with the W/IO signal on the oscilloscope. The W/IO signal on pin 14 is related to the I/O WRITE operation of this IC.

EXACT REPLACEMENT ESSENTIAL.

CHAPTER 4

8-BIT CPU

8-Bit CPU

PPS-8 (Rockwell) 8-Bit CPU

This device uses four-phase dynamic logic for operation. It contains: logic necessary to receive and decode the instructions, 8-bit parallel adder-accumulator for arithmetic and logical operations, 14-bit P-Register for sequencing through the ROM program, 16-bit L-Register for subroutine linkage, RAM operand addressing, and ROM indirect addressing, three 8-bit registers, (X, Y and Z) for RAM operand addressing, 5-bit stack pointer S for addressing a dedicated RAM area, logic for processing a priority interrupt structure, Direct Memory Access (DMA) mode, multiplexed receivers and drivers for interfacing with the 14-bit multiplexed address bus and the 8-bit bi-directional data/instruction bus.

PIN NAME	DESCRIPTION	TYPE
A/B1-A/B14	Address Bus	O
I/DI-I/D8	Instruction/Data Bus	I/O
INTO, INT1, INT2	Interrupt 0, 1, 2	I
A, $\bar{B}$	System Clock	I
W/IO	Write I/O	O
RIH	Read Inhibit	O
ACKO	I/O Interrupt Acknowledge	O
DMRA	DMA Request Acknowledge	I/O
PO	Power On	I
SPO	Synchronize Power-On	O
V_{DD}	Power Supply	
V_{SS}	Ground	

PIN CONFIGURATION

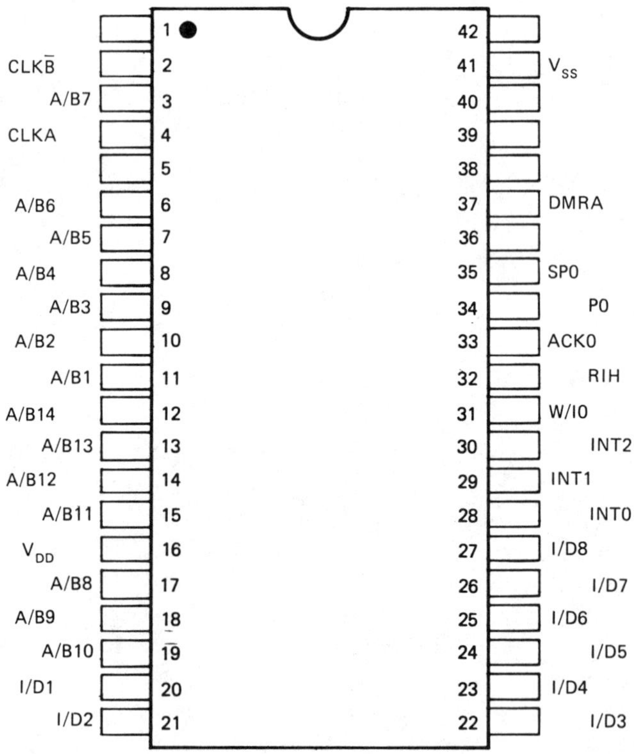

Special Features

- Two microsecond access time.
- Four microsecond complete instruction cycle time.
- Over 90 words instruction repertoire.
- (DMA) Direct Memory Access up to 8 prioritized channels at 256K bytes/sec.
- Program controller I/O at 60K bytes/sec.
- TTL-compatible interface.
- Three level interrupt structure.
- Bi-directional 8- or 16-bit parallel buses.

IN-CIRCUIT QUICK-TESTS

For 75% Confidence Level:

1. Volt-ohmmeter Measurements: The PC board ground should be connected directly to pin 41. Power supply voltage of no less than

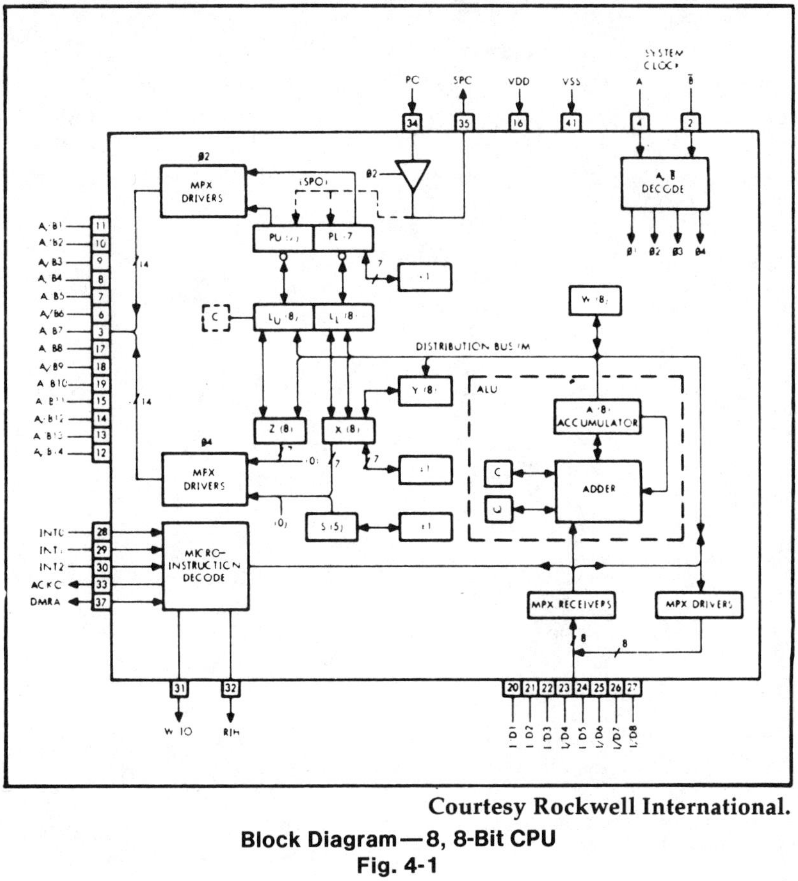

Courtesy Rockwell International.

Block Diagram—8, 8-Bit CPU
Fig. 4-1

−16 volts DC and no more than −18 volts DC should be measured from pin 16 to ground.

2. Oscilloscope Measurements: Clock signals with a frequency of 100 kHz to 256 kHz should appear at pins 2 and 4 with an amplitude of −10 to −17.8 volts peak. Also check the signal on pin 32. This should be a pulse train, synchronized to the clock and indicating the READ cycle.

For 90% Confidence Level:

All of the measurements made for the 75% confidence level must be correct. Add the following:

Monitor the clock on pins 2 and 4 in conjunction with the W/IO signal on the oscilloscope. The W/IO signal on pin 31 is related to the I/O WRITE operation of this IC.

EXACT REPLACEMENT ESSENTIAL.

Z 80/A (ZILOG) 8-Bit CPU[1]

This device has an instruction set compatible with all 78 of the 8080A instructions. Its duplicate set of general purpose and flag registers (16 total) allows single context switching, background-foreground programming and single level interrupt processing. Two 16-bit index registers allow processing of tables and arrays. It has a fully compatible family of peripheral circuits.

PIN NAME	DESCRIPTION	TYPE
A0–A15	Address Bus	O
D0–D7	Data Bus	I/O
$\overline{\text{M1}}$	Machine Cycle One	O
$\overline{\text{MREQ}}$	Memory Request	O
$\overline{\text{IORQ}}$	Input/Output Request	O
$\overline{\text{RD}}$	Read	O
$\overline{\text{WR}}$	Write	O
$\overline{\text{RFSH}}$	Refresh	O
$\overline{\text{HALT}}$	Halt	O
$\overline{\text{WAIT}}$	Wait	I
$\overline{\text{INT}}$	Interrupt	I
$\overline{\text{NMI}}$	Non-maskable Interrupt	I
$\overline{\text{RESET}}$	Reset	I

[1]NOTE: The same microprocessor is manufactured by:
MOSTEK—MK3880;
NEC Micro—μPD780;
SGS-ATES—Z80/A.

PIN NAME	DESCRIPTION	TYPE
$\overline{\text{BUSREQ}}$	Bus Request	I
$\overline{\text{BUSACK}}$	Bus Acknowledge	O
CLK	Clock	I
+5V	Power Supply	
GND	Ground	

Special Features

- 2.5MHz clock rate and 1.5μs instruction execution time—Z 80.
- 4MHz clock rate and 1.0μs instruction execution time—Z 80A.
- Instruction set includes: string, bit, byte, word operations, and block transfers along with addressing modes such as indexed and relative.
- All Z80 family components offer bus-request and prioritized interrupt request daisy chains that can be implemented without external logic.
- Three modes of high-speed interrupt processing: 8080 compatible, non Z-80 peripheral and Z-80 family peripheral daisy chain.

Pin Configuration

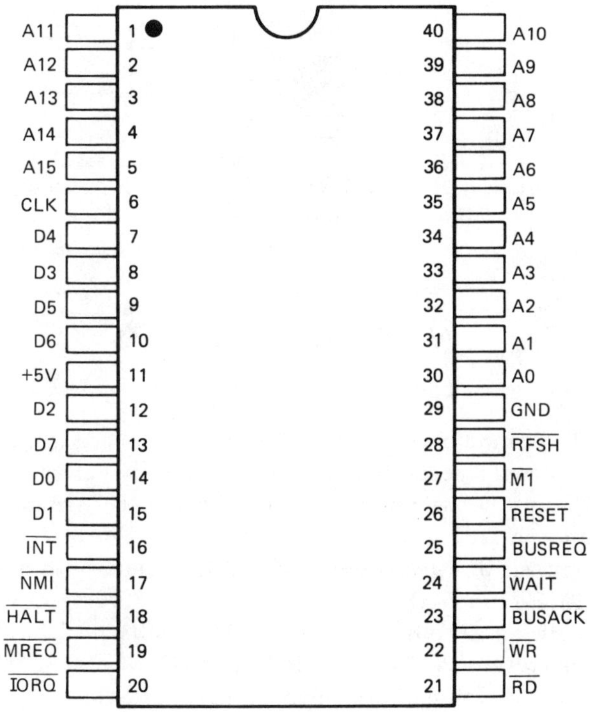

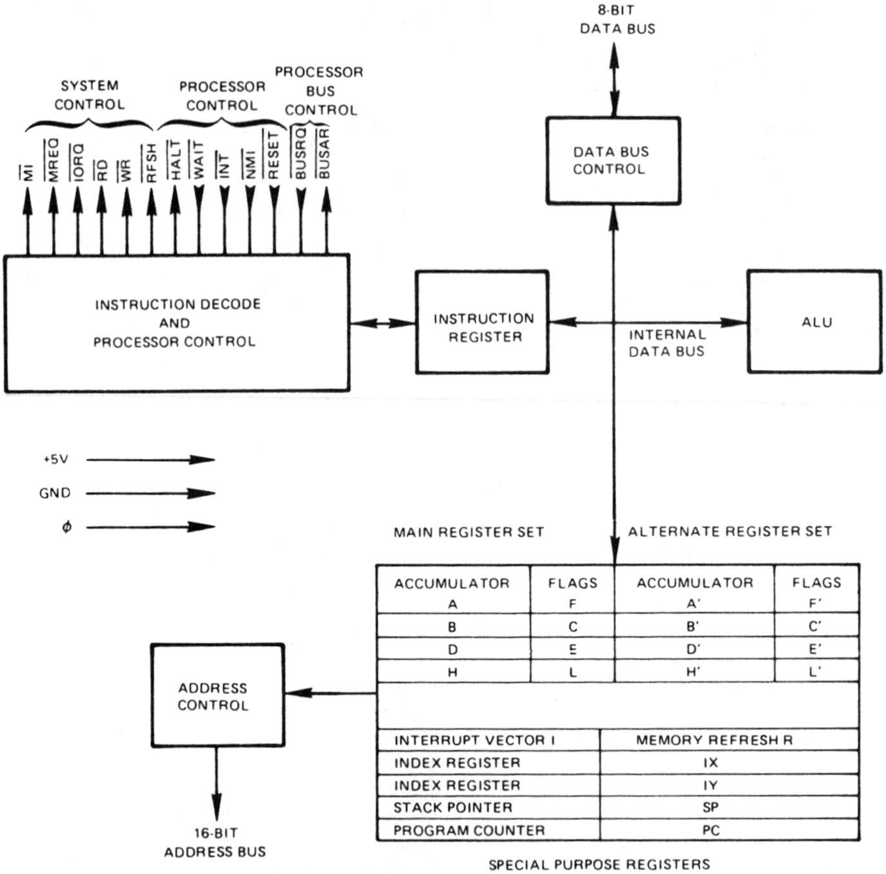

Courtesy NEC Electronics, U.S.A., Inc., Microcomputer Division.
Block Diagram—80/A, 8-Bit, CPU
Fig. 4-2

IN-CIRCUIT QUICK-TESTS

For 75% Confidence Level:

1. Volt-ohmmeter Measurements: The PC board ground should be connected directly to pin 29. Power supply voltage of no less than 4.75 volts DC and no more than 5.25 volts DC should be measured from pin 11 to ground.
2. Oscilloscope Measurements: Clock signals with a frequency of O.1MHz to 2.5MHz and 4MHz for the Z80A should appear at pin 6 with an amplitude of 4.0 to 5.75 volts peak. Also check the signal on pin 28. This should be a pulse train, synchronized to the clock indicating a refresh address is available.

For 90% Confidence Level:

All of the measurements made for the 75% confidence level must be correct. Add the following:

> Monitor the clock on pin 6 in conjunction with the M1 signal on the oscilloscope. The M1 signal on pin 27 is related to the op code fetch cycle of this IC.

EXACT REPLACEMENT PREFERRED—it may be possible to use the Z80A for the Z80 if the exact replacement is not available. The Z80 may not be suitable as replacement for the Z80A.

NSC 800 (National) 8-Bit CPU[2]

This device has the major functional areas: the ALU, register array, interrupt control, timing, and control logic. These areas are interconnected via the internal 8-bit data bus. Included on-chip are five levels of vectored, prioritized interrupts, bus controller, and clock generator.

PIN NAME	DESCRIPTION	TYPE
AD0-AD7	Multiplexed Address/Data	I/O
A8-A15	Address Bits	O
$\overline{\text{BACK}}$	Bus Acknowledge	O
RESET OUT	Reset Out	O
IO/$\overline{\text{M}}$	Input/Output/Memory	O
$\overline{\text{RFSH}}$	Refresh	O
ALE	Address Latch Enable	O
$\overline{\text{RD}}$	Read Strobe	O
$\overline{\text{WR}}$	Write Strobe	O
CLK	Clock	O
$\overline{\text{INTA}}$	Interrupt Acknowledge	O
SO, SI	Bus Status	O
XIN, XOUT	Crystal or RC Network	I,O
$\overline{\text{RESET IN}}$	Reset Input	I
$\overline{\text{BREQ}}$	Bus Request	I
$\overline{\text{NMI}}$	Non-Maskable Interrupt	I
$\overline{\text{RSTA}}$, $\overline{\text{RSTB}}$. $\overline{\text{RSTC}}$	Restart Interrupts A,B,C	I
$\overline{\text{INTR}}$	Interrupt Request	I
$\overline{\text{WAIT}}$	Wait	I
$\overline{\text{PS}}$	Power Save	I
V_{CC}	Power Supply	
GND	Ground	

[2]Note: The NSC 800A is the fast version of the same microprocessor with a 1μs Instruction Cycle at 4MHz.

8-Bit CPU

Special Features

- Fully compatible with Z80 instruction set.
- Set of 158 instructions.
- 10 addressing modes.
- 22 internal registers.
- Low power: 50mW at 5V.
- Multiplexed bus structure.
- On-chip, 8-Bit dynamic RAM refresh circuitry.
- Standard speed 1.6μs instruction cycle at 2.5MHz.
- Capable of addressing 64K bytes of memory and 256I/O devices.
- Schmitt trigger input on reset.
- Unique standby-current (power save) feature.

IN-CIRCUIT QUICK-TESTS

For 75% Confidence Level:

1. Volt-ohmmeter Measurements: The PC board ground should be connected directly to pin 20. Power supply voltage of no less than

Pin Configuration

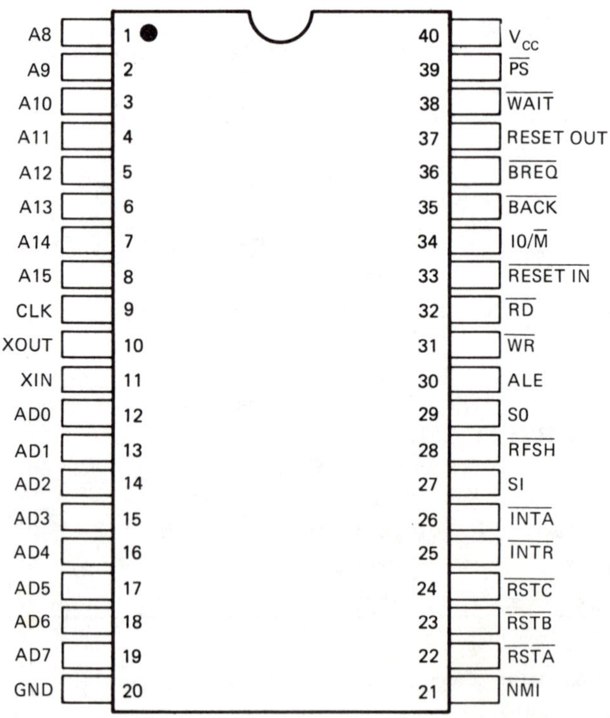

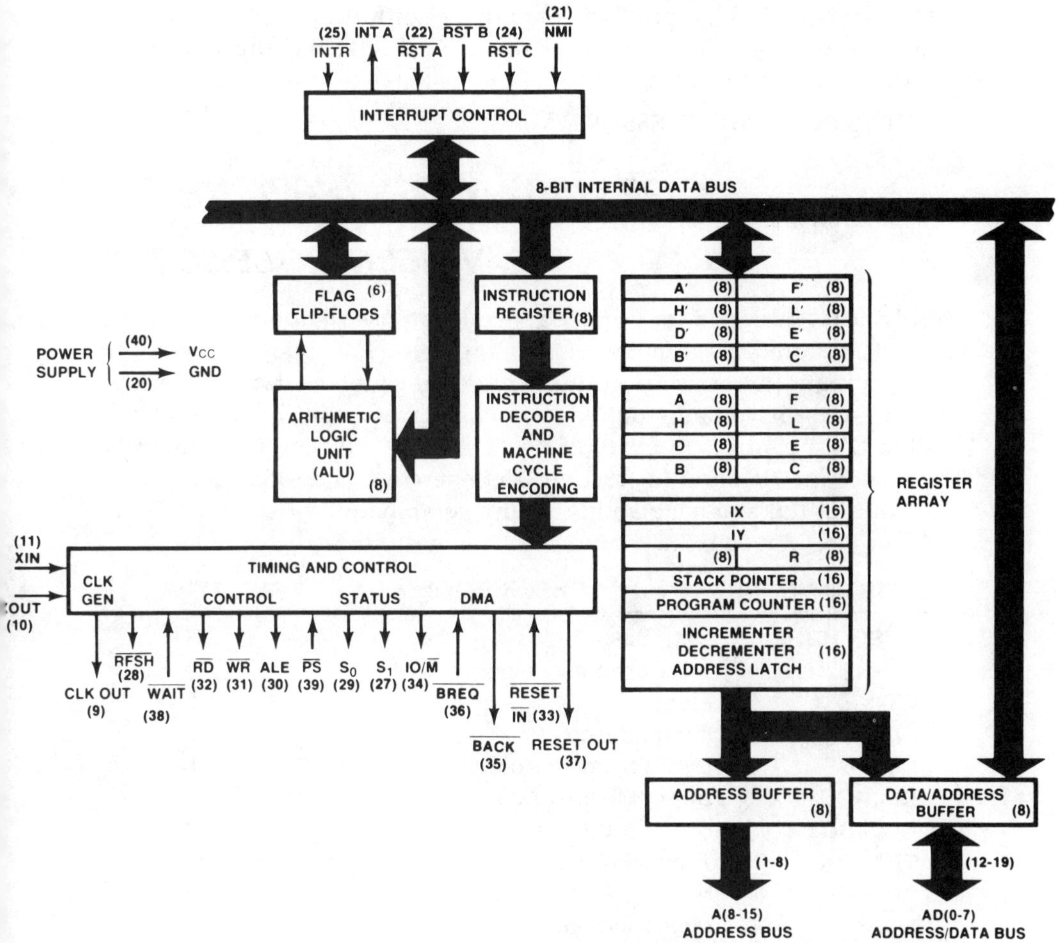

Courtesy of National Semiconductor Corporation.

Block Diagram—800
Fig. 4-3

4.5 volts DC and no more than 5.5 volts DC should be measured from pin 40 to ground.

2. Oscilloscope Measurements: Clock signals with a frequency of 0.1MHz to 2.5MHz should appear at pins 10 and 11 with an amplitude of 4 to 5 volts peak. Also check the signal on pin 9. This should be a square wave synchronized to the clock but ½ of the clock frequency.

FOR 90% CONFIDENCE LEVEL:

All of the measurements made for the 75% confidence level must be correct. Add the following:

Monitor the clock on pin 9 in conjunction with the RFSH signal on the oscilloscope. The RFSH signal on pin Z8 is related to the dynamic RAM refresh cycle of this IC.

EXACT REPLACEMENT ESSENTIAL.

CDP 1802/CDP 1802C (RCA)
MICROPROCESSOR[3a,b]

This device is designed for use as a general-purpose computing or control element in stored-program systems or products. It includes a 16×16-bit matrix of registers for use as multiple program counters, data pointers, or data registers. It contains optional on-chip crystal-controlled oscillator, on-chip DMA controls, simple RESET, LOAD, PAUSE, and RUN controls. The device has 91 basic instruction, 255 operation codes, programmable serial output (Q) and adaptability to any combination of standard RAM, ROM, or PROM memories.

PIN NAME	DESCRIPTION	TYPE
BUS0-BUS7	Data Bus	I/O
N0-N2	I/O Commands Lines	O
$\overline{\text{EF1-EF4}}$	Flags	I
$\overline{\text{INTERRUPT}}$	Interrupt Request	I
$\overline{\text{DMA-IN}}$	Direct Memory Access-in	I
$\overline{\text{DMA-OUT}}$	Direct Memory Access-out	I
SC0, SC1	State Codes Lines	O
TPA, TPB	Timing Pulses	O
A0-MA7	Memory Address Lines	O
$\overline{\text{MWR}}$	Memory Write	O
$\overline{\text{MRD}}$	Memory Read	O
Q	Set or Reset	O
CLOCK	Clock	I
$\overline{\text{XTAL}}$	Crystal	O

[3a]Note 1: The CDP 1802 is the higher speed, higher power device. It has: 4V to 10.5V operating voltage range; 2.5– or 3.75μs instruction time @25°C; 100mW power dissipation (typical operating conditions); 6.4MHz maximum clock input frequency at 10V @25°C.

The CDP 1802C has: 4V to 6.5V recommended operating voltage range; 5– or 7.5μs instruction time @25°C; 10mW power dissipation (typical operating conditions); 3.2MHz maximum clock input frequency at 5V @25°C.

[3b]Note 2: The same microprocessor is manufactured by:
HUGHES—HCMP 1802/HCMP 1802C;
SSS—SCP 1802/SCP 1802C.

PIN NAME	DESCRIPTION	TYPE
WAIT	Wait (Control Line)	I
$\overline{\text{CLEAR}}$	Clear (Control Line)	I
V_{CC}	Power Supply	
V_{DD}	Power Supply	
V_{SS}	Ground	

Special Features

- DC to 6.4MHz clock (single phase) at 25°C.
- Split-power-supply option that allows for 10V on internal parts of CPU and 5V on interfacing lines.
- Up to 65K addressable bytes of Memory.
- Maskable interrupt and four testable external flag lines.
- Operating temperature range:
  −55°C to +125°C (CDP 1802D, CDP 1802CD);
  −40°C to +85°C (CDP 1802E, CDP 1802CE).

PIN CONFIGURATION

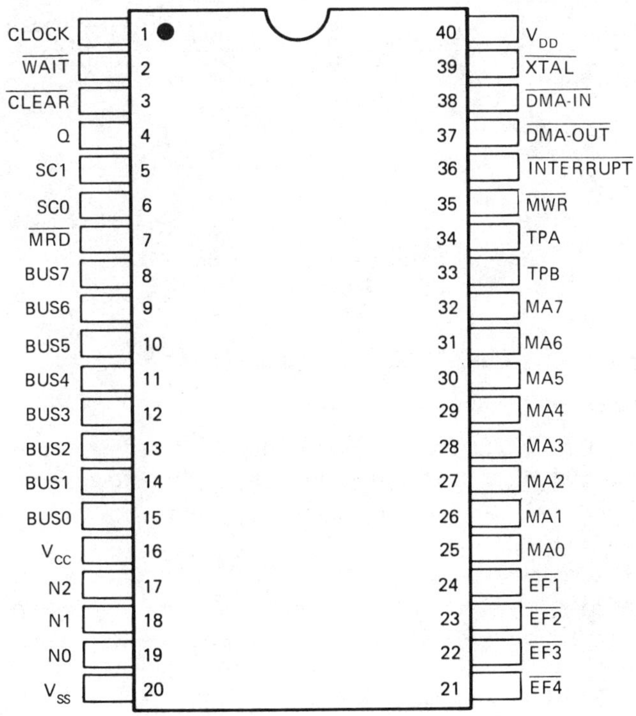

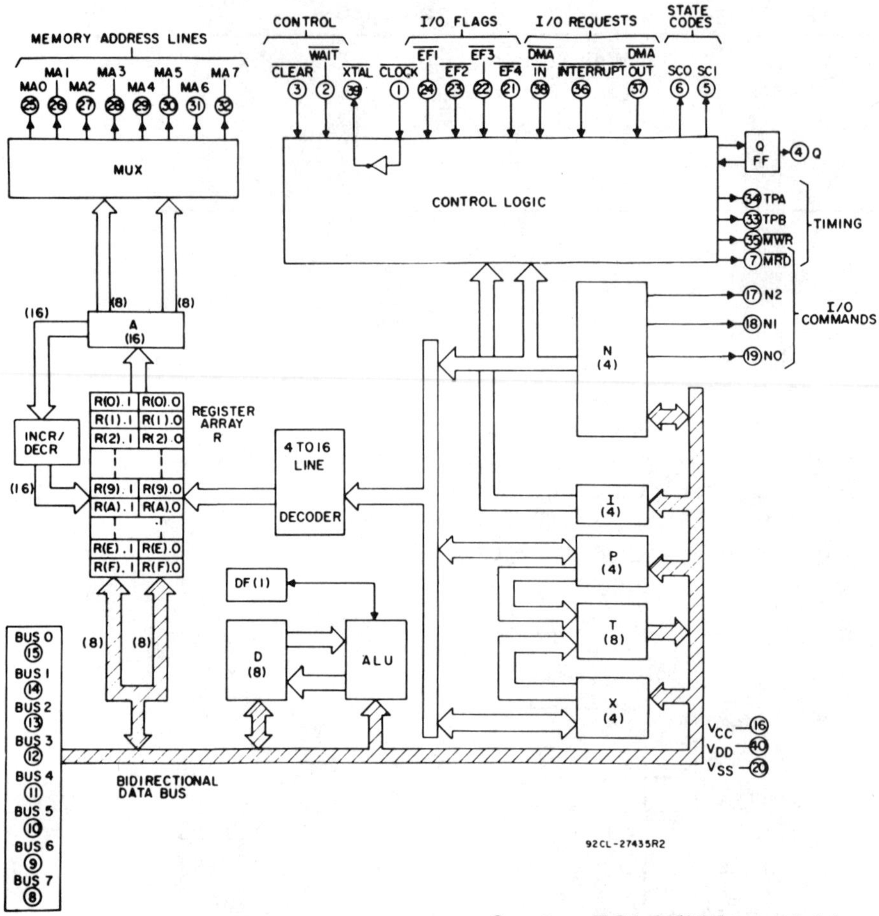

Courtesy RCA Solid State Division.

Block Diagram—1802/C, 8-Bit CPU
Fig. 4-4

IN-CIRCUIT QUICK-TESTS

FOR 75% CONFIDENCE LEVEL:

1. Volt-ohmmeter Measurements: The PC board ground should be connected directly to pin 20. Power supply voltage of no less than +5 volts DC and no more than +8 (+6 for 1802C) volts DC should be measured from pin 40 to ground.
2. Oscilloscope Measurements: Clock signals with a frequency of zero to 6.4MHz (3.2MHz for 1802C) should appear at pin 1 with an amplitude of 2.4 to 5.0 volts peak. Also check the signal on pins 33 and 34. This should be a pulse train, synchronized to the clock, but 1/8 of the clock frequency.

For 90% Confidence Level:

All of the measurements made for the 75% confidence level must be correct. Add the following:

> Monitor the clock on pin 1 in conjunction with the $\overline{\text{MRD}}$ signal on the oscilloscope. The $\overline{\text{MRD}}$ signal on pin 7 is related to the memory read operation of this IC.

EXACT REPLACEMENT PREFERRED—it may be possible to use the 1802C if the clock is below 3MHz if the exact replacement is not available. The 1802C can usually be used as replacement for the 1802.

CDP 1805/CDP 1805C (RCA)

Microprocessor

The CDP 1805 series is an improved and expanded version of the CDP 1802 microprocessor series, containing the same architectural features of a central 16 × 16 scratchpad register array that is used to generate all memory addressing and to store internal data. The additional features of separate I/O bussing, on-board DMA control, and serial I/O capability are also retained.

The CDP 1805 and CDP 1805C are functionally identical. They differ in that the CDP 1805 has an operating voltage range of 4 to 10.5V and the CDP 1805C has an operating voltage range of 4 to 6.5V.

PIN NAME	DESCRIPTION	TYPE
BUS0-BUS7	Data Bus	I/O
N0-N2	I/O Commands Lines	O
$\overline{\text{EF1}}$-$\overline{\text{EF4}}$	Flags	I
$\overline{\text{INTERRUPT}}$	Interrupt Request	I
$\overline{\text{DMA-IN}}$	Direct Memory Access-in	I
$\overline{\text{DMA-OUT}}$	Direct Memory Access-out	I
SC0, SC1	State Code Lines	O
TPA, TPB	Timing Pulses	O
MA0-MA7	Memory Address Lines	O
$\overline{\text{MWR}}$	Memory Write	O
$\overline{\text{MRD}}$	Memory Read	O
Q	Single Bit Output ROM CPU	O
CLOCK	Clock	I
$\overline{\text{XTAL}}$	Crystal	O
$\overline{\text{WAIT}}$	Wait	I
$\overline{\text{CLEAR}}$	Clear	I
$\overline{\text{ME}}$	Memory Enable	I

PIN NAME	DESCRIPTION	TYPE
V_{DD}	Power Supply	
V_{SS}	Ground	

Special Features

- ROM-less version of the CDP 1804A microcomputer.
- Emulates CDP 1804A function with single 2K-ROM device.
- Instruction fetch-execute time of 4 microsec. at $V_{DD} = 5V$ over full temperature range.
- 113 instructions; upwards software compatible with CDP 1802.
- Pin-out same as CDP 1802 except for V_{CC} terminal.
- 16 × 16 matrix of registers for use as memory pointers. (program counters, data pointers, stack pointers) or as data storage registers.
- On-chip crystal or RC controlled oscillator.
- 64K memory address capability.
- Fully static— no minimum clock frequency.

PIN CONFIGURATION

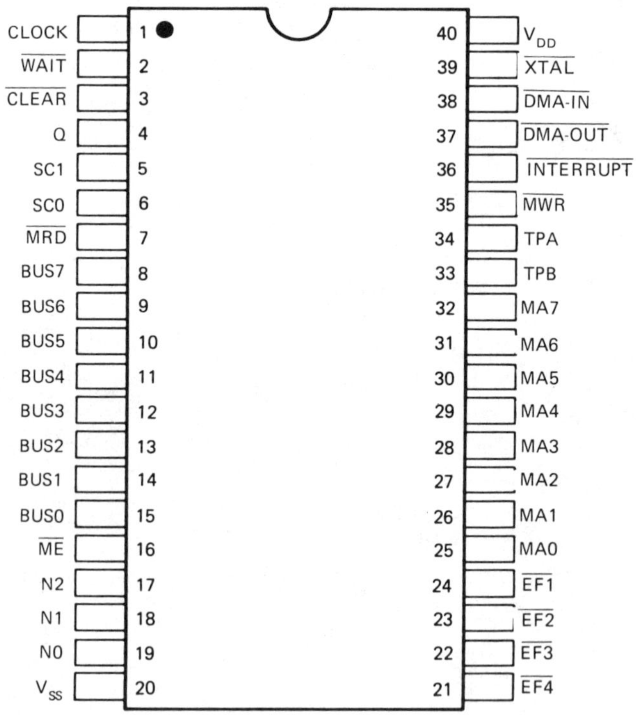

- Single voltage supply:
  4V to 10.5V (CDP 1805D, CDP 1805E)
  4V to 6.5V (CDP 1805CD, CDP 1805CE).
- Wide operating temperature range:
  −55°C to +125°C (CDP 1805D, CDP 1805CD)
  −40°C to +85°C (CDP 1805E, CDP 1805CE)

IN-CIRCUIT QUICK-TESTS

For 75% Confidence Level

1. Volt-ohmmeter Measurements: The PC board ground should be connected directly to pin 20. Power supply voltage of no less than 4.0 volts DC and no more than 10.5 (6.5 for 1805C) volts DC should be measured from pin 40 to ground.
2. Oscilloscope Measurements: Clock signals with a frequency of zero to 8.0MHz should appear at pin 1 with an amplitude of 2.4 to

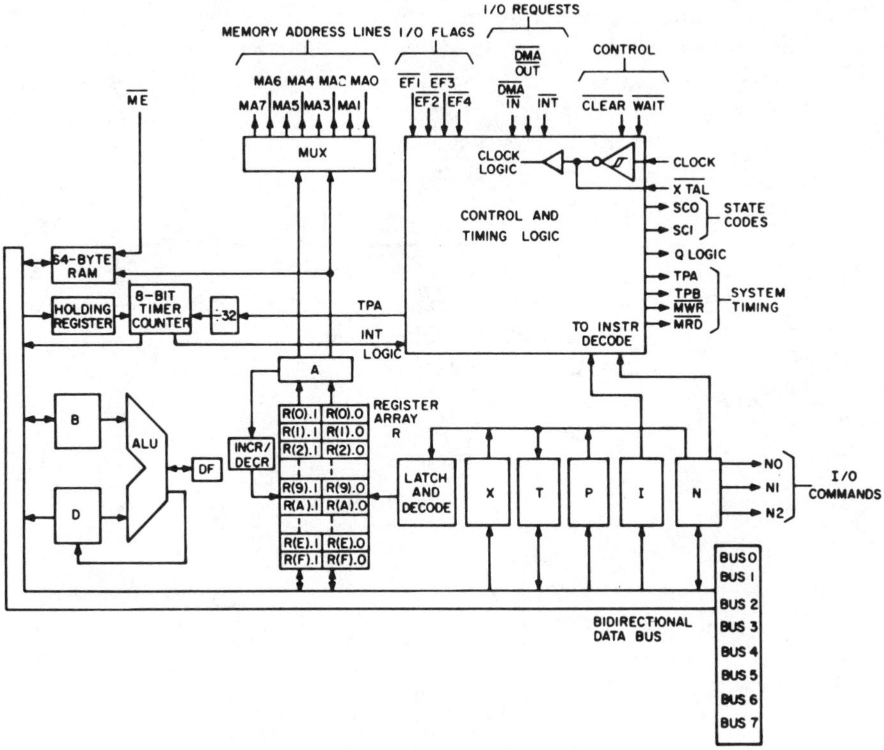

Courtesy RCA Solid State Division.

Block Diagram—1805/C, 8-Bit CPU
Fig. 4-5

5.0 (10 volt max.) volts peak. Also check the signal on pins 5 and 6. This should be a pulse train, synchronized to the clock and indicates the state of the CPU. When both signals are "O" it is in the "fetch" cycle. When both are "1", it is in the "INTERRUPT" mode.

For 90% Confidence Level:

All of the measurements made for the 75% confidence level must be correct. Add the following:

Monitor the clock on pin 1 in conjunction with the TPA signal on the oscilloscope. The TPA signal on pin 34 is related to the I/O operation of this IC.

EXACT REPLACEMENT PREFERRED—it may be possible to use CDP 1802 in some instances if the exact replacement is not available.

2650A, A-1 (Signetics) 8-Bit CPU

This device is manufactured using N-channel silicon gate MOS technology. It executes a fixed instruction set, with each instruction being one to three bytes in length. It contains a total of seven general purpose registers which may be used as a source or destination for arithmetic operations, as index registers, and for I/O memory transfers. An eight-level subroutine return address stack is included on the chip.

PIN NAME	DESCRIPTION	TYPE
ADR0-ADR12	Address Lines	O
ADR13-E/NE	Address 13-Extended/Non-extended	O
ADR14-D/C	Address 14-Data/Control	O
ADREN	Address Enable	I
DBUS0-DBUS7	Data Bus	I/O
DBUSEN	Data Bus Enable	I
OPREQ	Operation Request	O
OPACK	Operation Acknowledge	I
M/IO	Memory/Input-Output	O
R/W	Read/Write	O
WRP	Write Pulse	O
SENSE	Sense	I
FLAG	Flag	O
INTREQ	Interrupt Request	I
INTACK	Interrupt Acknowledge	O
PAUSE	Pause	I
RUN/WAIT	Run/Wait	O
RESET	Reset	I

PIN NAME	DESCRIPTION	TYPE
CLOCK	Clock	I
V_{CC}	Power Supply	
GND	Ground	

Special Features

- TTL level single phase clock.
- TTL compatible inputs and outputs.
- Variable length instructions of one, two, or three bytes.
- 32K byte addressing range.
- Coding efficiency with multiple addressing modes.
- Synchronous or asynchronous memory and I/O interface.
- Interfaces directly with industry standard memories.
- Single bit serial I/O path.
- Vectored interrupt.
- Cycle time: 1.5μs for 2650A-1; 2.4μs for 2650A.

PIN CONFIGURATION

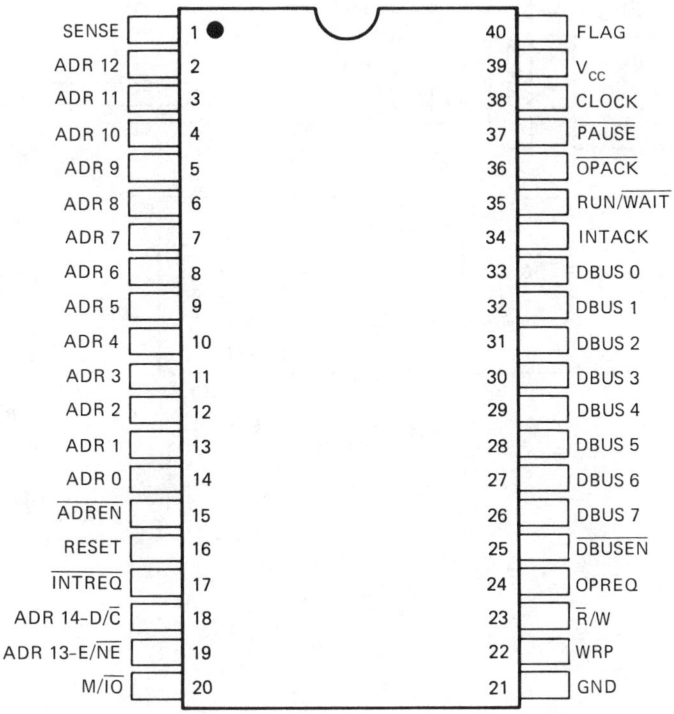

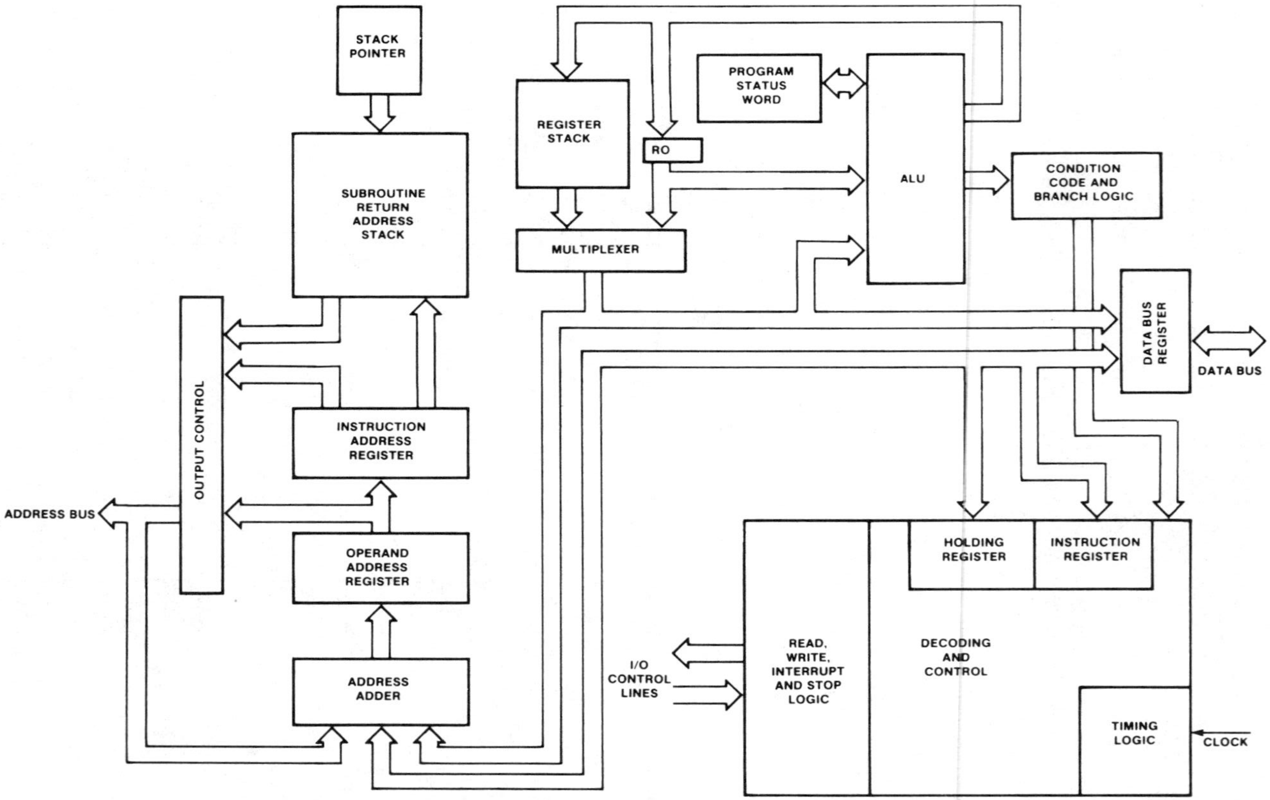

Courtesy of Signetics, 811 East Arques Avenue, Sunnyvale, CA 94086.

Block Diagram—2650A, A-1, 8-Bit CPU

Fig. 4-6

IN-CIRCUIT QUICK-TESTS

FOR 75% CONFIDENCE LEVEL:

1. Volt-ohmmeter Measurements: The PC board ground should be connected directly to pin 21. Power supply voltage of no less than 4.75 volts DC and no more than 5.25 volts DC should be measured from pin 39 to ground.
2. Oscilloscope Measurements: Clock signals with a frequency of 1.0MHz to 2.0MHz should appear at pin 38 with an amplitude of 2.4 to 5.25 volts peak. Also check the signal on pin 22. This should be a pulse train, synchronized to the clock, which indicates timing for WRITE operations.

FOR 90% CONFIDENCE LEVEL:

All of the measurements made for the 75% confidence level must be correct. Add the following:

Monitor the clock on pin 38 in conjunction with the R/W signal on the oscilloscope. The R/W signal on pin 23 is related to the READ/WRITE operation of this IC.

EXACT REPLACEMENT ESSENTIAL.

6500 SERIES (COMMODORE SEMICONDUCTOR GROUP) MICROPROCESSOR

The 6500 Series represents a totally software-compatible microprocessor family. This family of products includes a variety of microprocessors which provide a selection of addressable memory range, interrupt input options and on-chip clock oscillators and drivers. All of the microprocessors in the 6500 group are software-compatible within the group and are bus compatible with the M6800 product offering.

The family includes five microprocessors with on-board clock oscillators and drivers and four microprocessors driven by external clocks. The on-chip clock versions are aimed at high-performance, low-cost applications where single-phase inputs, crystal or RC oscillators, provide the time base. The external clock versions are geared for multi-processor system applications where maximum timing control is mandatory. All versions of the microprocessors are available in 1MHz and 2MHz ("A" suffix) maximum operating frequencies.

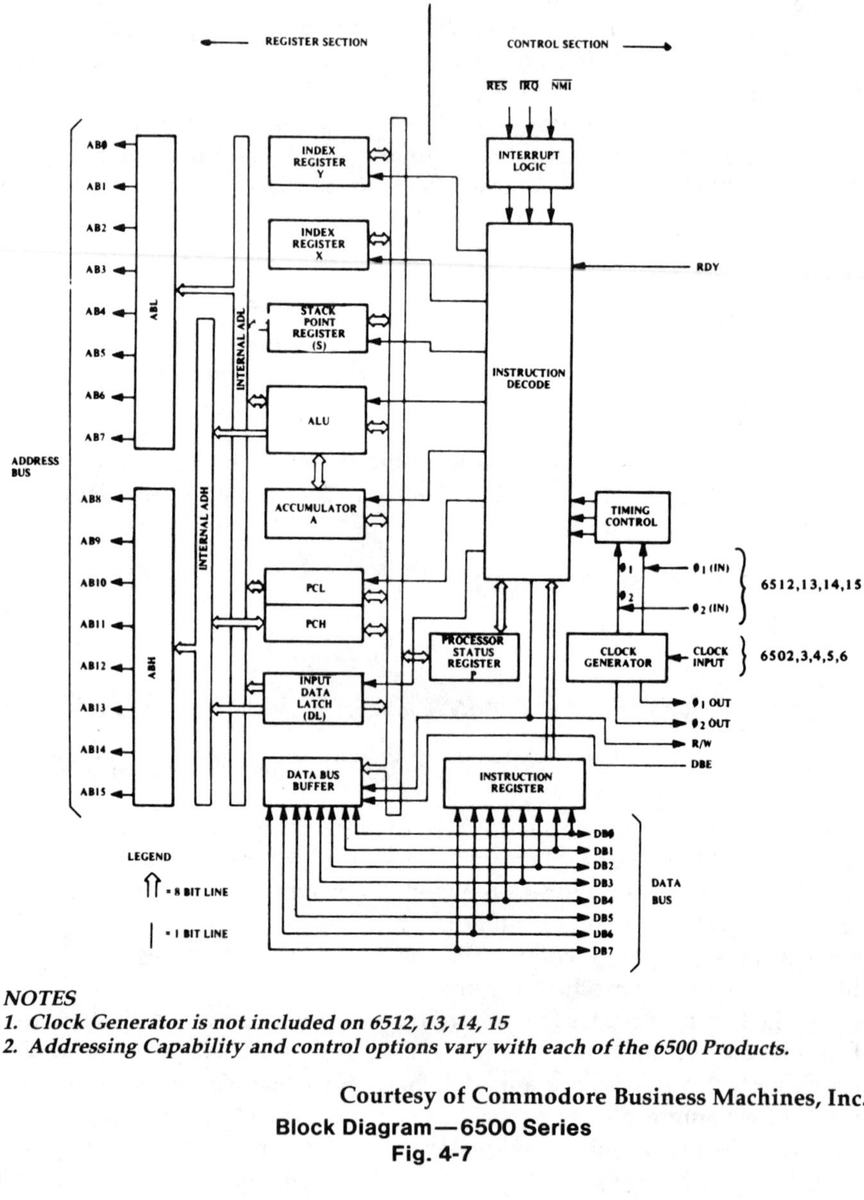

NOTES

1. *Clock Generator is not included on 6512, 13, 14, 15*
2. *Addressing Capability and control options vary with each of the 6500 Products.*

Courtesy of Commodore Business Machines, Inc.

Block Diagram—6500 Series

Fig. 4-7

PIN NAME	DESCRIPTION	TYPE
AB0-AB15	Address Bus	O
D0-D7	Data Bus	I/O
DBE	Data Bus Enable	I
Ø1	Clock	
Ø2	Clock	
RDY	Ready	I
$\overline{\text{IRQ}}$	Interrupt Request	I
$\overline{\text{NMI}}$	Non-maskable Interrupt	I
S.O.	Set Overflow Flag	I
SYNC	Syncronism	O
RESET	Reset	I
R/W	Read/Write	O
V_{CC}	Power Supply	
V_{SS}	Ground	

Special Features

- Single +5V power supply.
- 8-bit parallel processing.
- 56 instructions.
- Decimal and Binary Arithmetic.
- 13 addressing modes.
- Programmable Stack Pointer and Variable-length Stack.
- Usable with any type or speed memory.
- One or two MHz operation.
- Pipelined architecture.

6502 MICROPROCESSOR

Special Features

- 65K addressable bytes of memory.
- $\overline{\text{IRQ}}$ interrupt
- $\overline{\text{NMI}}$ interrupt.
- On-the-chip clock:
  TTL level single phase input;
  RC time base input;
  crystal time base input.
- SYNC signal (can be used for single instruction execution).
- RDY signal (can be used for single instruction execution).
- Two phase output clock for timing of support chips.

PIN CONFIGURATION

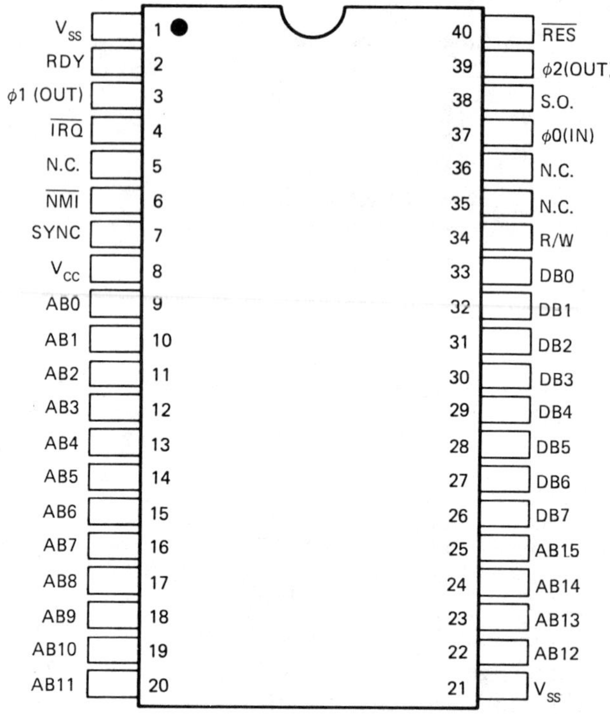

IN-CIRCUIT QUICK-TESTS

FOR 75% CONFIDENCE LEVEL:

1. Volt-ohmmeter Measurements: The PC board ground should be connected directly to pins 1 and 21. Power supply voltage of no less than 4.75 volts DC and no more than 5.25 volts DC should be measured from pin 8 to ground.
2. Oscilloscope Measurements: Clock signals with a frequency of 1.0MHz and 2.0MHz should appear at pins 3, 37 and 39 with an amplitude of 4.8 to 5.25 volts peak. Also check the signal on pin 7. This should be a pulse train, synchronized to the clock and indicates that an OP CODE fetch cycle is in progress.

FOR 90% CONFIDENCE LEVEL:

All of the measurements made for the 75% confidence level must be correct. Add the following:

Monitor the clock on pin 39 in conjunction with the A0-A15 signal on the oscilloscope. The A0-A15 signal on pins 9-25 is related to the address bus operation of this IC.

EXACT REPLACEMENT ESSENTIAL.

6503 MICROPROCESSOR

Special Features

- 4K addressable bytes of memory (AB00-AB11).
- On-the-chip clock.
- $\overline{\text{IRQ}}$ interrupt.
- $\overline{\text{NMI}}$ interrupt.
- 8-bit bidirectional data bus.

PIN CONFIGURATION

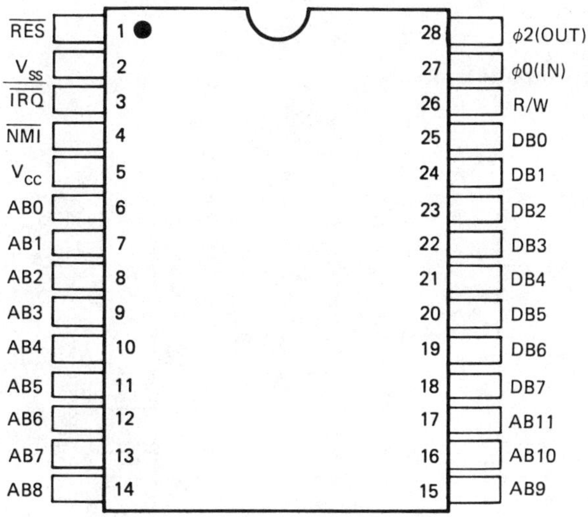

IN-CIRCUIT QUICK-TESTS

FOR 75% CONFIDENCE LEVEL:

1. Volt-ohmmeter Measurements: The PC board ground should be connected directly to pin 2. Power supply voltage of no less than 4.75 volts DC and no more than 5.25 volts DC should be measured from pin 5 to ground.
2. Oscilloscope Measurements: Clock signals with a frequency of 1.0MHz to 2.0MHz should appear at pins 27 and 28 with an

amplitude of 4.8 to 5.25 volts peak. Also check the signal on pin 26. This should be a pulse train, synchronized to the clock and controlling the READ/WRITE cycle.

For 90% Confidence Level:

All of the measurements made for the 75% confidence level must be correct. Add the following:

Monitor the clock on pin 28 in conjunction with the AB0-AB11 signal on the oscilloscope. The AB0-AB11 signal on pins 6–17 is related to the address bus operation of this IC.

EXACT REPLACEMENT ESSENTIAL.

6504 Microprocessor

Special Features

- 8K addressable bytes of memory (AB00-AB12).
- On-the-chip clock.
- $\overline{\text{IRQ}}$ interrupt.
- 8-Bit bidirectional data bus.

Pin Configuration

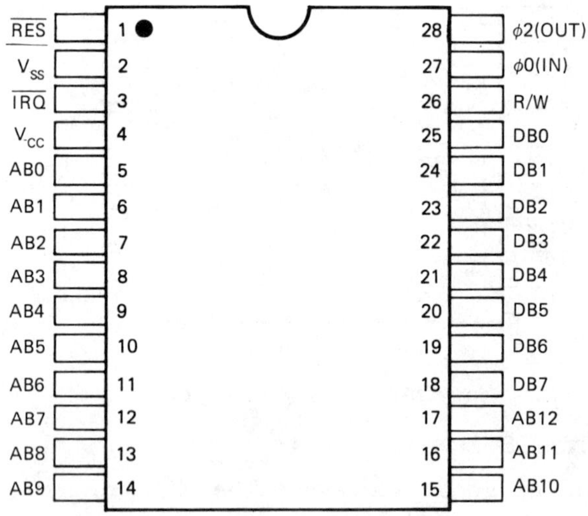

IN-CIRCUIT QUICK-TESTS

For 75% Confidence Level:

1. Volt-ohmmeter Measurements: The PC board ground should be connected directly to pin 2. Power supply voltage of no less than

4.75 volts DC and no more than 5.25 volts DC should be measured from pin 4 to ground.

2. Oscilloscope Measurements: Clock signals with a frequency of 1.0MHz to 2.0MHz should appear at pins 27 and 28 with an amplitude of 4.8 to 5.25 volts peak. Also check the signal on pin 26. This should be a pulse train, synchronized to the clock and controls the READ/WRITE cycle.

FOR 90% CONFIDENCE LEVEL:

All of the measurements made for the 75% confidence level must be correct. Add the following:

Monitor the clock on pin 28 in conjunction with the AB0-AB12 signal on the oscilloscope. The AB0-AB12 signal on pins 5–17 is related to the address bus operation of this IC.

EXACT REPLACEMENT ESSENTIAL.

6505 MICROPROCESSOR

Special Features

- 4K Addressable Bytes of Memory (AB00-AB11).
- On-the-chip clock.
- $\overline{\text{IRQ}}$ interrupt.
- RDY signal.
- 8-bit bidirectional data bus.
- See 6503 for IN-CIRCUIT QUICK-TESTS.

PIN CONFIGURATION

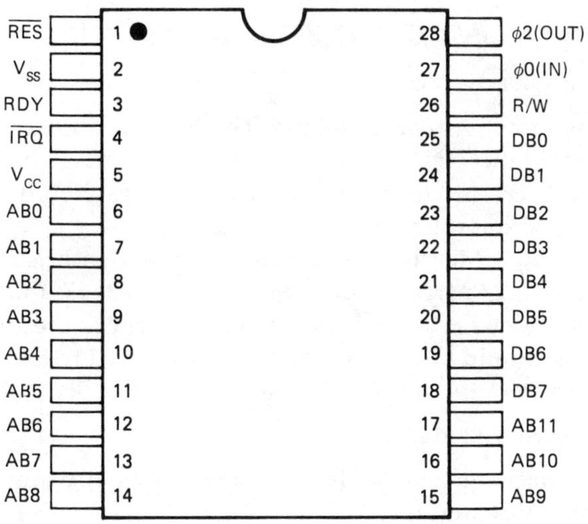

6506 MICROPROCESSOR

Special Features

- 4K addressable bytes of memory (AB00-AB11).
- On-the-chip clock.
- $\overline{\text{IRQ}}$ interrupt.
- Two phases off.
- 8-bit bidirectional data bus.

PIN CONFIGURATION

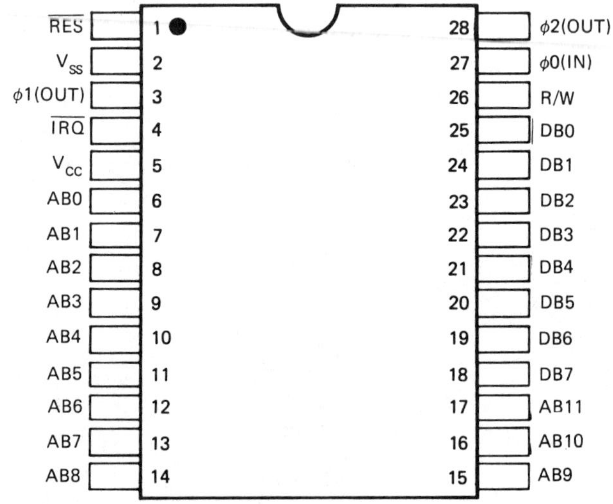

IN-CIRCUIT QUICK-TESTS

FOR 75% CONFIDENCE LEVEL:

1. Volt-ohmmeter Measurements: The PC board ground should be connected directly to pin 2. Power supply voltage of no less than 4.75 volts DC and no more than 5.25 volts DC should be measured from pin 5 to ground.
2. Oscilloscope Measurements: Clock signals with a frequency of 1.0MHz to 2.0MHz should appear at pins 3, 27 and 28 with an amplitude of 4.8 to 5.25 volts peak. Also check the signal on pin 26. This should be a pulse train, synchronized to the clock and it controls the READ/WRITE cycle.

FOR 90% CONFIDENCE LEVEL:

All of the measurements made for the 75% confidence level must be correct. Add the following:

Monitor the clock on pin 28 in conjunction with the AB0-AB11 signal on the oscilloscope. The AB0-AB11 signal on pins 6–17 is related to the address bus operation of this IC.

EXACT REPLACEMENT ESSENTIAL.

6507 MICROPROCESSOR

Special Features

- 8K addressable bytes of memory.
- On-the-chip clock.
- RDY signal.
- 8-bit bidirectional data bus.

See 6504 for IN-CIRCUIT QUICK-TEST.

PIN CONFIGURATION

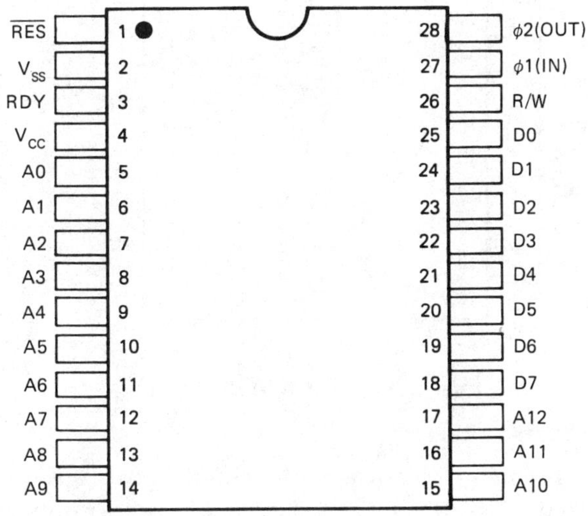

6512 MICROPROCESSOR

Special Features

- 65K addressable bytes of memory.
- $\overline{\text{IRQ}}$ interrupt.
- $\overline{\text{NMI}}$ interrupt.
- RDY signal.
- 8-bit bidirectional data bus.
- SYNC signal.

- Two phase input.
- Data bus enable.

PIN CONFIGURATION

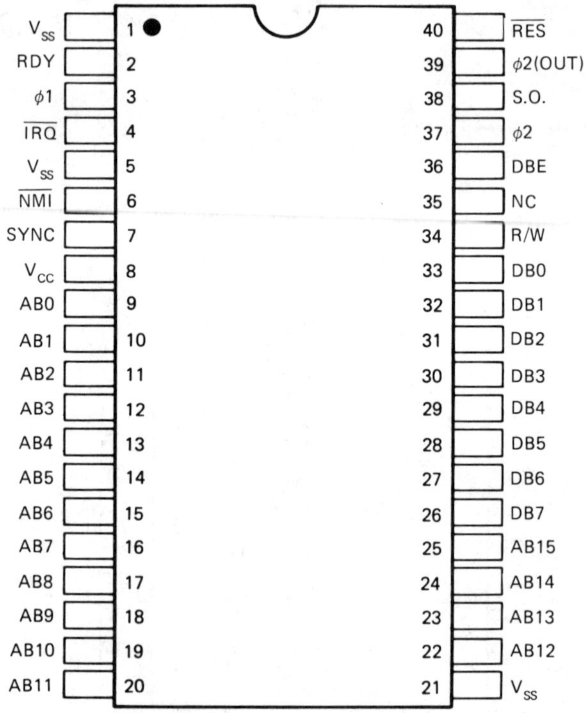

IN-CIRCUIT QUICK-TESTS

FOR 75% CONFIDENCE LEVEL:

1. Volt-ohmmeter Measurements: The PC board ground should be connected directly to pins 1, 5 and 21. Power supply voltage of no less than 4.75 volts DC and no more than 5.25 volts DC should be measured from pin 8 to ground.
2. Oscilloscope Measurements: Clock signals with a frequency of 1.0 MHz to 2.0 MHz should appear at pins 3, 37 and 39 with an amplitude of 4.8 to 5.25 volts peak. Also check the signal on pin 7. This should be a pulse train, synchronized to the clock and indicates that an OP CODE fetch cycle is in progress.

FOR 90% CONFIDENCE LEVEL:

All of the measurements made for the 75% confidence level must be correct. Add the following:

Monitor the clock on pin 39 in conjunction with the A0–A15 signal on the oscilloscope. The A0–A15 signal on pins 9–25 is related to the address bus operation of this IC.

EXACT REPLACEMENT ESSENTIAL.

6513 MICROPROCESSOR

Special Features

- 4K addressable bytes of memory (AB00–AB11).
- Two phase clock input.
- $\overline{\text{IRQ}}$ interrupt.
- $\overline{\text{NMI}}$ interrupt.
- 8-bit bidirectional data bus.

PIN CONFIGURATION

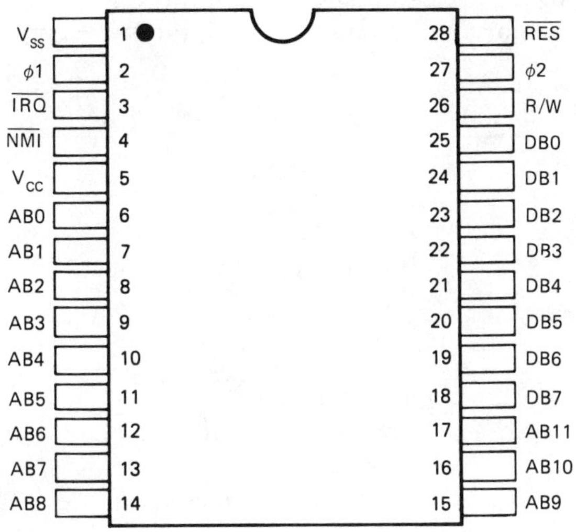

IN-CIRCUIT QUICK-TESTS

FOR 75% CONFIDENCE LEVEL:

1. Volt-ohmmeter Measurements: The PC board ground should be connected directly to pin 1. Power supply voltage of no less than 4.75 volts DC and no more than 5.25 volts DC should be measured from pin 5 to ground.
2. Oscilloscope Measurements: Clock signals with a frequency of 1.0 MHz to 2.0 MHz should appear at pins 2 and 27 with an amplitude of 4.8 and 5.25 volts peak. Also check the signal on pin

26. This should be a pulse train, synchronized to the clock and it controls the READ/WRITE cycle.

For 90% Confidence Level:

All of the measurements made for the 75% confidence level must be correct. Add the following:

Monitor the clock on pin 27 in conjunction with the AB0–AB11 signal on the oscilloscope. The AB0–AB11 signal on pins 6–17 is related to the address bus operation of this IC.

EXACT REPLACEMENT ESSENTIAL.

MC 6800 (Motorola) 8-bit CPU[4]

This device is TTL compatible, it does not require external TTL devices for bus interface. It is capable of addressing 65K bytes of memory with its 16-bit address lines. The 8-bit data bus is bidirectional as well as 3-state, making direct memory addressing and multiprocessing applications realizable.

PIN NAME	DESCRIPTION	TYPE
A0–A15	Address Bus	O
D0–D7	Data Bus	I/O
01, 02	Clock Phase	I
DBE	Data Bus Enable	I
BA	Bus Available	O
$R/\overline{W}$	Read/Write	O
$\overline{\text{RESET}}$	Reset	I
$\overline{\text{IRQ}}$	Interrupt Request	I
$\overline{\text{NMI}}$	Non-maskable Interrupt	I
TSC	Three State Control	I
VMA	Valid Memory Address	O
$\overline{\text{HALT}}$	Halt	I
V_{CC}	Power Supply	
V_{SS}	Ground	

[4]NOTE: The MC 6800 operates at 1.0MHz, the MC 68A00 operates at 1.5MHz, and the MC68B00 operates at 2MHz.

The same microprocessor is manufactured by:
FAIRCHILD—F 6800;
AMI—S 6800;
HITACHI—HD46800;
FUJITSU—MBM6800.

Special Features

- 72 variable length instructions.
- Seven addressing modes— direct, relative, immediate, indexed, extended, implied, and accumulator.
- Variable length stack.
- Vectored restart.
- Maskable interrupt vector.
- Separate non-maskable interrupt–internal registers saved in stack.
- Six internal registers—two accumulators, index register, program counter, stack pointer, and condition code register.
- Halt and single instruction execution capability.

PIN CONFIGURATION

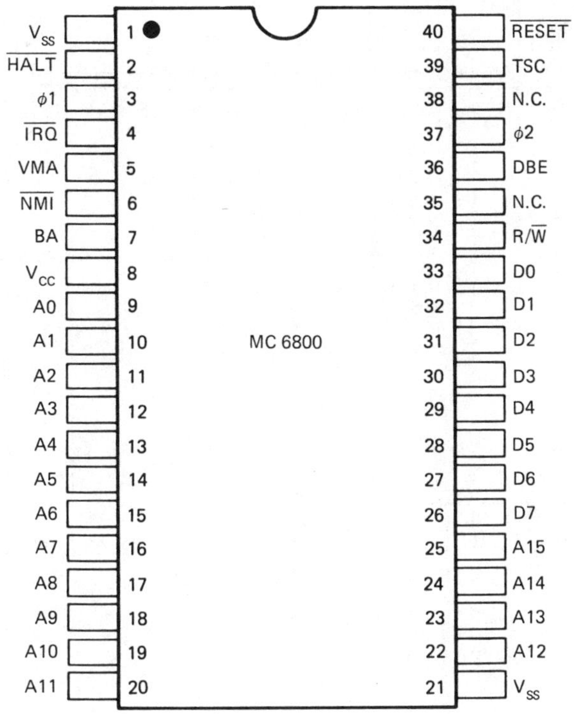

IN-CIRCUIT QUICK-TESTS

FOR 75% CONFIDENCE LEVEL:

1. Volt-ohmmeter Measurements: The PC board ground should be connected directly to pins 1 and 21. Power supply voltage of no

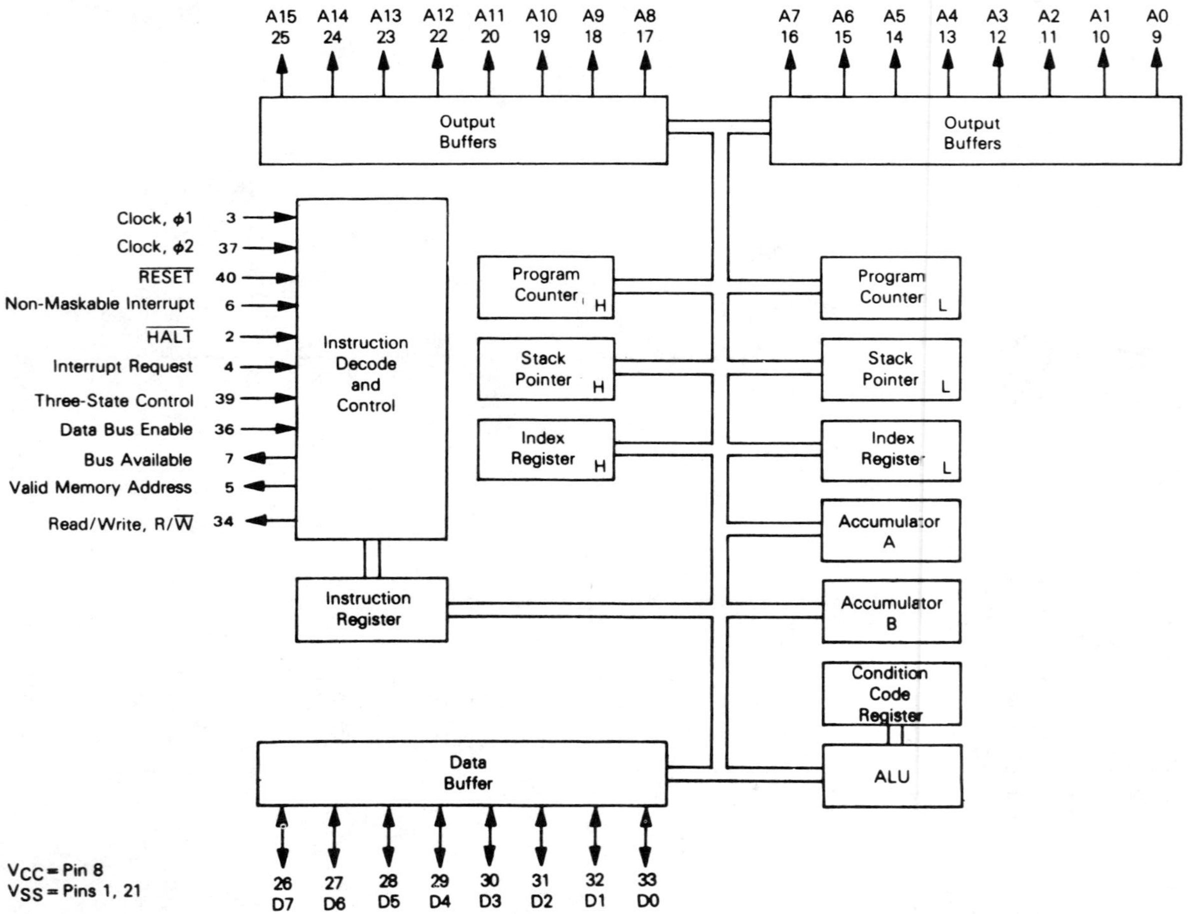

Courtesy Motorola, Inc.

Block Diagram—6800, 8-Bit CPU
Fig. 4-8

less than 4.0 volts DC and no more than 5.25 volts DC should be measured from pin 8 to ground.

2. Oscilloscope Measurements: Clock signals with a frequency of 0.1MHz to 1.0MHz should appear at pins 3 and 37 with an amplitude of 4.3 to 5.5 volts peak. Also check the signal on pin 5. This should be a pulse train, synchronized to the clock, indicating that a valid memory address is on the address bus. The VMA signal will change as machine cycles change.

For 90% Confidence Level:

All of the measurements made for the 75% confidence level must be correct. Add the following:

Monitor the 0_1 clock on pin 3 in conjunction with the 0_2 clock signal on the oscilloscope. The 0_1 signal on pin 3 is the exact opposite of 0_2 on pin 37. Check the 3A (Bus Available) signal on pin 7. It is normally "0", but will be "1" if $\overline{\text{HALT}}$ (pin 2) is "0" or if the WAIT instruction is being executed.

EXACT REPLACEMENT PREFERRED—it may be possible to use the 68A00 or 68B00 if the exact replacement is not available, but not the other way around.

MC 6802, MC 6808, MC 6802NS (Motorola) Microprocessor[5a,b]

These devices contain all the registers and accumulators of the present MC 6800, plus an internal clock oscillator and driver on the same chip. In addition, the MC 6802 has 128 bytes of on-board RAM. The first 32 bytes of RAM may be retained in a low power mode by utilizing V_{CC} standby, facilitating memory retention during a power-down situation.

The MC 6808 is identical to the MC 6802 without on-board RAM.

The MC 6802NS is identical to the MC 6802 without standby RAM features.

8-Bit CPU

[5a]NOTE 1:
The MC6802, MC6808, MC6802NS operating at 1MHz.
The MC68A02, and MC68A08 operating at 1.5MHz.
The MC68B02, and MC68B08 operating at 2.0MHz.

[5b]NOTE 2: The same microprocessor is manufactured by:
AMI—S6802;
FAIRCHILD—F6802;
HITACHI—HD46802;
FUJITSU—MBM6802.

PIN NAME	DESCRIPTION	TYPE
A0–A15	Address Bus	O
D0–D7	Data Bus	I/O
$\overline{\text{HALT}}$	Halt	I
R/$\overline{\text{W}}$	Read/Write	O
VMA	Valid Memory Address	O
BA	Bus Available	O
$\overline{\text{IRQ}}$	Interrupt Request	I
$\overline{\text{RESET}}$	Reset	I
$\overline{\text{NMI}}$	Non-maskable Interrupt	I
RE (MC6802, MC6802NS)	RAM Enable	I
EXTAL, XTAL	Crystal	I
MR	Memory Ready	I
E	Enable	O
V_{CC} STANDBY (MC6802)	Standby Power supply	
V_{CC}	Power supply	
V_{SS}	Ground	

Pin Configuration

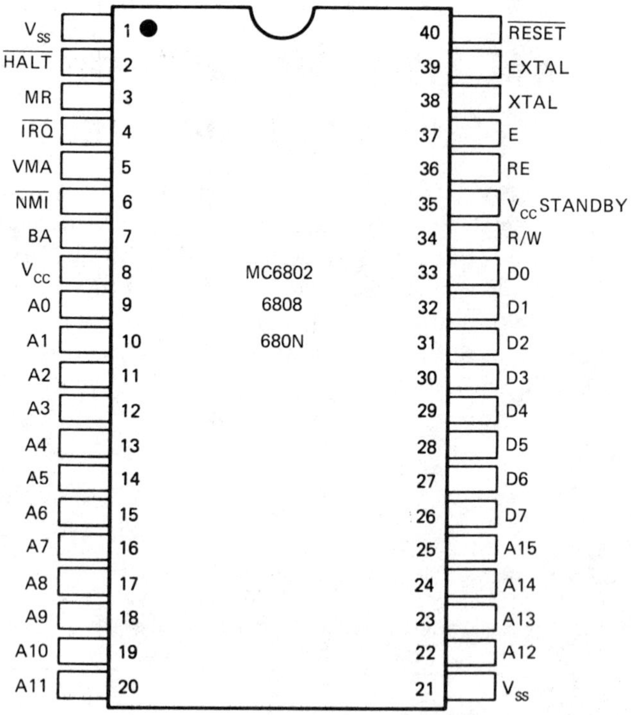

Note: Pin 35 must be tied to 5V on the MC6802NS; pin 36 must be tied to GND on the MC6808.

Special Features

- Software compatible with the MC6800.
- Expandable to 64K words.
- Standard TTL-compatible inputs and outputs.
- 8-bit word size.
- 16-bit memory addressing.
- Interrupt capability.

IN-CIRCUIT QUICK-TESTS

For 75% Confidence Level:

1. Volt-ohmmeter Measurements: The PC board ground should be connected directly to pins 1 and 21. Power supply voltage of no

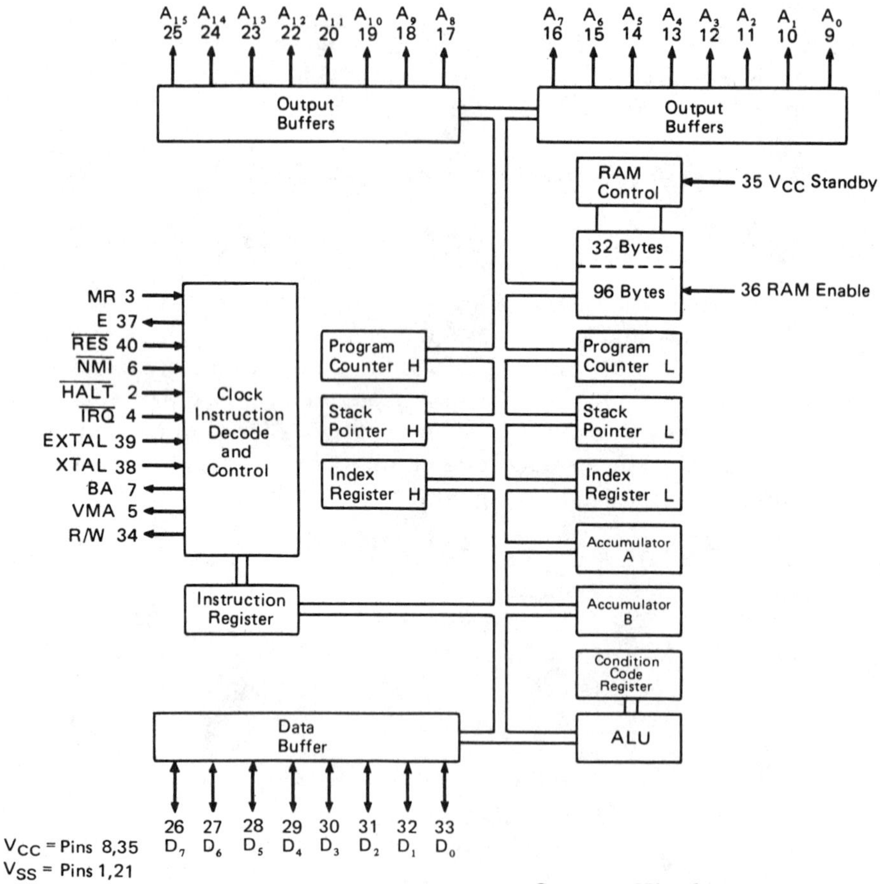

Courtesy Hitachi America, Ltd.

Block Diagram—6802, 6808, 6802NS, 8-Bit CPU
Fig. 4-9

less than 4.75 volts DC and no more than 5.25 volts DC should be measured from pins 8 and 35 to ground.

2. Oscilloscope Measurements: Clock signals with a frequency of 0.1MHz to 1.0MHz should appear at pin 37 with an amplitude of 4.0 to 4.5 volts peak. Also check the signal on pins 38 and 39. This should be a pulse train, synchronized to the clock either by a factor of 4× for external crystal or at clock frequency for oscillator.

FOR 90% CONFIDENCE LEVEL:

All of the measurements made for the 75% confidence level must be correct. Add the following:

Monitor the clock on pin 37 in conjunction with the VMA signal on the oscilloscope. The VMA signal on pin 5 is related to the address bus operation of this IC.

EXACT REPLACEMENT PREFERRED—it may be possible to use the 6802NS if the exact replacement is not available, but this eliminates the standby power RAM feature.

MC 6809/MC 68A09/MC 68B09 (MOTOROLA) 8-BIT CPU[6]

This device supports programming techniques such as position independence, reentrancy, and modular programming. It has 10 addressing modes, 1464 instructions with unique addressing modes, transfer/exchange all registers, push/pull any registers or any set of registers. It has an on-chip oscillator and the external clock inputs are provided to allow synchronization with peripherals, systems or other microprocessors. Although similar to the 6809E series, the pin configuration is different.

PIN NAME	DESCRIPTION	TYPE
A0–A15	Address Bus	O
D0–D7	Data Bus	I/O
R/$\overline{W}$	Read/Write	O
$\overline{RESET}$	Reset	I
$\overline{HALT}$	Halt	I
BA	Bus Available	O
BS	Bus Status	O
$\overline{NMI}$	Non-maskable Interrupt	I
$\overline{IRQ}$	Interrupt Request	I

[6]Note: The same microprocessor is manufactured by:
FAIRCHILD—F6809;
HITACHI—HD6809.

PIN NAME	DESCRIPTION	TYPE
FIRQ	Fast Interrupt Request	I
XTAL, EXTAL	Crystal	I
MRDY	Memory Ready	I
E, Q	Clock	O
$\overline{\mathrm{DMA/BREQ}}$	Direct Memory Access/Bus Request	I
V_{CC}	Power Supply	
V_{SS}	Ground	

Special Features

- 6800 upward compatible addressing modes.
- Direct addressing anywhere in memory map.
- True indirect addressing.
- $\overline{\mathrm{DMA/BREQ}}$ allows DMA operation on memory refresh.
- MRDY extends data access times for use with slow memory.
- Single bus-cycle $\overline{\mathrm{RESET}}$.
- Early address valid allows use with slower memories.
- Early write-data for dynamic memories.

PIN CONFIGURATION

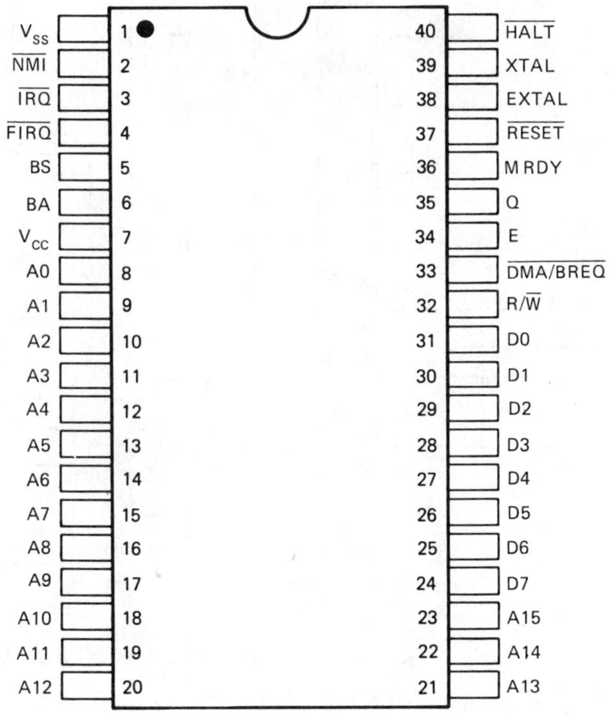

- 16–bit arithmetic.
- Frequency of operation:
  1. 0MHz MC6809;
  1. 5MHz MC68A09;
  2. 0MHz MC68B09.

IN CIRCUIT QUICK-TESTS

For 75% Confidence Level:

1. Volt-ohmmeter Measurements: The PC board ground should be connected directly to pin 1. Power supply voltage of no less than 4.75 volts DC and no more than 5.25 volts DC should be measured from pin 7 to ground.
2. Oscilloscope Measurements: Clock signals with a frequency of

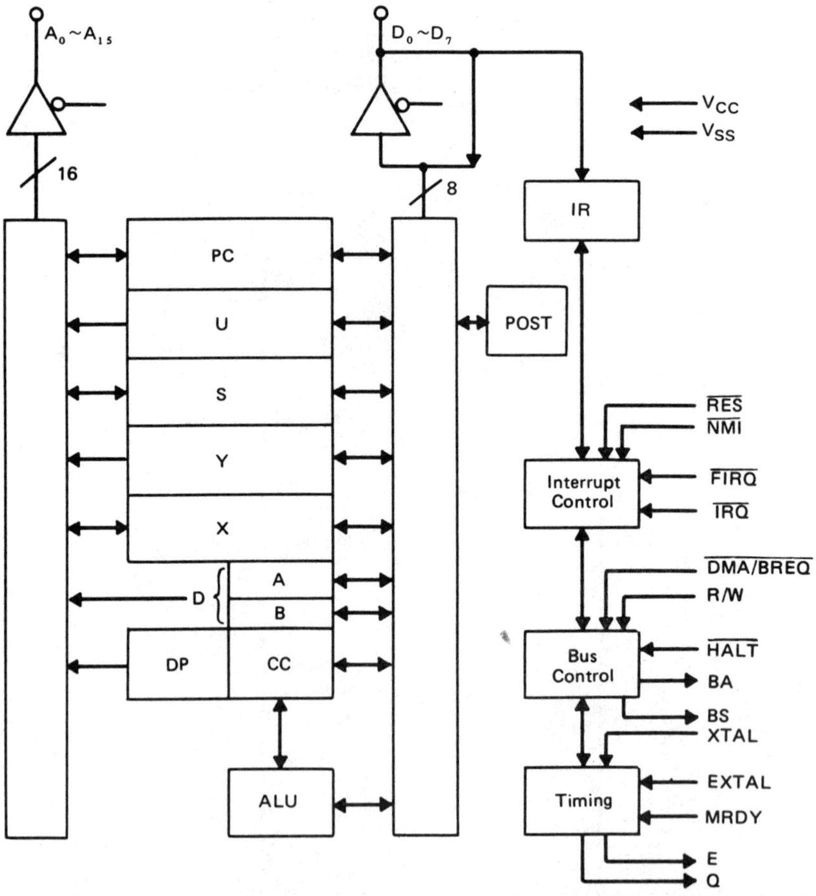

Courtesy Hitachi America, Ltd.

Block Diagram—6809, 68A09, 68B09, 8-Bit CPU
Fig. 4-10

0.4MHz to 4, 6 or 8 MHz (6809, 68A09, 68B09) should appear at pins 38 and 39 with an amplitude of 2 to 5.25 volts peak. Also check the signal on pins 34 and 35. This should be a pulse train, synchronized to the clock and indicating that addresses are valid (Q, pin 35) and data is Latched (E, pin 34).

FOR 90% CONFIDENCE LEVEL:

All of the measurements made for the 75% confidence level must be correct. Add the following:

Monitor the clock on pin 38 or 39 in conjunction with the R/$\overline{W}$ signal on the oscilloscope. The R/$\overline{W}$ signal on pin 32 is related to the READ/WRITE operation of this IC.

EXACT REPLACEMENT PREFERRED—it may be possible to use the 6809E, 68A09E or 68B09E if the exact replacement is not available.

MC6809E/MC68A09E/MC68B09E (MOTOROLA) 8-BIT CPU[7]

This device supports programming techniques such as position independence, reentrancy, and modular programming. It has 10 addressing modes, 1464 instructions with unique addressing modes, transfer/exchange all registers, push/pull any registers or any set of registers. It has an on-chip oscillator and the external clock inputs are provided to allow synchronization with peripherals, systems or other microprocessors. Although similar to the 6809 series, the pin configuration is different.

PIN NAME	DESCRIPTION	TYPE
A0-A15	Address Bus	O
D0-D7	Data Bus	I/O
R/$\overline{W}$	Read/Write	O
$\overline{RESET}$	Reset	I
$\overline{HALT}$	Halt	I
BA	Bus Available	O
BS	Bus Status	O
$\overline{NMI}$	Non-maskable Interrupt	I
$\overline{FIRQ}$	Fast Interrupt Request	I
$\overline{IRQ}$	Interrupt Request	I
E, Q	Clock	I
BUSY	Busy	O
AVMA	Advanced VMA	O
LIC	Last Instruction Cycle	O
TSC	Three State Control	I

[7]Note: The same microprocessor is manufactured by:
FAIRCHILD—F6809E;
HITACHI—HD46809E.

PIN NAME	DESCRIPTION	TYPE
V_{CC}	Power Supply	
V_{SS}	Ground	

Special Features

- M6800 upward compatible addressing modes.
- Direct addressing anywhere in memory map.
- True indirect addressing.
- TSC controls internal bus buffers.
- LIC indicates opcode fetch.
- AVMA allows use of common resources in a multiprocessor system.
- BUSY is a status line for multiprocessing.
- Single bus-cycle RESET.
- Early address valid allows use with slower memories.
- Early write-data for dynamic memories.
- 16-bit arithmetic.
- Frequency of operation:
  1. 0MHz MC6809E;
  1. 5MHz MC68A09E;
  2. 0MHz MC68B09E.

PIN CONFIGURATION

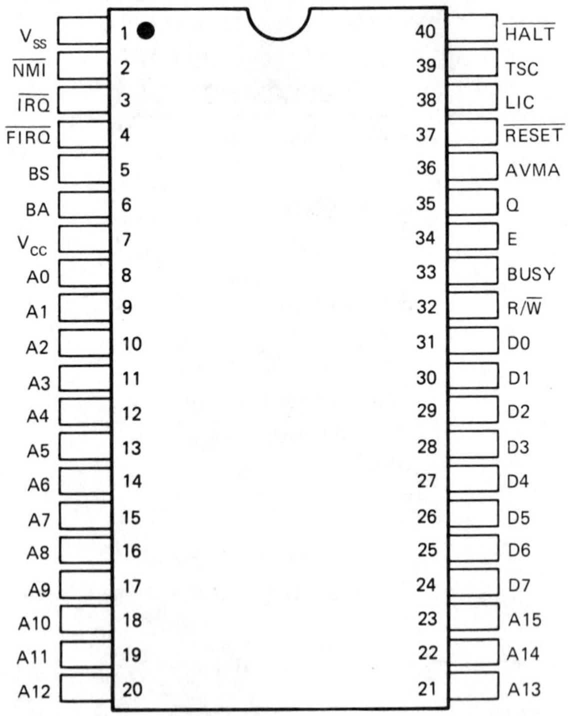

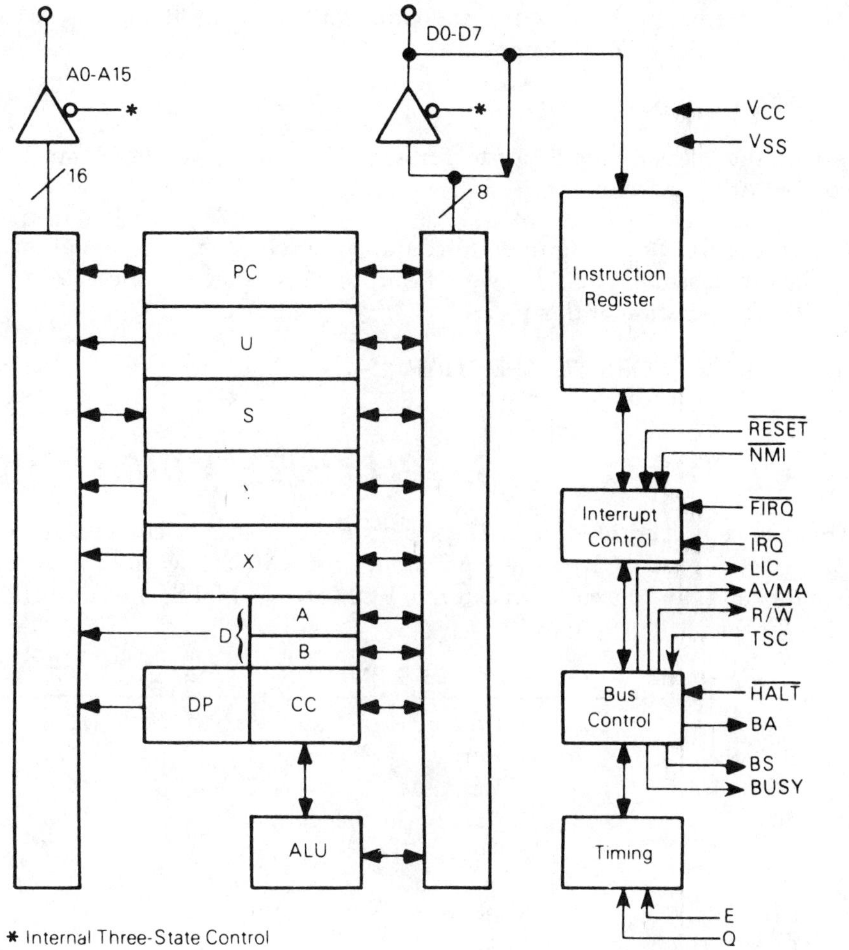

Courtesy Motorola, Inc.

Block Diagram—6809E, 68A09E, 68B09E, 8-Bit CPU
Fig. 4-11

IN-CIRCUIT, QUICK-TESTS

FOR 75% CONFIDENCE LEVEL:

1. Volt-ohmmeter Measurements: The PC board ground should be connected directly to pin 1. Power supply voltage of no less than 4.75 volts DC and no more than 5.25 volts DC should be measured from pin 7 to ground.
2. Oscilloscope Measurements: Clock signals with a frequency of 0.1MHz to 1, 1.5 and 2MHz (6809E, 68A09E, 68B09E) should appear at pins 34 and 35 with an amplitude of 2.0 to 5.25 volts peak. Also check the signal on pin 39. This should be a pulse

train, synchronized to the clock and indicates the status of the Tri-State Control signal.

For 90% Confidence Level:

All of the measurements made for the 75% confidence level must be correct. Add the following:

Monitor the clock on pin 34 in conjunction with the R/$\overline{W}$ signal on the oscilloscope. The R/$\overline{W}$ signal on pin 32 is related to the READ/WRITE operation of this IC.

EXACT REPLACEMENT ESSENTIAL.

8040H (INTEL) 8-BIT CPU

This device is fabricated on a single silicon chip using N-channel silicon gate HMOS process. It is the equivalent of the 8050H without program memory and can be used with external ROM and RAM. It is the equivalent CPU for the 8050H, 8-bit μC.

PIN NAME	DESCRIPTION	TYPE
P10-P17	Port 1	I/O
P20-P27	Port 2	I/O
DB0-DB7	Data Bus	I/O
T0	Test or Clock Input	I
T1	Test or Timer/Counter	I
$\overline{INT}$	Interrupt	I
$\overline{RD}$	Read	O
$\overline{RESET}$	Reset	I
$\overline{WR}$	Write	O
ALE	Address Latch Enable	O
$\overline{PSEN}$	Program Store Enable	O
$\overline{SS}$	Single Step	I
EA	External Access	I
XTAL1, XTAL2	Crystal	I
PROG	Port Extender Strobe	O
V_{CC}	Power Supply	
V_{DD}	Low Power Standby	
V_{SS}	Ground	

Special Features

- See the 8050H, an 8-bit μC.

Pin Configuration

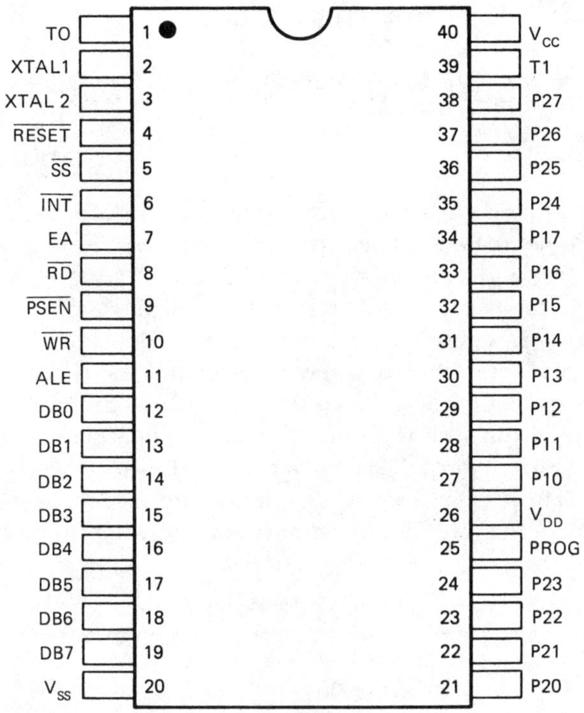

IN-CIRCUIT QUICK-TESTS

For 75% Confidence Level:

1. Volt-ohmmeter Measurements: The PC board ground should be connected directly to pin 20. Power supply voltage of no less than 4.5 volts DC and no more than 5.5 volts DC should be measured from pin 40 to ground.
2. Oscilloscope Measurements: Clock signals with a frequency of 0.1MHz to 6.0MHz should appear at pins 2 and 3 with an amplitude of 2.5 to 5.5 volts peak. Also check the signal on pin 11. This should be a pulse train, synchronized to the clock and it represents the ALE (Address Latch Enable) strobe.

For 90% Confidence Level:

All of the measurements made for the 75% confidence level must be correct. Add the following:

Monitor the clock on pins 2 and 3 in conjunction with the WR signal on the oscilloscope. The WR signal on pin 10 is related to the WRITE operation of this IC.

EXACT REPLACEMENT ESSENTIAL.

8080A/8080A-1/8080A-2 (INTEL)
8-BIT CPU[8]

This device contains six 8-bit general purpose working registers and an accumulator. The registers may be addressed individually or in pairs, providing both single and double precision operators. Arithmetic and logical instructions set or reset four testable flags. A fifth flag provides decimal arithmetic operation. The 8080A has an external stack feature wherein any portion of memory may be used as a last in/first out stack to store/retrieve the contents of the accumulator, flags, program counter, and all of the general purpose registers. The 16-bit stack pointer controls the addressing of this external stack. Separate 16-line address and 8-line bidirectional data busses are used to facilitate interface to memory and I/O. Signals to control the interface to memory and I/O are provided directly by the 8080A.

PIN NAME	DESCRIPTION	TYPE
A15-A0	Address Bus	O
D7-D0	Data Bus	I/O
SYNC	Synchronizing Signal	O
DBIN	Data Bus In	O
READY	Ready	I
WAIT	Wait	O
$\overline{WR}$	Write	O
HOLD	Hold	I
HLDA	Hold Acknowledge	O
INTE	Interrupt Enable	O
INT	Interrupt Request	I
RESET	Reset	I
01, 02	Clock Phases	
V_{DD}	$+12V \pm 5\%$	
V_{CC}	$+5V \pm 5\%$	
V_{BB}	$-5V \pm 5\%$	
V_{SS}	Ground	

[8]Note: The M 8080A is the military version of the 8080A. It has a military temperature range (−55°C to +125°C) and power supply tolerance (±10%).

Special Features

- TTL drive capability.
- Instruction Cycle: 2.0 μsec. for 8080A: 1.3 μsec. for 8080A-1; 1.5 μsec. for 8080A-2.
- 16-bit program counter for directly addressing up to 64K bytes of memory.
- 16-bit stack pointer and stack manipulation instructions for rapid switching of the program environment.
- Decimal, binary, and double precision arithmetic.
- Provides priority vectored interrupts.
- 512 directly addressed I/O ports.

IN-CIRCUIT QUICK-TESTS

For 75% Confidence Level:

1. Volt-ohmmeter Measurements: The PC board ground should be connected directly to pin 2. Power supply voltage of no less than

Pin Configuration

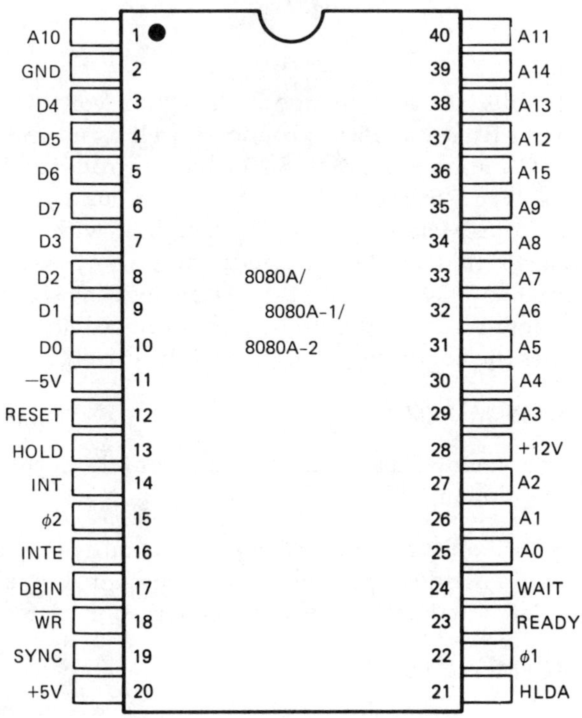

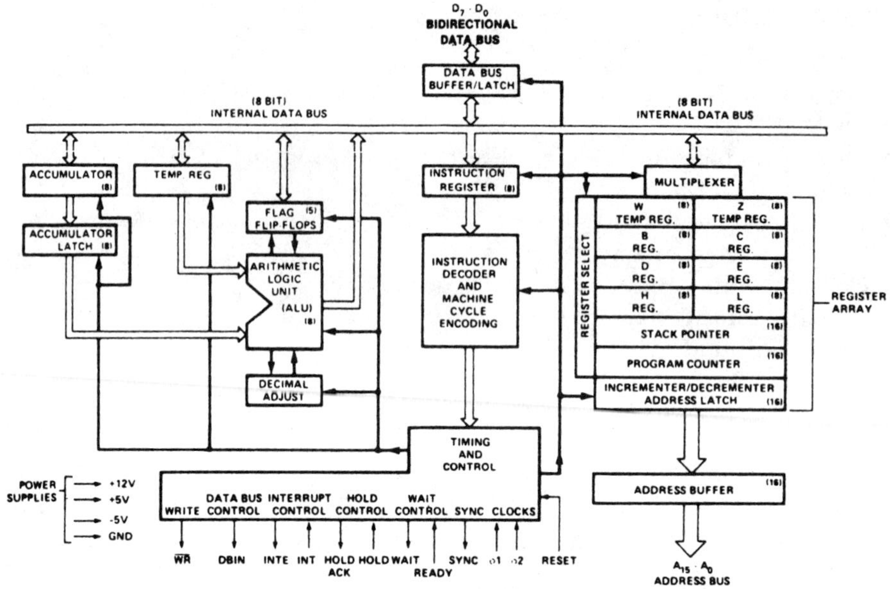

Reprinted by permission of Intel Corporation.

Block Diagram—8080A, −1, −2, 8-Bit CPU
Fig. 4-12

+11.6 volts DC and no more than 12.6 volts DC should be measured from pin 28 to ground as well as no less than +4.75 volts DC and no more than 5.25 volts DC from pin 20 to ground and −4.75 to −5.25 volts from pin 11 to ground.

2. Oscilloscope Measurements: Clock signals with a frequency of 10MHz to 18MHz should appear at pins 15 and 22 with an amplitude of 9 to 12 volts peak. Also check the signal on pin 19. This should be a pulse train, synchronized to the clock and indicates the beginning of each machine cycle.

For 90% Confidence Level:

All of the measurements made for the 75% confidence level must be correct. Add the following:

Monitor the clock on pins 15 or 22 in conjunction with the address bus signal on the oscilloscope. The address bus signal on pins 1, 26, 27, 29–40 is related to the memory and I/O operation of this IC.

EXACT REPLACEMENT ESSENTIAL.

8085A/8085A-2 (INTEL) 8-BIT CPU[9]

This device has an instruction set that is 100% software compatible with the 8080A and is designed to improve the present 8080A's performance by higher system speed. It incorporates all of the features that the 8224 (clock generator) and the 8228 (system controller) provided for the 8080A, thereby offering a high level of system integration. It uses a multiplexed data bus. The address is split between the 8-bit address bus and the 8-bit data bus.

The 8085A-2 is a faster version of the 8085A.

PIN NAME	DESCRIPTION	TYPE
A8-A15	Address Bus	O
AD0-AD7	Multiplexed Address/Data Bus	I/O
ALE	Address Latch Enable	O
SO, SI, IO/$\overline{M}$	Machine Cycle Status	O
$\overline{RD}$	Read	O
$\overline{WR}$	Write	O
READY	Ready	I
HOLD	Hold	I
HLDA	Hold Acknowledge	O
INTR	Interrupt Request	I
$\overline{INTA}$	Interrupt Acknowledge	O
RST 5.5 RST 6.5 RST 7.5	Restart Interrupts	I
TRAP	Trap Interrupt	I
$\overline{RESET\ IN}$	Reset In	I
RESET OUT	Reset Out	O
X1, X2	Crystal, LC, RC Network	I
CLK	Clock	O
SID	Serial Input Data Line	I
SOD	Serial Output Data Line	O
V_{CC}	Power supply	
V_{SS}	Ground	

[9]Note: The I 8085A is the industrial version of the 8085A and it has the industrial temperature range:-40°C to +85°C.

The M 8085M is the military version of the 8085A and it has the military temperature range:-55°C to +125°C.

The 8085AH/8085AH-2 are the HMOS version of the 8085A/8085A-2. The difference is that for the 8085AH/8085AH-2 the current I_{CC} 30% is less than for the 8085A/8085A-2.

Special Features

- Instruction cycle: 1.3 μsec (8085A); 0.8 μsec (8085A-2).
- On-chip clock generator (with external crystal, LC, or RC network).
- On-chip system controller, advanced cycle status information, available for large system control.
- Four Vectored Interrupt Inputs (One is Non-Maskable) plus an 8080A-compatible interrupt.
- Serial in/serial out port.
- Decimal, binary, and double precision arithmetic.
- Direct addressing capability to 64K bytes of memory.

IN-CIRCUIT QUICK-TESTS

FOR 75% CONFIDENCE LEVEL:

1. Volt-ohmmeter Measurements: The PC board ground should be connected directly to pin 20. Power supply voltage of no less than

PIN CONFIGURATION

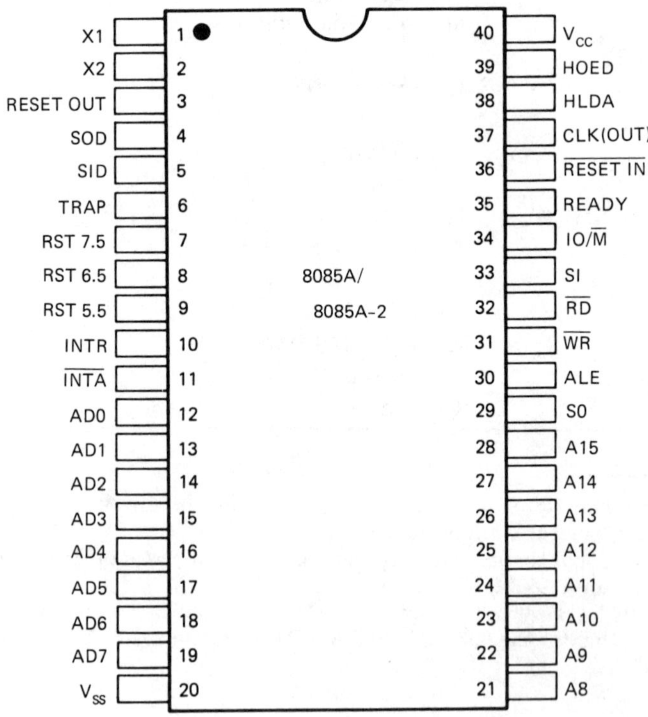

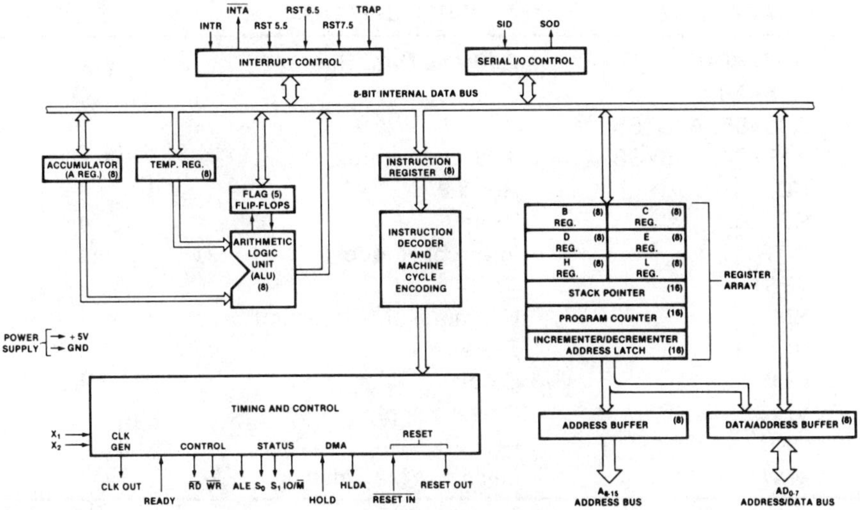

Block Diagram—8085A, –2, 8-Bit CPU
Fig. 4-13

4.75 volts DC and no more than 5.25 volts DC should be measured from pin 40 to ground.

2. Oscilloscope Measurements: Clock signals with a frequency of 1MHz to 6MHz should appear at pins 1 and 2 with an amplitude of 2.4 to 5.25 volts peak. Also check the signal on pin 37. This should be a pulse train, synchronized to the clock and one half of the frequency on pins 1 and 2.

FOR 90% CONFIDENCE LEVEL:

All of the measurements made for the 75% confidence level must be correct. Add the following:

Monitor the clock on pin 37 in conjunction with the ALE signal on the oscilloscope. The ALE signal on pin 30 is related to the address latch enable operation of this IC.

EXACT REPLACEMENT PREFERRED—it may be possible to use the industrial (I) or military (M) version if the exact replacement is not available.

IAPX 88/10 (8088) (INTEL) 8-BIT CPU

This device has attributes of both 8- and 16-bit microprocessors. It is directly compatible with IAPX 86/10 software and 8080/8085 hardware and peripherals.

PIN NAME	DESCRIPTION	TYPE
AD7-AD0	Address Data Bus	I/O
A15-A8	Address Bus	O
A19/S6, A18/S5 A17/S4, A16/S3	Address/Status	O
$\overline{RD}$	Read	I
READY	Ready	I
INTR	Interrupt Request	I
$\overline{TEST}$	Test	I
NMI	Non-maskable Interrupt	I
RESET	Reset	I
CLK	Clock	I
V_{CC}	Power Supply	
GND	Ground	
MN/$\overline{MX}$	Minimum/Maximum	I

The following pin function descriptions are for the 8088/8228 system in maximum mode (i.e. MN/$\overline{MX}$ = GND). Only the pin functions which are unique to maximum mode are described; all other pin functions are as described above.

$\overline{S2}$, $\overline{S1}$, $\overline{S0}$	Status	O
$\overline{RQ}/\overline{GT0}$, $\overline{RQ}/\overline{GT1}$	Request/Grant	I/O
$\overline{LOCK}$	Lock	O
QS1, QS0	Queue Status	O
HIGH	Always High in Max. Mode	O

The following pin function descriptions are for the 8088 in minimum mode (i.e. MN/$\overline{MX}$ = V_{CC}). Only the pin functions which are unique to minimum mode are described; all other pin functions are as described above.

IO/$\overline{M}$	Status Line	O
$\overline{WR}$	Write	O
$\overline{INTA}$	Interrupt Acknowledge	O
ALE	Address Latch Enable	O
DT/$\overline{R}$	Data Transmit/Receive	O
$\overline{DEN}$	Data Enable	O
HOLD	Hold	I
HLDA	Hold Acknowledge	O
$\overline{SSO}$	Status Line	O

Special Features

- 8-bit data bus interface.
- 16-bit internal architecture.

- Direct addressing capability up to 1M byte of memory.
- Direct software compatibility with IAPX 86/10 (8086 CPU).
- 14-word by 16-bit register set with symmetrical operations.
- 24 operand addressing modes.
- Byte, word, and block operations.
- 8-bit and 16-bit signed and unsigned arithmetic in binary or decimal, including multiply and divide.
- Compatible with 8155-2, 8755A-2, and 8185-2 multiplexed peripherals.

IN-CIRCUIT QUICK-TESTS

For 75% Confidence Level:

1. Volt-ohmmeter Measurements: The PC board ground should be connected directly to pins 1 and 20. Power supply voltage of no less than 4.5 volts DC and no more than 5.5 volts DC should be measured from pin 40 to ground.

Pin Configuration

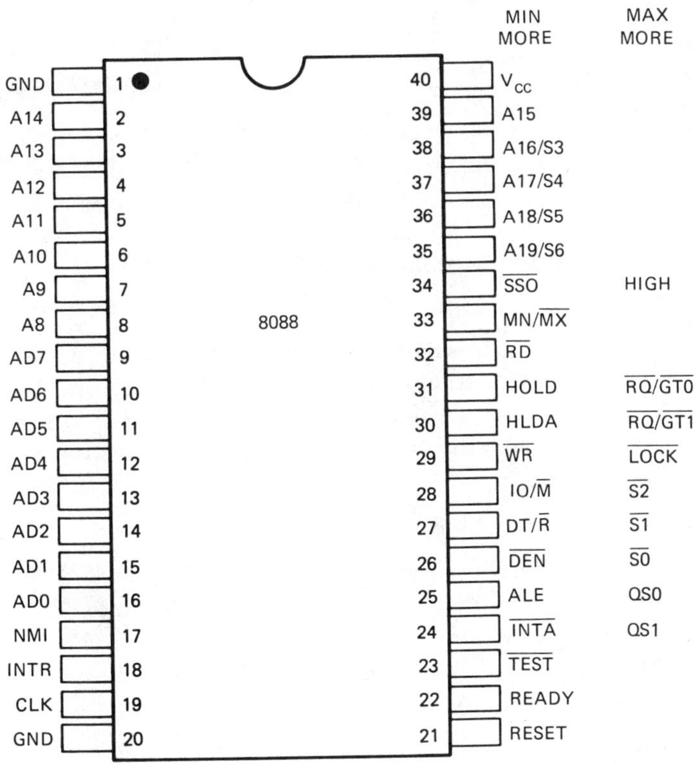

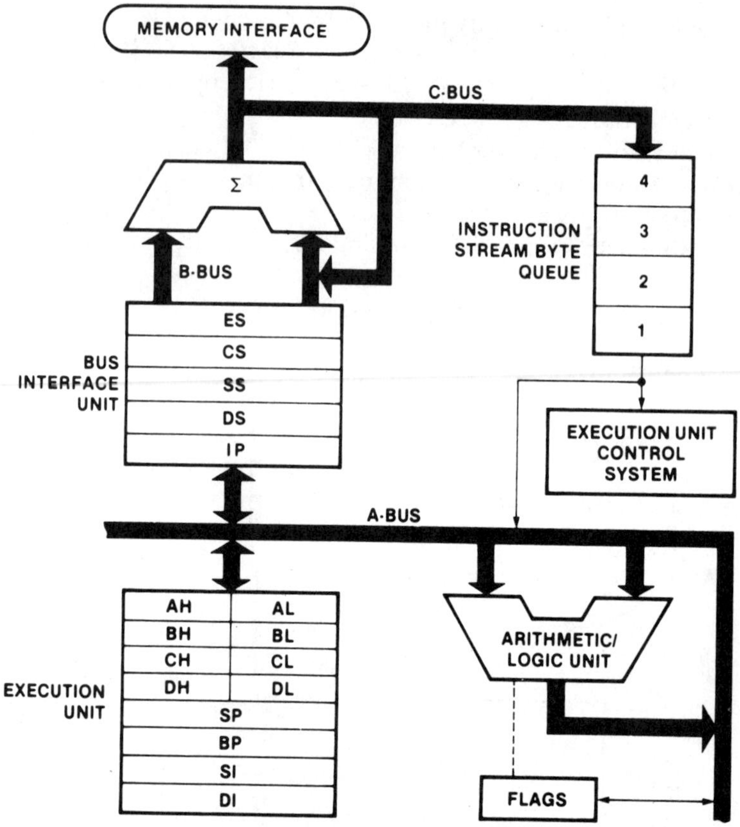

Reprinted by permission of Intel Corporation.

Block Diagram—8088, 88/10, 8-Bit CPU
Fig. 4-14

2. Oscilloscope Measurements: Clock signals with a frequency of 1MHz to 6MHz should appear at pin 19 with an amplitude of 2.4 to 5.5 volts peak. Also check the signal on pin 34. This should be a pulse train, synchronized to the clock and indicating the status of the bus cycle.

For 90% Confidence Level:

All of the measurements made for the 75% confidence level must be correct. Add the following:

Monitor the clock on pin 19 in conjunction with the ALE signal on the oscilloscope. The ALE signal on pin 25 is related to the address latch enable operation of this IC.

EXACT REPLACEMENT ESSENTIAL.

CHAPTER 5

12-BIT CPU

HM6100 (HARRIS) MICROPROCESSOR[1]

This is a device with a single address, fixed word length, parallel transfer, using 12-bit two's complement arithmetic. Standard features include indirect addressing and facilities for instruction skipping, program inter-

[1]Note: The same microprocessor is manufactured by:
INTERSIL—IM6100.

rupts as a function of input/output device conditions, and auto-start. The device design is optimized to minimize the number of external components required for interfacing with standard memory and peripheral devices.

PIN NAME	DESCRIPTION	TYPE
RUN	Run	O
DMAGNT	Direct Memory Access Grant	O
$\overline{\text{DMAREQ}}$	Direct Memory Access Request	I
$\overline{\text{CPREQ}}$	Control Panel Request	I
RUN/$\overline{\text{HLT}}$	Run/Halt	I
$\overline{\text{RESET}}$	Reset	I
$\overline{\text{INTREQ}}$	Interrupt Request	I
XTA, XTB, XTC	External Coded Minor Cycle Timing	O
LXMAR	Load External Address	O
$\overline{\text{WAIT}}$	Wait	I
OSC IN	Oscillator Input	I
OSC OUT	Oscillator Output	O
DX0-DX11	Data In, Data Out, Address	I/O
LINK	Link Flip-Flop	O
$\overline{\text{DEVSEL}}$	Device Selector	O
$\overline{\text{SWSEL}}$	Switch Register Select	O
$\overline{\text{C0}}$, $\overline{\text{C1}}$, $\overline{\text{C2}}$	Control Lines	I
$\overline{\text{SKP}}$	Skip	I
IFETCH	Instruction Fetch Cycle	O
$\overline{\text{MEMSEL}}$	Memory Select	O
$\overline{\text{CPSEL}}$	Control Panel Memory Select	O
INTGNT	Interrupt Grant	O
DATAF	Data Field	O
V_{cc}	Power Supply	
GND	Ground	

Special Features

- Fully static: 0 to 5.7 MHz.
- Single power supply: 5V (6100) or 10V (6100A).
- Single phase clock, on-chip crystal oscillator.
- Low power dissipation: less than 10 mW at 2.5 MHz, at 5V.
- Full temperature range: −55°C to +125°C.
- Provision for dedicated control panel.
- 128 general purpose registers.
- 8 autoindexing registers.
- Flexible programmed I/O transfers.
- Vectored interrupt capability.

Pin Configuration

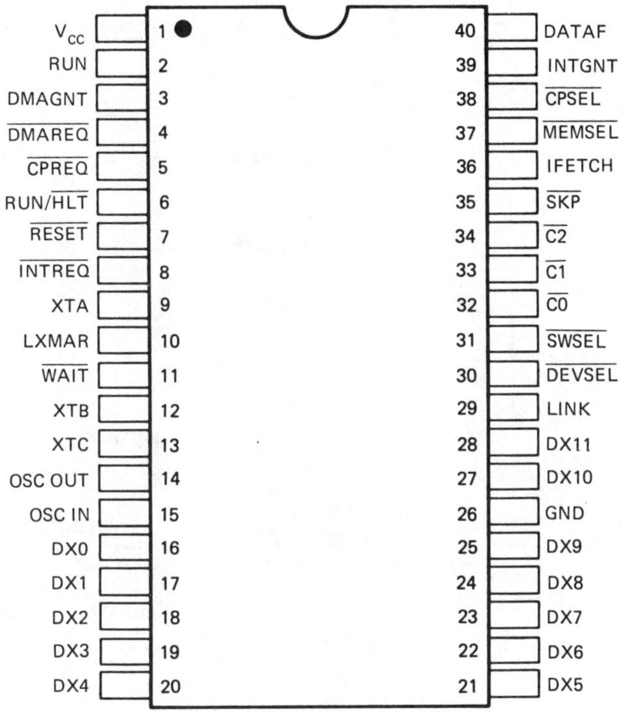

IN-CIRCUIT QUICK-TESTS

For 75% Confidence Level:

1. Volt-ohmmeter Measurements: The PC board ground should be connected directly to pin 26. Power supply voltage of no less than 4.5 volts DC for 6100 and 9.5 volts for 6100A and no more than 5.5 volts DC for 6100 and 10.5 volts for 6100A should be measured from pin 1 to ground.
2. Oscilloscope Measurements: Clock signals with a frequency of 0.1 MHz to 4.0 MHz for 6100 and 8.0 MHz for 6100A should appear at pins 14 and 15 with an amplitude of 4.0 to 5.0 volts peak for 6100 and 9.0 to 10.0 volts for 6100A. Also check the signal on pin 36. This should be a pulse train, synchronized to the clock and indicates the fetch cycle.

For 90% Confidence Level:

All of the measurements made for the 75% confidence level must be correct. Add the following:

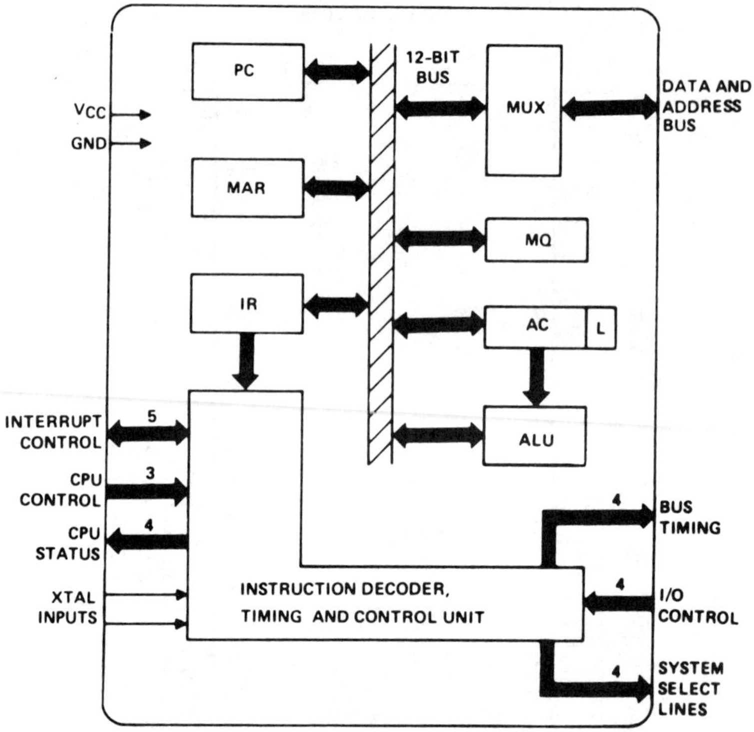

Technical data furnished courtesy of Harris Semiconductor, Melbourne, Florida.

Block Diagram—6100
Fig. 5-1

Monitor the clock on pins 14 or 15 in conjunction with the XTC signal on the oscilloscope. The XTC signal on pin 13 is related to the Read/Write operation of this IC.

EXACT REPLACEMENT ESSENTIAL.

AMU/PR (AMI) MICROPROCESSOR

This device is produced using a dual-poly CMOS silicongate technology. It features unique memory-to-memory architecture and separate interrupt-bus structure. The microprocessor has full minicomputer instruction set capability including multiply and divide and is compatible with 9940, as well as with all S9900 peripherals.

PIN NAME	DESCRIPTION	TYPE
A0(MSB)-A15/CRUOUT(LSB)	Address Bus/CRUOut	O
D0(MSB)-D7(LSB)	Data Bus	I/O
XTAL1, XTAL2	Crystal	I

PIN NAME	DESCRIPTION	TYPE
CLK	Clock	O
$\overline{\text{MEMEN}}$	Memory Enable	O
$\overline{\text{WE}}$	Write Enable	O
CRUCLK	CRU Clock	O
CRUIN	CRU Data In	I
DBIN	Data Bus In	O
$\overline{\text{HOLD}}$	Hold	I
HOLDA	Hold Acknowledge	O
$\overline{\text{INT1}}$, $\overline{\text{INT2}}$, $\overline{\text{INT3}}$	Interrupt 1, 2, 3	I
$\overline{\text{NMI}}$	Non-Maskable Interrupt	I
NMIACK	NMI Acknowledge	O
IAQ	Instruction Acquisition	O
$\overline{\text{RESET}}$	Reset	I
$\overline{\text{IDLE}}$	Idle State (for Power Down)	O
MS1, MS2	Signals-mode select	I
V_{CC}	Power Supply	
V_{SS}	Ground	

Special Features

- 16-bit instruction word.
- Up to 64K bytes of addressable memory.
- 16 general registers.
- 5 prioritized interrupts.
- Programmed and DMA I/O Capability.
- On-chip Clock Generator.
- 16 general purpose flags.
- Single 5V ± 10% power supply.
- Power Down State (IDLE).

IN-CIRCUIT QUICK-TESTS

FOR 75% CONFIDENCE LEVEL:

1. Volt-ohmmeter Measurements:
   a) Make sure PC board ground has good connection to pin 18.
   b) Measure power supply voltage of 4.5 to 6.0 volts DC at pins 19 and 44.
2. Oscilloscope Measurements:
   a) Observe clock signals at pins 20 and 21. They should be square waves with a frequency of 1.0 to 3.0 MHz.
   b) Observe the signal on pin 17. This signal is the system clock output and is synchronized to the clock. This signal must be ½ of the frequency on pins 20 and 21.

PIN CONFIGURATION 116-C

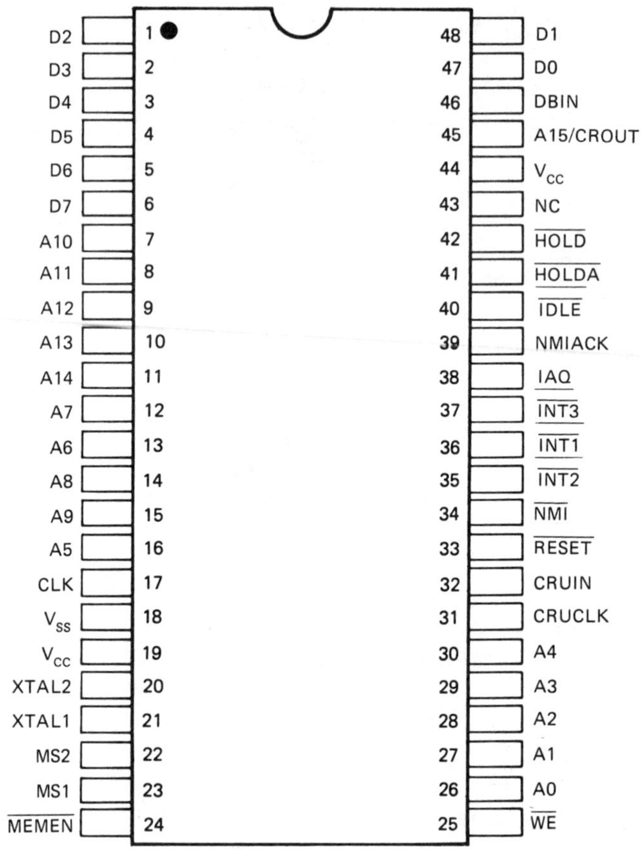

FOR 90% CONFIDENCE LEVEL:

In addition to the 75% confidence level tests, use a dual-trace oscilloscope to observe the following:

a) Monitor the clock signal on pin 17 on one trace, while observing the WE signal on pin 25 on the other.
b) Monitor the clock signal on pin 17 on one trace, while observing the IAQ signal on pin 38 on the other.

EXACT REPLACEMENT ABSOLUTELY ESSENTIAL

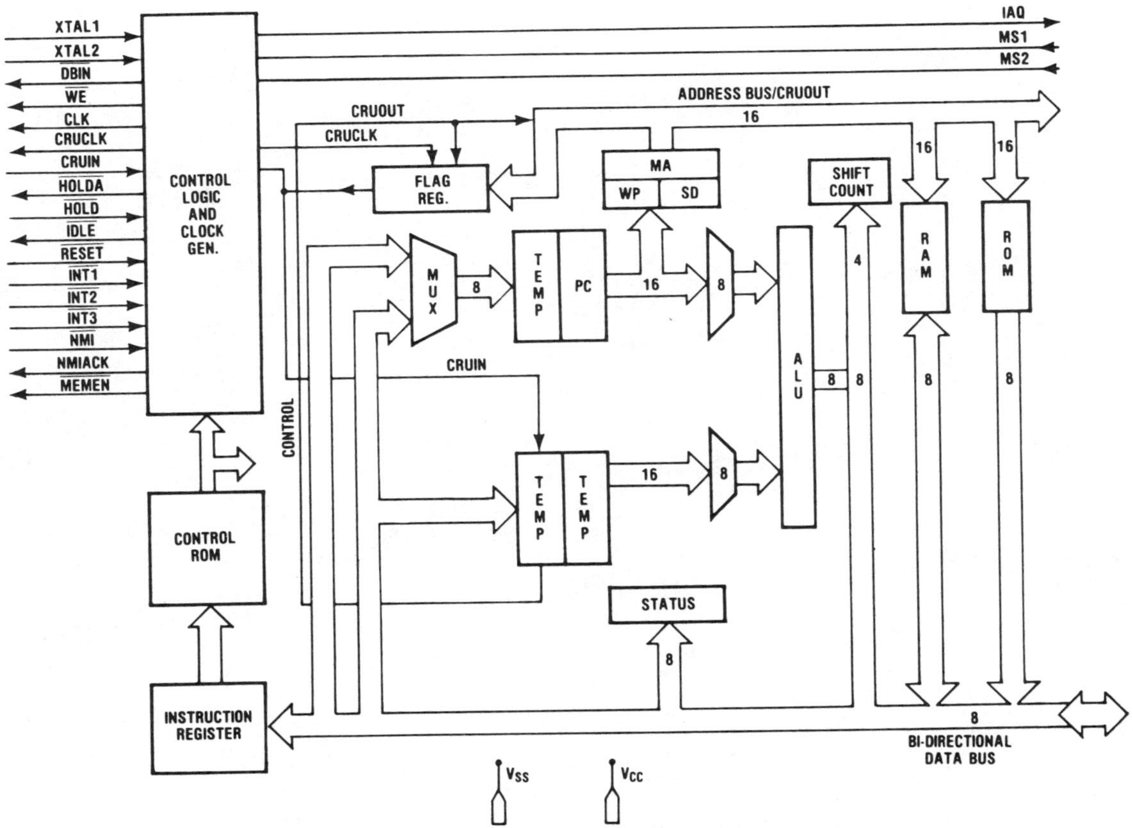

Courtesy of American Microsystems, Inc., Santa Clara, California.

Block Diagram—AMU/PR, 16-Bit CPU
Fig. 5-2

CHAPTER 6

16-BIT CPU

MN 601 (Data General) 16-Bit CPU

This device provides the central processing functions for Data General's microNOVA family. It features NOVA[R] 16-bit architecture including hardware multiply/divide; multiple addressing modes including absolute, relative, index, deferred, and auto-increment/decrement; multiple accumulators, including two that can be used as index registers; hardware stack and frame pointers with stack overflow protection; programmed priority interrupt to 16 levels; and separate memory and I/O buses.

PIN NAME	DESCRIPTION	TYPE
MBO-MB15	Address/Data Bus	I/O
01, 02	Clocks Phase One and Phase Two	I
P	Memory Synchronization	O
SAE	Memory Read Enable	O
WE	Memory Write Enable	O
I/O DATA1, I/O DATA2	Data and Control (I/O Bus)	I/O
I/O CLOCK	I/O Synchronization	I/O
I/O INPUT	Directions of I/O Transfers	O
$\overline{\text{EXT INT}}$	External Interrupt	I
$\overline{\text{DCH INT}}$	DMA Request	I
HALT	Halt	O
CLAMP	Power On Reset	I
PAUSE	Memory Bus Grant	O
V_{CC}	Power Supply: 5±.25V	
V_{BB}	Power Supply: +4.25±.25V	
V_{GG}	Power Supply: 14±1.0V	
V_{DD}	Power Supply: 10±1.0V	
V_{SS}	Ground	

Special Features

- Integral data channel, real time clock, and multiply/divide.
- Integral hidden refresh and control logic for dynamic RAMs.
- SAVE and RETURN instructions for subroutine calls.
- System memory support up to 32K words of RAM/PROM.
- Single word instruction format in a variety of addressing modes: absolute, relative, indexed, deferred, and auto-increment/decrement.
- I/O bus provides functional equivalent of 47-line NOVA I/O bus.
- Master clock 8.3MHz.
- Clock frequency (Ø1,Ø2): maximum 4.166MHz.

IN-CIRCUIT QUICK-TESTS

FOR 75% CONFIDENCE LEVEL:

1. Volt-ohmmeter Measurements: The PC board ground should be connected directly to pins 8, 26 and 40. Power supply voltage of

Pin Configuration

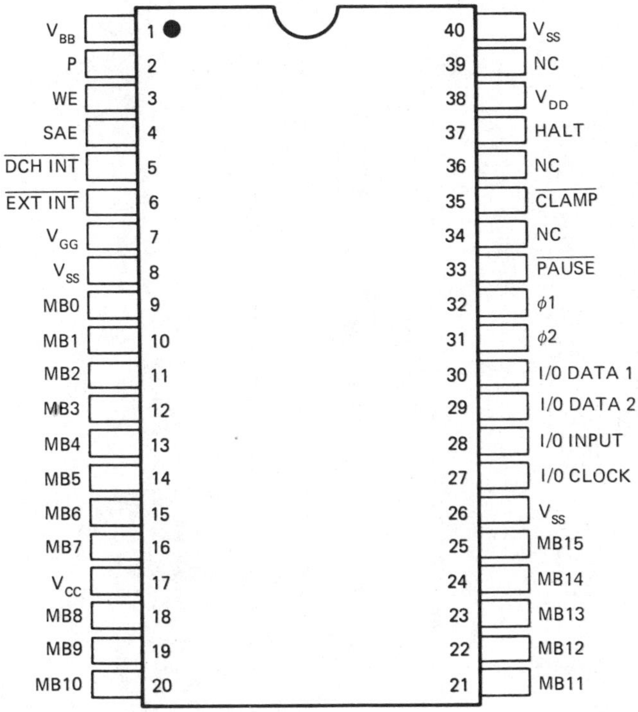

no less than 4.75 volts DC and no more than 5.25 volts DC should be measured from pin 17 to ground. About 14 volts should be measured at pin 7 and 10 volts at pin 38.

2. Oscilloscope Measurements: Clock signals with a frequency of 1.0 MHz to 8.3 MHz should appear at pins 31 and 32 with an amplitude of 13 to 14 volts peak. Also check the signal on pin 27. This should be a pulse train, synchronized to the clock, which synchronizes all I/O information transfers.

For 90% Confidence Level:

All of the measurements made for the 75% confidence level must be correct. Add the following:

Monitor the clock on pins 31 and 32 in conjunction with the WE signal on the oscilloscope. The WE signal on pin 3 is related to the WRITE/REFRESH operation of this IC.

EXACT REPLACEMENT ESSENTIAL.

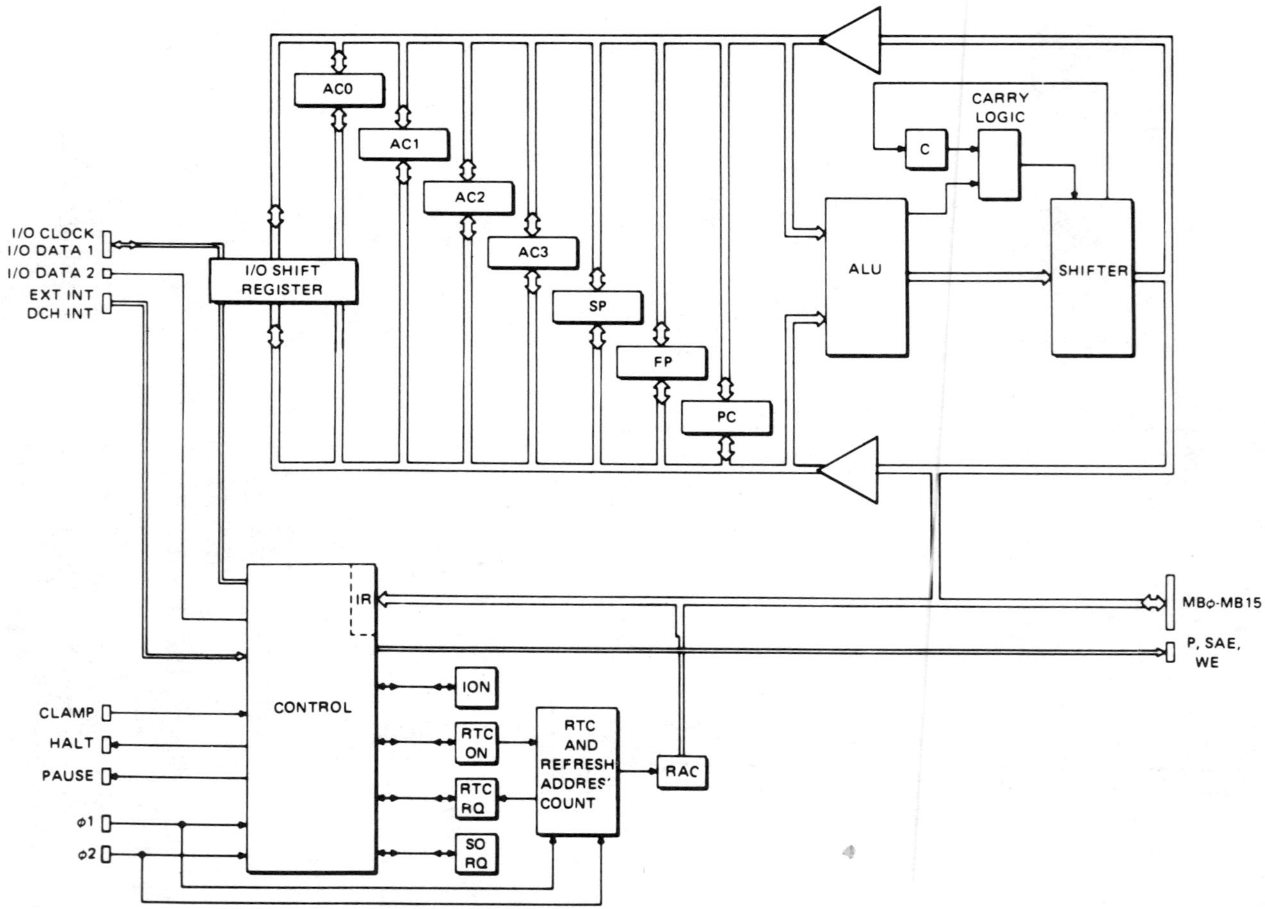

Courtesy of Data General Corp.

Block Diagram—601, 16-Bit CPU
Fig. 6-1

MN 602 (DATA GENERAL) 16-BIT CPU

This device provides the central processing functions for DATA GENERAL's MP/100 family of microcomputers. It executes the entire NOVA instruction set. It provides a 2.08Mbyte/s parallel data channel via the memory bus for applications requiring large bandwidth between peripheral devices and memory.

PIN NAME	DESCRIPTION	TYPE
MB0-MB15	Address/Data Bus	I/O
01, 02	Clocks Phase 1 and Phase 2	I
P	Memory Synchronization	O
SAE	Memory Read Enable	O
WE	Memory Write Enable	O
WAIT	Wait	I
I/O DATA 1, I/O DATA 2	Data and Control (I/O Bus)	I/O
I/O CLOCK	I/O Synchronization	I/O
I/O INPUT	Directions of I/O Transfers	O
EXT INT	External Interrupt	I
DCH INT	DMA Request	I
FDCHR	High-speed Data Channel Request	I
FDCHE	High-speed Data Channel Control	O
HALT	Halt	O
MAPON	Map On	O
SCEN	Status Condition Enable	
CLAMP	Power on Reset	
A2	Sync. Fact Data Channel Request	
V_{BB}	Power Supply:-2 to -7V	
V_{CC}	Power Supply: -.3 to +7V	
V_{DD}	Power Supply: -.8 to -15V	
V_{SS}	Ground	

Special Features

- 16-bit multi-accumulator architecture with frame-oriented stack support and 16-level interrupt facility.
- Executes the full NOVA[R] instruction set, including integer multiply, integer divide, push, pop, state save, and state restore instructions.
- Integral real-time clock, power monitor, and transparent refresh for 4K and 16K dynamic RAMs.
- Support for 128K bytes of RAM/PROM memory in two address spaces (primary and secondary).
- Serial I/O bus functionally equivalent to the NOVA I/O bus, supports programmed I/O and data channel transactions.

- Independent non-maskable interrupt.
- Memory cycle time 960ns.
- Add time 2.4μs.
- Memory reference time 2.9μs.
- Direct memory access channel: input—296K bytes/s standard; 2 M bytes/s high speed. Output—344K bytes/s standard; 2 M bytes/s high speed.

IN-CIRCUIT QUICK-TESTS

FOR 75% CONFIDENCE LEVEL:

1. Volt-ohmmeter Measurements: The PC board ground should be connected directly to pin 8. Power supply voltage of no less than 4.75 volts DC and no more than 5.25 volts DC should be measured from pin 17 to ground—5 volts should be measured at pin 1 and 12 volts at pin 38.
2. Oscilloscope Measurements: Clock signals with a frequency of 0.1

PIN CONFIGURATION

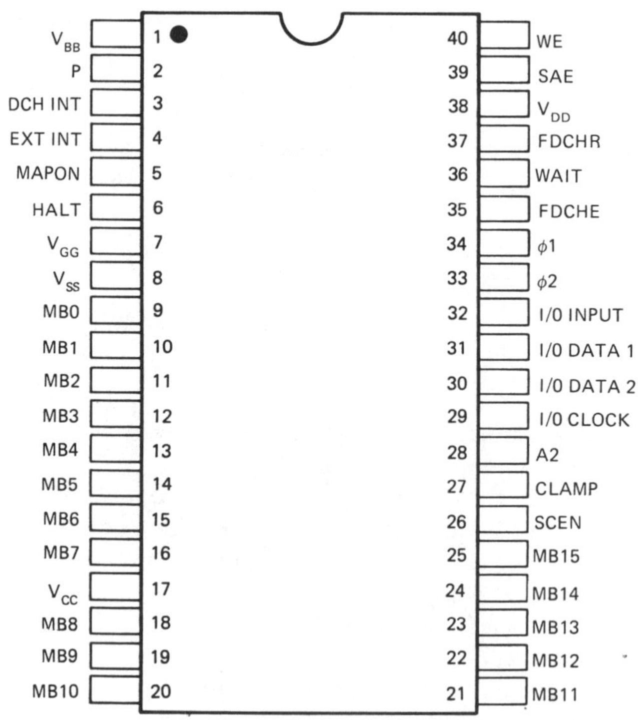

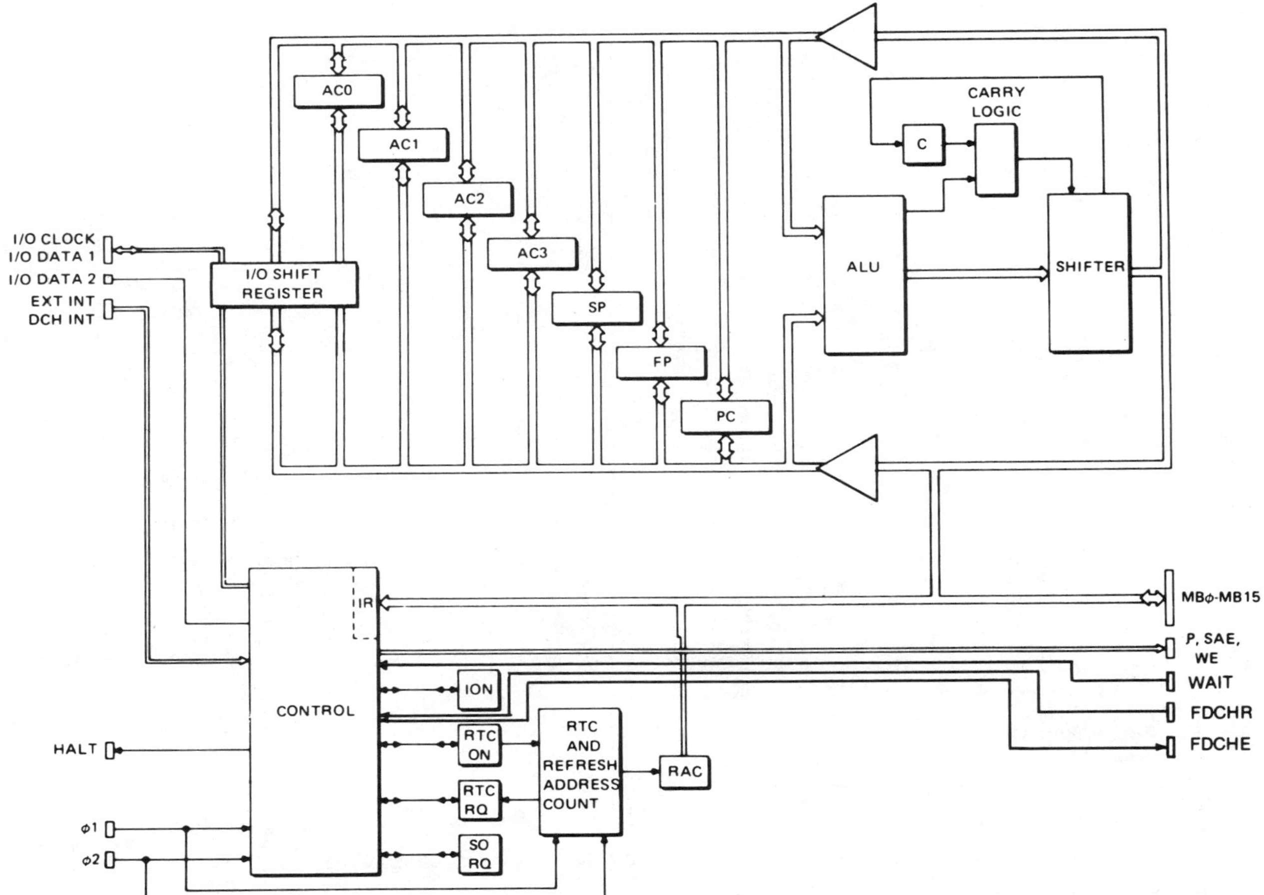

Courtesy of Data General Corp.

Block Diagram—602, 16-Bit CPU
Fig. 6-2

MHz to 8.3 MHz should appear at pins 33 and 34 with an amplitude of 9 to 11 volts peak. Also check the signal on pin 29. This should be a pulse train, synchronized to the clock and it controls I/O information transfers.

For 90% Confidence Level:

All of the measurements made for the 75% confidence level must be correct. Add the following:

Monitor the clock on pins 33 or 34 in conjunction with the WE signal on the oscilloscope. The WE signal on pin 40 is related to the WRITE/REFRESH operation of this IC.

EXACT REPLACEMENT ESSENTIAL.

AM Z8001 (AMD) 16-Bit CPU[1]

This device belongs to the AM Z8000 family. Its architecture is centered around 16 16-bit general registers. The device deals with 23-bit address spaces, therefore can address directly 8MB of memory. The 23-bit address consists of two components: 7-bit segment number and 16-bit offset. Facilities are provided to maintain three distinct address spaces: code data and stack. The CPU also contains an on-chip memory refresh facility.

PIN NAME	DESCRIPTION	TYPE
AD0-AD15	Address/Data Bus	I/O
$\overline{AS}$	Address Strobe	O
$\overline{DS}$	Data Strobe	O
R/$\overline{W}$	Read/Write	O
B/$\overline{W}$	Byte/Word	O
ST0-ST3	Status	O
$\overline{WAIT}$	Wait	I
N/$\overline{S}$	Normal/System Mode	O
$\overline{MREQ}$	Memory Request	O
$\overline{BUSRQ}$	Bus Request	O
$\overline{BUSAK}$	Bus Acknowledge	O
$\overline{NMI}$	Non-maskable Interrupt	I
$\overline{VI}$	Vectored Interrupt	I
$\overline{NVI}$	Non-Vectored Interrupt	I
$\overline{\mu I}$	Micro-In	I
$\overline{\mu O}$	Micro-Out	O
$\overline{RESET}$	Reset	I
CLK	Clock	I

[1]Note: The same microprocessor is manufactured by: ZILOG—Z8001.

PIN NAME	DESCRIPTION	TYPE
DECOUPLE	Output From Substrate Bias Generator	O
STOP	Stop	I
SN0-SN6	Segment Number	O
SEGT	Segment Trap	I
V_{CC}	Power Supply	
GND	Ground	

Special Features

- Software compatible with AM Z8002 microprocessor.
- Privileged/non-privileged (System/Normal) mode of operation.
- TTL compatible inputs and outputs.
- Single phase clock.

PIN CONFIGURATION

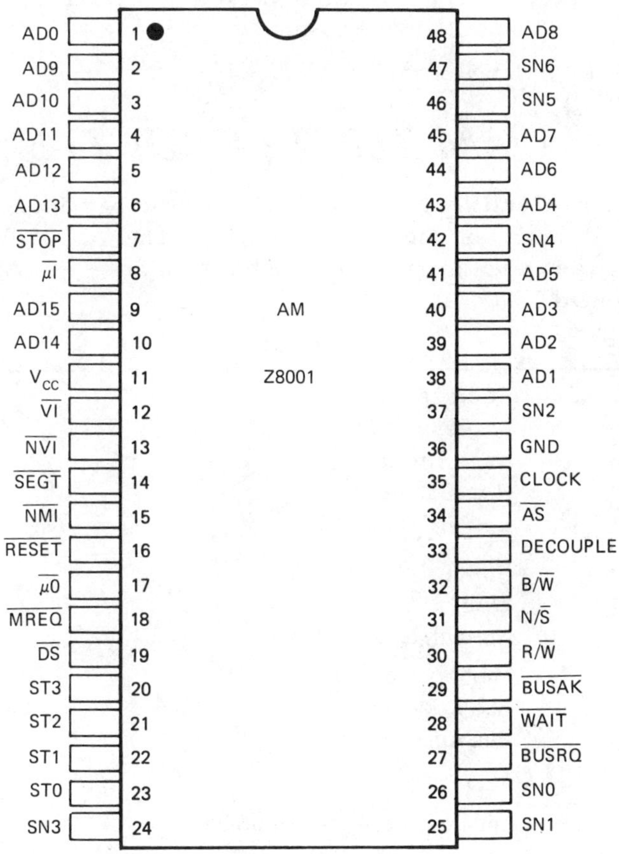

IN-CIRCUIT QUICK-TESTS

FOR 75% CONFIDENCE LEVEL:

1. Volt-ohmmeter Measurements: The PC board ground should be connected directly to pin 36. Power supply voltage of no less than 4.5 volts DC and no more than 5.5 volts DC should be measured from pin 11 to ground.
2. Oscilloscope Measurements: Clock signals with a frequency of 0.4 MHz to 2.0 MHz should appear at pin 35 with an amplitude of 4.5 to 5.5 volts peak. Also check the signal on pin 30. This should be a pulse train, synchronized to the clock and it indicates READ/WRITE cycles.

FOR 90% CONFIDENCE LEVEL:

All of the measurements made for the 75% confidence level must be correct. Add the following:

Monitor the clock on pin 35 in conjunction with the STATUS signals on the oscilloscope. The STATUS signals on pins 20, 21, 22 and 23 are related to the status of the processor.

EXACT REPLACEMENT ESSENTIAL.

AM Z8002 (AMD) 16-BIT CPU[2]

This device is essentially the same as AM Z8001. They differ only in the manner and range of memory addressing. The AM Z8002 directly addresses 64K bytes of memory with 16 bits of address. It is referred to as non-segmented CPU.

PIN NAME	DESCRIPTION	TYPE
AD0-AD15	Address/Data Bus	I/O
$\overline{AS}$	Address Strobe	Output
$\overline{DS}$	Data Strobe	Output
R/$\overline{W}$	Read/Write	Output
B/$\overline{W}$	Byte/Word	Output
ST0-ST3	Status	Output
$\overline{WAIT}$	Wait	Input
N/$\overline{S}$	Normal/System Mode	Output
$\overline{MREQ}$	Memory Request	Output
$\overline{BUSRQ}$	Bus Request	Input
$\overline{BUSAK}$	Bus Acknowledge	Output

[2]Note: The same microprocessor is manufactured by: ZILOG—Z8002.

PIN NAME	DESCRIPTION	TYPE
NMI	Non-maskable Interrupt	Input
$\overline{VI}$	Vectored Interrupt	Input
$\overline{NVI}$	Non-Vectored Interrupt	Input
$\overline{\mu I}$	Micro-In	Input
$\overline{\mu O}$	Micro-Out	Output
$\overline{RESET}$	Reset	Input
CLK	Clock	Input
DECOUPLE	Output From Substrate Bias Generator	Output
$\overline{STOP}$	Stop	Input
V_{CC}	Power Supply	
GND	Ground	

Special Features

- Software compatible with AM Z8001 microprocessor.

PIN CONFIGURATION

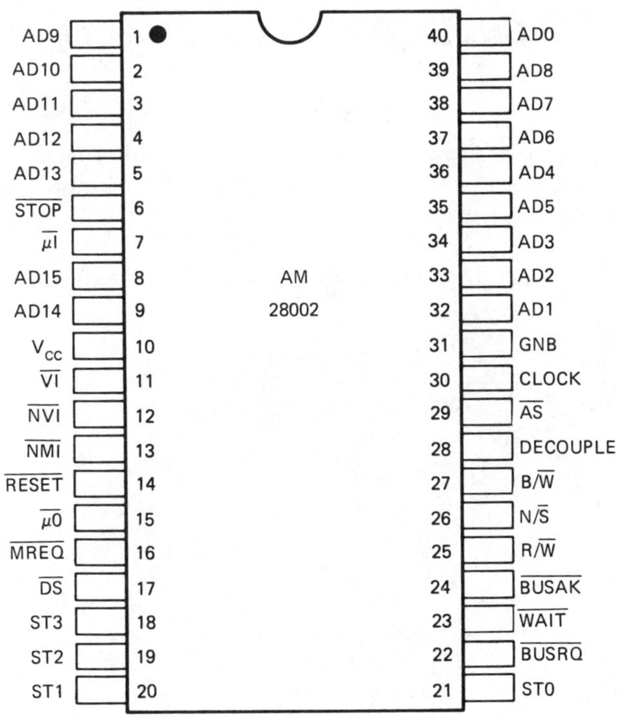

IN-CIRCUIT QUICK-TESTS

FOR 75% CONFIDENCE LEVEL:

1. Volt-ohmmeter Measurements: The PC board ground should be connected directly to pin 31. Power supply voltage of no less than 4.5 volts DC and no more than 5.5 volts DC should be measured from pin 10 to ground.
2. Oscilloscope Measurements: Clock signals with a frequency of 0.4 MHz to 2.0 MHz should appear at pin 30 with an amplitude of 4.5 to 5.5 volts peak. Also check the signal on pin 25. This should be a pulse train, synchronized to the clock, and indicating the READ/WRITE cycle.

FOR 90% CONFIDENCE LEVEL:

All of the measurements made for the 75% confidence level must be correct. Add the following:

Monitor the clock on pin 30 in conjunction with the status signals on the oscilloscope. The status signals on pins 18, 19, 20 and 21 are related to the status of the processor.

EXACT REPLACEMENT ESSENTIAL.

INS 8070–8072 (NATIONAL SEMICONDUCTOR) 16-BIT CPU

These devices are designed for use in systems requiring single chip, multiprocessing bus architecture and 16-bit arithmetic operations. INS8070 has 64 bytes RAM and no ROM. INS8072 has 64 bytes of RAM and 2.5K ROM.

Both 8070 and 8072 are fabricated using N-channel, silicon gate, depletion load, MOS technology.

PIN NAME	DESCRIPTION	TYPE
A0–A15	Address Bus	O
D0–D7	Data Bus	I/O
NRST	Reset	I
NHOLD	Hold	I
SA/INTA	Sense A/Interrupt A	I
SB/INTB	Sense B/Interrupt B	I
NENIN	Enable Input	I
NWDS	Write Data Strobe	O
NRDS	Read Data Strobe	O
NENOUT	Enable Output	O
F1, F2, F3	Flags 1, 2, 3	O

PIN NAME	DESCRIPTION	TYPE
NBREQ	Bus Request	I/O
X_{IN}, X_{OUT}	Clock	I/O
V_{CC}	Power Supply	
V_{SS}	Ground	

Special Features

- 8-bit data bus.
- 16-bit address bus (64K addressing capability).
- Set of 8 and 16-bit arithmetic, logic and stack manipulation instructions.
- Hardware 16 × 16 bit multiply (37 μs) and divide (42 μs).
- Built-in multiprocessing and DMA logic.
- Interfaces with memory and standard 8080 peripherals at any clock speed.
- On-chip clock generation.
- Single instruction character search and single instruction ASCII to decimal conversion.

PIN CONFIGURATION

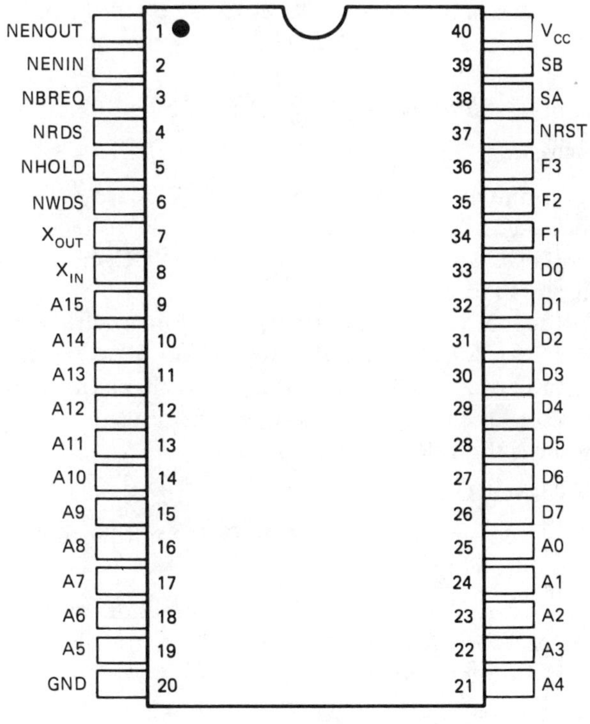

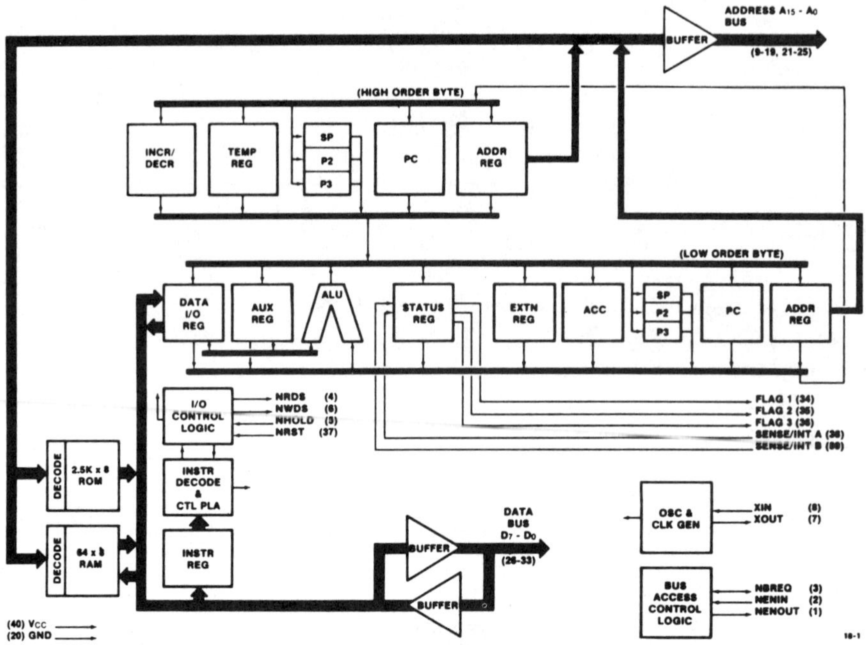

Courtesy of National Semiconductor Corporation.

Block Diagram—8070, 8072, 16-Bit CPU
Fig. 6-3

IN-CIRCUIT QUICK-TESTS

FOR 75% CONFIDENCE LEVEL:

1. Volt-ohmmeter Measurements: The PC board ground should be connected directly to pin 20. Power supply voltage of no less than 4.5 volts DC and no more than 5.5 volts DC should be measured from pin 40 to ground.
2. Oscilloscope Measurements: Clock signals with a frequency of 1.0MHz to 4.0MHz should appear at pins 7 and 8 with an amplitude of 2.4 to 5.5 volts peak. Also check the signal on pin 6. This should be a pulse train, synchronized to the clock and represents the WRITE strobe output.

FOR 90% CONFIDENCE LEVEL:

All of the measurements made for the 75% confidence level must be correct. Add the following:

Monitor the clock on pins 7 and 8, in conjunction with the NRDS signal on the oscilloscope. The NRDS signal on pin 4 is related to the READ CYCLE timing of this IC.

EXACT REPLACEMENT ESSENTIAL.

8086 (INTEL) 16-BIT CPU[3]

This device is a multiple processor designed for modular programming as well as assembly languages. It has an 8-bit external data path to memory and I/O. The chip is contained in standard 40-pin dual-in-line package and operates from a single −5V power supply.

PIN NAME	DESCRIPTION	TYPE
	COMMON SIGNALS	
AD15–AD0	Address/Data Bus	I/O
A19/S6–A16/S3	Address/Status	O
$\overline{BHE}$/S7	Bus High Enable/Status	O
MN/$\overline{MX}$	Minimum/Maximum Mode Control	I
$\overline{RD}$	Read Control	O
$\overline{TEST}$	Wait-on Test Control	I
READY	Wait State Control	I
RESET	System Reset	I
NMI	Non-maskable Interrupt Request	I
INTR	Interrupt Request	I
CLK	System Clock	I
V_{CC}	Power supply	
GND	Ground	
	MINIMUM MODE SIGNALS (MN/$\overline{MX}$ = V_{CC})	
HOLD	Hold Request	I
HLDA	Hold Acknowledge	O
$\overline{WR}$	Write Control	O
M/$\overline{IO}$	Memory/I/O Control	O
DT/$\overline{R}$	Data Transmit/Receive	O
$\overline{DEN}$	Data Enable	O
ALE	Address Latch Enable	O
$\overline{INTA}$	Interrupt Acknowledge	O
	MAXIMUM MODE SIGNALS (MN/$\overline{MX}$ = GND)	
$\overline{RQ}$/$\overline{GT1,0}$	Request/Grant Bus Access Control	I/O
$\overline{LOCK}$	Bus Priority Lock Control	O
$\overline{S2}$–$\overline{S0}$	Bus Cycle Status	O
QS1, QS0	Instruction Queue Status	O

[3]Note: The 8086-1 is identical to the 8086; the only difference is 10MHz clock rate. The 8086-2 is also identical but has a clock rate of 8.0MHz.

The same microprocessor is manufactured by:
MOSTEK—MK 8086
NEC MICROCOMPUTERS—uPD8086.

Special Features

- Multiple asynchronous bus structures supported.
- 24 operand addressing modes, one megabyte addressability.
- Implements the proposed IEEE floating point standard.
- 14 general data processing registers plus an 8 × 80 bit numeric register stack.
- Bit, byte, word, real, decimal, and block operations.
- 5MHz (200ns cycle time), and 8MHz (8086/10) are available.
- System can be constructed for both 8 and 16 bit data paths.
- Processor operates on 8-, 16-, 32-, 64-bit, character, and string data types; internal data paths are at least 16-bits wide.
- Up to one megabyte of memory can be addressed, along with a separate 64K byte I/O.

IN-CIRCUIT QUICK-TESTS

For 75% Confidence Level:

1. Volt-ohmmeter Measurements: The PC board ground should be connected directly to pins 1 and 20. Power supply voltage of no

Pin Configuration

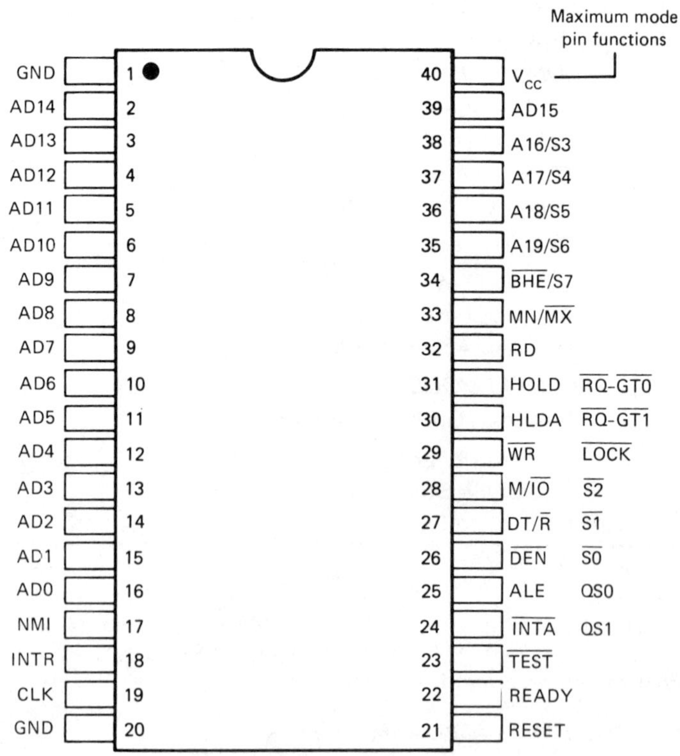

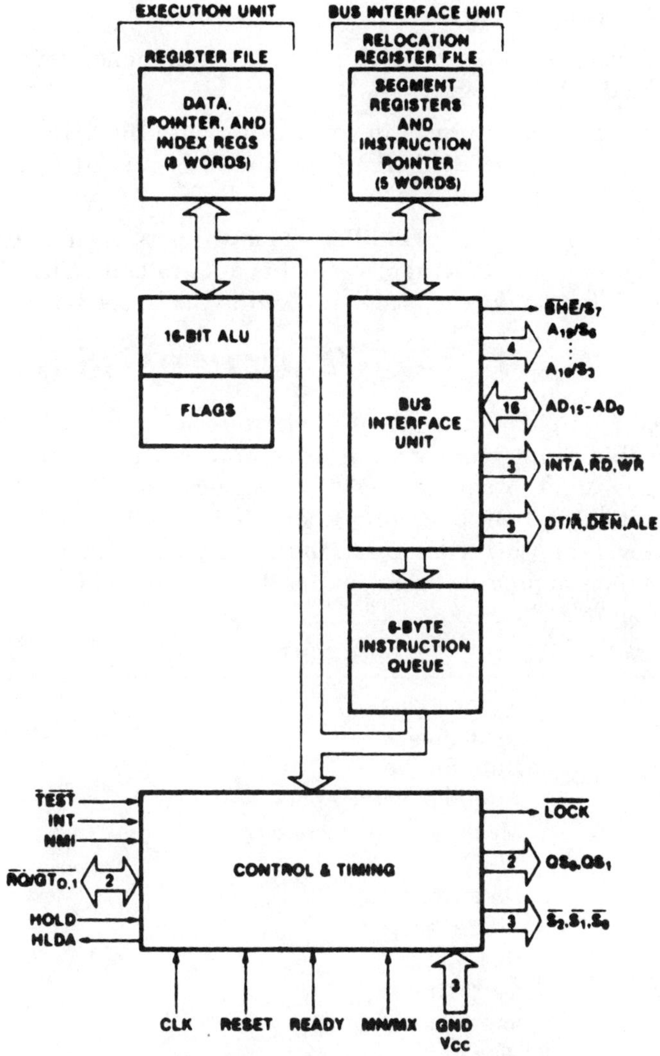

Courtesy NEC Electronics, U.S.A., Inc., Microcomputer Division.

Block Diagram—8086, 16-Bit CPU
Fig. 6-4

less than 4.5 volts DC and no more than 5.5 volts DC should be measured from pin 40 to ground.

2. Oscilloscope Measurements: Clock signals with a frequency of 1.0MHz to 10MHz should appear at pin 19 with an amplitude of 4.5 to 5.5. volts peak. Also check the signal on pin 32. This should be a pulse train, synchronized to the clock and indicating the READ cycle.

For 90% Confidence Level:

All of the measurements made for the 75% confidence level must be correct. Add the following:

> Monitor the clock on pin 19 in conjunction with the BHE signal on the oscilloscope. The BHE signal on pin 34 is related to the BUS operation of this IC.

EXACT REPLACEMENT PREFERRED—it may be possible to use an 8086-1 or 2 to replace it if the exact replacement is not available. The 8086-1 can replace the -2, but not vice versa because of the clock speed differences.

F 9445 (Fairchild) 16-Bit CPU

This device is implemented using bipolar technology which, combined with a pipeline architecture, gives the microprocessor very fast execution times. It has eight program-accessible registers and the capability of directly addressing 128K bytes of memory. It can address 62 I/O devices, handle 16 levels of priority interrupt, and perform direct memory access. It has control lines to provide operator-console functions and has an on-chip self-test program.

PIN NAME	DESCRIPTION	TYPE
IB0–IB15	Information Bus	I/O
SYN	Synchronize	O
STRBD	Data Strobe	O
STRBA	Strobe Memory Address Register	O
$\overline{M}$, 01, 00	Memory or I/O function	O
$\overline{W}$	Write	O
RDYD	Data Ready	I
RDYA	Address Ready	I
RUN	Run Status	O
CARRY	Carry Status	O
INTON	Interrupt-on Status	O
CLK	Single-phase Clock	I
$\overline{BUSREQ}$	Bus Request	O
$\overline{BUSLOCK}$	Bus Lock	O
$\overline{BUSGNT}$	Bus Grant	I
$\overline{MR}$	Master Reset	I
$\overline{DCHREQ}$	Data Channel Request	I
$\overline{CONREQ}$	Console Request	I
$\overline{INTREQ}$	Interrupt Request	I
$\overline{ABORT}$	Abort	I
V_{CC}	Power supply	
GND	Ground	
I_{INJ}	Injection Current Input	

Special Features

- Execution times: 25Onsec. Register to Register; 2.9μsec. 16 × 16-Bit Multiply.
- 11 addressing modes.
- Eight program-accessible registers (AC0, AC1, AC2, AC3, SP, FP, PC, PSW).
- Instruction set includes memory reference, ALU, I/O, stack, multiply/divide, and floating point assist (scale/normalize) instructions with 8-bit byte, 16-bit word or 32-bit double-word data.
- Static operation with single-phase clock up to 24MHz.
- LS TTL I/O structure with I^3L (isoplanar integrated injection logic) internal circuits.
- Full military temperature and voltage ranges:–65°C to +150°C; –.5V to 6.0V.
- Radiation-tolerant technology.

PIN CONFIGURATION

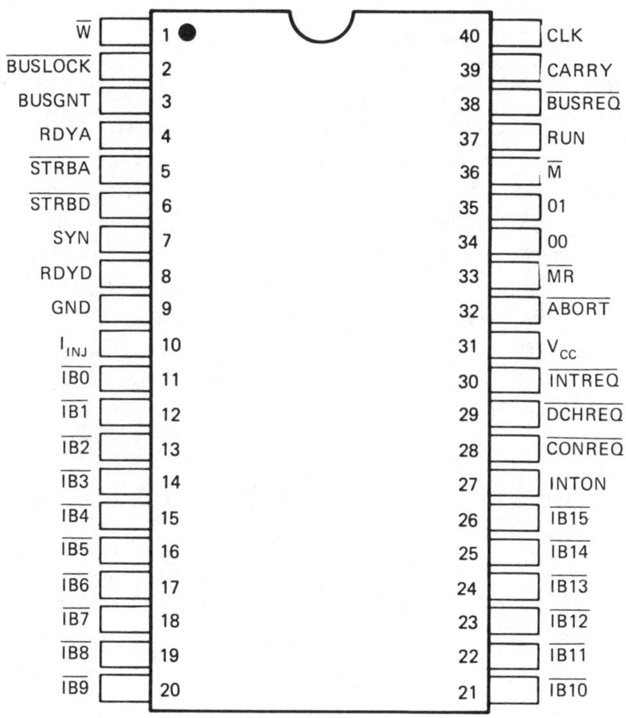

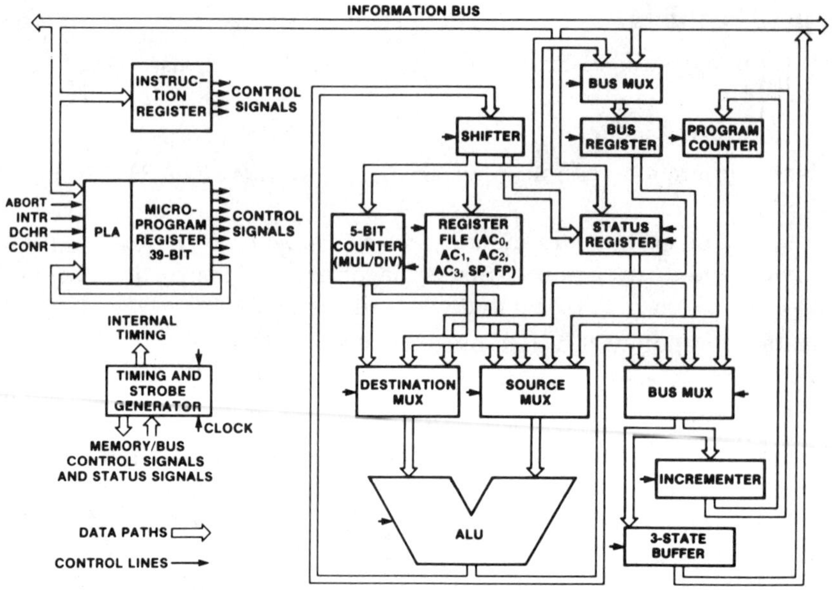

Reprinted by permission of Fairchild Camera and Instrument Corp.

Block Diagram—9445, 16-Bit CPU
Fig. 6-5

IN-CIRCUIT QUICK-TESTS

For 75% Confidence Level

1. Volt-ohmmeter Measurements: The PC board ground should be connected directly to pin 9. Power supply voltage of no less than 4.5 volts DC and no more than 5.5 volts DC should be measured from pin 31 to ground. Also check pin 10 where about 1.0 V at 300 to 400 mA should be provided.
2. Oscilloscope Measurements: Clock signals with a frequency of 0.1 MHz to 24 MHz should appear at pin 40 with an amplitude of 4.5 to 5.5 volts peak. Also check the signal on pin 7. This should be a pulse train, synchronized to the clock and it indicates every machine cycle.

For 90% Confidence Level

All of the measurements made for the 75% confidence level must be correct. Add the following:

Monitor the clock on pin 40 in conjunction with the RDY signal on the oscilloscope. The RDY signal on pin 4 is related to the address bus status of this IC.

EXACT REPLACEMENT ESSENTIAL.

TMS 9900 (Texas Instruments) 16-Bit CPU[4]

This device is produced using N-channel silicon-gate MOS technology. It has a minicomputer Instruction set, including multiply, and divide capability. The memory-to-memory architecture features multiple register files, resident in memory, which allow fast response to interrupts and programming flexibility.

PIN NAME	DESCRIPTION	TYPE
A0(MSB)-A14(LSB)	Address Bus	O
D0(MSB)-D15 (LSB)	Data Bus	I/O
01-04	Phase 1-Phase 4 clock	I
DBIN	Data Bus In	O
MEMEN	Memory Enable	O
WE	Write Enable	O
CRUCLK	CRU Clock	O
CRUIN	CRU In	I
CRUOUT	CRU Out	O
INTREQ	Interrupt Request	I
IC0(MSB)-IC3(LSB)	Interrupt Codes	I
HOLD	Hold	I
HOLDA	Hold Acknowledge	O
READY	Ready	I
WAIT	Wait	O
IAQ	Instruction Acquisition	O
LOAD	Load	I
RESET	Reset	I
V_{BB}	-5V Power Supply	
V_{CC}	+5V Power Supply	
V_{DD}	12V Power Supply	
V_{SS}	Ground	

Special Features

- Up to 65,536 Bytes of memory can be addressed.
- Separate memory, I/O, and interrupt-bus structure.
- 16 prioritized interrupts.
- Programmed and DMA I/O capability.
- 0–70°C ambient temperature range.
- Directly TTL compatible I/O.
- 3.3MHz speed (The TMS 9900-40 version has 4.0MHz speed).

[4]Note: The same microprocessor is manufactured by: AMI—S9900.

Pin Configuration

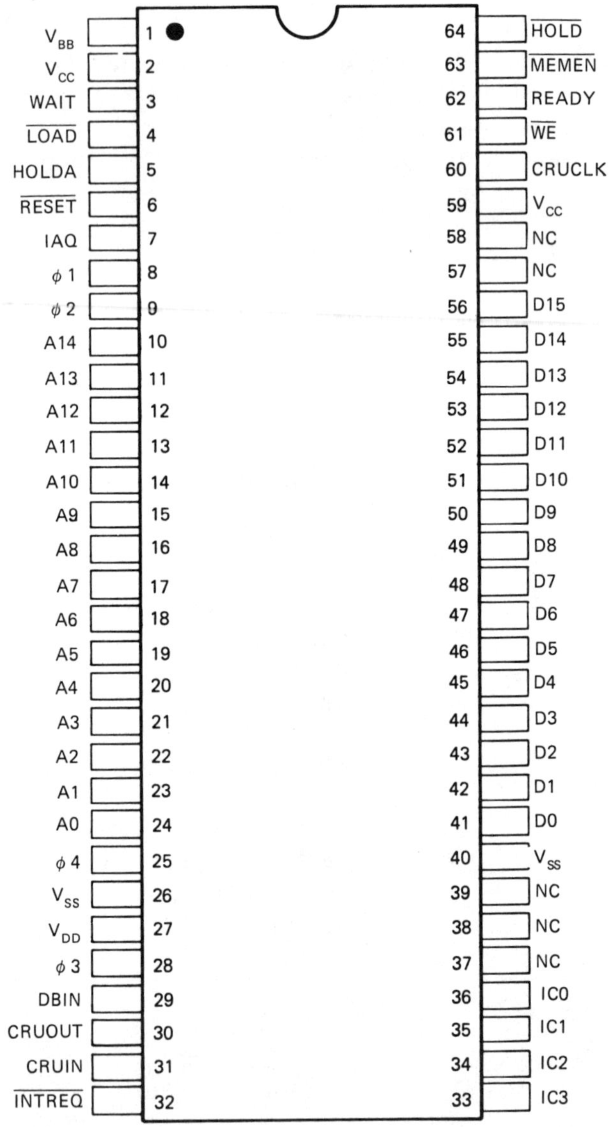

IN-CIRCUIT QUICK-TESTS

For 75% Confidence Level:

1. Volt-ohmmeter Measurements: The PC board ground should be connected directly to pins 26 and 40. Power supply voltage of no less than 4.75 volts DC and no more than 5.25 volts DC should be

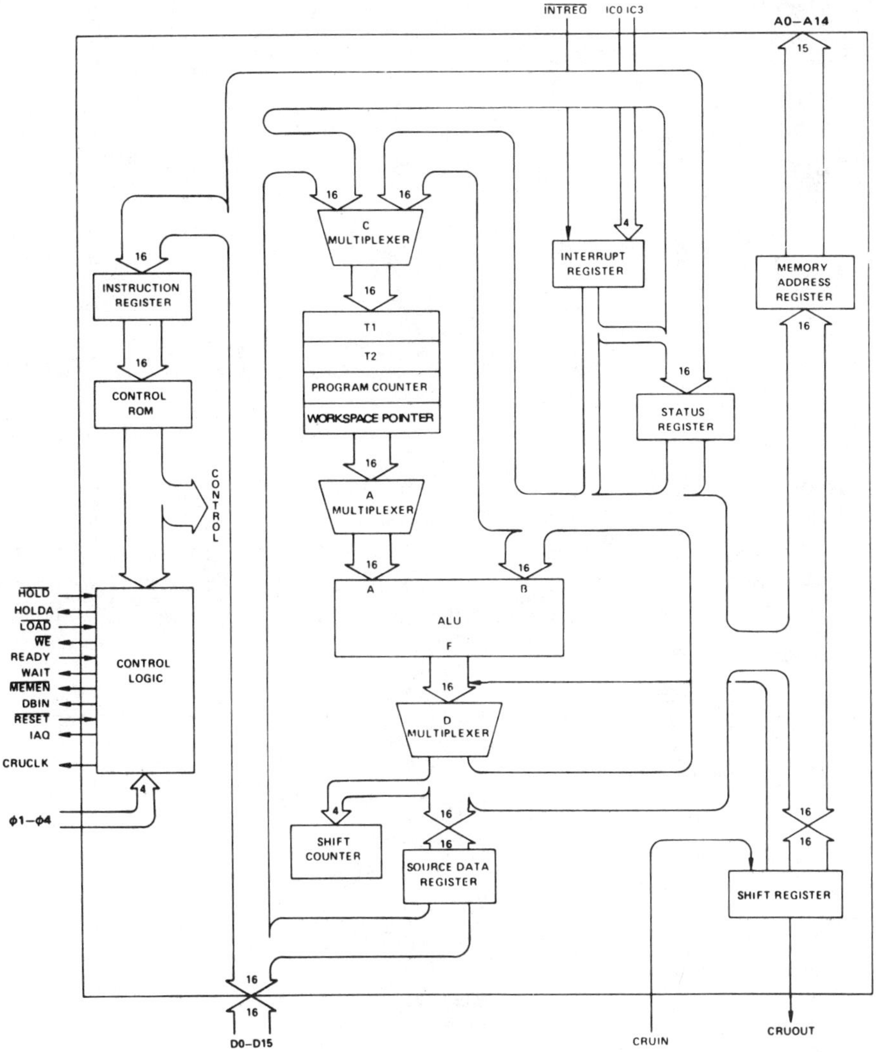

Courtesy Texas Instruments Incorporated.

Block Diagram—9900, 16-Bit CPU
Fig. 6-6

measured from pins 2 and 59 to ground. −4.75 to −5.25 volts should be measured at pin 1 and 11.4 to 12.6 volts at pin 27.

2. Oscilloscope Measurements: Clock signals with a frequency of 0.1MHz to 3.3 MHz should appear at pins 8, 9, 25 and 28 with an amplitude of 10 to 12 volts peak. Also check the signal on pin 60. This should be a pulse train, synchronized to the clock and it indicates that data is available.

For 90% Confidence Level:

All of the measurements made for the 75% confidence level must be correct. Add the following:

> Monitor the clock on pins 8, 9, 25 or 28 in conjunction with the WE signal on the oscilloscope. The WE signal on pin 61 is related to the WRITE ENABLE operation of this IC.

EXACT REPLACEMENT PREFERRED—it may be possible to use the 9900-40 16-BIT CPU if the exact replacement is not available.

SPB 9900A (Texas Instruments) 16-Bit CPU

This device is basically the same as the TMS 9900, but it employs I^2L technology to enhance enviromental specifications. It is a static, bipolar microprocessor operating from a single phase clock over the frequency range from 0 to 3MHz. The power supply is specified as a single input injector current which may be varied over the range from 10mA to 1A with a corresponding change in speed.

PIN NAME	DESCRIPTION	TYPE
A0(MSB)-A14 (LSB)	Address Bus	O
D0(MSB)-D15 (LSB)	Data Bus	I/O
CLOCK	Clock	I
DBIN	Data Bus In	O
$\overline{\text{MEMEN}}$	Memory Enable	O
$\overline{\text{WE}}$	Write Enable	O
CRUCLK	CRU Clock	O
CRUIN	CRU In	I
CRUOUT	CRU Out	O
$\overline{\text{INTREQ}}$	Interrupt Request	I
IC0(MSB)-IC3 (LSB)	Interrupt Codes	I
$\overline{\text{HOLD}}$	Hold	I
HOLDA	Hold Acknowledge	O
READY	Ready	I
WAIT	Wait	O
IAQ	Instruction Acquisition	I
$\overline{\text{CYCEND}}$	Cycle End	O
$\overline{\text{LOAD}}$	Load	I
$\overline{\text{RESET}}$	Reset	I
INJ	Injector-Supply-Current	
GND	Ground	

Special Features

- Up to 65,536 bytes of memory can be addressed.
- 3MHz speed.
- 16 prioritized interrupts.

PIN CONFIGURATION

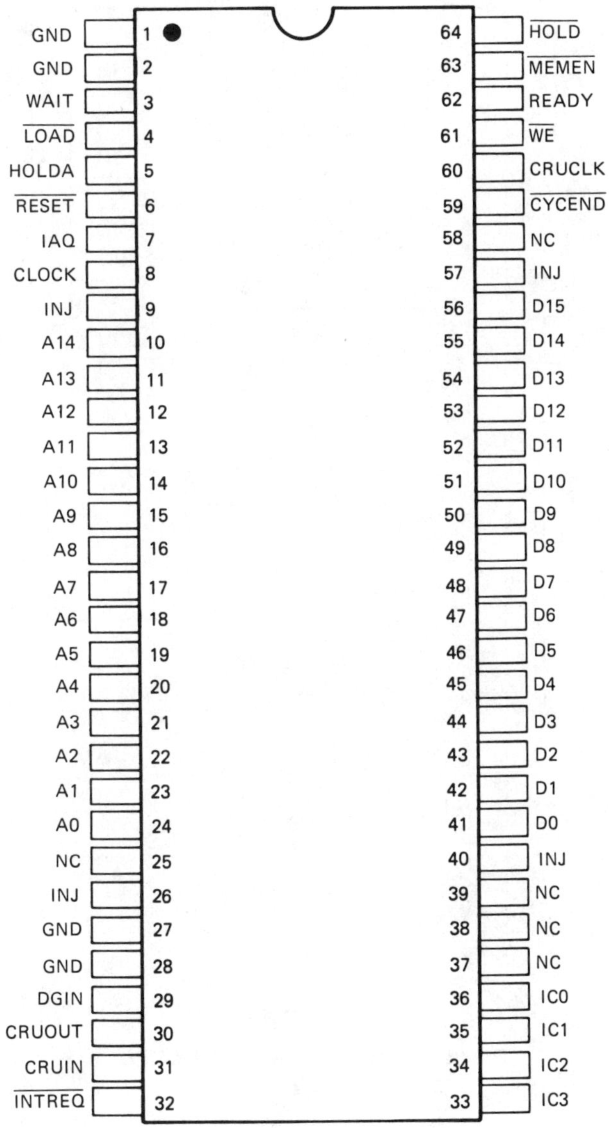

- I²L technology.
- −55 to +125°C ambient temperature range.
- Single DC power supply.
- Directly TTL compatible I/O.

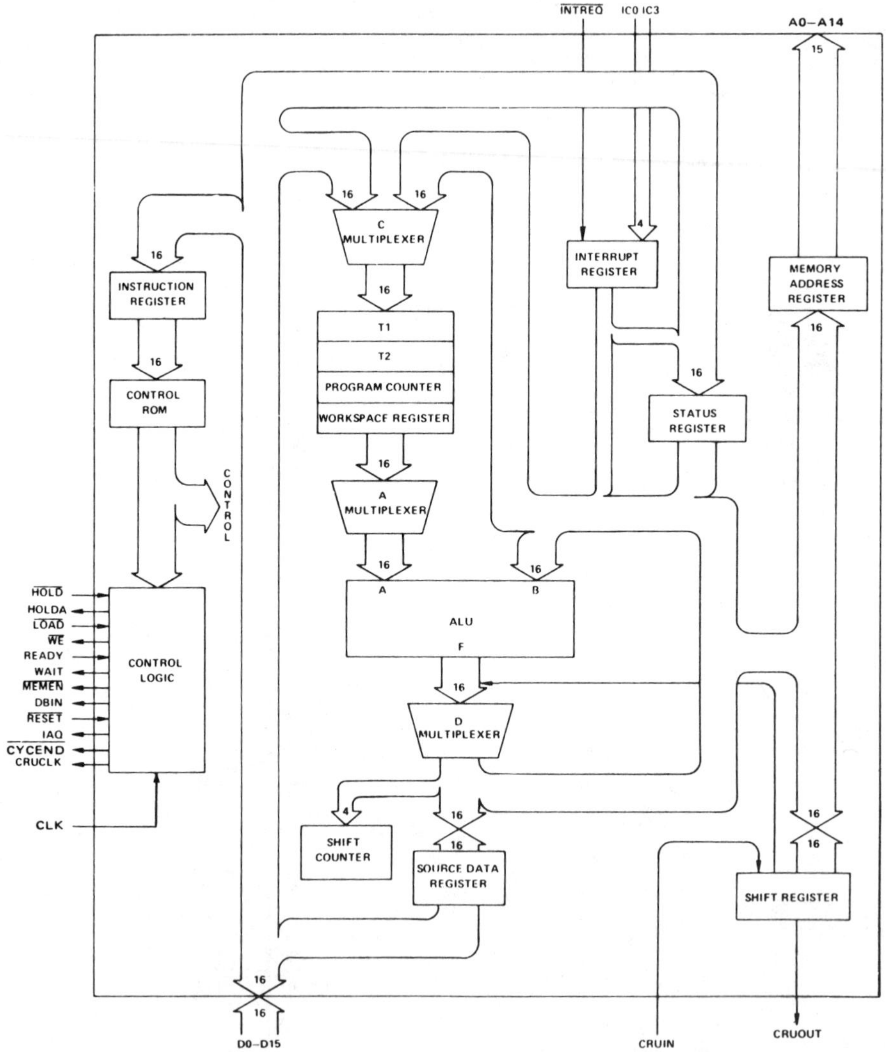

Courtesy Texas Instruments Incorporated.

Block Diagram—9900A, 16-Bit CPU
Fig. 6-7

IN-CIRCUIT QUICK-TESTS

FOR 75% CONFIDENCE LEVEL:

1. Volt-ohmmeter Measurements: The PC board ground should be connected directly to pins 1, 2, 27 and 28. Power supply voltage of no less than 1.0 volts DC and no more than 1.3 volts DC should be measured from pins 9, 26, 40 and 57 to ground at an "injector supply current" of 450 to 550 mA.
2. Oscilloscope Measurements: Clock signals with a frequency of zero to 2.0 MHz should appear at pin 8 with an amplitude of 2.0 to 2.4 volts peak. Also check the signal on pin 60. This should be a pulse train, synchronized to the clock and it indicates that data is available.

FOR 90% CONFIDENCE LEVEL:

All of the measurements made for the 75% confidence level must be correct. Add the following:

Monitor the clock on pin 8 in conjunction with the WE signal on the oscilloscope. The WE signal on pin 61 is related to the WRITE ENABLE operation of this IC.

EXACT REPLACEMENT ESSENTIAL.

TMS 9980 A (TEXAS INSTRUMENTS) 16-BIT CPU[5]

This device is a software compatible member of the 9900 family of microprocessors and microcomputers. It has an 8-bit data bus and an on-chip clock. The instruction set is exactly the same as the 9900's. The unique memory-to-memory architecture features multiple register files, resident in memory, which allow faster response to interrupts and increased programming flexibility. The separate bus structure simplifies the system design effort.

PIN NAME	DESCRIPTION	TYPE
A0 (MSB)-A12	Address Bus	O
A13/CRUOUT	Address Bus/CRU Output	O
D0 (MSB)-D7 (LSB)	Data Bus	I/O
CKIN	Clock In	I

[5]Note: The same microprocessor is manufactured by:
AMI—S9980
SMC—SMC9980.

PIN NAME	DESCRIPTION	TYPE
$\overline{0}3$	Clock Phase Three	O
DBIN	Data Bus In	O
$\overline{\text{MEMEN}}$	Memory Enable	O
$\overline{\text{WE}}$	Write Enable	O
CRUCLK	CRU Clock	O
CRUIN	CRU In	I
INT0-INT2	Interrupt Code	I
$\overline{\text{HOLD}}$	Hold	I
HOLDA	Hold Acknowledge	O
READY	Ready	I
IAQ	Instruction Acquisition	O
V_{BB}	-5V Power Supply	
V_{CC}	+5V Power Supply	
V_{DD}	12V Power Supply	
V_{SS}	Ground	

Pin Configuration

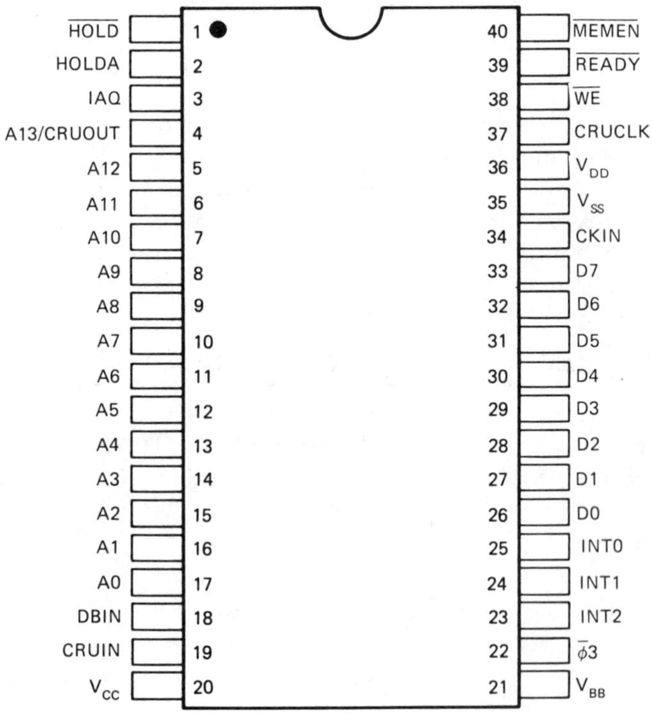

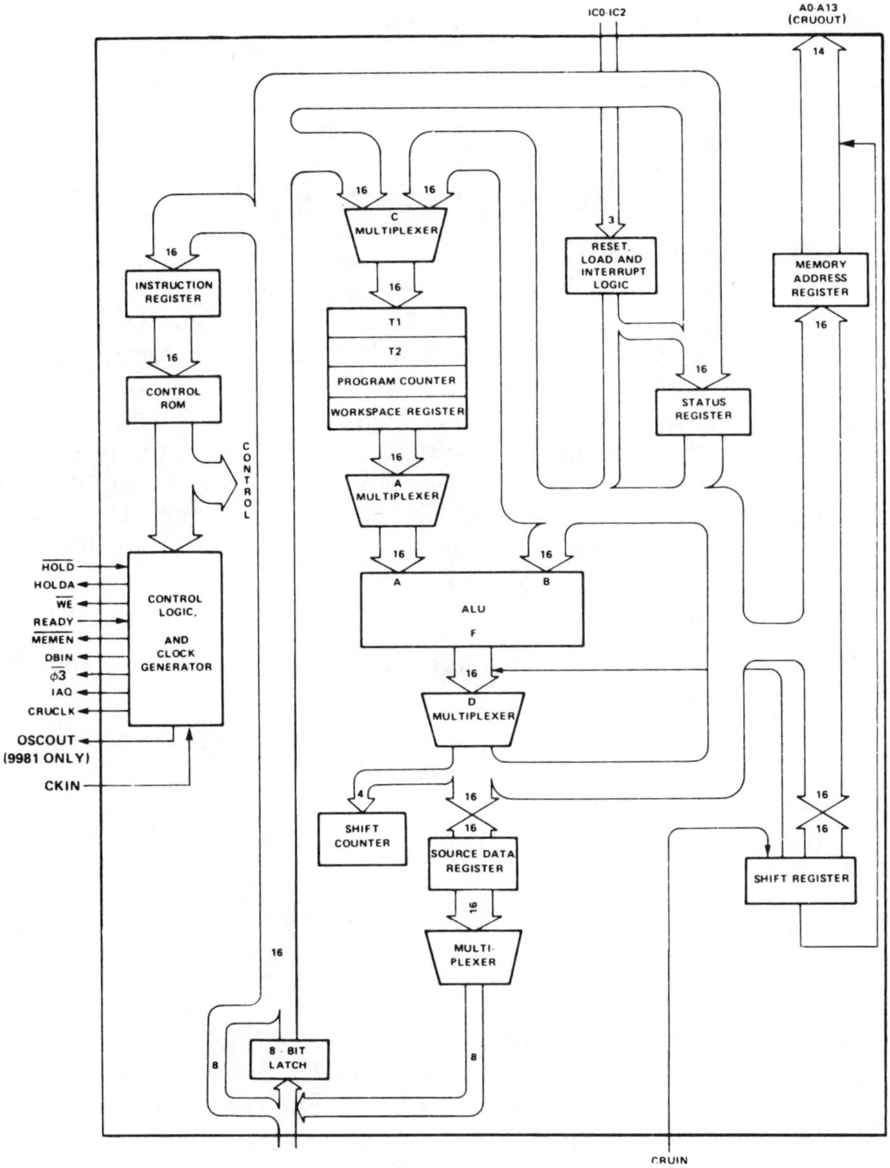

Courtesy Texas Instruments Incorporated.

Block Diagram—9980A 16-Bit CPU
Fig. 6-8

Special Features

- 10MHz speed.
- Up to 16,384 addressable bytes of memory.
- 8-bit memory bus.
- Four prioritized interrupts.
- On-chip four-phase clock generator.
- 0 to 70°C ambient temperature range.

IN-CIRCUIT QUICK-TESTS

FOR 75% CONFIDENCE LEVEL

1. Volt-ohmmeter Measurements: The PC board ground should be connected directly to pin 35. Power supply voltage of no less than 4.75 volts DC and no more than 5.25 volts DC should be measured from pin 20 to ground. −5.25 to −4.75 volts should be measured at pin 21 and 11.4 to 12.6 volt at pin 36.
2. Oscilloscope Measurements: Clock signals with a frequency of 6.0MHz to 10.0MHz should appear at pin 34 with an amplitude of 2.0 to 5.0 volts peak. Also check the signal on pin 22. This should be a pulse train, synchronized to the clock and ¼ of the clock input frequency measured on pin 34.

FOR 90% CONFIDENCE LEVEL:

All of the measurements made for the 75% confidence level must be correct. Add the following:

Monitor the clock on pin 34 in conjunction with the WE signal on the oscilloscope. The WE signal on pin 38 is related to the WRITE ENABLE operation of this IC.

EXACT REPLACEMENT ESSENTIAL.

TMS 9981 (TEXAS INSTRUMENTS) 16-BIT CPU[6]

This is a device very similar to the TMS 9980A. The differences concern the power supplies, the clock and the pin configuration compatibility. The TMS 9981 has an internal charge pump to generate V_{BB} from V_{CC} and V_{DD}; it has an optional on-chip oscillator in addition to the external clock mode. The pinouts are not compatible for D0-D7, INT0-INT2, and $\overline{0}3$.

PIN NAME	DESCRIPTION	TYPE
A0 (MSB)-A12	Address Bus	O
A13/CRUOUT	Address Bus/CRU Out	O

[6]*Note:* The block diagram is the same as the 9980A.

PIN NAME	DESCRIPTION	TYPE
D0 (MSB)-D7 (LSB)	Data Bus	I/O
CKIN	Clock In	I
OSCOUT	Oscillator Out	O
$\overline{0}3$	Clock Phase Three	O
DBIN	Data Bus In	O
$\overline{\text{MEMEN}}$	Memory Enable	O
$\overline{\text{WE}}$	Write Enable	O
CRUCLK	CRU Clock	O
CRUIN	CRU In	I
INT0-INT2	Interrupt Code	I
$\overline{\text{HOLD}}$	Hold	I
HOLD A	Hold Acknowledge	O
READY	Ready	I
IAQ	Instruction Acquisition	O
V_{CC}	5V Power Supply	
V_{DD}	12V Power Supply	
V_{SS}	Ground	

Special Features

The same as for the TMS 9980A.

IN-CIRCUIT QUICK-TESTS

For 75% Confidence Level:

1. Volt-ohmmeter Measurements: The PC board ground should be connected directly to pin 35. Power supply voltage of no less than 4.75 volts DC and no more than 5.25 volts DC should be measured from pin 20 to ground. 11.4 to 12.6 volts should be measured from pin 36 to ground.
2. Oscilloscope Measurements: Clock signals with a frequency of 6.0 MHz to 10.0 MHz should appear at pins 33 and 34 with an amplitude of 2.4 to 5.5 volts peak. Also check the signal on pin 21. This should be a pulse train, synchronized to the clock but 1/4 of its frequency.

For 90% Confidence Level:

All of the measurements made for the 75% confidence level must be correct. Add the following:

Monitor the clock on pin 33 or 34 in conjunction with the WE signal on the oscilloscope. The WE signal on pin 38 is related to the WRITE ENABLE operation of this IC.

EXACT REPLACEMENT ESSENTIAL.

PIN CONFIGURATION

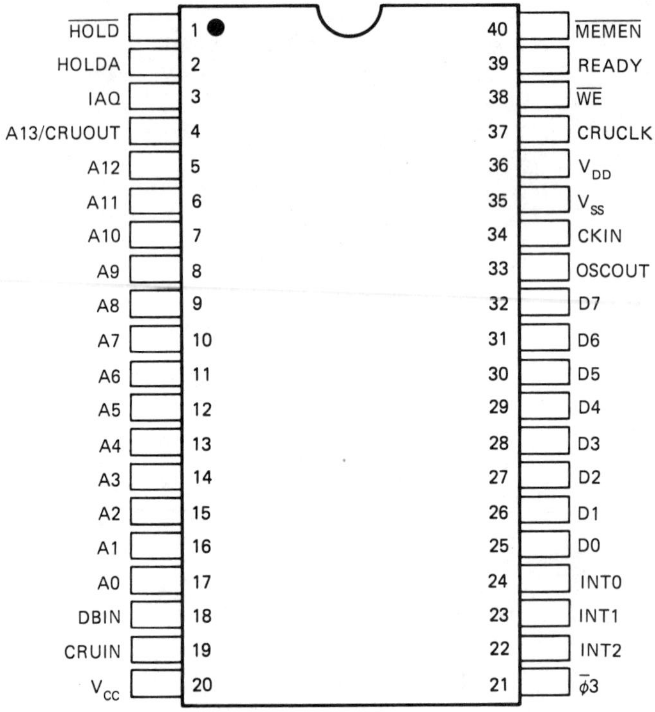

TMS 9985 (Texas Instruments) 16-Bit CPU[7]

This device is a software compatible member of the 9900 family of microprocessors and microcomputers. It contains a 16-bit CPU, 256 bytes of RAM, on-chip timer/event counter, external 16-bit address bus and 8-bit data bus. The unique memory-to-memory architecture features multiple register files, resident in memory which allows faster response to interrupts and increased programming flexibility. All members of the TMS 9900 family of peripheral circuits are compatible with the TMS 9985.

PIN NAME	DESCRIPTION	TYPE
XTAL1	Crystal 1	I
XTAL2	Crystal 2 or External Oscillator	I

[7]Note: The same microprocessor is manufactured by: AMI—S9985.

PIN NAME	DESCRIPTION	TYPE
0	Clock	O
$\overline{RST}$	Reset	I
$\overline{INT1}$	Interrupt 1	I
$\overline{INT2/EC}$	Interrupt 2/Event Counter	I
$\overline{LOAD}$	Load	I
AO/$\overline{TC}$	Address Bit 0/Transfer Clock	I/O
A1/TD	Address Bit 1/Transfer Data	I/O
A2–A14	Address Bus	O
A15/CRUOUT	Address Bit 15/CRU Output	O
D0–D7	Data Bus	I/O
DBIN	Data Bus In	O
$\overline{MEMEN}$	Memory Enable	O
$\overline{WE}$	Write Enable	O
CRUIN	CRU In	I
CRUCLK	CRU Clock	O
RDY/$\overline{HLD}$	Ready/Hold	I
IAQ/HOLD A	Instruction Acquisition/Hold Acknowledge	O
V_{CC}	Power Supply	
V_{SS}	Ground	

PIN CONFIGURATION

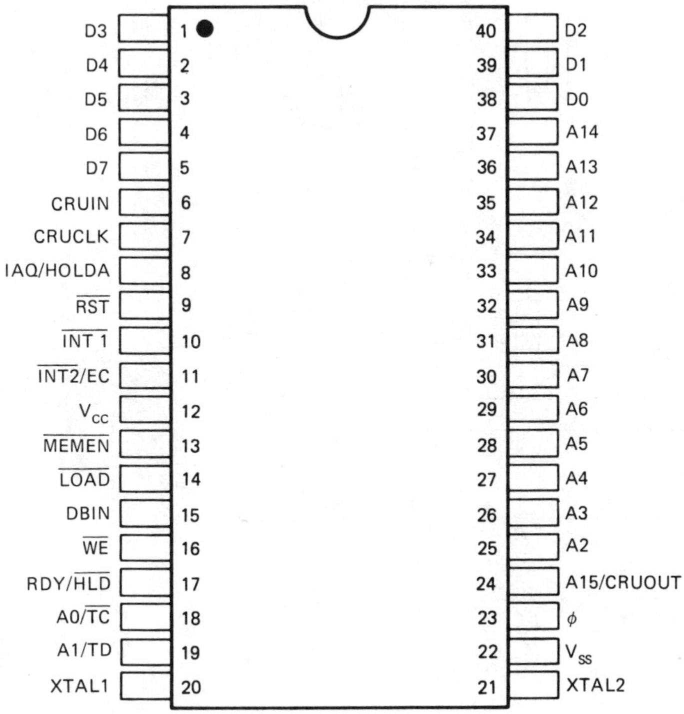

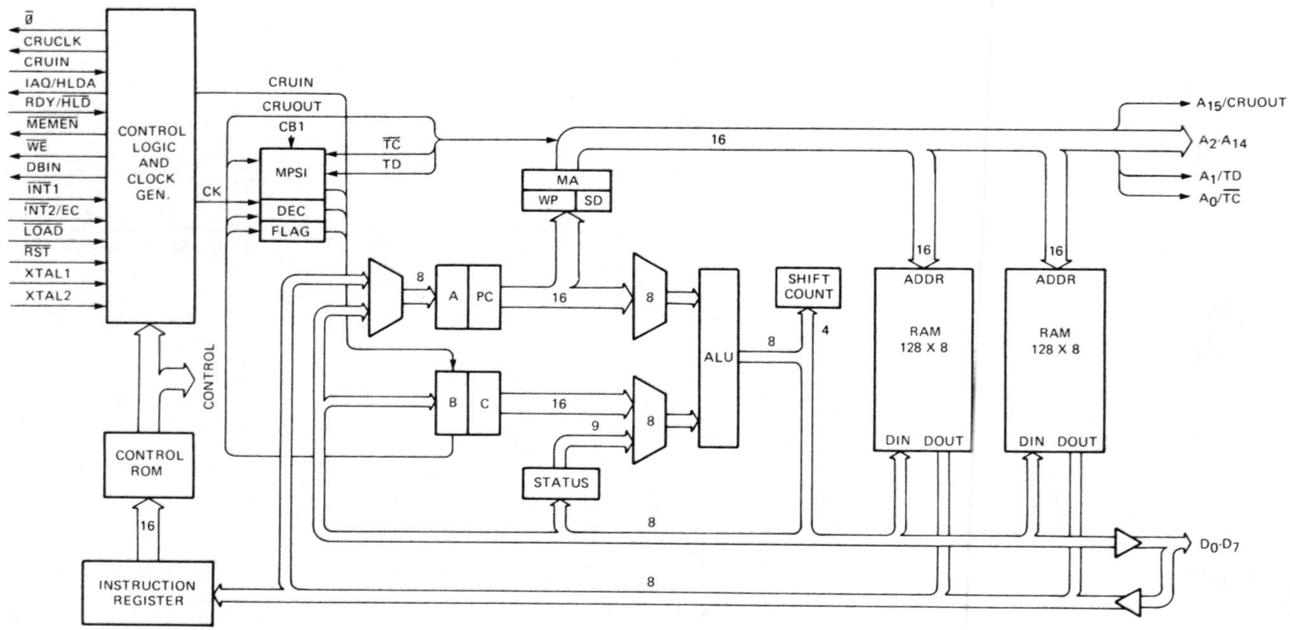

Courtesy Texas Instruments Incorporated.

Block Diagram—9985, 16-Bit CPU
Fig. 6-9

Special Features

- 5MHz speed.
- 8-Bit Memory Data Bus.
- Separate Memory, I/O and Interrupt Bus Structures.
- Five Prioritized Interrupts.
- On-chip timer/event counter.
- 256 bits of RAM on chip.
- Up to 65,536 addressable bytes of memory.
- Multiprocessor system interface.
- Single 5V power supply.
- 0 to 70°C ambient temperature range.

IN-CIRCUIT QUICK-TESTS

FOR 75% CONFIDENCE LEVEL:

1. Volt-ohmmeter Measurements: The PC board ground should be connected directly to pin 22. Power supply voltage of no less than 4.75 volts DC and no more than 5.25 volts DC should be measured from pin 12 to ground.
2. Oscilloscope Measurements: Clock signals with a frequency of 0.1MHz to 5.0MHz should appear at pins 20 and 21 with an amplitude of 2.4 to 5.25 volts peak. Also check the signal on pin 23. This should be a pulse train, synchronized to the clock and ½ the frequency of the clock.

FOR 90% CONFIDENCE LEVEL:

All of the measurements made for the 75% confidence level must be correct. Add the following:

Monitor the clock on pin 20 and 21 in conjunction with the WE signal on the oscilloscope. The WE signal on pin 16 is related to the WRITE ENABLE operation of this IC.

EXACT REPLACEMENT ESSENTIAL.

AM 29116 (ADVANCED MICRO DEVICES) 16-BIT CPU

This device is designed for use in microprogrammed systems, particularly peripheral controllers, communication controllers, industrial controllers, or in microprogrammed processor applications. In addition to the normal one- and two-operand logical and arithmetic instructions, the instruction set contains the following instructions in a single microcycle: rotate and merge, rotate and compare, and prioritize. It also has instructions which perform CRC (Cyclic-Redundancy Check), calculations for any CRC polynomial of 16 bits or less.

PIN NAME	DESCRIPTION	TYPE
I0–I15	Port I	I
Y0–Y15	Port Y	I/O
T1–T4	Port T	I/O
$\overline{OE}_Y$	Output Enable	I
OE_T	Output Enable	I
$\overline{DLE}$	Data Latch Enable	I
$\overline{SRE}$	Status Register Enable	I
CT	Conditional Test	O
CP	Clock Pulse	I
$\overline{IEN}$	Instruction Enable	I
V_{CC}	Power Supply	
GND	Ground	
NC	No Connection	

Special Features

- 100ns microcycle time for all instructions.
- 10MHz clock rate.
- 16-bit data path with full carry look ahead over all 16 bits in the ALU during arithmetic operation.
- 32 working registers arranged in a single port RAM architecture.
- 16-bit barrel shifter which can rotate an input up to 15 positions.
- Status manipulation capability for condition code initiated branching and user definable flag manipulation.
- Power supply: 5V ± 5% (±10% for the military AM29116).

IN-CIRCUIT QUICK-TESTS

FOR 75% CONFIDENCE LEVEL:

1. Volt-ohmmeter Measurements: The PC board ground should be connected directly to pins 11, 25, 35 and 44. Power supply voltage of no less than 4.5 volts DC and no more than 5.5 volts DC should be measured from pins 12, 40 and 41 to ground.
2. Oscilloscope Measurements: Clock signals with a frequency of 0.1MHz to 10.0MHz should appear at pin 18 with an amplitude of 2.5 to 5.5 volts peak. Also check the signal on pin 27. This should

Pin Configuration

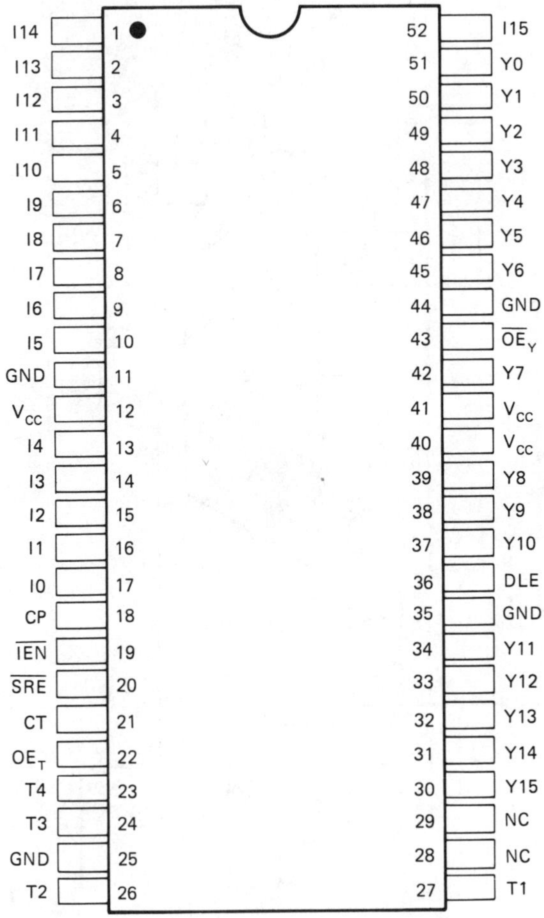

be a pulse train, synchronized to the clock and it represents an I/O status indicator.

For 90% Confidence Level:

All of the measurements made for the 75% confidence level must be correct. Add the following:

> Monitor the clock on pin 18 in conjunction with the CT signal on the oscilloscope. The CT signal on pin 21 is related to the MUX LOGIC operation of this IC.

EXACT REPLACEMENT ESSENTIAL.

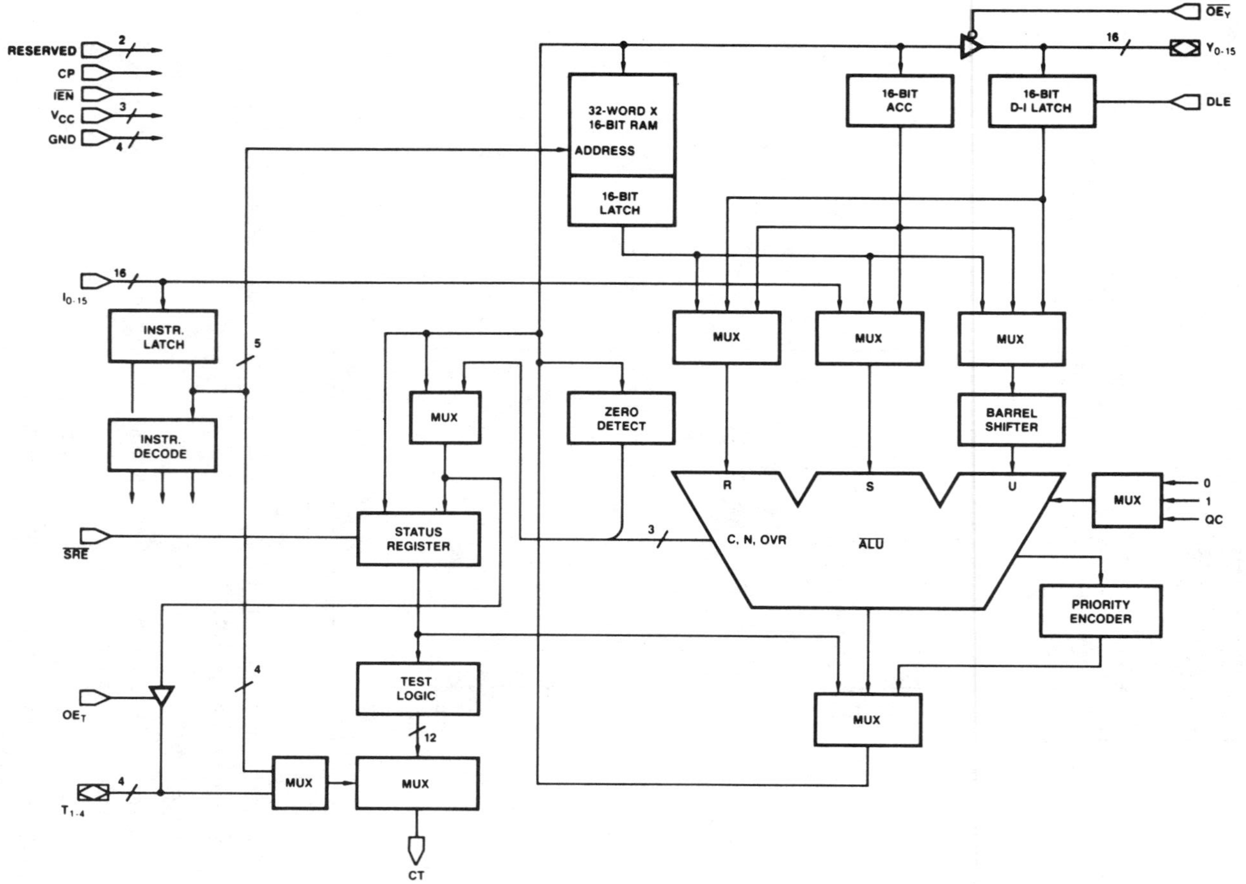

Courtesy Advanced Micro Devices, Inc.

Block Diagram—29116, 16-Bit CPU
Fig. 6-10

HD 68000 (HITACHI) 16-BIT CPU[8]

This is an advanced device that offers seventeen 32-bit registers in addition to the 32-bit program counter and a 16-bit status register. The first eight registers (D0–D7) are used as data registers for byte (8-bit), word (16-bit) and long word (32-bit) data operations. The second set of seven registers (A0–A6) and the system stack pointer may be used as software stack pointers and base address registers. In addition, these registers may be used for word and long word address operations. All seventeen registers may be used as index registers.

PIN NAME	DESCRIPTION	TYPE
A1-A23	Address Bus	O
D0-D15	Data Bus	I/O
$\overline{AS}$	Address Strobe	O
R/$\overline{W}$	Read/Write	O
$\overline{UDS}$	Upper Data Strobe	O
$\overline{LDS}$	Lower Data Strobe	O
$\overline{DTACK}$	Data Transfer Acknowledge	I
$\overline{BR}$	Bus Request	I
$\overline{BG}$	Bus Grant	O
$\overline{BGACK}$	Bus Grant Acknowledge	I
$\overline{IPL0}$-$\overline{IPL2}$	Interrupt Control	I
$\overline{BERR}$	Bus Error	I
$\overline{RES}$	Reset	I/O
$\overline{HALT}$	Halt	I/O
E	Enable	O
$\overline{VPA}$	Valid Peripheral Address	I
$\overline{VMA}$	Valid Memory Address	O
FC0-FC2	Processor Status	O
CLK	Clock	I
V_{CC}	Power Supply	
GND	Ground	

Special Features

- 32-bit data and address registers.
- 16 megabyte direct addressing range.
- 56 powerful instruction types.
- Operations on five main data types.
- Memory mapped I/O.
- 14 addressing modes.

---

[8]Note: The same microprocessor is manufactured by:
MOTOROLA—MC 68000L (4: 4MHz; 6:6MHz; 8:8MHz; 10:10MHz).

Pin Configuration

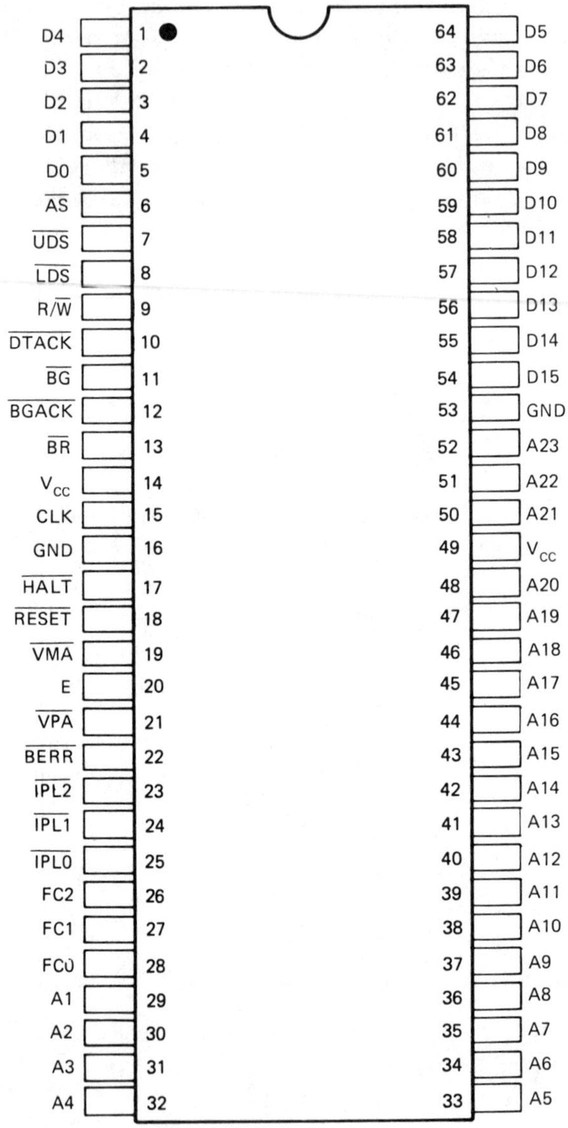

IN-CIRCUIT QUICK-TESTS

For 75% Confidence Level:

1. Volt-ohmmeter Measurements: The PC board ground should be connected directly to pin 16 and 53. Power supply voltage of no

less than 4.75 volts DC and no more than 5.25 volts DC should be measured from pins 14 and 49 to ground.

2. Oscilloscope Measurements: Clock signals with a frequency of 2.0MHZ to 4.0, 6.0 on 8.0MHz should appear at pin 15 with an amplitude of 2.4 to 5.5 volts peak. Also check the signal on pin 9. This should be a pulse train, synchronized to the clock and indicates the READ/WRITE status.

FOR 90% CONFIDENCE LEVEL:

All of the measurements made for the 75% confidence level must be correct. Add the following:

Monitor the clock on pin 15 in conjunction with the AS signal on the oscilloscope. The AS signal on pin 6 is related to the ADDRESS BUS operation of this IC.

EXACT REPLACEMENT ESSENTIAL.

CHAPTER 7

32-Bit CPU

32-BIT CPU

NS 16032 (National Semiconductor) 32-Bit CPU

This device functions as a central processing unit in National Semiconductor's NS 16000 microcomputer family. It has been designed to support the use of a large addressing space for large programs and/or data structures. Its instruction set provides general two-address capability, high degree of symmetry, addressing modes for high-level language references and expansion via slave processors.

PIN NAME	DESCRIPTION	TYPE
A16-A23	Address Bits	O
AD0-AD15	Address/Data	I/O
PHI1, PHI2	Two-phase Clocking Signals	I
RDY	Ready	I
$\overline{HOLD}$	Hold	I
$\overline{HLDA}$	Hold Acknowledge	O
$\overline{INT}$	Interrupt	I
$\overline{NMI}$	Non-maskable Interrupt	I
$\overline{RST}/\overline{ABT}$	Reset/Abort	I
$\overline{ADS}$	Address Strobe	O
$\overline{DDIN}$	Data Direction In	O
$\overline{HBE}$	High Byte Enable	O
ST0-ST3	Status	O
$U/\overline{S}$	User/Supervisor	O
$\overline{ILO}$	Interlocked Operation	O
$\overline{PFS}$	Program Flow Status	O
$\overline{AT}/\overline{SPC}$	Address Translation/Slave Processor Control	I/O
$\overline{DS}/\overline{FLT}$	Data Strobe/Float	I/O
BBG	Back-Bias Generator	
V_{CC}	Power Supply	
GNDL	Logical Ground	
GNDB	Buffer Ground	

Special Features

- 32-bit architecture and implementation.
- 16 Mbyte uniform addressing space.
- High-speed XMOS technology.

IN-CIRCUIT QUICK-TESTS

FOR 75% CONFIDENCE LEVEL:

1. Volt-ohmmeter Measurements: The PC board ground should be connected directly to pin 24 and 25. Power supply voltage of no less than 4.75 volts DC and no more than 5.25 volts DC should be measured from pin 48 to ground.
2. Oscilloscope Measurements: Clock signals with a frequency of 0.2MHz to 10MHz should appear at pins 26 and 27 with an amplitude of 4.5 to 6.25 volts peak. Also check the signal on pin

PIN CONFIGURATION

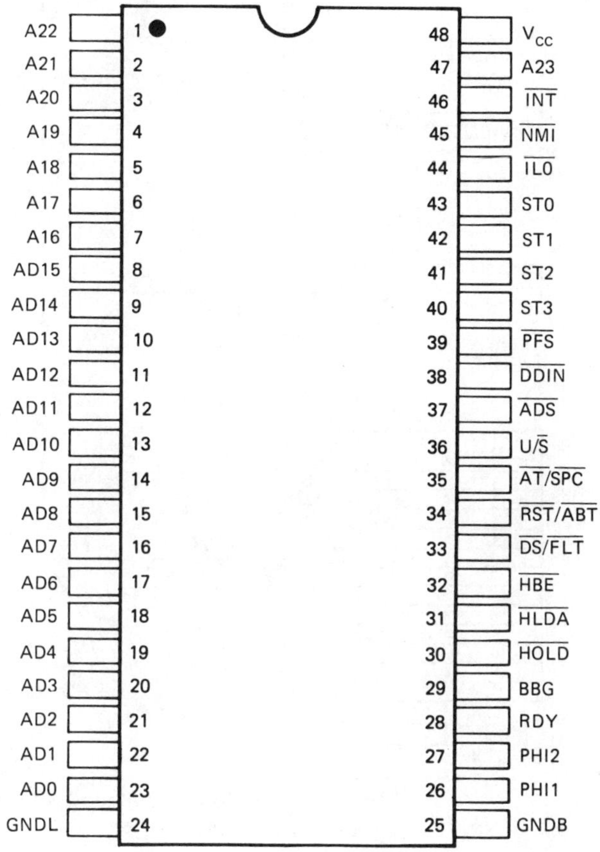

39. This should be a pulse train, synchronized to the clock and indicates the beginning of an instruction cycle.

FOR 90% CONFIDENCE LEVEL:

All of the measurements made for the 75% confidence level must be correct. Add the following:

Monitor the clock on pins 26 or 27 in conjunction with the ADS signal on the oscilloscope. The ADS signal on pin 37 is related to the bus cycle operation of this IC.

EXACT REPLACEMENT ESSENTIAL.

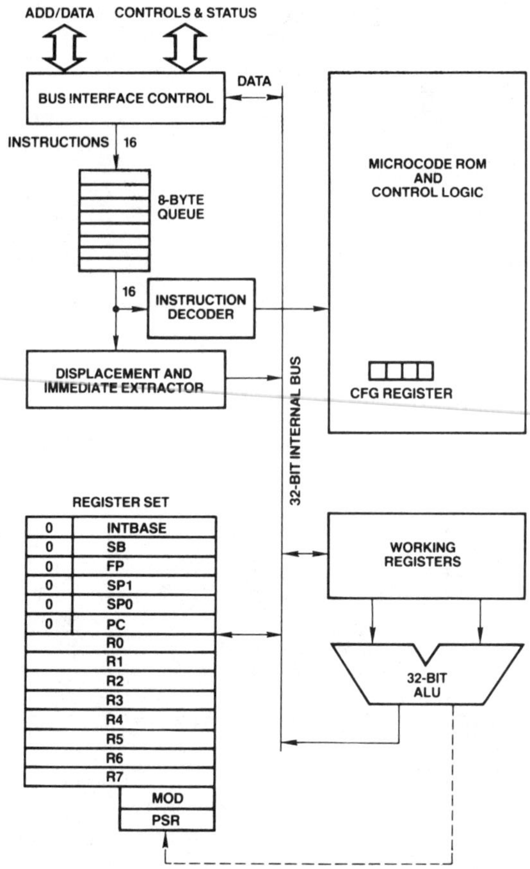

Courtesy of National Semiconductor Corporation.

Block Diagram—16032, 32-Bit CPU
Fig. 7-1

CHAPTER 8

4-BIT MICROCOMPUTER (μC)

4-Bit μC

MM75 (PPS-4/1 FAMILY) (ROCKWELL) 4-BIT MICROCOMPUTER

This device contains the following functions: a CPU, instruction decode, program save register, 640 bytes of program memory (ROM), 48 4-bit words of data memory (RAM), program counter (P), data address register (B), nine input/output discrete drivers/receivers, two 4-bit parallel input/

output channels, one 4-bit parallel input channel, interrupt and control logic, and a self-contained clock generator circuit.

PIN NAME	DESCRIPTION	TYPE
DI/00-DI/08	Discrete I/O Ports	I/O
RI01-RI04	Channel A I/O Ports	I/O
RI05-RI08	Channel B I/O Ports	I/O
PI1-PI4	Channel one Input Ports	I
INTO, INT1	Interrupt 0, 1	I
A	Clock	O
PO	Power On	I
VC	Oscillator Power Supply	
V_{DD}	Power Supply	
V_{SS}	Ground	

Special Features

- 16 8-bit word decode matrix.
- TTL and CMOS compatible.
- Arithmetic logic unit and four working registers.
- Over 50 instructions.
- Power supply operation range: –15V ±5%
- Maximum negative voltage: –30V (Vacuum Fluorescent Drive); –15V (Standard).
- Low power: 75mW typical, 125mW max.

PIN CONFIGURATION

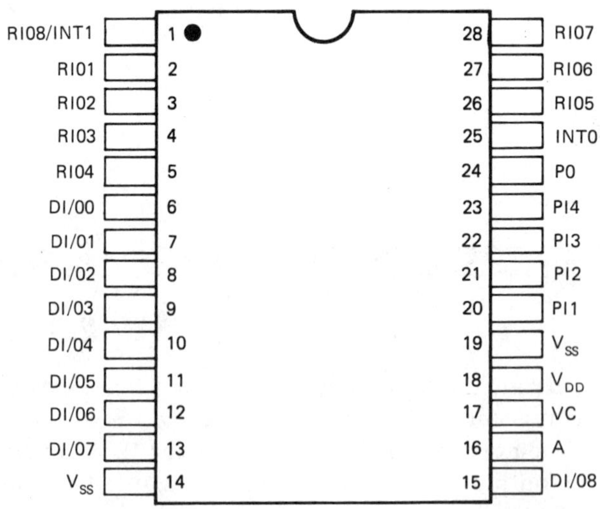

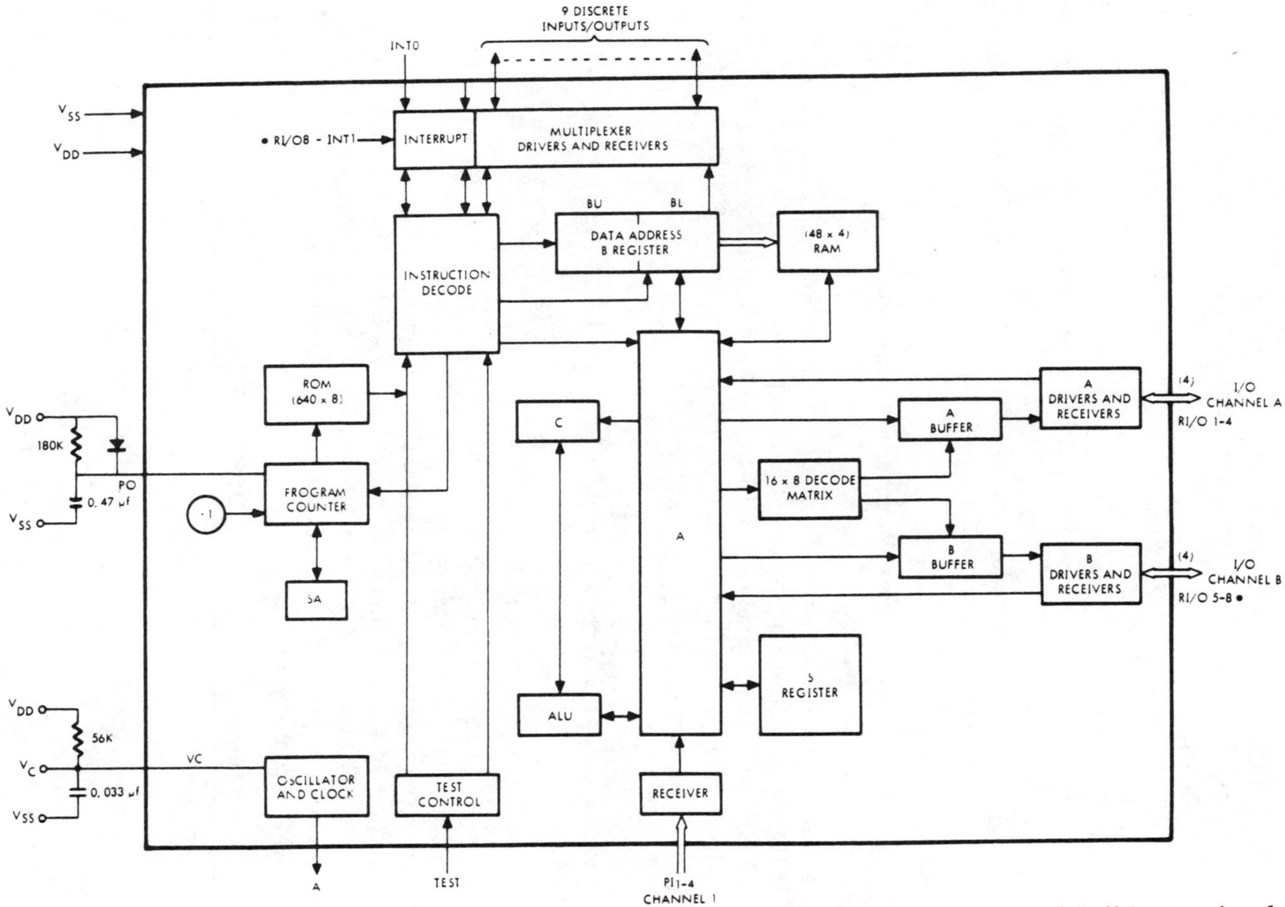

Courtesy Rockwell International.

Block Diagram—75, 4-Bit μC
Fig. 8-1

IN-CIRCUIT QUICK-TESTS

FOR 75% CONFIDENCE LEVEL:

1. Volt-ohmmeter Measurements:
   a) Make sure PC board ground has good connection to pins 14 and 19.
   b) Measure power supply voltage of –14.25 to –15.75 volts DC at pin 18.
2. Oscilloscope Measurements:
   a) Observe clock signals at pin 17. They should be square waves with a frequency of 0.09 to 0.1 MHz.
   b) Observe the signal on pin 16. This signal is the A clock output and is synchronized to the clock.

FOR 90% CONFIDENCE LEVEL:

In addition to the 75% confidence level tests, use a dual-trace oscilloscope to observe the following:

a) Monitor the A signal on pin 16 on one trace, while observing the R101 signal on pin 2 on the other. R101 is part of channel A I/O.
b) Monitor the A signal on pin 16 on one trace, while observing the DI/01 signal on pin 7 on the other. DI/01 is part "DISCRETE" I/O.

EXACT REPLACEMENT ESSENTIAL

MM78 (PPS-4/1 FAMILY) (ROCKWELL) 4-BIT MICROCOMPUTER

This device contains the following functions: CPU, program memory (ROM), data memory (RAM), program counter, (P), instruction decode, two program save registers, data address register (B), ten I/O discrete drivers/receivers, two 4-bit parallel I/O channels, two 4-bit parallel input channels, a serial input/output port, interrupt and control logic, and a self-contained four-phase clock generator circuit. The microcomputer is TTL and CMOS compatible.

PIN NAME	DESCRIPTION	TYPE
DI/00-DI/09	Discrete I/O Ports	I/O
PI1-PI4	Channel one Input Port	I
PI5-PI8	Channel two Input Port	I
RI01-RI04	Channel A I/O Port	I/O
RI05-RI08	Channel X I/O Port	I/O
CLOCK	Shift Clock	I/O
CLKIN	Clock In	I
EXCLK	External Clock	I
INT0, INT1	Interrupt 0, 1	I

PIN NAME	DESCRIPTION	TYPE
DATA I, DATA 0	Data In, Out	I/O
A, BP	Clock Signal	O
PO	Power On	I
VC	Clock Power Supply	
V_{DD}	Power Supply	
V_{SS}	Ground	

Special Features

- 2048 bytes of program memory and 128 4-bit data words.
- Clocked simultaneous serial input/output capability.
- Externally controlled serial input/output capability.
- Two interrupt request lines.
- Arithmetic logic unit and six working registers.
- Two-level subroutine nesting.
- 31 input/output ports.

PIN CONFIGURATION

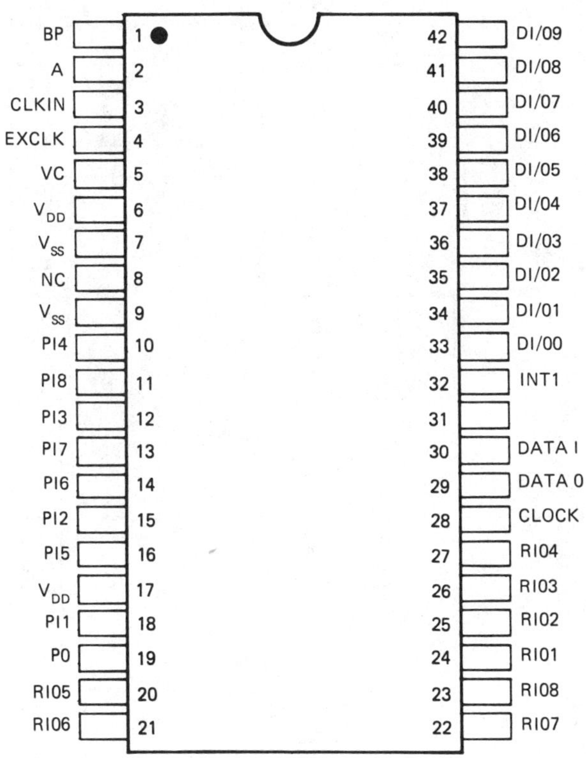

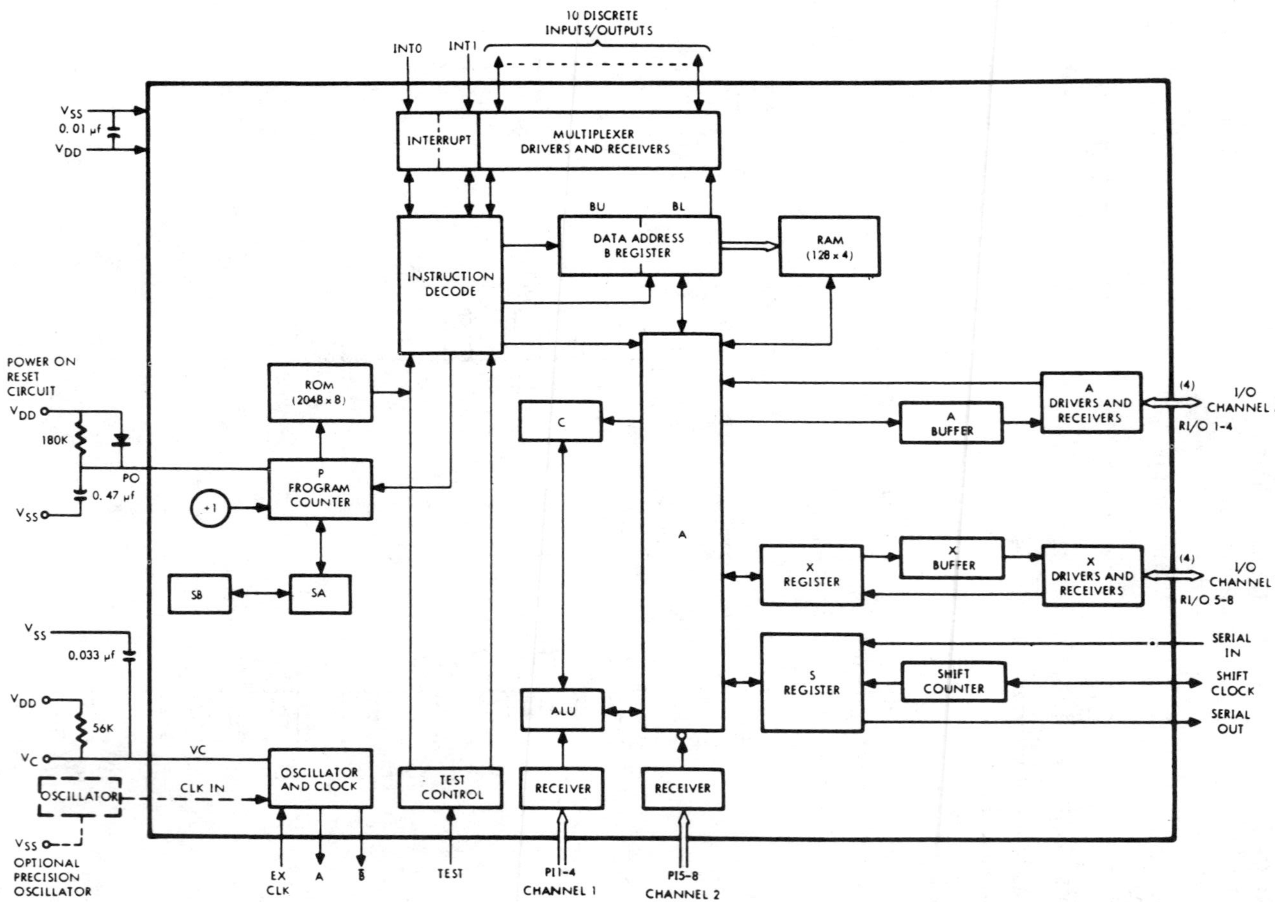

Courtesy Rockwell International.

Block Diagram—78, 4-Bit μC
Fig. 8-2

- Over 60 instructions.
- Power supply operation: -15V ± 5%.
- Maximum negative voltage: -30V (Vacuum Fluorescent Drive); -15V (Standard).
- Low power: 75mW typical, 125mW max.

IN-CIRCUIT QUICK-TESTS

FOR 75% CONFIDENCE LEVEL:

1. Volt-ohmmeter Measurements:
   a) Make sure PC board ground has good connection to pins 7 and 9.
   b) Measure power supply voltage of -14.25 to -15.75 volts DC at pins 6 and 17.
2. Oscilloscope Measurements:
   a) Observe clock signals at pins 1 and 2. They should be square waves with a frequency of 0.09 to 0.1 MHz.
   b) Observe the signal on pin 28. This signal is the shift clock output and is synchronized to the clock. The VC signal on pin 5 is the power supply voltage for the internal clock. It should measure -10 to -15 volts DC.

FOR 90% CONFIDENCE LEVEL:

In addition to the 75% confidence level tests, use a dual-trace oscilloscope to observe the following:

a) Monitor the clock signal on pin 28 on one trace, while observing the DATA OUT signal on pin 29 on the other. The two signals should change in synch.
b) Monitor the clock signal on pin 28 on one trace, while observing the DATA IN signal on pin 30 on the other.

EXACT REPLACEMENT ESSENTIAL

MM78L (PPS-4/1 FAMILY) (ROCKWELL) 4-BIT MICROCOMPUTER

This device contains the following functions: central processing unit (CPU), instruction decode, two program save registers, 2048 bytes of program memory (ROM), 128 4-bit words of data memory (RAM), program counter (P), data address register (B), ten I/O drivers/receivers, two 4-bit parallel I/O channels, two 4-bit input channels, a serial I/O port, interrupt and control logic, and a self-contained four-phase clock generator circuit.

PIN NAME	DESCRIPTION	TYPE
DI/00-DI/09	Discrete I/O Ports	I/O
PI1-PI4	Channel 1 Input Ports	I
PI5-PI8	Channel 2 Input Ports	I
RI01-RI04	Channel A I/O Ports	I/O
RI05-RI08	Channel X I/O Ports	I/O
INT0, INT1	Interrupt 0, 1	I
XTLIN, XTLOUT	Crystal	I
A, BP	Clock Signal	I/O
CLOCK	Shift Clock	I/O
DATA I, DATA O	Data In, Out	I, O
TEST	Test	I
PO	Power On	I
VC	Clock Power Supply	
V_{DD}	Power Supply	
V_{SS}	Ground	

Pin Configuration

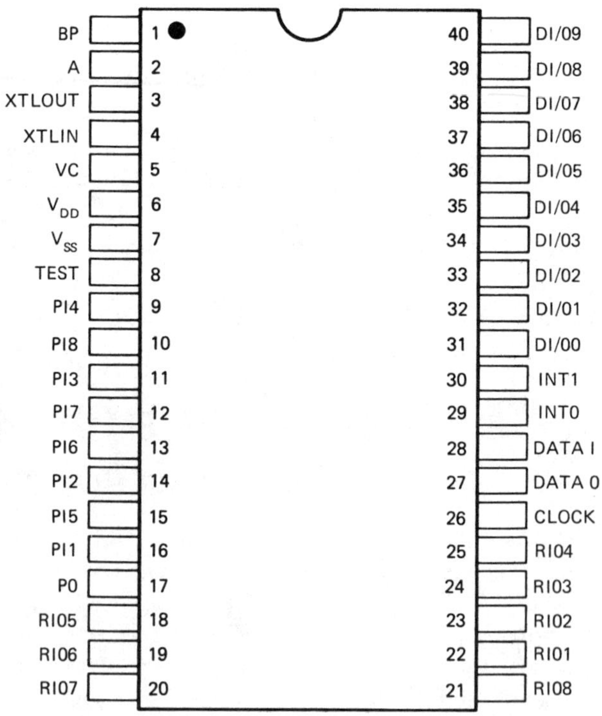

Special Features

- Six working registers.
- Over 60 instructions.
- Power supply operation: -8.5V, -2.5V, +2.0V.
- Low power 15mW nominal @ -8.5V.
- Maximum negative I/O voltage: -11V(Standard); -30V(Vacuum Fluorescent Drive).
- Nominal internal clock frequency 100kHz (±30%) with VC to V_{DD}.
- Low impedance drivers: DI/O less than 100ohm @ 10mA; RIO less than 250ohm @ 6mA.
- Mask programmed pull-down resistors on outputs.
- Mask programmed enhancement FET pull-downs on inputs.

IN-CIRCUIT QUICK-TESTS

FOR 75% CONFIDENCE LEVEL:

1. Volt-ohmmeter Measurements:
   a) Make sure PC board ground has good connection to pin 7.
   b) Measure power supply voltage of -7.0 to -10.0 volts DC at pin 6.
2. Oscilloscope Measurements:
   a) Observe clock signals at pins 1 and 2. They should be square waves with a frequency of 0.09 and 0.1 MHz.
   b) Observe the signal on pin 26. This signal is the shift clock output and is synchronized to the clock.

FOR 90% CONFIDENCE LEVEL:

In addition to the 75% confidence level tests, use a dual-trace oscilloscope to observe the following:

a) Monitor the clock signal on pin 26 on one trace, while observing the DATA OUT signal on pin 27 on the other.
b) Monitor the clock signal on pin 26 on one trace, while observing the DATA IN signal on pin 28 on the other.

EXACT REPLACEMENT ESSENTIAL

MM78LA (PPS-4/1 FAMILY) (ROCKWELL) 4-BIT MICROCOMPUTER

This device is low voltage, very low power member of the PPS-4/1 one chip microcomputer family. It is similar to the MM78L and its instruction set is compatible with the exception of those instructions that have been

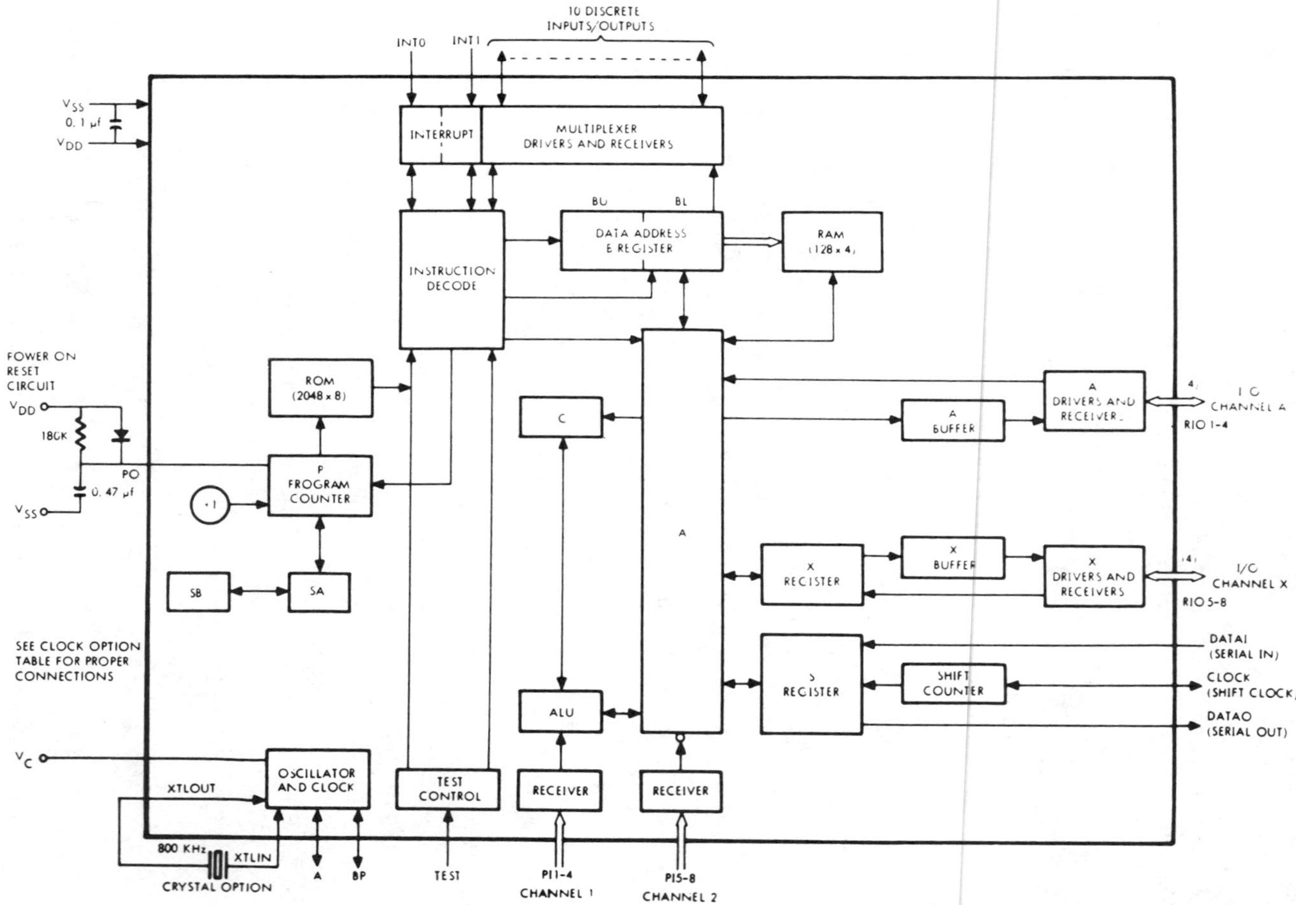

Courtesy Rockwell International.

Block Diagram—78L, 4-Bit μC
Fig. 8-3

changed to meet the needs of the added features. The MM78LA contains the following functions: a CPU, Instruction Decode, two Program Save Registers, 2048 bytes of program memory (ROM), 128 4-bit words of data memory (RAM), program counter (P), data address register (B), I/O drivers/receivers, two 4-bit parallel input channels, a tone generator, two speaker drivers, 32 14-bit words of programmable logic array (PLA) for output pattern generation, 14 parallel output drivers, and a self-contained four-phase clock generator circuit.

PIN NAME	DESCRIPTION	TYPE
DIO0-DIO9	Discrete I/O Ports	I/O
PI1-PI4	Channel One Input Ports	I
PI5-PI8	Channel Two Input Ports	I
RO01-RO14	Output Ports	O
A, BP	Clock	O
SPK R1, SPK R2	Speaker Driver	O
TEST	Test	I
PO	Power On	I
VC	Oscillator Power Supply	
$V_{DD\ SPK}$	Speaker Power Supply	
V_{DD}	Power Supply	
V_{SS}	Ground	

Special Features

- Software compatible with the MM78.
- One interrupt request input line.
- TTL and CMOS compatible.
- Six working registers.
- Over 60 instructions.
- Power supply operation range: -6.5 to -11.0V.
- Low power: 15mW nominal @ -8.5V.
- Built-in tone generator with two piezo-electric speaker drivers.
- Direct LED or vacuum fluorescent drive capability.
- Three clock modes.
- Low impedance drivers: DIO's less than 150ohms @ 60mA (Dynamic); RO's less than 105ohms @ 6mA (Dynamic), w/o swamping resistor.

IN-CIRCUIT QUICK-TESTS

FOR 75% CONFIDENCE LEVEL:

1. Volt-ohmmeter Measurements:
   a) Make sure PC board ground has good connection to pin 6.
   b) Measure power supply voltage of -6.5 to -11.0 volts DC at pins 3 and 32. (If speakers are not used, pin 32 may be unconnected.

PIN CONFIGURATION

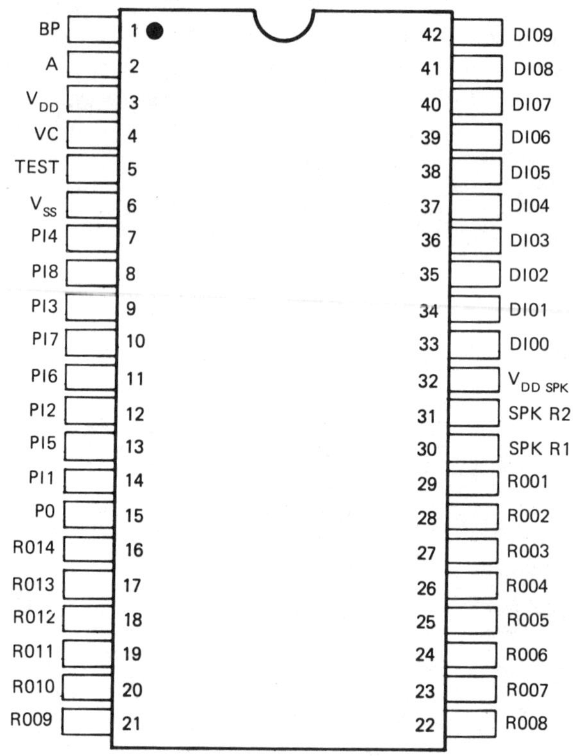

2. Oscilloscope Measurements:
   a) Observe clock signals at pins 1 and 2. They should be square waves with a frequency of 0.05 to 0.1 MHz.
   b) Observe the signal on pins 30 and 31. This signal is the speaker output.

FOR 90% CONFIDENCE LEVEL:

In addition to the 75% confidence level tests, use a dual-trace oscilloscope to observe the following:

a) Monitor the clock signal on pins 1 or 2 on one trace, while observing the DI01 signal on pin 34 on the other. This is one of the "DISCRETE" I/O signals.
b) Monitor the clock signal on pins 1 or 2 on one trace, while observing the R001 signal on pin 29 on the other.

EXACT REPLACEMENT ESSENTIAL

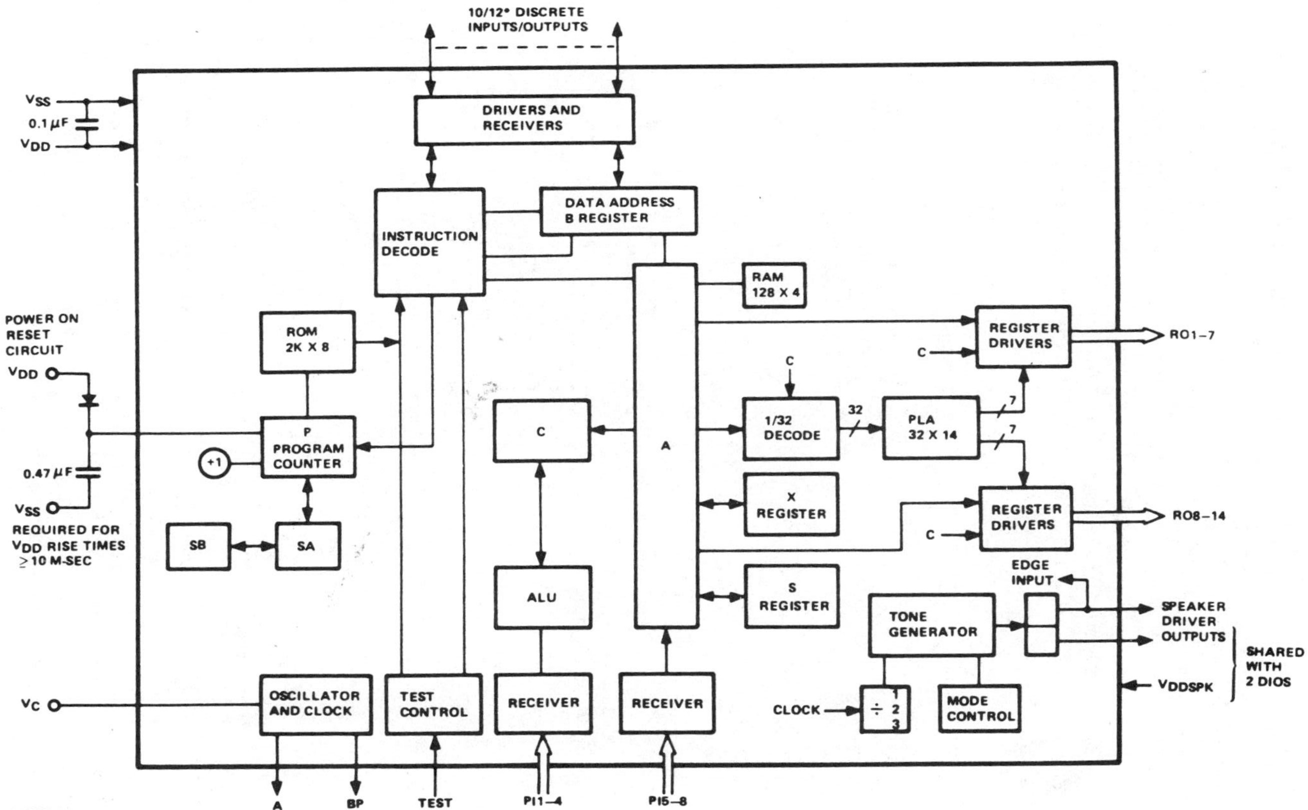

NOTE:
* 12 IF SPEAKER OUTPUTS NOT USED

Courtesy Rockwell International.

Block Diagram—78LA, 4-Bit μC
Fig. 8-4

TMS 1000 FAMILY (TEXAS INSTRUMENTS) 4-BIT MICROCOMPUTER

This family of 4-bit microcomputers offers a variety of devices which use the same block diagram, the same logic functions and the same instruction set, but are available in different memory capacities, power levels, pin configurations and I/O characteristics. These combinations result in a number of different microcomputer ICs and these are presented, together with their pin configurations and IN-SERVICE QUICK-TESTS in the following pages.

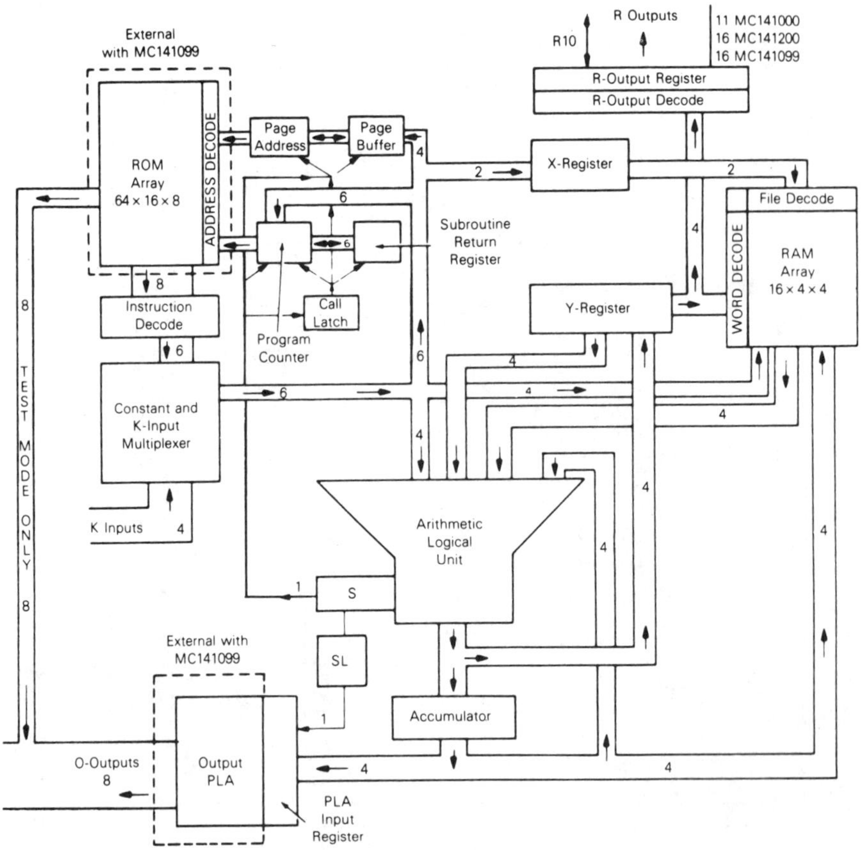

Courtesy Motorola, Inc.

Block Diagram — 1000 Family
Fig. 8-5

TMS 1000NLL, TMS 1100NLL, TMS 1070NLL, TMS 1170NLL[1]

Special Features

- Instruction read only: 1024 × 8 bits (TMS 1000, and TMS 1070); 2048 × 8 bits (TMS 1100, and TMS 1170).
- Data random access memory: 64 × 4 bits (TMS 1000, and TMS 1070), 128 × 4 bits (TMS 1100, and TMS 1170).
- "R" individually addressed output latches: 11.
- "O" parallel latched data outputs: 8 bits.
- Maximum rated voltage (O, R, K): –15V (TMS 1000, and TMS 1100); –30V (TMS 1070, and TMS 1170).
- Working registers: 2–4 bits.
- Programmable instruction decoder.
- On-chip oscillator.
- Power supply/typical dissipation: 9V/36mW (TMS 1000); 9V/45mW (TMS1100, TMS1070, TMS1170).

PIN CONFIGURATION

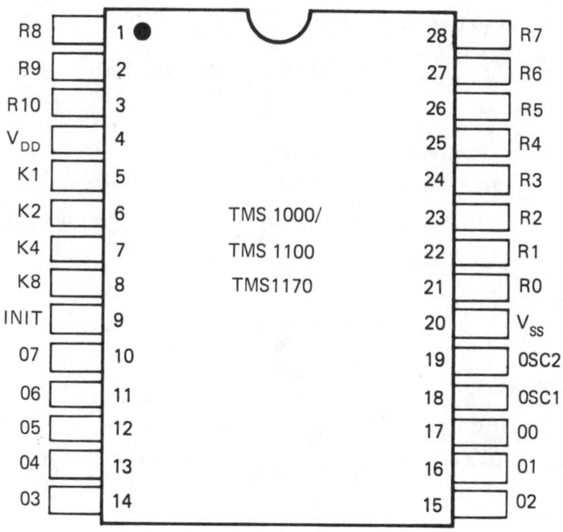

[1]Note: The same microprocessor is manufactured by MOTOROLA—MC141000.

PIN NAME	DESCRIPTION	TYPE
K1, K2, K4, K8	Data Input	I
R0–R10	Control Output	O
OSC1, OSC2	Oscillator one, two	I
INIT	Initialize	I
HLT (TMS1000C)	Low Power Halt	I
V_{DD}	Power Supply	
V_{SS}	Ground	
00–07	Data Output	O

IN-CIRCUIT QUICK-TESTS

For 75% Confidence Level:

1. Volt-ohmmeter Measurements:
   a) Make sure PC board ground has good connection to pin 20.
   b) Measure power supply voltage of –7.5 to –10.0 volts DC at pin 4.
2. Oscilloscope Measurements:
   a) Observe clock signals at pins 18 and 19. They should be square waves with a frequency of 0.1 to 0.35 MHz.
   b) Observe the signal on pin 21. This signal is the control output and is synchronized to the clock.

For 90% Confidence Level:

In addition to the 75% confidence level tests, use a dual-trace oscilloscope to observe the following:

a) Monitor the clock signal on pins 18 or 19 on one trace, while observing the 00 signal on pin 17 on the other. "00" is part of the data output.

EXACT REPLACEMENT ESSENTIAL

IN-CIRCUIT QUICK-TESTS

For 75% Confidence Level:

1. Volt-ohmmeter Measurements:
   a) Make sure PC board ground has good connection to pin 21.
   b) Measure power supply voltage of –7.5 to –10.0 volts DC at pin 4.
2. Oscilloscope Measurements:
   a) Observe clock signals at pins 18 and 19. They should be square waves with a frequency of 0.1 to 0.35 MHz.
   b) Observe the signal on pin 20. This signal is the control output and is synchronized to the clock.

PIN CONFIGURATION

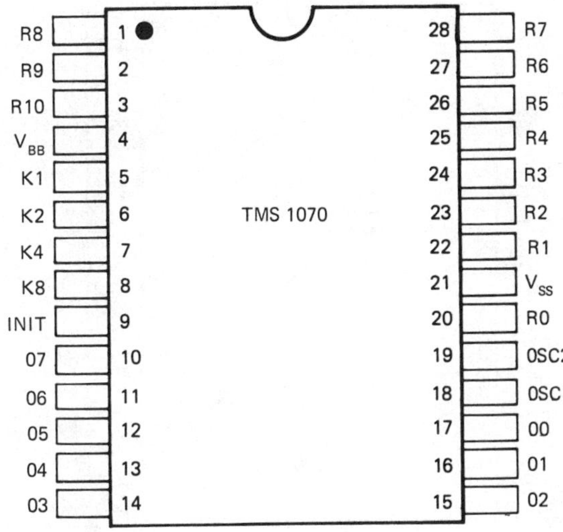

FOR 90% CONFIDENCE LEVEL:

In addition to the 75% confidence level tests, use a dual-trace oscilloscope to observe the following:

a) Monitor the clock signal on pins 18 or 19 on one trace, while observing the 00 signal on pin 17 on the other. "00" is part of the data output.

EXACT REPLACEMENT ESSENTIAL

IN-CIRCUIT QUICK-TESTS

FOR 75% CONFIDENCE LEVEL:

1. Volt-ohmmeter Measurements:
   a) Make sure PC board ground has good connection to pin 5.
   b) Measure power supply voltage of -7.5 to -10.0 volts DC at pin 26.
2. Oscilloscope Measurements:
   a) Observe clock signals at pins 24 and 25. They should be square waves with a frequency of 0.1 to 0.35 MHz.
   b) Observe the signal on pin 23. This signal is the control output and is synchronized to the clock.

FOR 90% CONFIDENCE LEVEL:

In addition to the 75% confidence level tests, use a dual-trace oscilloscope to observe the following:

PIN CONFIGURATION

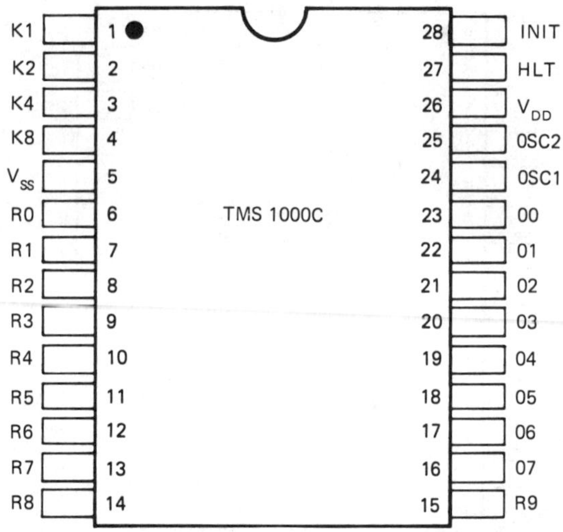

a) Monitor the clock signal on pins 24 or 25 on one trace, while observing the 00 signal on pin 23 on the other. "00" is part of the data output.

EXACT REPLACEMENT ESSENTIAL

TMS 1200NLL, TMS 1300NLL, TMS 1270NLL, TMS 1370NLL[2]

Special Features

- Instruction read only: 1024 × 8 Bits (TMS 1200 and TMS 1270); 2048 × 8 Bits (TMS 1300 and TMS 1370).
- Data random access memory: 64 × 4 Bits (TMS 1200 and TMS 1270); 128 × 4 Bits (TMS 1300 and TMS 1370).
- "R" individually addressed output latches: 13 (TMS 1200 and TMS 1270); 16 (TMS 1300 and TMS 1370).
- "0" parallel latched data outputs: 8 bits (TMS1200, TMS1300, TMS1370); 10 Bits (TMS1270).
- Maximum rated voltage (O,R,K): –15V (TMS 1200, and TMS 1300); 30V (TMS 1270, and TMS 1370).

---

[2]Note: The same microprocessor is manufactured by MOTOROLA—MC141200.

- Working registers: 2–4 bits.
- Programmable instruction decoder.
- On-chip oscillator.
- Power supply/typical dissipation: 9V/36mW (TMS 1200); 9V/45mW (TMS1300, TMS1270, TMS1370).

PIN NAME	DESCRIPTION	TYPE
K1, K2, K4, K8	Data Input	I
L1, L2, L4, L8 (TMS1200C)	Data Input	I
00–07 (09 for TMS1270)	Data Output	O
R0–R10 R0–R12, R13–R15 TMS1200; R0–R12, TMS1270; R0–R15, TMS1300.	Control Output	O
OSC1, OSC2	Oscillator one, two	I
INIT	Initialize	I
HLT (TMS1200C)	Low Power Halt	I
K/L (TMS1200C)	K/L Input Select	I
MODE (TMS1200C)	Latched Mode Select	I
V_{DD}	Power Supply	
V_{SS}	Ground	

PIN CONFIGURATION

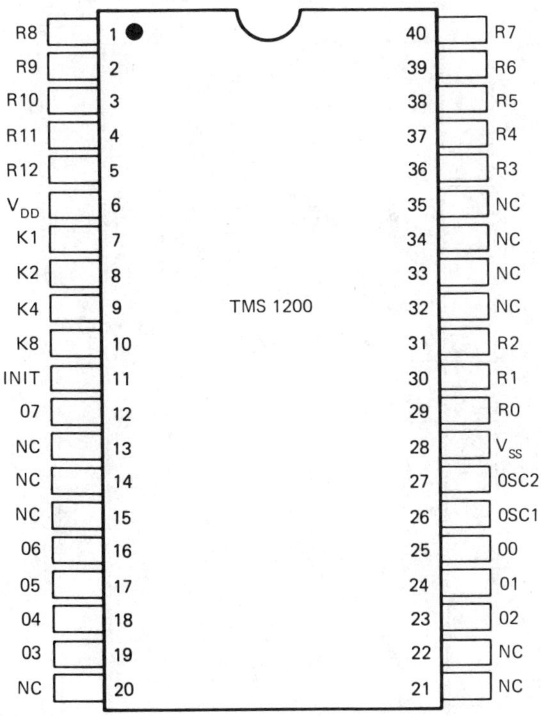

IN-CIRCUIT QUICK-TESTS

FOR 75% CONFIDENCE LEVEL:

1. Volt-ohmmeter Measurements:
   a) Make sure PC board ground has good connection to pin 28.
   b) Measure power supply voltage of -7.5 to -10.0 volts DC at pin 6.
2. Oscilloscope Measurements:
   a) Observe clock signals at pins 26 and 27. They should be square waves with a frequency of 0.1 to 0.35 MHz.
   b) Observe the signal on pin 29. This signal is the control output and is synchronized to the clock.

FOR 90% CONFIDENCE LEVEL:

In addition to the 75% confidence level tests, use a dual-trace oscilloscope to observe the following:

a) Monitor the clock signal on pins 26 or 27 on one trace, while observing the 00 signal on pin 25 on the other. "00" is the data output.

EXACT REPLACEMENT ESSENTIAL

PIN CONFIGURATION

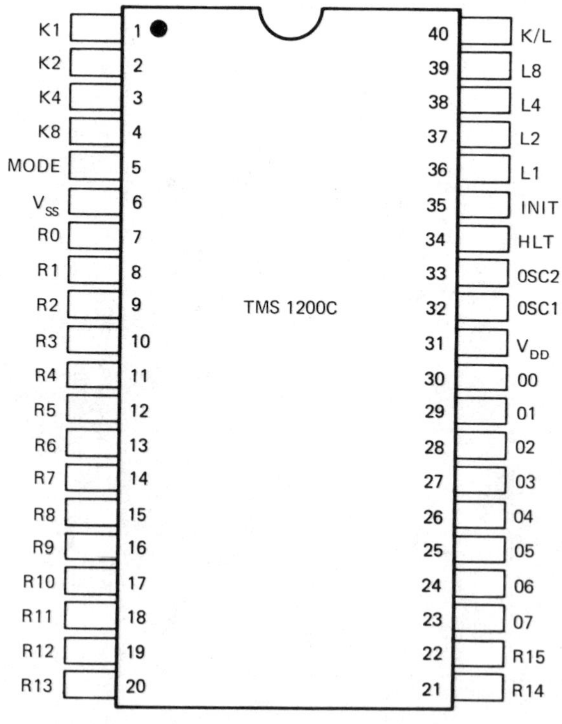

IN-CIRCUIT QUICK-TESTS

FOR 75% CONFIDENCE LEVEL:

1. Volt-ohmmeter Measurements:
   a) Make sure PC board ground has good connection to pin 6.
   b) Measure power supply voltage of -7.5 to -10.0 volts DC at pin 31.
2. Oscilloscope Measurements:
   a) Observe clock signals at pins 32 and 33. They should be square waves with a frequency of 0.1 to 0.35 MHz.
   b) Observe the signal on pin 7. This signal is the control output and is synchronized to the clock.

FOR 90% CONFIDENCE LEVEL:

In addition to the 75% confidence level tests, use a dual-trace oscilloscope to observe the following:

a) Monitor the clock signal on pins 32 or 33 on one trace, while observing the 00 signal on pin 30 on the other. "00" is the data output.

EXACT REPLACEMENT ESSENTIAL

PIN CONFIGURATION

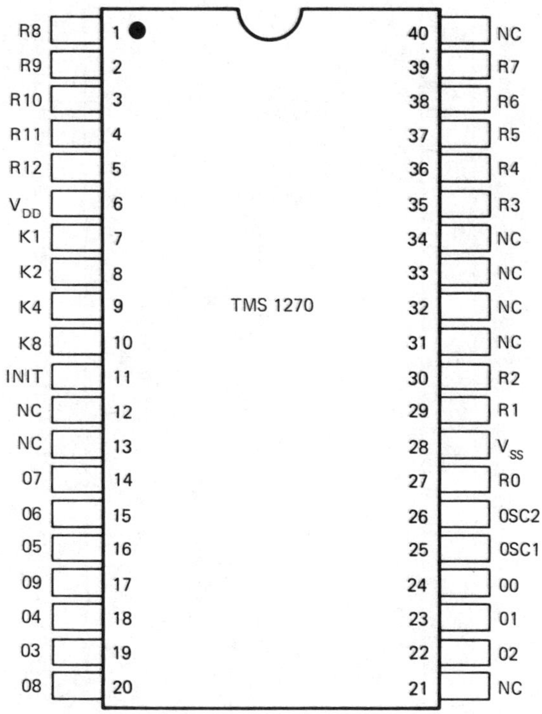

IN-CIRCUIT QUICK-TESTS

For 75% Confidence Level:

1. Volt-ohmmeter Measurements:
   a) Make sure PC board ground has good connection to pin 28.
   b) Measure power supply voltage of –7.5 to –10.0 volts DC at pin 6.
2. Oscilloscope Measurements:
   a) Observe clock signals at pins 25 and 26. They should be square waves with a frequency of 0.1 to 0.35 MHz.
   b) Observe the signal on pin 27. This signal is the control output and is synchronized to the clock.

For 90% Confidence Level:

In addition to the 75% confidence level tests, use a dual-trace oscilloscope to observe the following:

a) Monitor the clock signal on pins 25 or 26 on one trace, while observing the 00 signal on pin 24 on the other. "00" is the data output.

EXACT REPLACEMENT ESSENTIAL

Pin Configuration

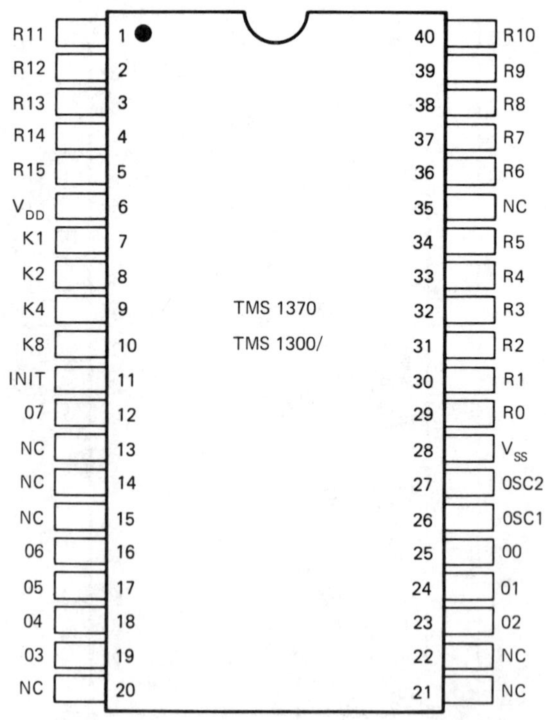

IN-CIRCUIT QUICK-TESTS

FOR 75% CONFIDENCE LEVEL:

1. Volt-ohmmeter Measurements:
   a) Make sure PC board ground has good connection to pin 28.
   b) Measure power supply voltage of –7.5 to –10.0 volts DC at pin 6.
2. Oscilloscope Measurements:
   a) Observe clock signals at pins 26 and 27. They should be square waves with a frequency of 0.1 to 0.35 MHz.
   b) Observe the signal on pin 29. This signal is the control output and is synchronized to the clock.

FOR 90% CONFIDENCE LEVEL:

In addition to the 75% confidence level tests, use a dual-trace oscilloscope to observe the following:

a) Monitor the clock signal on pins 26 or 27 on one trace, while observing the 00 signal on pin 25, on the other. "00" is the data output.

EXACT REPLACEMENT ESSENTIAL

SERIES 40 (OKI SEMICONDUCTOR) 4-BIT MICROCOMPUTERS

This is a family of five CMOS microcomputers and support devices. Each microcomputer in the series contains CPU, ROM, RAM, I/O, plus a timer/counter. Their features are:

- Low power consumption: battery powered operation, and battery back-up operation.
- Power supply voltage range 3–6VDC.
- Accurate, crystal-controlled oscillator: 100% static operation. Built-in timer/counter.
- 8-bit bi-directional bus: byte input/output; Code conversion; Easily interfaced.
- High noise immunity.
- TTL compatible. The members of the series are: MSM5840/MSM5840XX, MSM5845XX,
- MSM5842XX, MSM58421-XX, MSM58423-XX.

4-Bit μC

MSM 5840/MSM 5840RS

- Typical/max. supply current @ 5V: .8/3mA.
- Clock rate: 4MHz.
- Basic instruction execution time: 8μsec. @ 4MHz.

- Instruction set: 96 with 93 single byte.
- ROM size: MSM5840: 4096 × 8 external. MSM5840RS: 2048 × 8 internal, 2048 × 8 external.
- RAM size: 128 × 4.
- SAVE/Working Registers: 4/4.
- Input port: 1 × 4 and 1 × 2 latched.
- Output port: 4 × 4.
- I/O port: 2 × 4.
- Four levels of stack.
- One (8 Bit) R/W timer/counter.
- Two levels interrupt.

PIN NAME	DESCRIPTION	TYPE
A0–A3	Port A	I/O
B0–B3	Port B	I/O
D0–D3	Port D	O
E0–E3	Port E	O
F0–F3	Port F	O
G0–G3	Port G	O
$\overline{H0}$, $\overline{H1}$	Port H	I
K0–K3	Port K	I
OSC0, $\overline{OSC1}$	Crystal	I
$\overline{RESET}$	Reset	I
$\overline{MODE}$	Operation Mode	I
INT	Interrupt	I
$\overline{CIN}$	Count In	I
$\overline{RD}$	Read	O
$\overline{WR}$	Write	O
$\overline{IF}$	Interface	O
SYNC	Synchronize	O
V_{DD}	Power Supply	
GND	Ground	

IN-CIRCUIT QUICK-TESTS

For 75% Confidence Level:

1. Volt-ohmmeter Measurements:
   a) Make sure PC board ground has good connection to pin 21.
   b) Measure power supply voltage of 4.5 to 5.5 volts DC at pin 42.
2. Oscilloscope Measurements:
   a) Observe clock signals at pins 9 and 10. They should be square waves with a frequency of 0.1 to 4.0 MHz.
   b) Observe the signal on pin 11. This signal is the WRITE output and is synchronized to the clock.

Pin Configuration

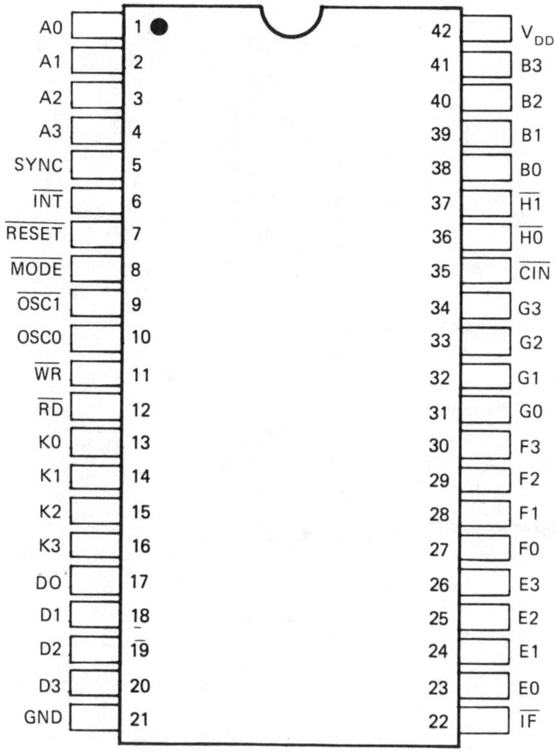

For 90% Confidence Level:

In addition to the 75% confidence level tests, use a dual-trace oscilloscope to observe the following:

a) Monitor the clock signal on pins 9 or 10 on one trace, while observing the RD signal on pin 12 on the other. "RD" occurs when part A or B is read.

b) Monitor the clock signal on pins 9 or 12 on one trace, while observing the SYNC signal on pin 5 on the other.

EXACT REPLACEMENT ESSENTIAL

MSM 5842RS

- Typical/Max. supply current @ 5V: 1.5/4mA.
- Clock rate: 4MHz maximum.
- Basic instruction time: 8μsec. @ 4MHz.

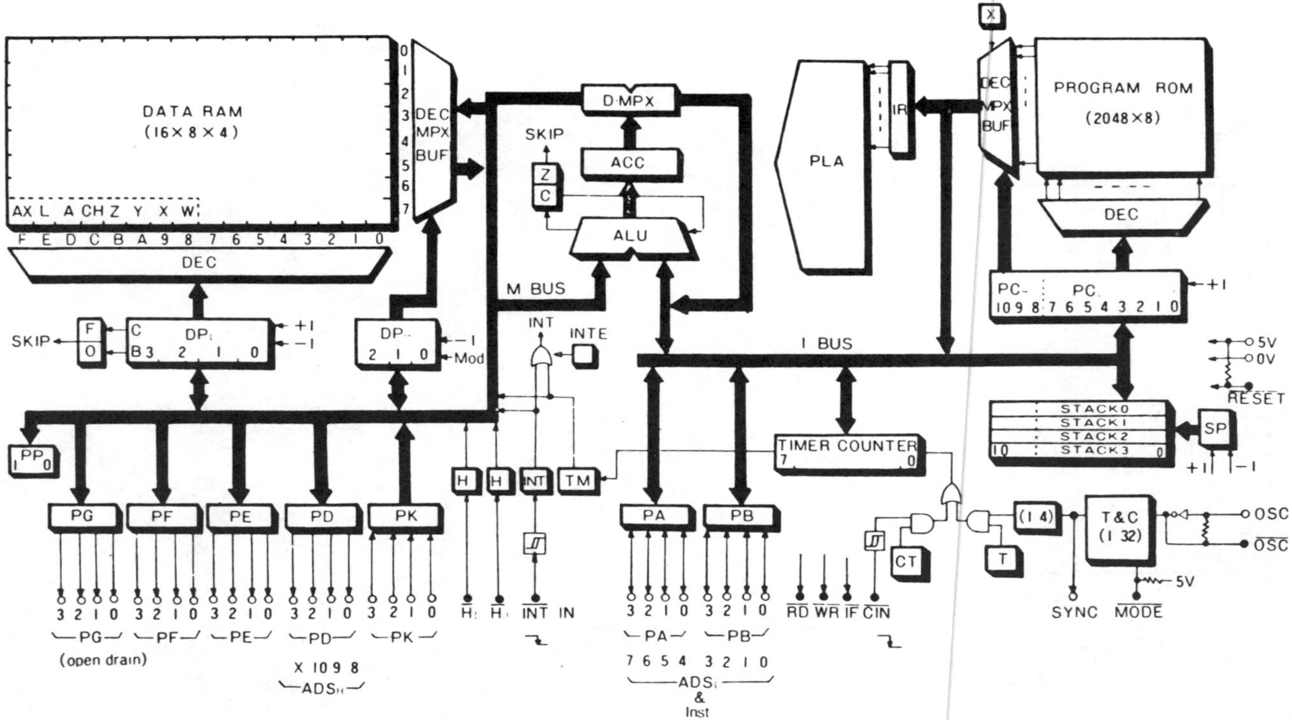

Courtesy of OKI Semiconductor, Inc.

Block Diagram—5840RS, 4-Bit μC
Fig. 8-6

- Instruction set: 52 instructions with 50 single byte.
- ROM size: 768 × 8.
- RAM size: 32 × 4.
- SAVE/Working Registers 0/1.
- Input port: 1 × 4 and 1 latched.
- Output port: 2 × 4.
- I/O port: 2 × 4.
- One level of stack.
- One (8-bit) timer/counter.

PIN NAME	DESCRIPTION	TYPE
A0–A3	Port A	I/O
B0–B3	Port B	I/O
D0–D3	Port D	O
E0–E3	Port E	O
$\overline{\text{HO}}$	Port H	I
K0–K3	Port K	I
OSC0, $\overline{\text{OSC1}}$	Crystal	I
$\overline{\text{RESET}}$	Reset	I
$\overline{\text{CIN}}$	Count In	I
SYNC	Synchronize	O
V_{DD}	Power Supply	
GND	Ground	

PIN CONFIGURATION

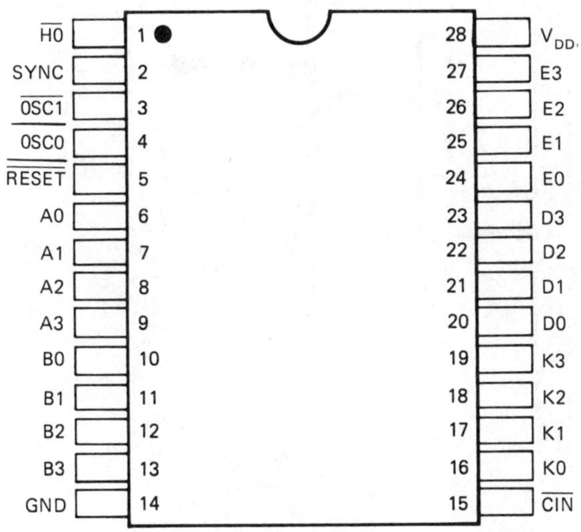

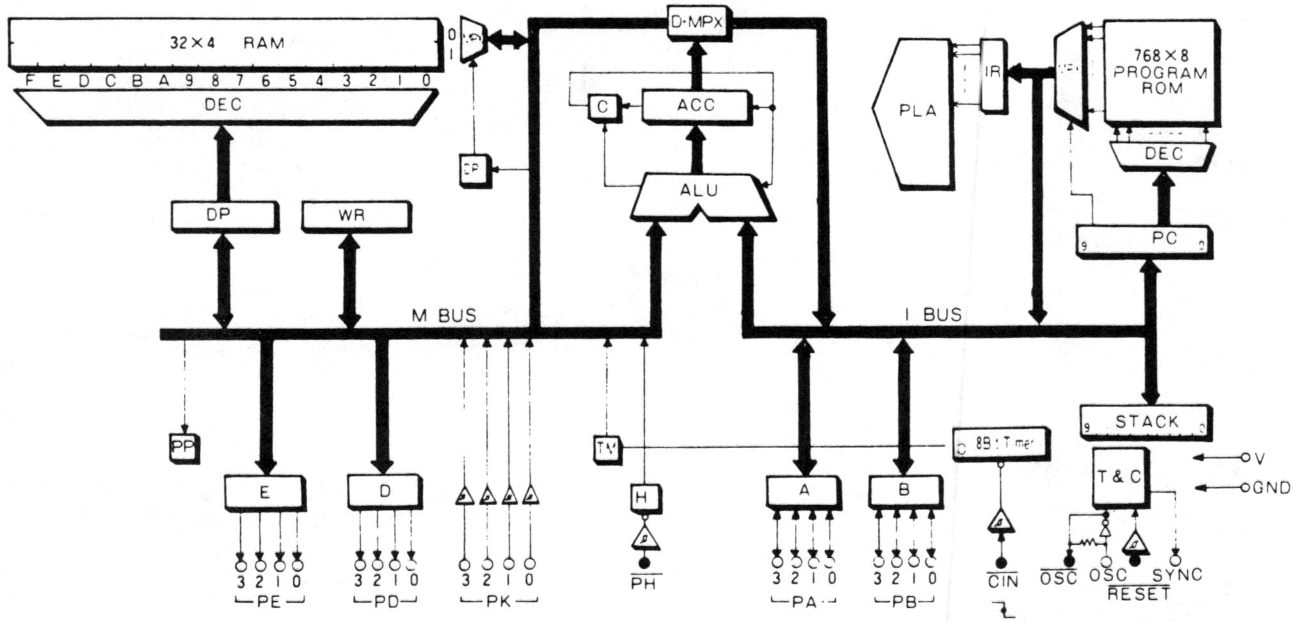

Courtesy of OKI Semiconductor, Inc.

Block Diagram—5842RS, 4-bit μC
Fig. 8-7

IN-CIRCUIT QUICK-TESTS

For 75% Confidence Level:

1. Volt-ohmmeter Measurements:
   a) Make sure PC board ground has good connection to pin 14.
   b) Measure power supply voltage of 4.5 to 5.5 volts DC at pin 28.
2. Oscilloscope Measurements:
   a) Observe clock signals at pins 3 and 4. They should be square waves with a frequency of 0.1 to 4.0 MHz.
   b) Observe the signal on pin 2. This signal is the SYNC output and is synchronized to the clock. SYNC occurs at the start of each machine cycle.

For 90% Confidence Level:

In addition to the 75% confidence level tests, use a dual-trace oscilloscope to observe the following:

a) Monitor the clock signal on pins 3 or 4 on one trace, while observing the DO signal on pin 21 on the other. DO is the data output for port D.
b) Monitor the clock signal on pins 3 or 4 on one trace, while observing the AO signal on pin 6 on the other.

EXACT REPLACEMENT ESSENTIAL

MSM 5845RS

- Typical/max. supply current @ 5V: 2/3mA.
- Clock rate: 4MHz maximum.
- Basic instruction execution time: 8μsec. @ 4MHz.
- Instruction Set: 49 instructions with 46 single byte.
- ROM size: 1280 × 8.
- RAM size: 64 × 4.
- SAVE/Working Registers: 3/1.
- Input port: 1 × 4 and 1 × 2 latched.
- Output port: 4 × 4.
- I/O port: 2 × 4.
- Two levels of stack.
- One (8-bit) timer/counter.
- One level of interrupt.

PIN NAME	DESCRIPTION	TYPE
PA0-PA3	Port A	I/O
PB0-PB3	Port B	I/O
PD0-PD3	Port D	O
PE0-PE3	Port E	O

PIN NAME	DESCRIPTION	TYPE
PF0–PF3	Port F	O
PG0–PG3	Port G	O
$\overline{\text{PH0}}$–$\overline{\text{PH1}}$	Port H	I
PK0–PK3	Port K	I
OSC0, $\overline{\text{OSC1}}$, OSC2	Crystal	I
$\overline{\text{RESET}}$	Reset	I
$\overline{\text{HOLD}}$	Hold	I
$\overline{\text{INT}}$	Interrupt In	I
$\overline{\text{C IN}}$	Count In	I
$\overline{\text{C OUT}}$	Count Out	O
SYNC	Synchronize	O
V_{DD}	Power supply	
GND	Ground	

Pin Configuration

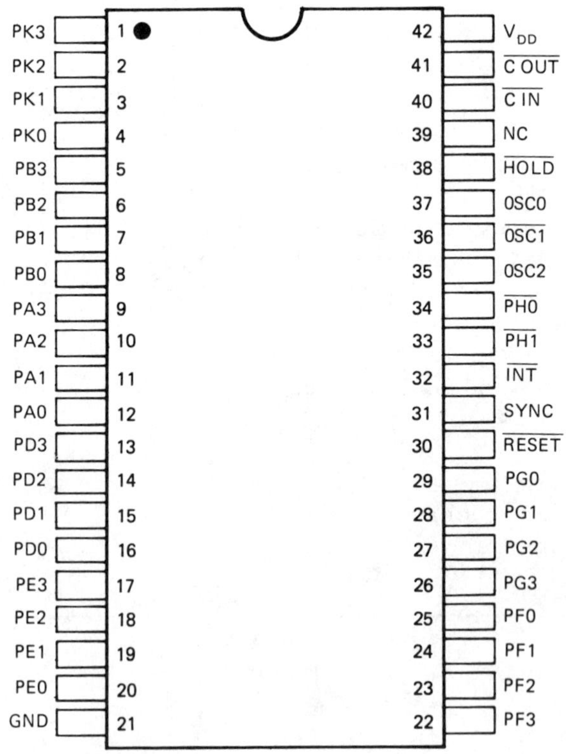

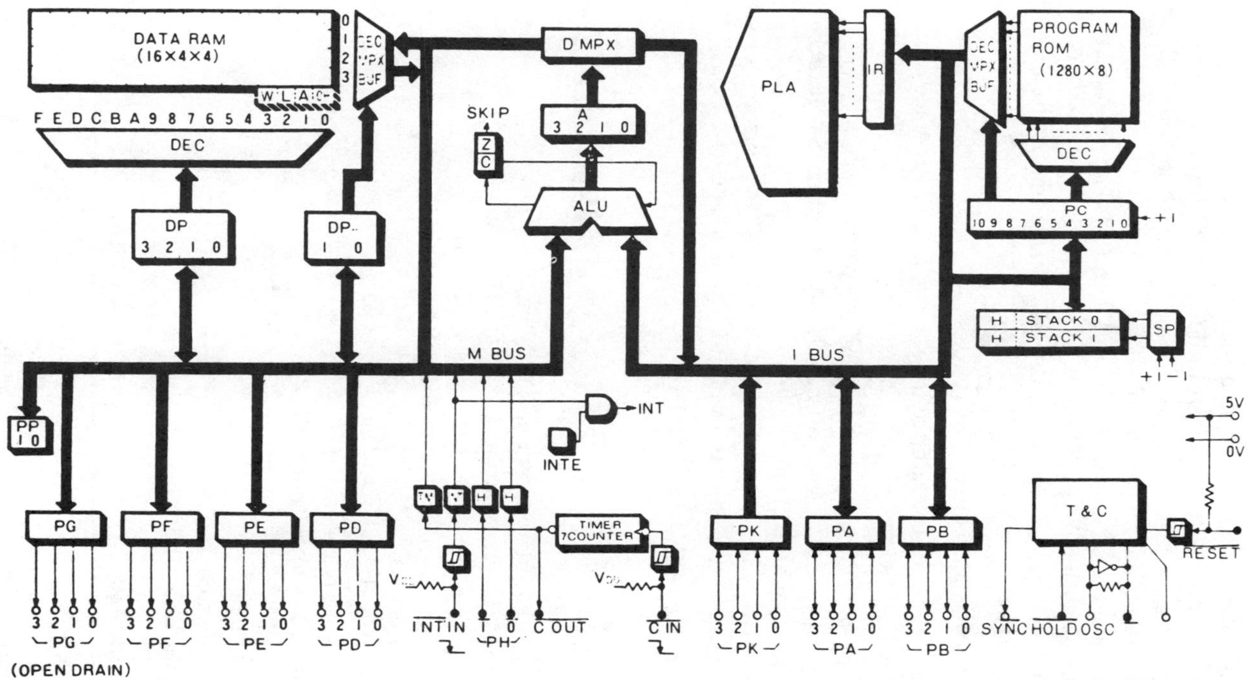

Courtesy of OKI Semiconductor, Inc.

Block Diagram—5845RS, 4-Bit μC
Fig. 8-8

IN-CIRCUIT QUICK-TESTS

FOR 75% CONFIDENCE LEVEL:

1. Volt-ohmmeter Measurements:
   a) Make sure PC board ground has good connection to pin 21.
   b) Measure power supply voltage of 4.5 to 5.5 volts DC at pin 42.
2. Oscilloscope Measurements:
   a) Observe clock signals at pins 9 and 37. They should be square waves with a frequency of 0.1 to 4.0 MHz.
   b) Observe the signal on pin 35. This signal is the OSC output and is synchronized to the clock.

FOR 90% CONFIDENCE LEVEL:

In addition to the 75% confidence level tests, use a dual-trace oscilloscope to observe the following:

a) Monitor the clock signal on pins 9 and 37 on one trace, while observing the SYNC signal on pin 31 on the other. SYNC occurs at start of each machine cycle.
b) Monitor the clock signal on pins 9 or 37 on one trace, while observing the COUT, signal on pin 41 on the other.

EXACT REPLACEMENT ESSENTIAL

MSM 58421 GS

- Typical/max. supply current @ 5V: 2/5mA.
- Clock rate: 4MHz. maximum.
- Basic instruction execution time: 8μsec. @ 4MHz.
- Instruction set: 52 instructions with 50 single byte.
- ROM size: 1536 × 8.
- RAM size: 40 × 4.
- SAVE/working registers 0/1.
- Input port: 1 × 4 and 1 latched.
- Output port: 5 × 7 (segment) and 1 × 5 (discrete).
- I/O port: 2 × 4.
- One level of stack.
- One (12 Bit) timer/counter.

PIN NAME	DESCRIPTION	TYPE
A0-A3	Port A	I/O
B0-B3	Port B	I/O
PLCD1a-PLCD1g	Port LCD 1	O
PLCD2a-PLCD2g	Port LCD 2	O

PIN NAME	DESCRIPTION	TYPE
PLCD3a-PLCD3g	Port LCD 3	O
PLCD4a-PLCD4g	Port LCD 4	O
PLCD5a-PLCD5g	Port LCD 5	O
PLCD61-PLCD65	Port LCD 6	O
COMMON	Common	O
$\overline{HO}$	Port H	I
K0-K3	Port K	I
OSC0.$\overline{OSC1}$	Crystal	I
SYNC	Synchronize	O
$\overline{RESET}$	Reset	I
V_{DD}	Power Supply	
GND	Ground	

Pin Configuration

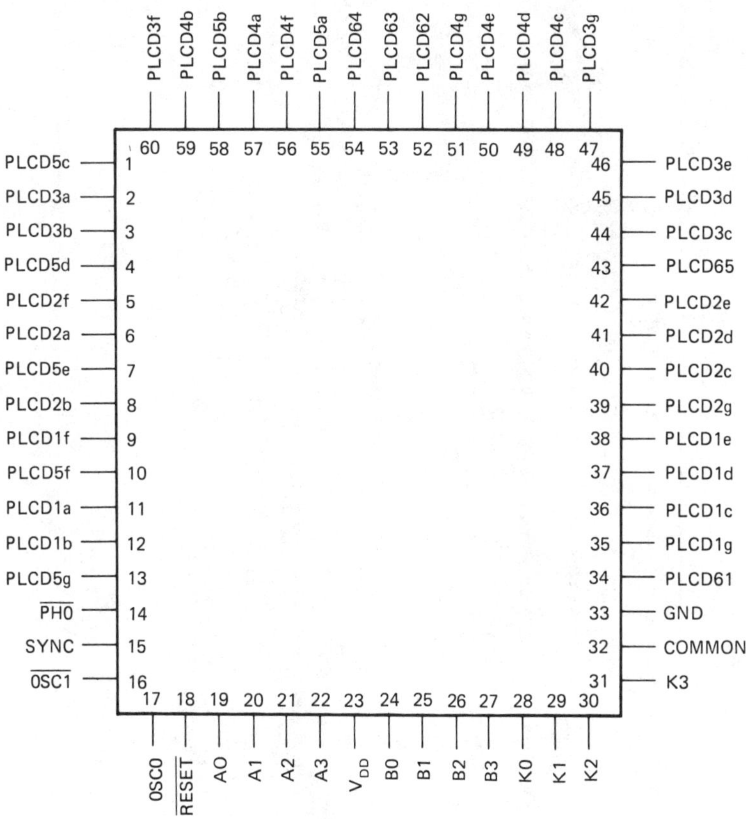

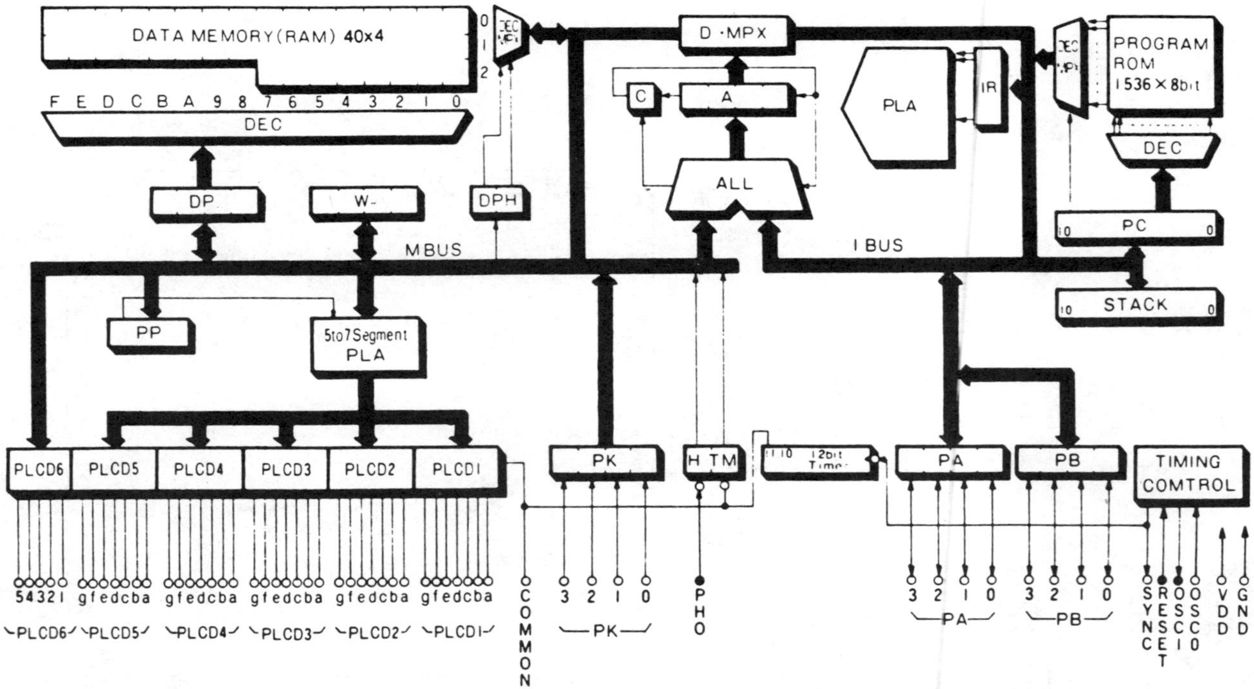

Courtesy of OKI Semiconductor, Inc.

Block Diagram—58421GS, 4-Bit μC
Fig. 8-9

IN-CIRCUIT QUICK-TESTS

For 75% Confidence Level:

1. Volt-ohmmeter Measurements:
   a) Make sure PC board ground has good connection to pin 33.
   b) Measure power supply voltage of 4.5 to 5.5 volts DC at pin 23.
2. Oscilloscope Measurements:
   a) Observe clock signals at pin 16 and 17. They should be square waves with a frequency of 0.1 to 4.0 MHz.
   b) Observe the signal on pin 15. This signal is the SYNC output and is synchronized to the clock. SYNC occurs at the start of each machine cycle.

For 90% Confidence Level:

In addition to the 75% confidence level tests, use a dual-trace oscilloscope to observe the following:

a) Monitor the clock signal on pins 16 or 17 on one trace, while observing the PLCD16 signal on pin 12 on the other. The PLCD16 is one of the LCD drive signals.
b) Monitor the clock signal on pins 16 or 17 on one trace, while observing the PLCD3a signal on pin 2 on the other. The PLCD3a is one of the LCD drive signals.

EXACT REPLACEMENT ESSENTIAL

MSM 58423 RS

- Typical/max. supply current @ 5V: 1mA (typical).
- Clock Rate: 2MHz maximum.
- Basic instruction execution time: 8μs @ 2MHz.
- Instruction set: 50 instructions with 48 single byte.
- ROM size: 1280 × 8.
- RAM size: 32 × 4.
- SAVE/Working Registers 0/1.
- Input port: 1 × 4 and 1 latched.
- Output port: 12 × 14 multiplexed VF high voltage outputs.
- I/O port: 1 × 4.
- Two levels of stack.
- One (8-bit) timer/counter.
- One level interrupt.

PIN NAME	DESCRIPTION	TYPE
A0–A3	Port A	I/O
B0–B3	Port B	O
D0–D3	Port D	O

4-Bit μC

PIN NAME	DESCRIPTION	TYPE
E0-E3	Port E	O
F0-F3	Port F	O
G0-G3	Port G	O
$\overline{\text{H0}}$	Port H	I
K0-K3	Port K	I
L0-L3	Port L	O
M0-M1	Port M	O
OSC0, $\overline{\text{OSC1}}$	Crystal	I
$\overline{\text{RESET}}$	Reset	I
SYNC	Synchronize	O
V_{DD}	Positive Power Supply	
V_{DP}	Negative Power Supply	
V_{SS}	Ground	

The ports: B, D, E, F, G, L, and M are vacuum fluorescent outputs (–35V max.).

PIN CONFIGURATION

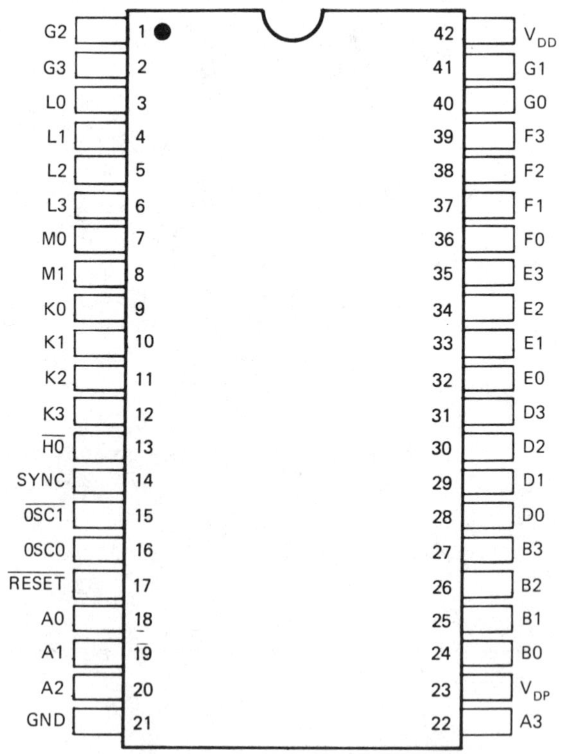

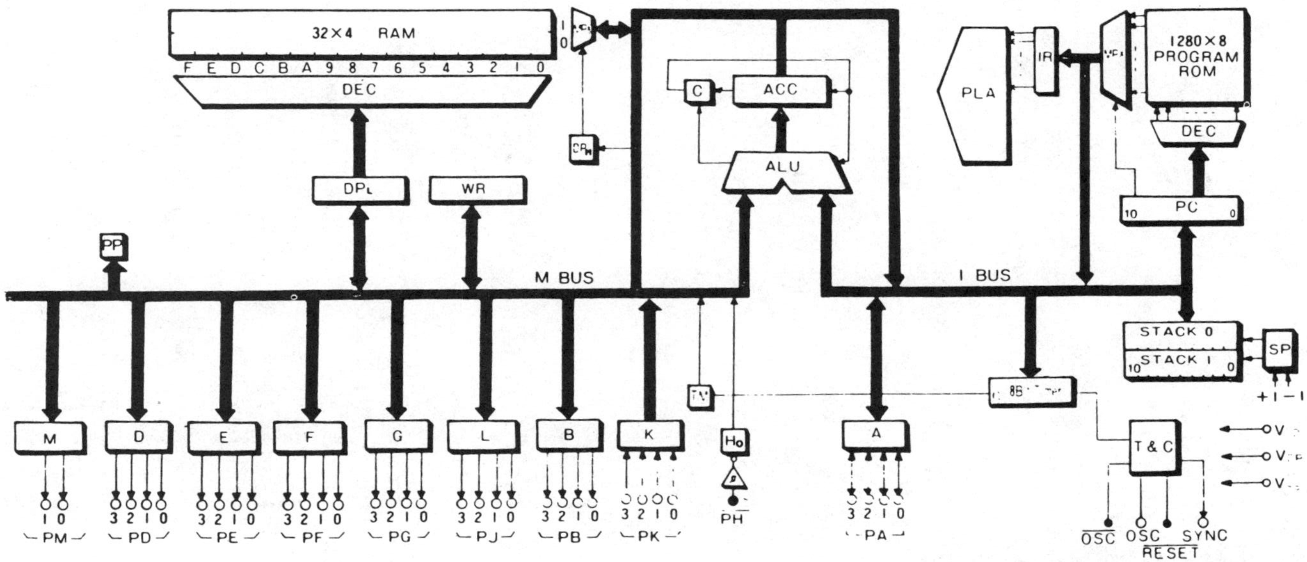

Courtesy of OKI Semiconductor, Inc.

Block Diagram—58423RS, 4-Bit μC
Fig. 8-10

IN-CIRCUIT QUICK-TESTS

FOR 75% CONFIDENCE LEVEL:

1. Volt-ohmmeter Measurements:
   a) Make sure PC board ground has good connection to pin 21.
   b) Measure power supply voltage of 4.5 to 5.5 volts DC at pin 42.
2. Oscilloscope Measurements:
   a) Observe clock signals at pins 15 and 16. They should be square waves with a frequency of 0.1 to 2.0 MHz.
   b) Observe the signal on pin 14. This signal is the SYNC output and is synchronized to the clock. SYNC occurs at the start of each machine cycle.

FOR 90% CONFIDENCE LEVEL:

In addition to the 75% confidence level tests, use a dual-trace oscilloscope to observe the following:

a) Monitor the clock signal on pins 15 or 16 on one trace, while observing the AO signal on pin 18 on the other. AO is one of the I/O terminals of Port A.
b) Monitor the clock signal on pins 15 or 16 on one trace, while observing the BO signal on pin 24 on the other. BO is one of the vacuum fluorescent display outputs.

EXACT REPLACEMENT ESSENTIAL

μCOM-43 (NEC MICROCOMPUTER INC.) 4-BIT MICROCOMPUTER

These devices are members of the μCOM-4 microcomputer family. They are distinguished from other μCOM-4 products by their larger ROM and RAM, their 35 line I/O capability, and the 22 additional instructions of the instruction set. The members of the μCOM-43 are: μPD 546, μPD 553, μPD 557L, and μPD 650. All of them provide all the hardware features of the μCOM-43 family, and execute all 80 instructions of the μCOM-43 instruction set.

The μPD546 is the original μCOM-43 4-bit microcomputer. It is manufactured using a low power consumption PMOS process.

The μPD553 is a μCOM-43 with high voltage outputs that can be pulled to −35V for direct interfacing to vacuum fluorescent display. It is manufactured using a low power consumption PMOS process.

The μPD557L is a μCOM-43 with high voltage outputs, and low power consumption. It is manufactured using a low power consumption PMOS process.

The μPD650 is a μCOM-43 manufactured with a low power consumption CMOS process.

PIN NAME	DESCRIPTION	TYPE
PA_0-PA_3	Port A	I
PB_0-PB_3	Port B	I
PC_0-PC_3	Port C	I/O
PD_0-PD_3	Port D	I/O
PE_0-PE_3	Port E	O
PF_0-PF_3	Port F	O
PG_0-PG_3	Port G	O
PH_0-PH_3	Port H	O
PI_0-PI_2	Port I	O
$\overline{INT}$	Interrupt	I
CL0-CL1	External Clock	I
RESET	Reset	I
V_{GG}	Power Supply Negative	
V_{SS}	Power Supply Positive	
TEST	Factory Test Pin (Connect to V_{SS})	
V_{CC} (μPD650)	Power Supply (Positive)	
V_{SS} (μPD650)	Ground	

Special Features

- 2000 × 8 ROM.
- 96 × 4 RAM: six 4-bit Working Registers; one 4-bit Flag Register.
- Typical instruction cycle time: 10μsec.
- 80 instructions—Table Look Up capability with CZP and JPA instructions. Single bit manipulation of RAM or I/O ports. Ten transfer and exchange instructions for working registers. Four flag instructions.
- 3-Level subroutine stack.
- Extensive I/O capability: two 4-bit input ports (μPD557L has one); two 4-bit I/O ports; four 4-bit output ports (μPD557L has two); one 3-bit output port (μPD557L has one 1-bit; output port instead).
- Programmable 8-bit timer.
- Hardware interrupt.
- Built-in clock signal generation circuitry.
- Built-in reset circuitry.

4-Bit μC

IN-CIRCUIT QUICK-TESTS

For 75% Confidence Level:

1. Volt-ohmmeter Measurements:
   a) Make sure PC board ground has good connection to pins 20 and 21 (For 650 the ground is pin 41).

PIN CONFIGURATION

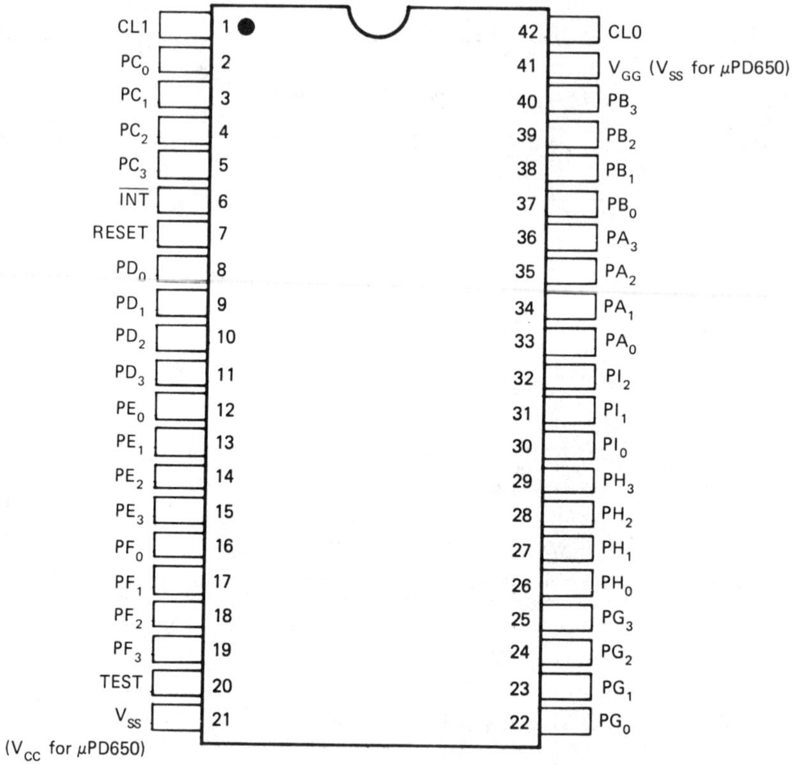

b) Measure power supply voltage of −9.0 to −11.0 volts DC at pin 41 (For 650 the voltage is 4.5 to 5.5 volts DC on pin 21).

2. Oscilloscope Measurements:
a) Observe clock signals at pins 1 and 42. They should be square waves with a frequency of 0.1 to 0.18 MHz.
b) Observe the signal on pin 30. This signal is one Port I output line and is synchronized to the clock.

FOR 90% CONFIDENCE LEVEL:

In addition to the 75% confidence level tests, use a dual-trace oscilloscope to observe the following:

a) Monitor the clock signal on pins 1 or 42 on one trace, while observing the PHO signal on pin 26 on the other.
b) Monitor the clock signal on pins 1 or 42 on one trace, while observing the PGO signal on pin 22 on the other.

EXACT REPLACEMENT ESSENTIAL

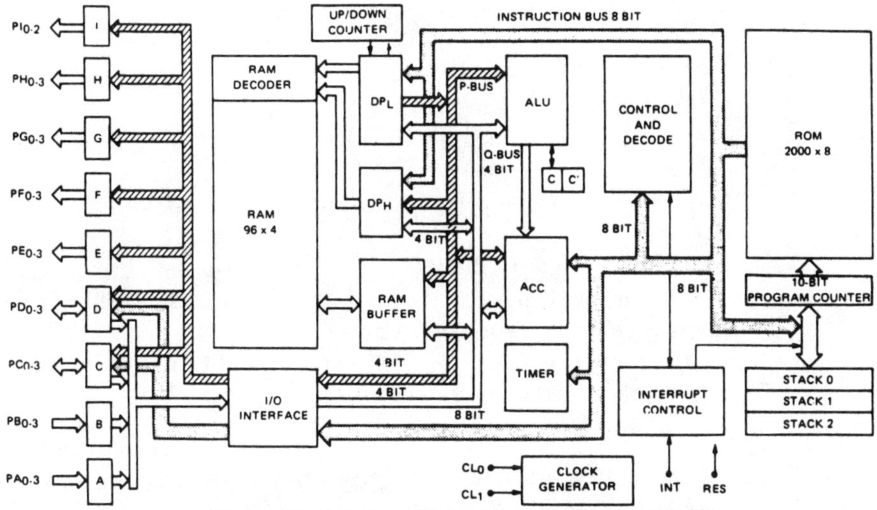

Note: Block diagram above applies to μPD546, μPD553, and μPD650 4-bit microcomputers. The μPD557L block diagram is similar to the above, except that PB_{0-3}, PG_{1-3}, PH_{0-3}, and PI_{0-2} have been eliminated to accommodate the μPD557L's 28-pin package.

Courtesy NEC Electronics, U.S.A., Inc., Microcomputer Division.

Block Diagram—43 Family, 4-Bit μC

Fig. 8-11

Pin Configuration

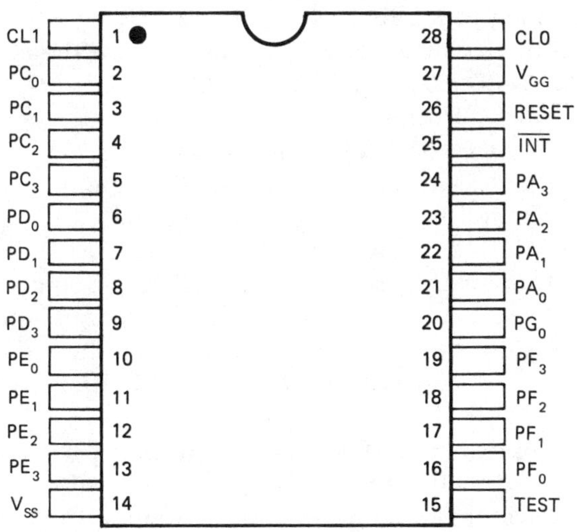

IN-CIRCUIT QUICK-TESTS

FOR 75% CONFIDENCE LEVEL:

1. Volt-ohmmeter Measurements:
   a) Make sure PC board ground has good connection to pins 14 and 15.
   b) Measure power supply voltage of −7.2 to −8.8 volts DC at pin 27.
2. Oscilloscope Measurements:
   a) Observe clock signals at pins 1 and 28. They should be square waves with a frequency of 0.1 and 0.18 MHz.
   b) Observe the signal on pin 20. This signal is one of the Port G outputs and is synchronized to the clock.

FOR 90% CONFIDENCE LEVEL:

In addition to the 75% confidence level tests, use a dual-trace oscilloscope to observe the following:

a) Monitor the clock signal on pins 1 or 28 on one trace, while observing the PEO signal on pin 10 on the other.
b) Monitor the clock signal on pins 1 or 28 on one trace, while observing the PFO signal on pin 16 on the other.

EXACT REPLACEMENT ESSENTIAL

μCOM-44 (NEC MICROCOMPUTER INC.) 4-BIT MICROCOMPUTER

These devices are members of the μCOM-4 microcomputer family. They are distinguished from other μCOM-4 products by their ROM and RAM, and their 35 line I/O capability. The members of the μCOM-44 are: μPD 547, μPD 547L, μPD 552, μPD 651C, and μPD 651G. All of them provide all of the hardware features of the μCOM-44 family and execute all 58 instructions of the μCOM-44 instruction set.

The μPD547 is the original μCOM-44. It is manufactured with a standard PMOS process, allowing use of a single −10V power supply.

The μPD547L is manufactured with the low power consumption PMOS process, allowing use of a single −8V power supply.

The μPD552 is a μCOM-44 with high voltage outputs that can be pulled to −35V for direct interfacing to vacuum fluorescent displays. It is manufactured with a standard PMOS process allowing use of a single −10V power supply.

The μPD651 is a μCOM-44 manufactured with a low power consumption CMOS process, allowing use of a single +5V power supply. It has two subroutine stack levels. It is available either in a 42-pin dual-in-line package (μPD651C), or in a space saving 52-pin Flat-package (μPD651G).

PIN NAME	DESCRIPTION	TYPE
PA0-PA3	Port A	I
PB0-PB3	Port B	I
PC0-PC3	Port C	I/O
PD0-PD3	Port D	I/O
PE0-PE3	Port E	O
PF0-PF3	Port F	O
PG0-PG3	Port G	O
PH0-PH3	Port H	O
PI0-PI2	Port I	O
$\overline{INT}$	Interrupt	I
CL0-CL1	External Clock	I
RESET	Reset	I
V_{GG}	Power Supply Negative	
V_{SS}	Power Supply Positive (Ground for μPD651)	
V_{CC}	Power Supply for μPD651	
TEST	Factory Test Pin (Connect to V_{SS})	

Special Features

- 1000 × 8 ROM.
- 64 × 4 RAM.
- Typical instruction cycle time: 10 μSec.
- 58 instructions: Table Look Up capability with CZP and JPA instructions. single bit manipulation of RAM or I/O ports.
- One-level subroutine stack (μPD651 has a 2-level stack).
- Extensive I/O capability: two 4-bit input ports; two 4-bit I/O ports; four 4-bit output ports; one 3-bit output port.
- Software testable interrupt.
- Built-in clock signal generation circuitry.
- Built-in reset circuitry.

4-Bit μC

IN-CIRCUIT QUICK-TESTS

FOR 75% CONFIDENCE LEVEL:

1. Volt-ohmmeter Measurements:
   a) Make sure PC board ground has good connection to pins 20 and 21. On 651C pin 41 is ground.
   b) Measure power supply voltage of −9.0 to −11.0 volts DC at pin 41. On 651C the voltage is 4.5 to 5.5 volts DC on pin 21. (For 651C FLATPACK ground is pin 5 and power supply is pins 7 and 33).
2. Oscilloscope Measurements:
   a) Observe clock signals at pins 1 and 42. They should be square waves with a frequency of 0.14 to 0.44 MHz.

PIN CONFIGURATION

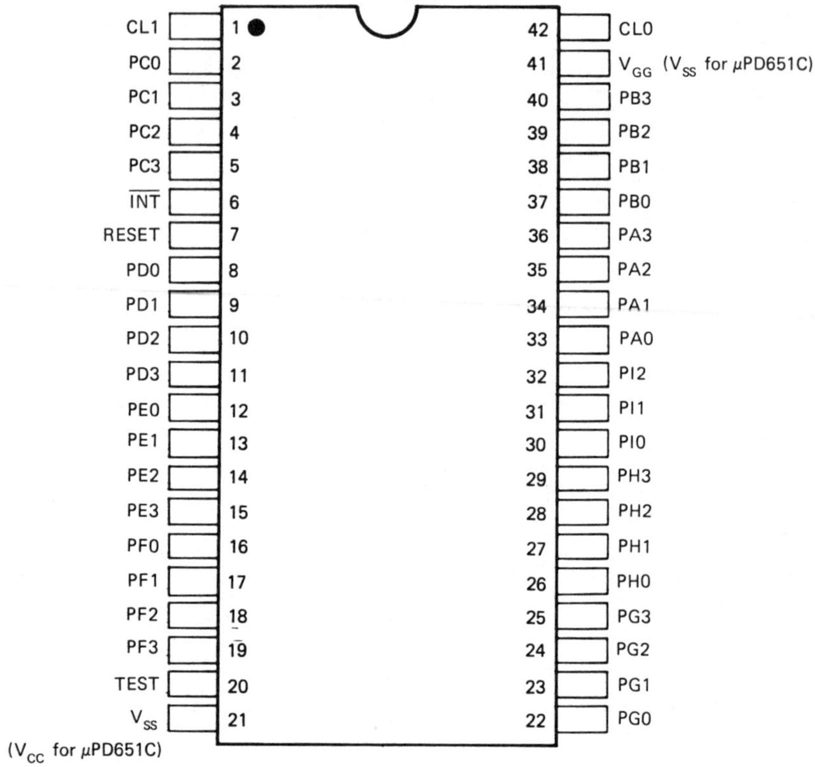

b) Observe the signal on pin 30. This signal is one of the Port I outputs and is synchronized to the clock. (For 651C FLATPACK clock is at pins 6 and 8. Port I is observed on pin 45).

FOR 90% CONFIDENCE LEVEL:

In addition to the 75% confidence level tests, use a dual-trace oscilloscope to observe the following:

a) Monitor the clock signal on pins 1 or 42 on one trace, while observing the PHO signal on pin 26 on the other. (For 651C FLATPACK clock is at pins 6 or 8. PHO is at pin 38).
b) Monitor the clock signal on pins 1 or 42 on one trace, while observing the PGO signal on pin 22 on the other. (For 651C FLAT-PACK clock is at pins 6 or 8. PGO is at pin 34).

EXACT REPLACEMENT ESSENTIAL

PIN CONFIGURATION

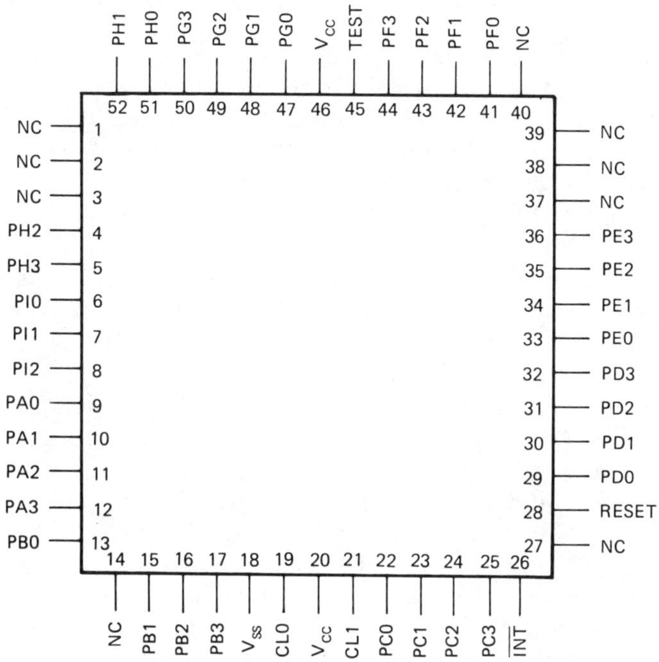

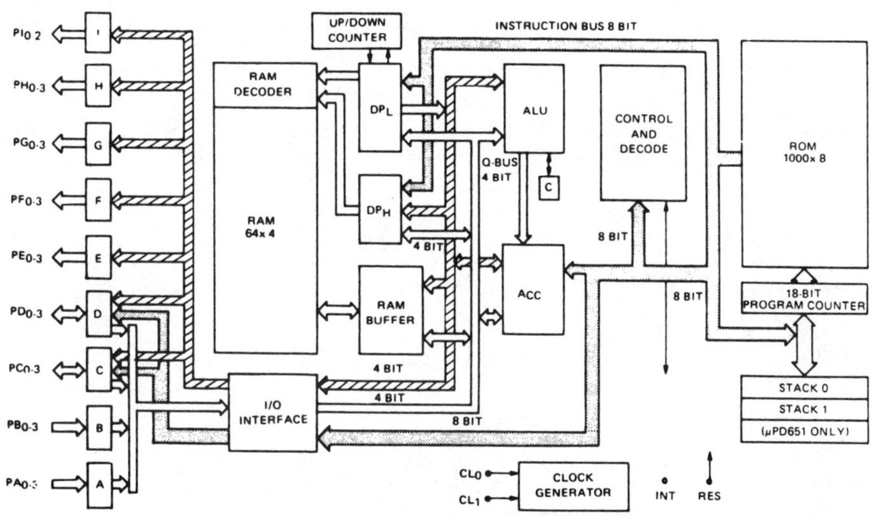

Courtesy NEC Electronics, U.S.A., Inc., Microcomputer Division.

Block Diagram—44 Family 4-Bit μC

Fig 8-12

μCOM-45 (NEC Microcomputer Inc.) 4-Bit Microcomputer

These devices are members of the μCOM-4 family. They are distinguished from other μCOM-45 products by their smaller ROM and RAM, and their reduced 21 line I/O capability. The members of the μCOM-45 are: μPD 550, μPD 550L, μPD 554, μPD554L, and μPD 652. All of them execute all 58 instructions of the μCOM-45 instruction set.

The μPD550 is a μCOM-45 with high voltage outputs that can be pulled to −35V for direct interfacing to vacuum fluorescent displays. It is manufactured with a standard PMOS process, allowing use of a single −10V power supply. It provides all of the hardware features of the μCOM-45 family, except that it has a 640 × 8-bit ROM to reduce device cost.

The μPD550L is a μCOM-45 with high voltage outputs and low power consumption. The outputs can be pulled to −35V for direct interfacing to vacuum fluorescent displays. It is manufactured with a low power consumption PMOS process, allowing use of a −8V, low current power supply. It provides all of the hardware features of the μCOM-45 family.

The μPD554 is the standard μCOM-45 with high voltage outputs that can be pulled to −35V for direct interfacing to vacuum fluorescent displays. It is manufactured with a standard PMOS process, allowing use of a single −10V power supply. It provides all of the hardware features of the μCOM-45 family.

The μPD554L is a μCOM-45 with high voltage outputs and low power consumption. It is manufactured with a low power consumption PMOS process, allowing use of a −8V, low current power supply.

The μPD652 is a μCOM-45 manufactured with a low power consumption CMOS process, allowing use of a single +5V power supply. It provides all the hardware features of the μCOM-45 family.

PIN NAME	DESCRIPTION	TYPE
PA0-PA3	Port A	I
PC0-PC3	Port C	I/O
PD0-PD3	Port D	I/O
PE0-PE3	Port E	O
PF0-PF3	Port F	O
PG0	Port G	O
CL0-GL1	External Clock Signals	I
$\overline{\text{INT}}$	Interrupt	I
RESET	Reset	I
V_{GG} (V_{SS} for μPD652)	Power Supply Negative	

PIN NAME	DESCRIPTION	TYPE
V_{SS} (V_{CC} for μPD652)	Power Supply Positive	
TEST	Factory Test Pin (Connect to V_{SS}, V_{CC} Respectively)	

Special Features

- 1000 × 8 ROM (μPD550 and μPD550L have 640 × 8 ROM).
- 32 × 4 RAM.
- Typical instruction cycle time: 10 μsec.
- 58 instructions. Table Look Up capability with CZP and JPA instructions. Single bit manipulation of RAM or I/O ports.
- One-Level subroutine stack.
- Extensive I/O capability: one 4-bit input port; two 4-bit I/O ports; two 4-bit output ports; one 1-bit output port.
- Software testable interrrupt.
- Built-in clock signal generation circuitry.
- Built-in reset circuitry.

PIN CONFIGURATION

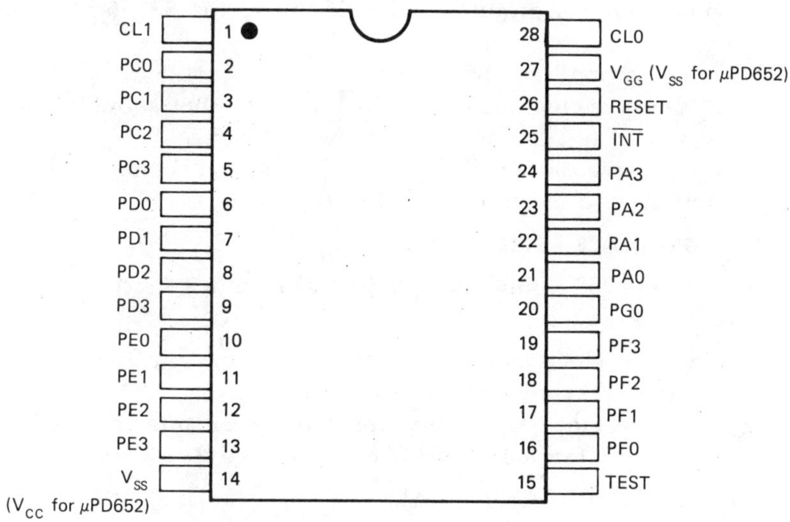

IN-CIRCUIT QUICK-TESTS

FOR 75% CONFIDENCE LEVEL:

1. Volt-ohmmeter Measurements:

   a) Make sure PC board ground has good connection to pins 14 and 15.

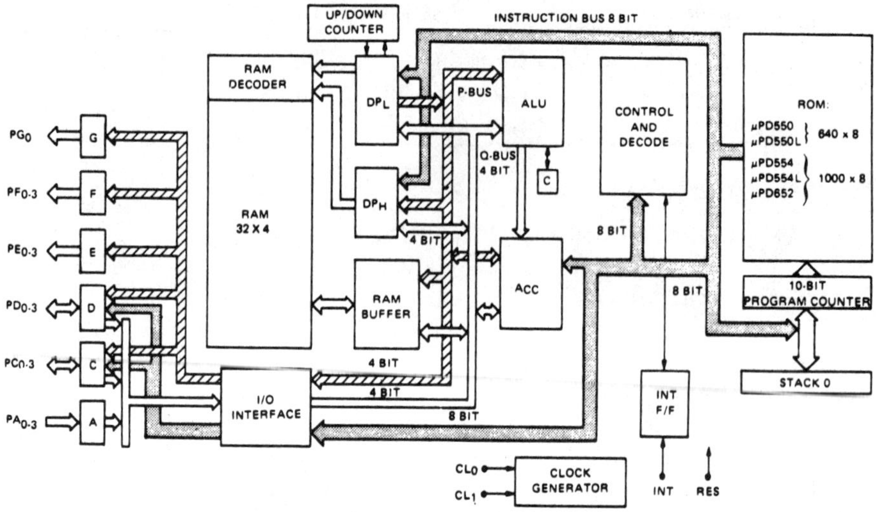

Courtesy NEC Electronics, U.S.A., Inc., Microcomputer Division.

Block Diagram—45 Family, 4-Bit μC
Fig. 8-13

b) Measure power supply voltage of −9.0 to −11.0 volts DC at pin 27. On 652 ground is at pin 27 and 4.5 to 5.5 volts DC is at pin 14.

2. Oscilloscope Measurements:
   a) Observe clock signals at pins 1 and 28. They should be square waves with a frequency of 0.1 to 0.44 MHz.
   b) Observe the signal on pin 20. This signal is one of the Port G outputs and is synchronized to the clock.

For 90% Confidence Level:

In addition to the 75% confidence level tests, use a dual-trace oscilloscope to observe the following:

a) Monitor the clock signal on pins 1 or 28 on one trace, while observing the PFO signal on pin 16 on the other.
b) Monitor the clock signal on pins 1 or 28 on one trace, while observing the PEO signal on pin 10 on the other.

EXACT REPLACEMENT ESSENTIAL

LM 6400 Series (Sanyo) 4-Bit Microcomputer

This series contains devices designed for controller applications in commercial systems. These devices are N-channel E/D MOS, containing a 4-bit parallel processing arithmetic logic unit (ALU), program memory (ROM), data memory (RAM), I/O ports, general-purpose times, prescaler, and clock generator. The instruction set has 82 instructions including the bit handling instruction and single bit or 4-bit accessing input/output instruction, binary addition and decimal addition and subtraction, logical operation. Programmable timer and programmable logic array (PLA) are self-contained.

The members of the LM6400 series are: LM6401, LM6402, LM6403, LM6404, LM6405, LM6406, and LM6499 (evaluation chip).

Special Features

- 4-level subroutine nesting (used jointly with interrupt).
- Interrupt (external interrupt, internal general purpose timer interrupt).
- Built-in 14-bit general-purpose timer (with programmable 6-bit prescaler, usable as programmable timer, event counter, or pulse width measure).
- Input/Output ports (single bit, 4-bit accessing capability).
- TTL/CMOS (at V_{DD} - 5V) compatible input voltage level.
- Open drain output/pull-up resistance, built-in output selectable.
- Built-in clock generator circuit (ceramic resonator, or externally attached).

LM 6401 / LM 6404

- ROM: 2048 × 8 bits (LM 6401); 1024 × 8 bits (LM 6404).
- RAM: 128 × 4 bits (LM 6401); 64 × 4 bits (LM 6404).
- On-chip A/D converter.

PIN NAME	DESCRIPTION	TYPE
PA0-PA3	Port A	I/O
PB0-PB3	Port B	I/O
PC0-PC3	Port C	I/O
PD0-PD3	Port D	I/O
PE0-PE3 (PLA0-PLA3)	Port E (PLA)	O
PF0-PF3 (PLA4-PLA7)	Port F (PLA)	O
I_{in}, I_{ref}, A_{out}, Z_{adj}	Pin for A/D Convert	
PH0-PH3	Port H	I/O
PI0-PI2	Port I	I/O
Xtal, EXtal	Crystal	I
$\overline{INT}$	Interrupt	I
$\overline{RES}$	Reset	I

4-Bit μC

PIN NAME	DESCRIPTION	TYPE
TEST	Test	I
V_{DD}	Power Supply	
V_{SS}	Ground	

IN-CIRCUIT QUICK-TESTS

FOR 75% CONFIDENCE LEVEL:

1. Volt-ohmmeter Measurements:
   a) Make sure PC board ground has good connection to pins 20 and 21.
   b) Measure power supply voltage of 4.5 to 5.5 volts DC at pin 41.
2. Oscilloscope Measurements:
   a) Observe clock signals at pins 1 and 42. They should be square waves with a frequency of 0.1 to 0.44 MHz.

PIN CONFIGURATION

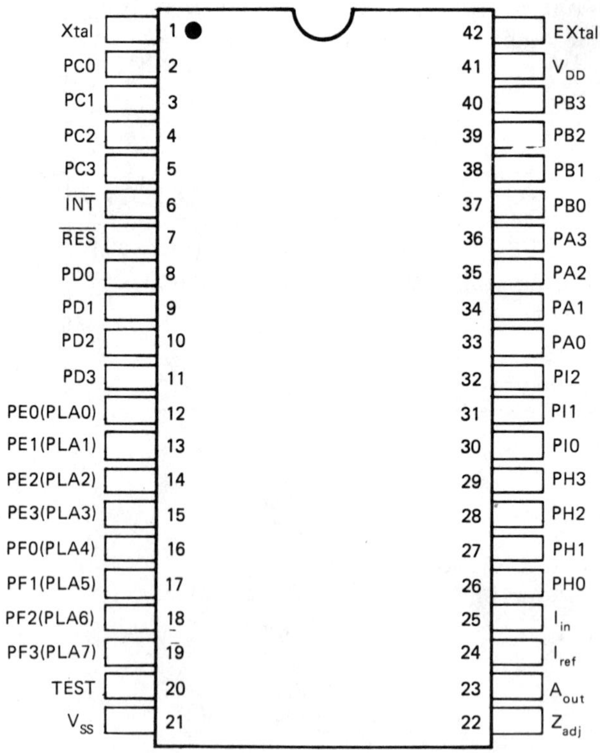

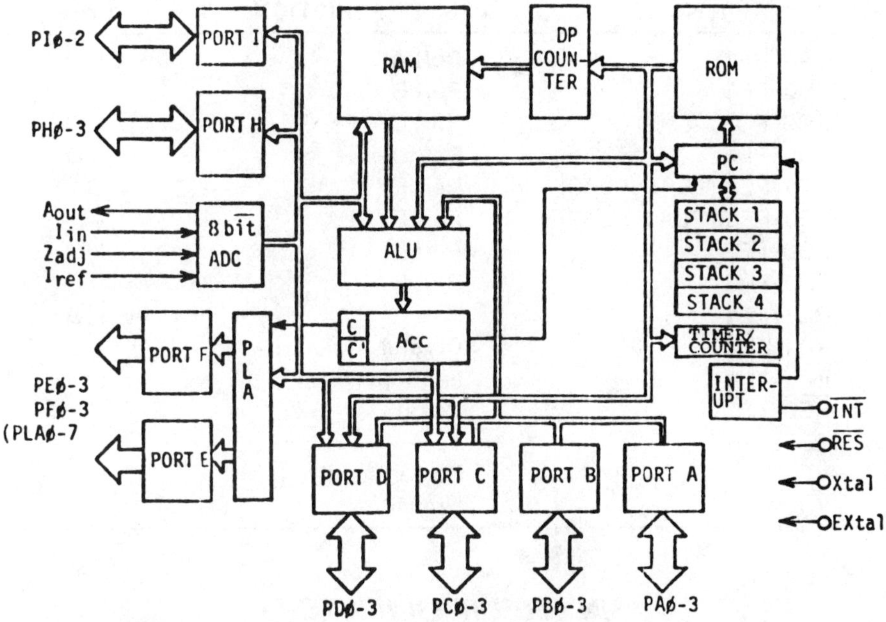

Courtesy Sanyo Semiconductor, Inc., 7 Pearl Court, Allendale, NJ 07401.

Block Diagram—6401, 6404, 4-Bit μC
Fig. 8-14

b) Observe the signal on pin 12. This signal is one of the PORT E outputs and is synchronized to the clock.

For 90% Confidence Level:

In addition to the 75% confidence level tests, use a dual-trace oscilloscope to observe the following:

a) Monitor the clock signal on pins 1 or 42 on one trace, while observing the PF0 signal on pin 16 on the other.
b) Monitor the clock signal on pins 1 or 42 on one trace, while observing the PF1 signal on pin 17 on the other.

EXACT REPLACEMENT ESSENTIAL

LM 6402/LM 6405

- ROM: 2048 × 8 bits (LM 6402); 1024 × 8 bits (LM 6405).
- RAM: 128 × 4 bits (LM 6402; 64 × 4 bits (LM 6405).

PIN NAME	DESCRIPTION	TYPE
PA0-PA3	Port A	I/O
PB0-PB3	Port B	I/O
PC0-PC3	Port C	I/O
PD0-PD3	Port D	I/O
PE0-PE3 (PLA0-PLA3)	Port E (PLA)	O
PF0-PF3 (PLA4-PLA7)	Port F (PLA)	O
PG0-PG3	Port G	I/O
PH0-PH3	Port H	I/O
PI0-PI2	Port I	I/O
Xtal, EXtal	Crystal	I
$\overline{INT}$	Interrupt	I
$\overline{RES}$	Reset	I
TEST	Test	I
V_{DD}	Power Supply	
V_{SS}	Ground	

IN-CIRCUIT QUICK-TESTS

For 75% Confidence Level:

1. Volt-ohmmeter Measurements:
   a) Make sure PC board ground has good connection to pin 20 and 21.
   b) Measure power supply voltage of 4.5 to 5.5 volts DC at pin 41.
2. Oscilloscope Measurements:
   a) Observe clock signals at pins 1 and 42. They should be square waves with a frequency of 0.1 to 0.44 MHz.
   b) Observe the signal on pin 12. This signal is one of the PORT E outputs and is synchronized to the clock.

For 90% Confidence Level:

In addition to the 75% confidence level tests, use a dual-trace oscilloscope to observe the following:

a) Monitor the clock signal on pins 1 or 42 on one trace, while observing the PF0 signal on pin 16 on the other.
b) Monitor the clock signal on pins 1 or 42 on one trace, while observing the PF1 signal on pin 17 on the other.

EXACT REPLACEMENT ESSENTIAL

PIN CONFIGURATION

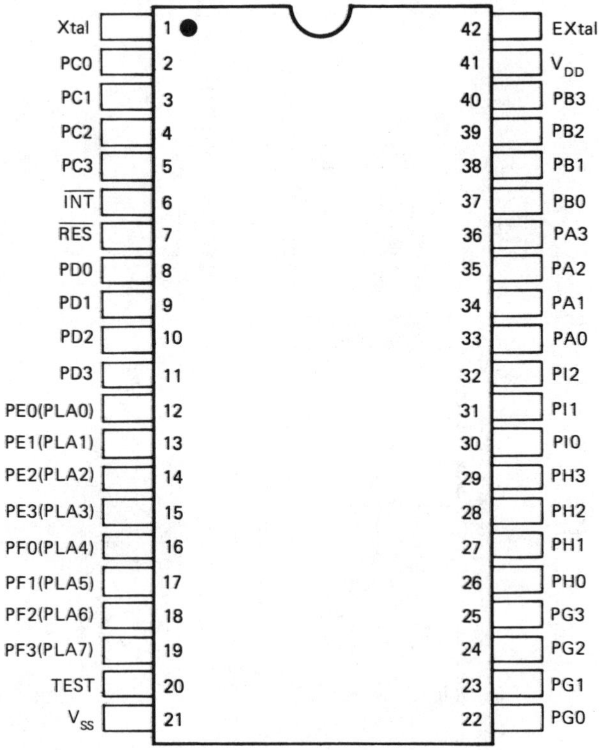

LM 6403/LM 6406

- ROM: 2048 × 8 bits (LM 6403); 1024 × 8 bits (LM 6406).
- RAM: 128 × 4 bits (LM 6403]; 64 × 4 bits (LM 6406).

PIN NAME	DESCRIPTION	TYPE
PA0–PA3	Port A	I/O
PC0–PC3	Port C	I/O
PD0–PD3	Port D	I/O
PE0–PE3 (PLA0–PLA3)	Port E (PLA)	O
PF0–PF3 (PLA4–PLA7)	Port F (PLA)	O
PG0	Port G	I/O
Xtal, EXtal	Crystal	I

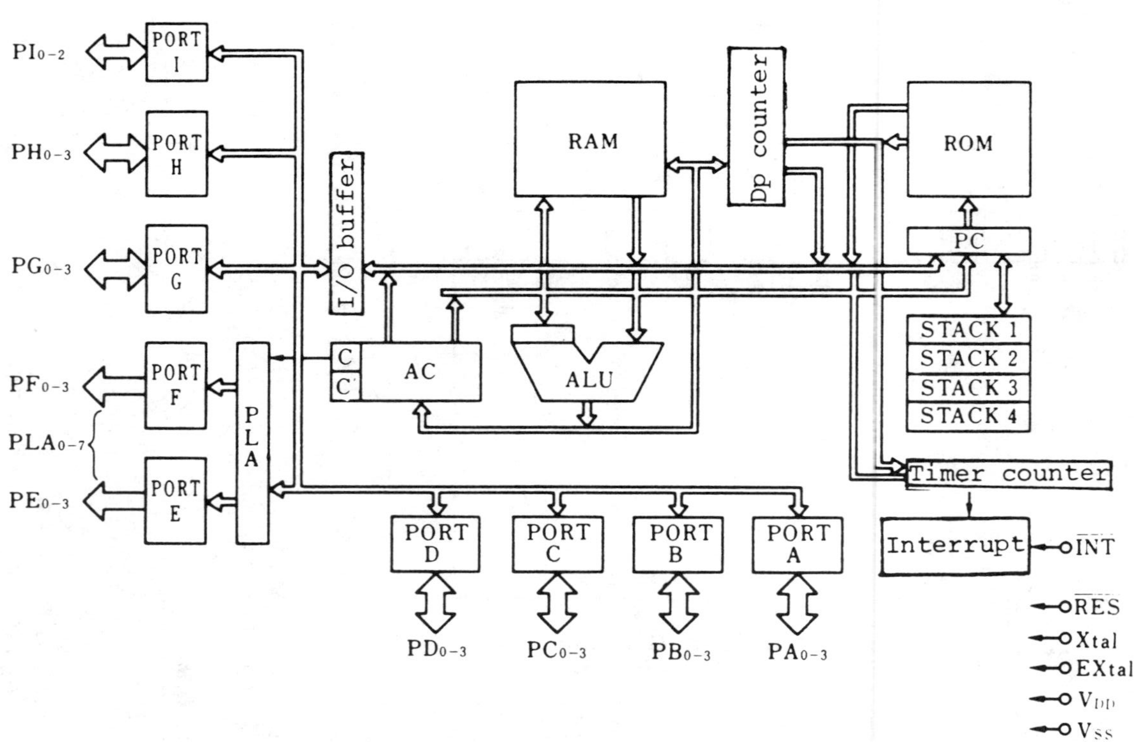

Courtesy Sanyo Semiconductor, Inc., 7 Pearl Court, Allendale, NJ 07401.

Block Diagram—6402, 6405, 4-Bit μC
Fig. 8-15

PIN NAME	DESCRIPTION	TYPE
$\overline{INT}$	Interrupt	I
$\overline{RES}$	Reset	I
TEST	Test	I
V_{DD}	Power Supply	
V_{SS}	Ground	

PIN CONFIGURATION

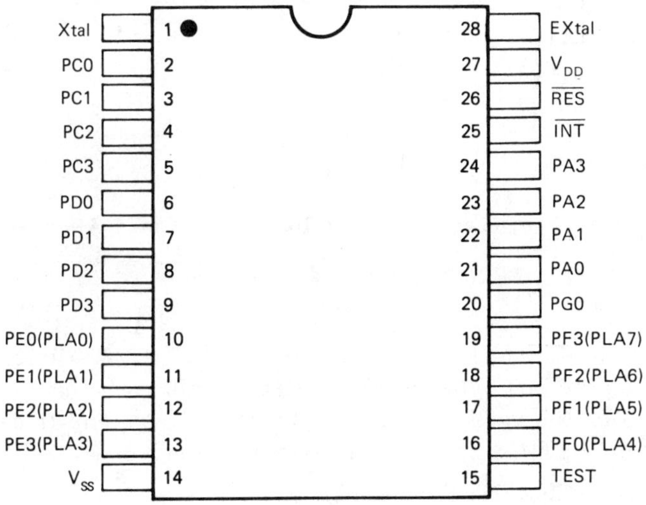

IN-CIRCUIT QUICK-TESTS

FOR 75% CONFIDENCE LEVEL:

1. Volt-ohmmeter Measurements:
   a) Make sure PC board ground has good connection to pins 14 and 15.
   b) Measure power supply voltage of 4.5 to 5.5 volts DC at pin 27.
2. Oscilloscope Measurements:
   a) Observe clock signals at pin 1 and 27. They should be square waves with a frequency of 0.1 to 0.44 MHz
   b) Observe the signal on pin 10. This signal is one of the PORT E outputs and is synchronized to the clock.

FOR 90% CONFIDENCE LEVEL:

In addition to the 75% confidence level tests, use a dual-trace oscilloscope to observe the following:

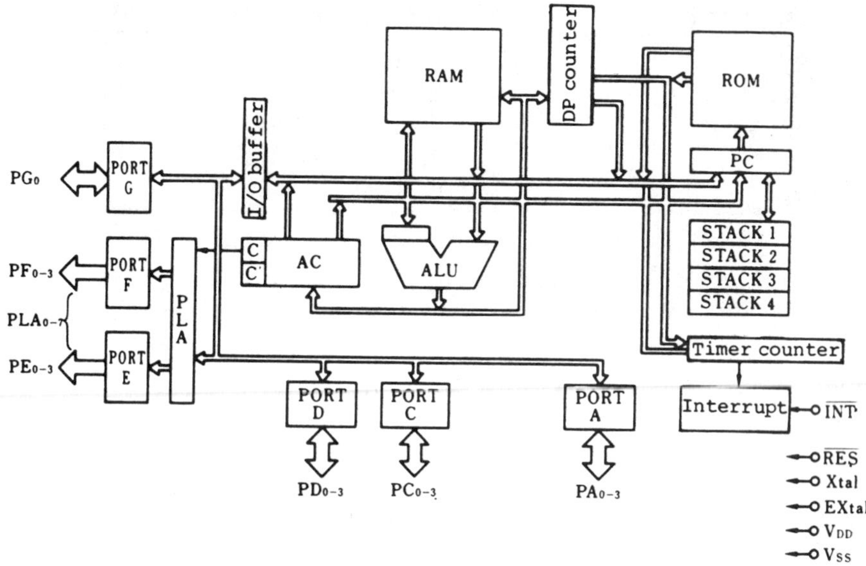

Courtesy Sanyo Semiconductor, Inc., 7 Pearl Court, Allendale, NJ 07401.

Block Diagram—6403, 6406, 4-Bit μC
Fig. 8-16

a) Monitor the clock signal on pins 1 or 27 on one trace, while observing the PF0 signal on pin 16 on the other.
b) Monitor the clock signal on pins 1 or 27 on one trace, while observing the PF1 signal on pin 17 on the other.

EXACT REPLACEMENT ESSENTIAL

μPD 7500 (NEC MICROCOMPUTERS) 4-BIT MICROCOMPUTER

This device is a μCOM-75 capable of addressing 8,192 bytes of external memory, and also functions as the prototype evaluation chip for the μPD 750X family of 4-bit single chip microcomputers. It is manufactured with a low power consumption CMOS process, allowing use of a single power supply between 2.7 and 5.5V, and providing programmable power-down capability. It executes 102 instructions of the μCOM-75 instruction set.

PIN NAME	DESCRIPTION	TYPE
BUS0–BUS13	Address/Instruction Bus	I/O
P00	Port 00	I
P01/$\overline{SCK}$	Port 01/Serial Clock	I
P02/SO	Port 02/Serial Output	I/O

PIN NAME	DESCRIPTION	TYPE
P03/SI	Port 03/Serial Input	I/I
P10-P13	Port 1	I/O
P20/$\overline{STB}$	Port 20/Port 1 Strobe Output	O/O
P21/PT_{OUT}	Port 21/Timer Output	O/O
P20-P23	Port 2	O
P30-P33	Port 3	O
P40-P43	Port 4	I/O
P50-P53	Port 5	I/O
P60-P63	Port 6	I/O
P70-P73	Port 7	I/O
INT0, INT1, INT2	Interrupt 0, 1, 2	I
CL1, CL2	System Clock	I, O
X1, X2	Crystal Clock	I, O
ALE	Address Latch Enable	O
$\overline{CSOUT}$	Chip Select OUTPUT	O
$\overline{DOUT}$	Data Out	O
LCD CL	LCD Clock	O
$\overline{PSEN}$	Program Store Enable	O
$\overline{STB}$	Strobe 1	O
RESET	Reset	I
V_{DD}	Power Supply Positive	
V_{SS}	Ground	
$\overline{TEST}$	Factory Test Pin	
NC	No Connection	

Special Features

- 256 × 4-Bit RAM.
- 10 μsec. instruction cycle time.
- 102 instructions. Table Look Up capability with LHLT and LAMTL instructions. Indirect indexed addressing with CALT instruction.
- RAM stack.
- Extensive I/O capability: one 4-bit input port; two 4-bit output ports; four 4-bit I/O ports, of which two are 8-bit byte accessible; one 4-bit I/O port with output strobe; one 14-bit address/instruction port; one 8-bit serial I/O port.
- Programmable 8-bit timer/event counter with crystal clock generator.
- Vectored, prioritized interrupts: three external; two internal (timer and serial I/O).
- Programmable power-down operation with HALT and STOP instructions.
- Built-in system clock generator.
- Built-in reset circuitry.

PIN CONFIGURATION

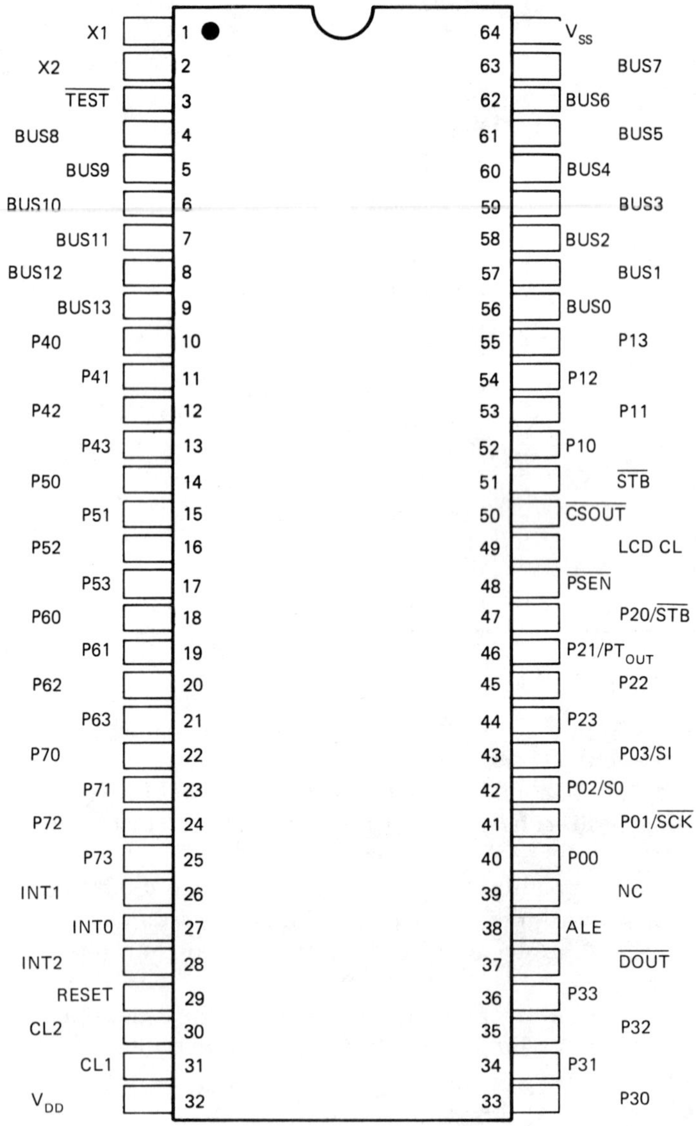

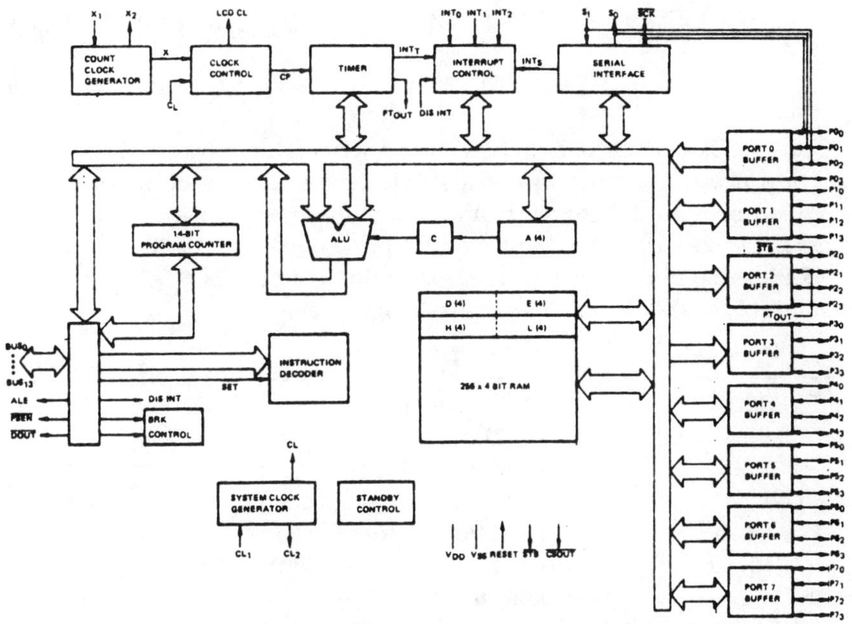

Courtesy NEC Electronics, U.S.A., Inc., Microcomputer Division.

Block Diagram—7500, 4-Bit μC
Fig. 8-17

IN-CIRCUIT QUICK-TESTS

For 75% Confidence Level:

1. Volt-ohmmeter Measurements:
   a) Make sure PC board ground has good connection to pin 3 and 64.
   b) Measure power supply voltage of 2.7 to 5.5 volts DC at pin 32.
2. Oscilloscope Measurements:
   a) Observe clock signals at pins 1 and 2 or at pins 30 and 31. They should be square waves with a frequency of 0.01 and 0.20 MHz.
   b) Observe the signal on pin 47. This signal is the PORT 1 Strobe output and is synchronized to the clock.

For 90% Confidence Level:

In addition to the 75% confidence level tests, use a dual-trace oscilloscope to observe the following:

a) Monitor the clock signal on pin 30 on one trace, while observing the P21/PT OUT signal on pin 46 on the other.
b) Monitor the clock signal on pin 30 on one trace, while observing the ALE signal on pin 38 on the other.

EXACT REPLACEMENT ESSENTIAL

μPD-7502 (NEC Microcomputers) 4-Bit Microcomputer[1]

This device is a μCOM-75 manufactured with a low power consumption CMOS process, allowing use of a single power supply between 2.7 and 5.5V, and providing programmable power-down capability. It has 23 I/O lines, organized into one 3-bit parallel port, five 4-bit parallel ports, and one 8-bit serial port. It executes 92 instructions of the μCOM-75 instruction set, and it is available in a 64-pin plastic flat package.

PIN NAME	DESCRIPTION	TYPE
S0-S23	LCD Segment	O
COM0-COM3	LCD Backplane	O
PO3/SI	Input Port 03/Serial Input	I/O
PO2/SO	Input Port 02/Serial Output	I/O
P01/$\overline{SCK}$	Input Port 01/Serial Clock	I
P10/INT0	Input Port 10/Interrupt 0	I
INT1	Interrupt 1	I
P10-P13	Input Port 1	I
P30-P33	Output Port 3	O
P40-P43	I/O Port 4	I/O
P50-P53	I/O Port 5	I/O
P60-P63	I/O Port 6	I/O
X1, X2	Crystal Clock Input, Output	I, O
C1, C2	System Clock Input, Output	I, O
RESET	Reset	I
V_{LCD1}-V_{LCD3}	LCD Power Supply	
V_{DD}	Power Supply Positive	
V_{SS}	Ground	

Special Features

- 2048 × 8-bit ROM.
- 128 × 4-bit RAM.
- 15 μsec. instruction cycle time.
- 92 instructions. ROM Data Table Look Up capability with LHLT and LAMT instructions. Sub-routine address table look up capability with CALT instruction.
- RAM stack.
- Four general purpose 4-bit registers (D, E, H, and L)
- Extensive I/O capability: one 3-bit input port; one 4-bit input port; one

[1]*Note:* The μPD7503 is identical to the μPD7502, except for the memory; the μPD7503 has a 4096 × 8 Bit ROM and a 224 × 4 Bit RAM.

4-bit output port; three 4-bit I/O ports, of which two are 8-bit byte accessible; one 8-bit serial I/O Port.

- Programmable LCD controller. 24 segment outputs and 4 backplane outputs. Can directly drive three or four backplane multiplexed LCD's. Automatic synchronization of segment and backplane signals, transparent to program execution.
- Programmable 8-bit timer/event counter with crystal clock generator.
- Vectored, prioritized interrupts—two external; two internal (timer and serial I/O).
- Programmable power-down operation with HALT and STOP instructions.
- Built-in system clock generator.
- Built-in reset circuitry.

PIN CONFIGURATION

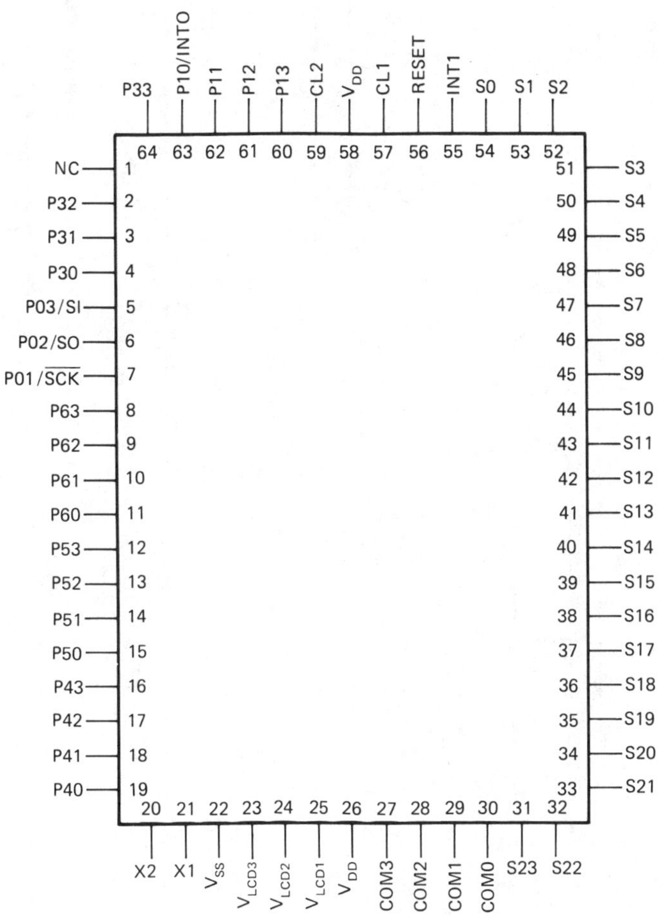

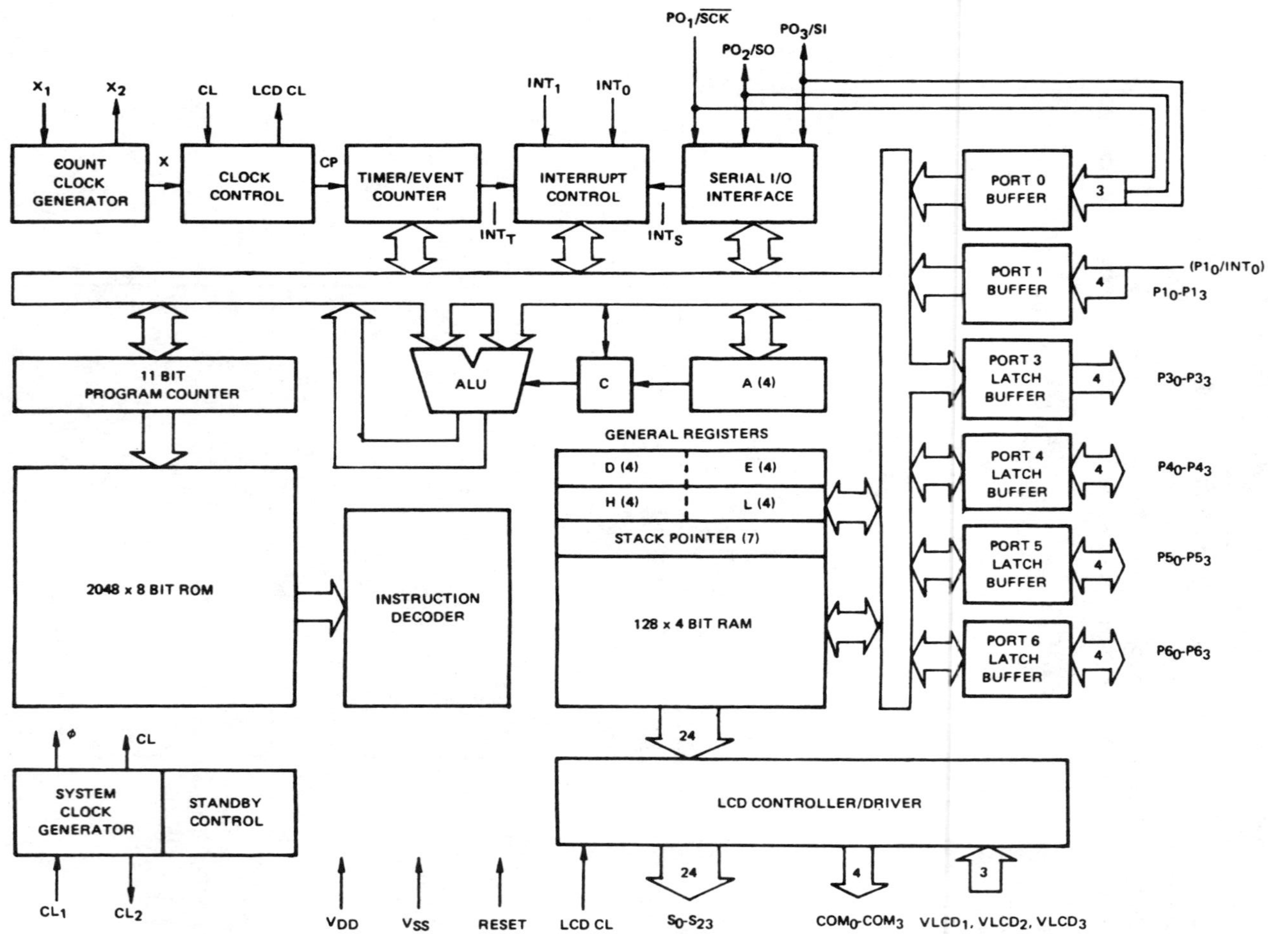

Courtesy NEC Electronics, U.S.A., Inc., Microcomputer Division.

Block Diagram—7502, 4-Bit μC
Fig. 8-18

IN-CIRCUIT QUICK-TESTS

FOR 75% CONFIDENCE LEVEL:

1. Volt-ohmmeter Measurements:
   a) Make sure PC board ground has good connection to pin 22.
   b) Measure power supply voltage of 2.7 to 5.5 volts DC at pins 26 and 58.
2. Oscilloscope Measurements:
   a) Observe clock signals at pins 20 and 21 or at pins 57 and 59. They should be square waves with a frequency of 0.01 to 0.20 MHz.
   b) Observe the signal on pin 6. This signal is the PORT O Serial output and is synchronized to the clock.

FOR 90% CONFIDENCE LEVEL:

In addition to the 75% confidence level tests, use a dual-trace oscilloscope to observe the following:

a) Monitor the clock signal on pin 59 on one trace, while observing the PO1/ECK signal on pin 7 on the other.
b) Monitor the clock signal on pin 59 on one trace, while observing the P40 signal on pin 19 on the other.

EXACT REPLACEMENT ESSENTIAL

μPD 7507 (NEC MICROCOMPUTERS) 4-BIT MICROCOMPUTER

This device is a μCOM-75 manufactured with a low power consumption CMOS process, allowing use of a single power supply between 2.7 and 5.5V, and providing programmable power-down capability. It has 32 I/O lines, organized into eight 4-bit parallel ports and one 8-bit serial port. The μPD 7507 executes 92 instructions of the μCOM-75 instruction set, and it is available in a 50 pin dual-in-line package.

PIN NAME	DESCRIPTION	TYPE
P00/INTO	Port 00/Interrupt 0	I
P01/$\overline{SCK}$	Port 01/Serial Clock	I
P02/SO	Port 02/Serial Output	I
P03/SI	Port 03/Serial Input	I
P10-P13	Port 1	I/O
P20/$\overline{STB}$	Port 20/Port 1 Strobe	O
P21/T_{OUT}	Port 21/Timer	O
P22-P23	Port 2	O
P30-P33	Port 3	O
P40-P43	Port 4	I/O

4-Bit μC

PIN NAME	DESCRIPTION	TYPE
P50–P53	Port 5	I/O
P60–P63	Port 6	I/O
P70–P73	Port 7	I/O
INT 1	Interrupt 1	I
CL 1, CL 2	System Clock	I, O
X1, X2	Crystal Clock	I, O
RESET	Reset	I
V_{DD}	Power Supply Positive	
V_{SS}	Ground	

Special Features

- 2048 × 8 bit ROM.
- 128 × 4 bit RAM.
- 10 μSec. instruction cycle time.
- 92 instructions: Table Look Up capability with LHLT and LAMT1 instructions. Indirect indexed addressing with CALT instruction.

PIN CONFIGURATION

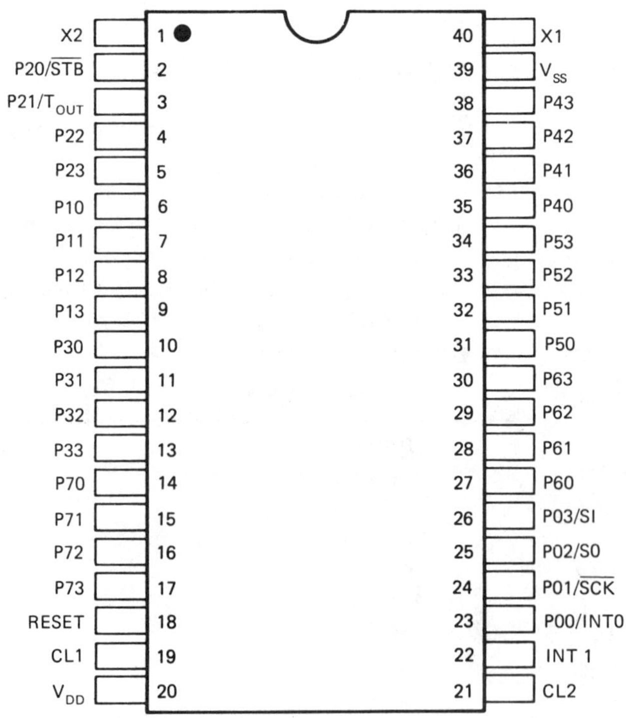

- RAM stack.
- Extensive I/O capability: one 4-bit input port; two 4-bit output ports; four 4-bit I/O ports, of which two are 8-bit byte accessible; one 4-bit I/O port with output strobe; one 8-bit serial I/O port.
- Programmable 8-bit timer/event counter with crystal clock generator.
- Vectored, prioritized interrupts: two external; two internal (timer and serial I/O).
- Programmable power-down operation with HALT and STOP instructions.
- Built-in system clock generator.
- Built-in reset circuitry.

IN-CIRCUIT QUICK-TESTS

For 75% Confidence Level:

1. Volt-ohmmeter Measurements:
   a) Make sure PC board ground has good connection to pin 39.
   b) Measure power supply voltage of 2.7 to 5.5 volts DC at pin 20.

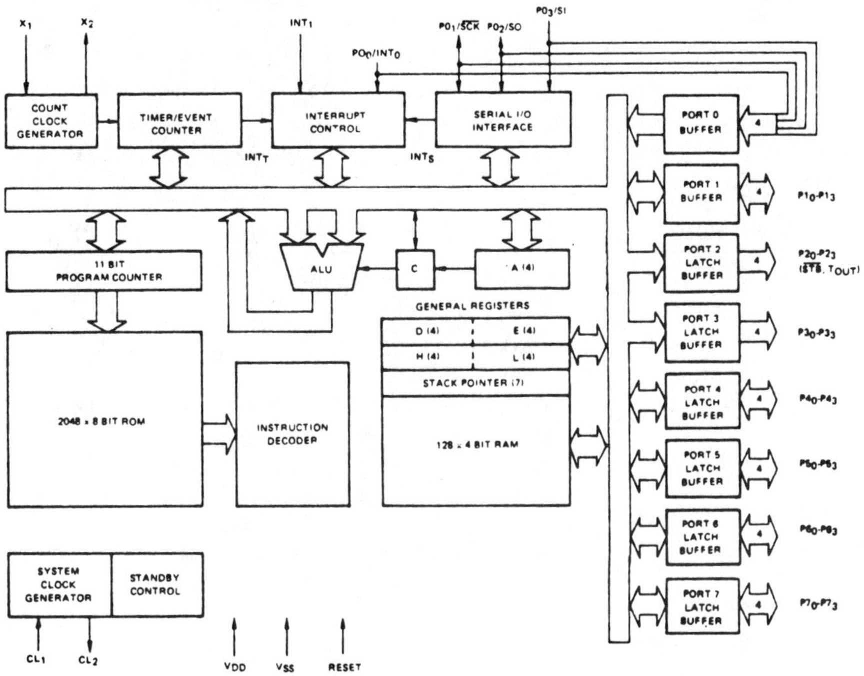

Courtesy NEC Electronics, U.S.A., Inc., Microcomputer Division.

Block Diagram—7507, 4-Bit μC
Fig. 8-19

4-Bit μC

2. Oscilloscope Measurements:
   a) Observe clock signals at pins 1 and 40 or at pins 19 and 21. They should be square waves with a frequency of 0.01 to 0.20 MHz.
   b) Observe the signal on pin 2. This signal is the PORT 1 strobe output and is synchronized to the clock.

For 90% Confidence Level:

In addition to the 75% confidence level tests, use a dual-trace oscilloscope to observe the following:

a) Monitor the clock signal on pin 21 on one trace, while observing the PO2/SO signal on pin 25 on the other.
b) Monitor the clock signal on pin 21 on one trace, while observing the P20 signal on pin 2 on the other.

EXACT REPLACEMENT ESSENTIAL

μPD 7520 (NEC Microcomputers) 4-Bit Microcomputer

This device is a μCOM-75 with a programmable display controller capable of directly driving a multiplexed eight segment, eight digit LED Display. It is manufactured with a low power consumption PMOS process, allowing use of a single power supply between −6V and −10V. It executes 47 instructions of the μCOM-75 instruction set,

PIN NAME	DESCRIPTION	TYPE
S0-S7	Port S Segment Drive	O
T0-T5	Port T Digit Drive	O
P10-P13	Port 1	I
P30-P31	Port 3	O
P40-P43	Port 4	I/O
CLK	Clock	I
RESET	Reset	I
V_{GG}	Power Supply Negative	
V_{SS}	Ground	

Special Features

- 768 × 8 Bit ROM.
- 48 × 4 Bit RAM.
- 20 μsec. typical instruction cycle time.
- 47 instructions. Table Look Up capability with LAMT instructions.
- Two-level subroutine stack.

- One 4-bit input port, one 4-bit I/O port, one 2-bit output port (capable of driving piezo element).
- Programmable display controller. Six LED direct drive outputs (possibly eight if using P40–P41) Eight LED direct segment drive outputs. Selection of a four, five, six, or eight digit display strobe cycle. Can directly drive eight Segment, multiplexed displays, or up to an 8 × 8 dot matrix. Automatic synchronization of segment and digit signals, transparent to program execution. Segment outputs also function as latched, 8-bit parallel output port.
- Built-in clock signal generation circuitry.
- Built-in reset circuitry.

Pin Configuration

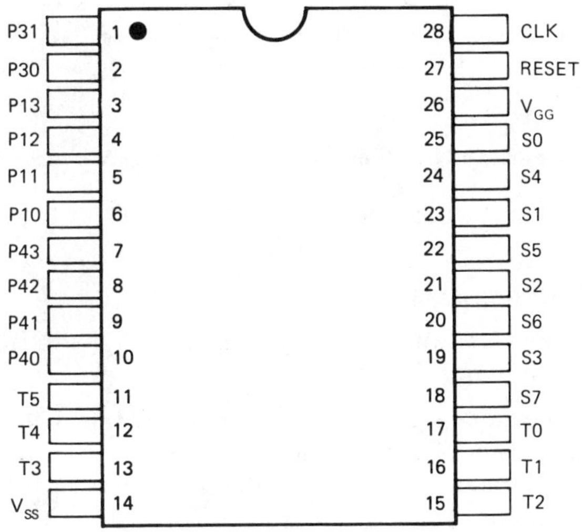

IN-CIRCUIT QUICK-TESTS

For 75% Confidence Level:

1. Volt-ohmmeter Measurements:
   a) Make sure PC board ground has good connection to pin 14.
   b) Measure power supply voltage of −6.0 to −10.0 volts DC at pin 26.
2. Oscilloscope Measurements:
   a) Observe clock signals at pin 28. They should be square waves with a frequency of 0.01 to 0.20 MHz.
   b) Observe the signal on pin 2. This signal is the PORT 3 output and is synchronized to the clock.

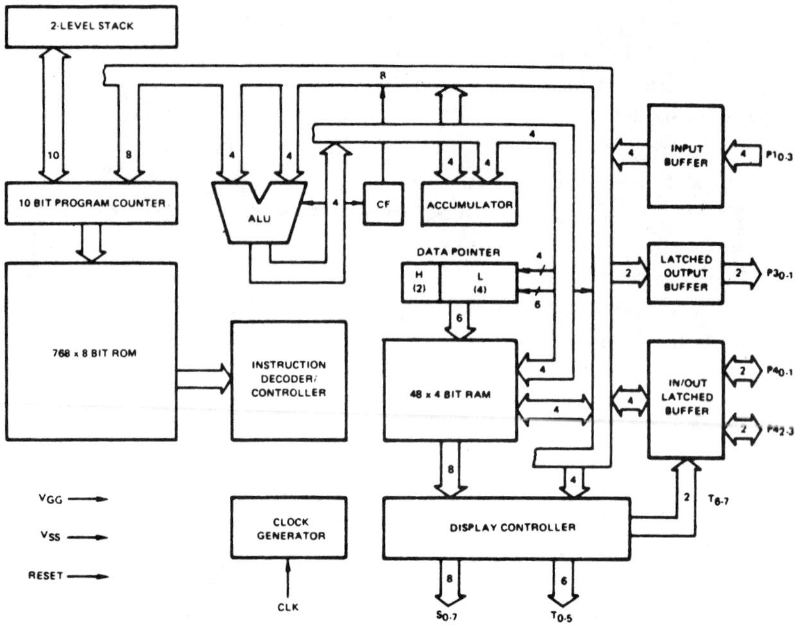

Courtesy NEC Electronics, U.S.A., Inc., Microcomputer Division.

Block Diagram—7520, 4-Bit μC
Fig. 8-20

For 90% Confidence Level:

In addition to the 75% confidence level tests, use a dual-trace oscilloscope to observe the following:

a) Monitor the clock signal on pin 28 on one trace, while observing the T0 signal on pin 17 on the other.
b) Monitor the clock signal on pin 28 on one trace, while observing the T1 signal on pin 16 on the other.

EXACT REPLACEMENT ESSENTIAL

CHAPTER 9

8-BIT MICROCOMPUTER (μC)

PIC 1650A (General Instrument) 8-Bit Microcomputer

This device contains 32 8-bit RAM registers, a 512 × 12-bit programmable ROM, four sets of eight TTL compatible input/output lines and a central processing unit. Keyboard scanning, display driving, and other system control functions can be done at the same time.

PIN NAME	DESCRIPTION	TYPE
RA0-RA7	Port A	I/O
RB0-RB7	Port B	I/O
RC0-RC7	Port C	I/O
RD0-RD7	Port D	I/O
OSC	Oscillator	I
$\overline{RTCC}$	Real Time Clock Counter	I
$\overline{MCLR}$	Master Clear	I
CLK OUT	Clock Output	O
TEST	Test	
V_{DD}	Power Supply	
V_{XX}	Output Buffer Power	
V_{SS}	Ground	

Special Features

- Arithmetic logic unit.
- Real time clock counter.

PIN CONFIGURATION

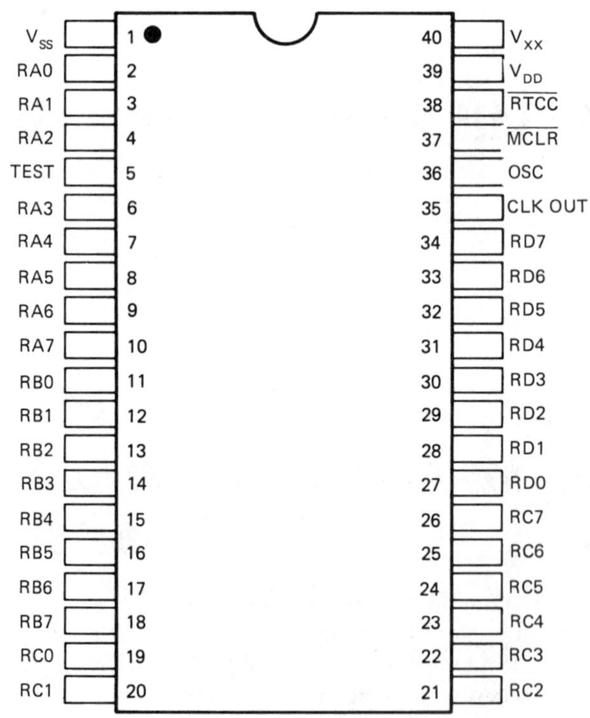

- Access to RAM registers.
- Power supply operating range: 4.5V to 7.0V.
- Available in two temperature ranges: 0°C to 70°C, and −40°C to 85°C.
- Two-level stack.
- Schmitt trigger inputs.
- Self-contained oscillator and external oscillator input available.
- V_{XX} output buffer supply voltage drives only the I/O ports and has a range within 4.5V to 10.0V.

IN-CIRCUIT QUICK-TESTS

FOR 75% CONFIDENCE LEVEL:

1. Volt-ohmmeter Measurements:
   a) Make sure PC board ground has good connection to pins 1 and 5.
   b) Measure power supply voltage of 4.5 to 5.5 volts DC at pin 39 and 4.5 to 10.0 volts DC on pin 40.
2. Oscilloscope Measurements:
   a) Observe clock signals at pin 36. They should be square waves with a frequency of 0.2 to 1.0 MHz.

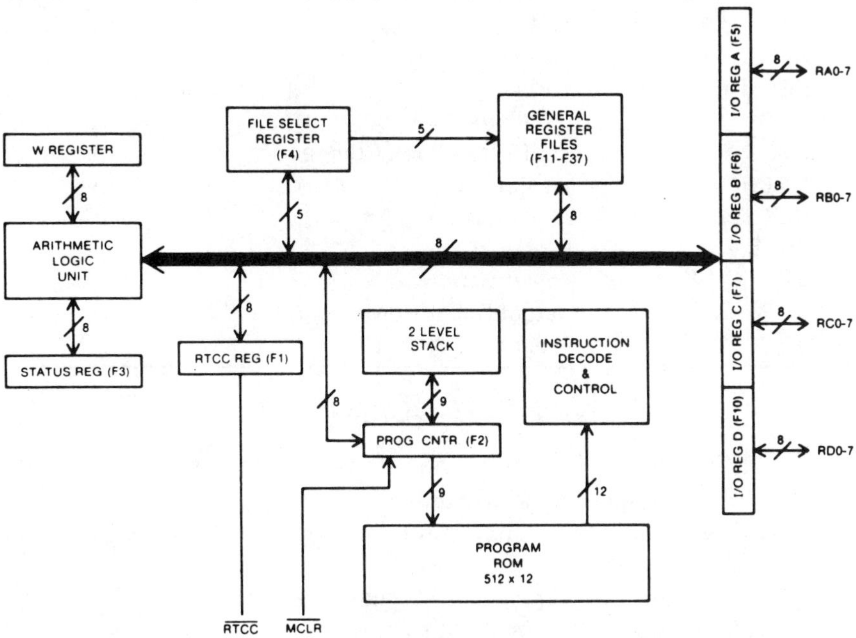

Courtesy of General Instrument Microelectronics.

Block Diagram—1650A, 8-Bit μC
Fig. 9-1

b) Observe the signal on pin 35. This signal is the clock output and is synchronized to the clock. This signal should be ¼ of the signal on pin 36.

For 90% Confidence Level:

In addition to the 75% confidence level tests, use a dual-trace oscilloscope to observe the following:

a) Monitor the clock signal on pin 35 on one trace, while observing the RA0 signal on pin 2 on the other.
b) Monitor the clock signal on pin 35 on one trace, while observing the RB0 signal on pin 11 on the other.

EXACT REPLACEMENT ESSENTIAL

PIC 1655A (General Instrument) 8-Bit Microcomputer

This device is essentially the same as PIC1650A, except for the type and number of the input/output lines and therefore the pin configuration.

PIN NAME	DESCRIPTION	TYPE
RA0-RA3	Port A	I
RB0-RB7	Port B	O
RC0-RC7	Port C	I/O
OSC	Oscillator	I
$\overline{RTCC}$	Real Time Clock Counter	I
$\overline{MCLR}$	Master Clear	I
CLK OUT	Clock Output	O
TEST	Test	I
V_{DD}	Power Supply	
V_{XX}	Output Buffer Power Supply	
V_{SS}	Ground	

IN-CIRCUIT QUICK-TESTS

For 75% Confidence Level:

1. Volt-ohmmeter Measurements:
   a) Make sure PC board ground has good connection to pins 4 and 5.
   b) Measure power supply voltage of 4.5 to 5.5 volts DC at pin 2 and measure 4.5 to 10.0 volts DC on pin 3.
2. Oscilloscope Measurements:
   a) Observe clock signals at pin 27. They should be square waves with a frequency of 0.2 to 1.0 MHz

PIN CONFIGURATION

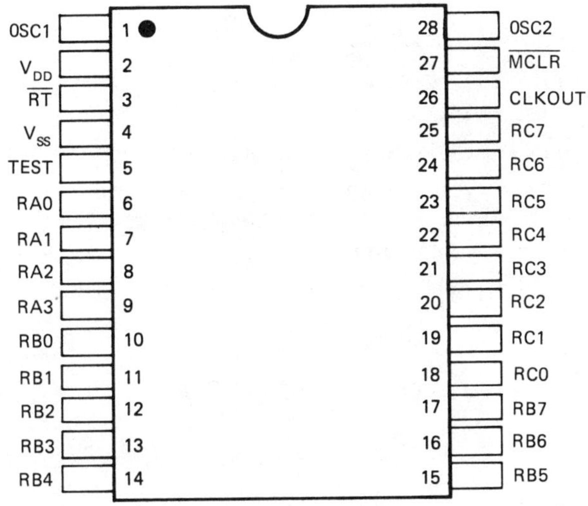

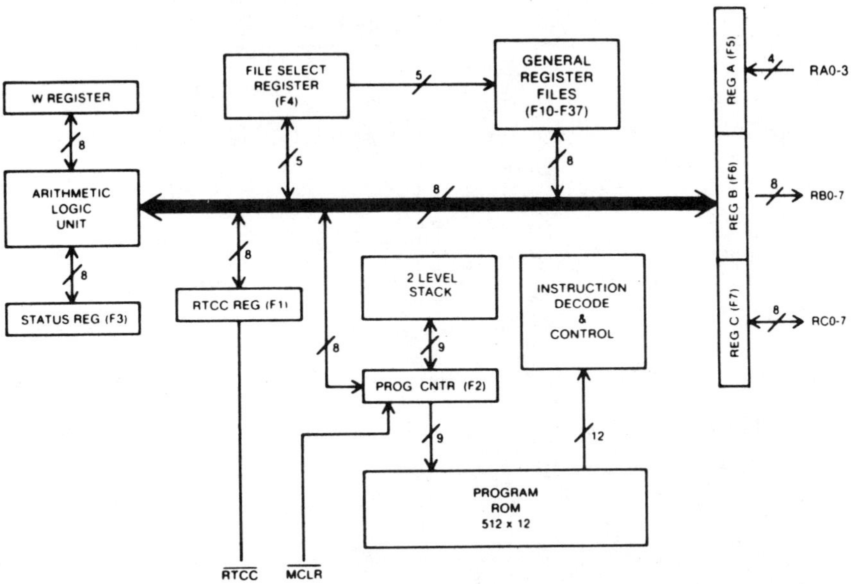

Courtesy of General Instrument Microelectronics.

Block Diagram — 1655A, a 8-Bit μC
Fig. 9-2

b) Observe the signal on pin 26. This signal is the clock output and is synchronized to the clock. This signal is ¼ of the signal on pin 27.

FOR 90% CONFIDENCE LEVEL:

In addition to the 75% confidence level tests, use a dual-trace oscilloscope to observe the following:

a) Monitor the clock signal on pin 26 on one trace, while observing the RA0 signal on pin 6 on the other.
b) Monitor the clock signal on pin 26 on one trace, while observing the RB0 signal on pin 10 on the other.

EXACT REPLACEMENT ESSENTIAL

PIC 1656 (GENERAL INSTRUMENT) 8-BIT MICROCOMPUTER

This device contains RAM, I/O, and a central processing unit as well as customer defined ROM. It is designed for real-time control applications requiring external and internal clock-driven interrupts. It has 20 I/O lines organized as two 8-bit registers and the four LSB's of a third register.

PIN NAME	DESCRIPTION	TYPE
RA0-RA3	Dedicated Input Lines	I
RB0-RB7	Dedicated Output Lines	O
RC0-RC7	User Programmable I/O Lines	I/O
OSC1, OSC2	Oscillator	I
$\overline{RT}$	Real-time	I
$\overline{MCLR}$	Master Clear	I
CLKOUT	Clock Output	O
TEST	Test	I
V_{DD}	Power Supply	
V_{SS}	Ground	

Special Features

- 32 8-bit RAM registers.
- 512 × 12-bit program ROM.
- Arithmetic logic unit.
- Real time clock counter.
- Event counter capability.
- Three-level stack.
- Vectored interrupt.

- Available in two temperature ranges: 0°C to 70°C, and −40°C to +85°C.
- Power supply operating range: 4.5 to 7.0V.

PIN CONFIGURATION

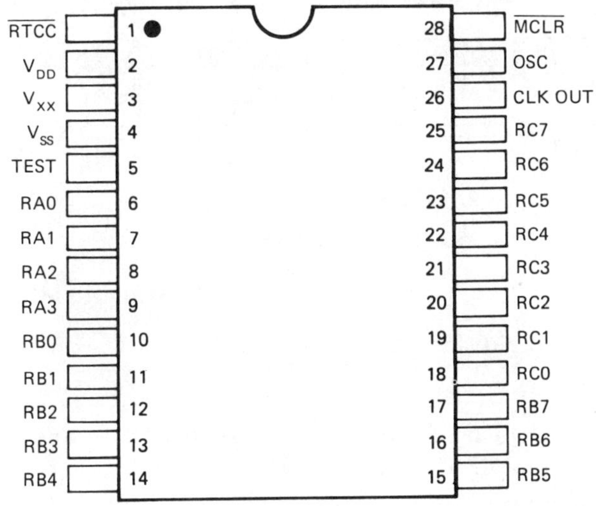

IN-CIRCUIT QUICK-TESTS

FOR 75% CONFIDENCE LEVEL:

1. Volt-ohmmeter Measurements:
   a) Make sure PC board ground has good connection to pins 4 and 5.
   b) Measure power supply voltage of 4.5 to 5.5 volts DC at pin 2.
2. Oscilloscope Measurements:
   a) Observe clock signals at pins 1 and 28. They should be square waves with a frequency of 0.8 to 4.0 MHz.
   b) Observe the signal on pin 26. This signal is the clock output and is synchronized to the clock. This signal is 1/16 of the signal on pins 1 and 28.

FOR 90% CONFIDENCE LEVEL:

In addition to the 75% confidence level tests, use a dual-trace oscilloscope to observe the following:

a) Monitor the clock signal on pin 26 on one trace, while observing the RB0 signal on pin 10 on the other.

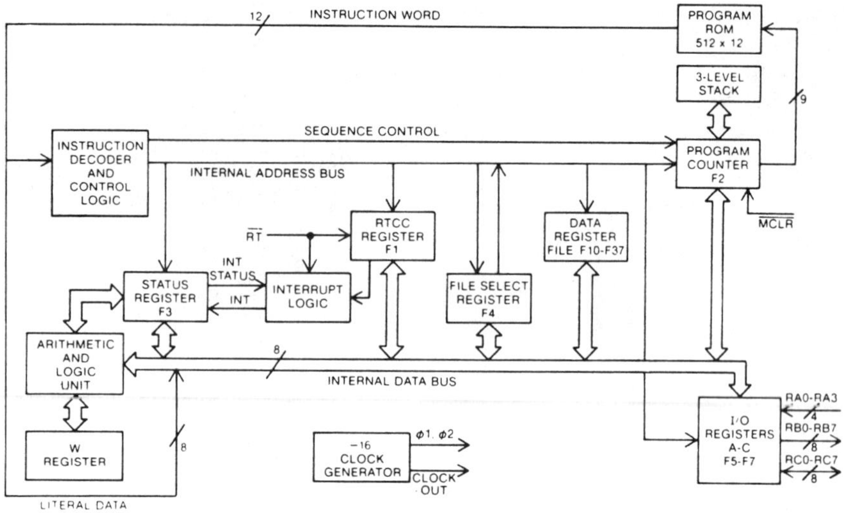

Courtesy of General Instrument Microelectronics.

Block Diagram—1656, 8-Bit μC
Fig. 9-3

b) Monitor the clock signal on pin 26 on one trace, while observing the RB7 signal on pin 17 on the other.

EXACT REPLACEMENT ESSENTIAL

PIC 1670 (General Instrument) 8-Bit Microcomputer

This device contains RAM, I/O, and a central processing unit as well as a customer defined ROM. It is fabricated using N-channel silicon gate technology. The on-chip oscillator provides the operating clock with either an external crystal or RC network. Inputs and outputs are TTL compatible, with open drain option available.

PIN NAME	DESCRIPTION	TYPE
RA0-RA7	Port A	I/O
RB0-RB7	Port B	I/O
RC0-RC7	Port C	I/O
RD0-RD7	Port D	I/O
OSC1, OSC2	Oscillator	I
$\overline{RT}$	Real Time	I
$\overline{MCLR}$	Master Clear	I

PIN NAME	DESCRIPTION	TYPE
TEST	Test	I
CLKOUT	Clock Output	O
V_{DD}	Power Supply	
V_{SS}	Ground	

Special Features

- 1024 × 13-bit Program ROM.
- 64 × 8-bit RAM (16 special purpose registers).
- Arithmetic logic unit.
- Six-level pushdown stack.
- 2μsec instruction execution time.
- Available in two temperature ranges: 0°C to 70°C, and −40°C to +85°C.
- Single power supply: 4.5 to 7.0V.

PIN CONFIGURATION

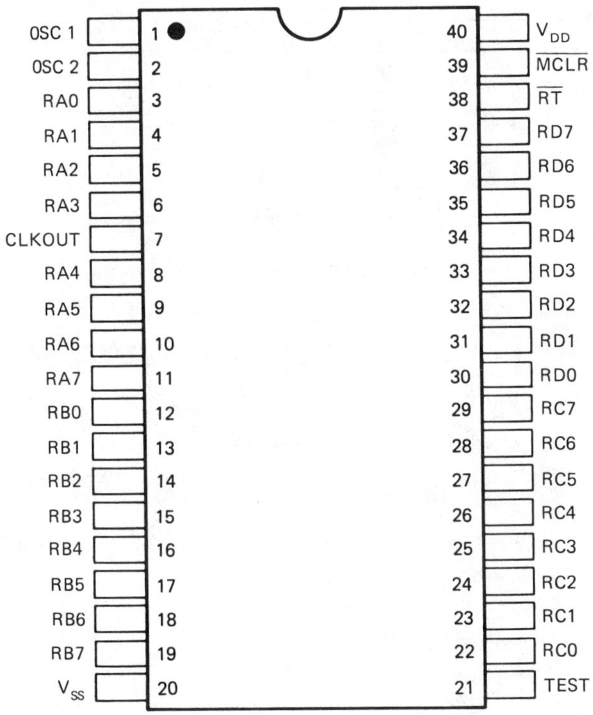

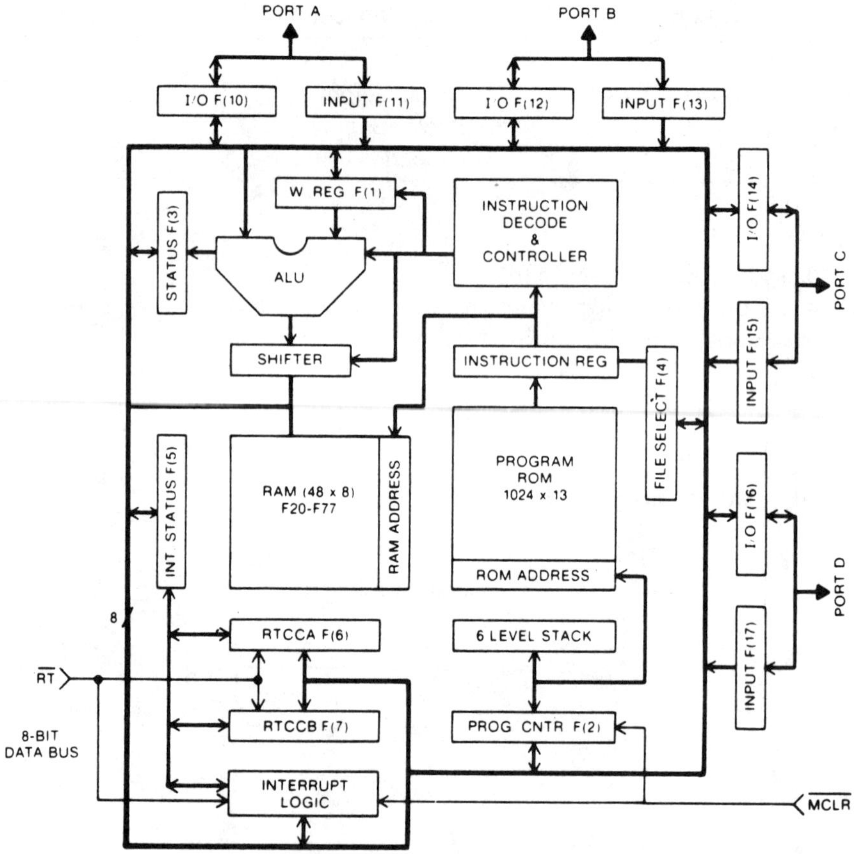

Courtesy of General Instrument Microelectronics.

Block Diagram — 1670, 8-Bit μC
Fig. 9-4

IN-CIRCUIT QUICK-TESTS

For 75% Confidence Level:

1. Volt-ohmmeter Measurements:

   a) Make sure PC board ground has good connection to pins 20 and 21.

   b) Measure power supply voltage of 4.5 to 5.5 volts DC at pin 40.

2. Oscilloscope Measurements:

   a) Observe clock signals at pins 1 and 2. They should be square waves with a frequency of 0.8 to 4.0 MHz.

   b) Observe the signal on pin 7. This signal is the clock output and is synchronized to the clock. This signal is 1/8 of the signal on pins 1 and 2.

For 90% Confidence Level:

In addition to the 75% confidence level tests, use a dual-trace oscilloscope to observe the following.

a) Monitor the clock signal on pin 7 on one trace, while observing the RA0 signal on pin 13 on the other.
b) Monitor the clock signal on pin 7 on one trace, while observing the RB0 signal on pin 12 on the other.

EXACT REPLACEMENT ESSENTIAL.

CDP 1804/CDP 1804C (RCA)

Microprocessor

This device is designed for use in a variety of general-purpose computing and control applications. It contains a 2048-byte, mask-programmable, ROM , 64 bytes of executable RAM, and an 8-bit presettable down-counter with a conditional or 32 prescaler, in addition to the standard architecture of the CDP 1802 microprocessor. Upwards software compatibility is maintained since the CDP 1804 contains the entire instruction set of the CDP 1802 plus 22 added instructions.

The CDP 1804 and CDP 1804C are functionally identical. They differ in that the CDP 1804 has an operating voltage range of 4 to 10.5V and the CDP 1804C has an operating voltage range of 4 to 6.5V.

PIN NAME	DESCRIPTION	TYPE
BUS0-BUS7	Data Bus	I/O
N0-N2	I/O Commands Lines	O
EF1-EF4	Flags	I
INTERRUPT	Interrupt Request	I
DMA-IN	Direct Memory Access-in	I
DMA-OUT	Direct Memory Access-out	I
SC0, SC1	State Code Lines	O
TPA, TPB	Timing Pulses	O
MA0-MA7	Memory Address Lines	O
MWR	Memory Write	O
MRD	Memory Read	O
Q	Single Bit Output From CPU	O
CLOCK	Clock	I
XTAL	Crystal	O
WAIT	Wait	I
CLEAR	Clear	I

PIN NAME	DESCRIPTION	TYPE
$\overline{EMS}$	External Memory Selection	O
V_{DD}	Power Supply	
V_{SS}	Ground	

Special Features

- Typical instruction fetch-execute time of 2.5 or 3.75μSec. at $V_{DD} = 5V$.
- Static CMOS circuitry—no minimum clock frequency.
- Single voltage supply.
- High noise immunity; wide operating voltage range.
- Low power.
- Operating temperature range −55°C to +125°C (CDP 1804D, and CDP 1804CD). −40°C to +85 °C (CDP 1804E, and CDP 1804CE).
- 8-bit parallel organization.
- Pin-out same as CDP 1802 except for V_{CC} terminal.
- Contains ROM, RAM, I/O, and timer/counter.

PIN CONFIGURATION

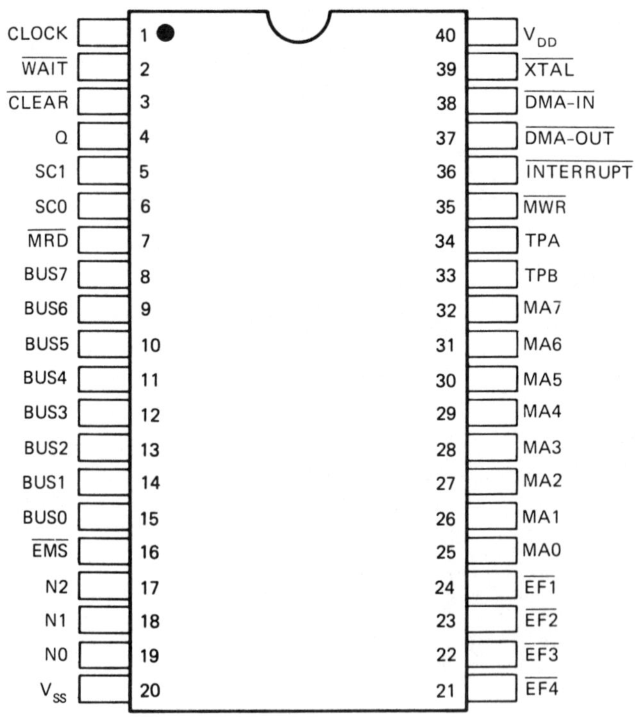

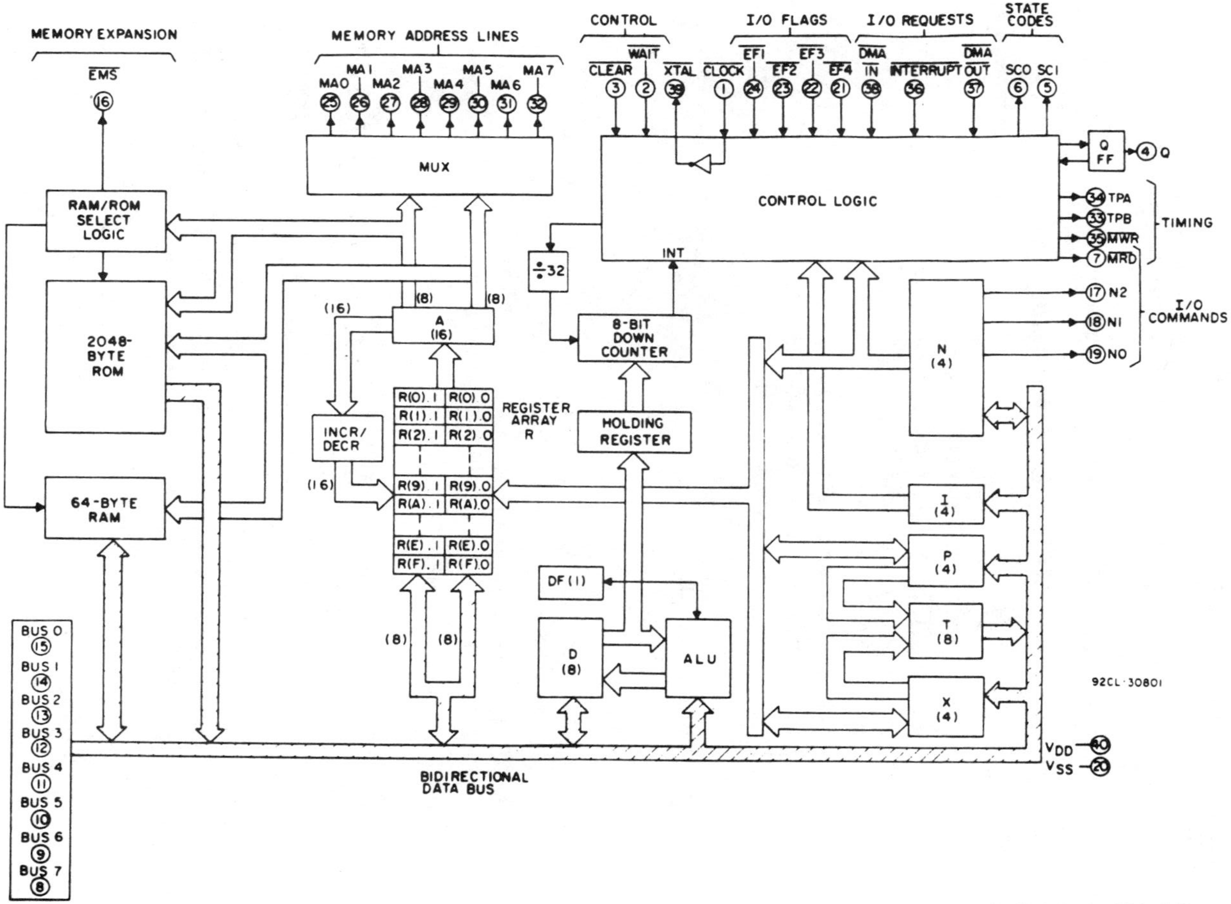

Courtesy RCA Solid State Division.

Block Diagram—1804, 1804C, 8-Bit μC
Fig. 9-5

- Expandable in memory and I/O.
- On-chip oscillator controlled by crystal or RC network; single phase clock.
- Upwards software compatible with CDP 1802.
- 113 instructions.
- 16 × 16 matrix of registers for use as multiple program counters, data pointers or data registers.
- Test mode allows prototyping with external memory.

IN-CIRCUIT QUICK-TESTS

FOR 75% CONFIDENCE LEVEL:

1. Volt-ohmmeter Measurements:
   a) Make sure PC board ground has good connection to pin 20.
   b) Measure power supply voltage of 4.5 to 5.5 volts DC at pin 40.
2. Oscilloscope Measurements:
   a) Observe clock signals at pins 1 and 39. They should be square waves with a frequency of 0.0 to 4.0 MHz.
   b) Observe the signal on pin 35. This signal is the WRITE output and is synchronized to the clock.

FOR 90% CONFIDENCE LEVEL:

In addition to the 75% confidence level tests, use a dual-trace oscilloscope to observe the following:

a) Monitor the clock signal on pins 1 or 39 on one trace, while observing the MRD signal on pin 7 on the other.
b) Monitor the clock signal on pins 1 or 39 on one trace, while observing the SC0 signal on pin 6 on the other.

EXACT REPLACEMENT ESSENTIAL.

MC 3870 (MOTOROLA) 8-BIT MICROCOMPUTER[1]

This device uses ion implanted, N-channel silicon gate technology for single voltage, low power operations. It is software compatible with the F8 family and is designed for control and logic applications.

PIN NAME	DESCRIPTION	TYPE
$\overline{\text{P0-0}}$-$\overline{\text{P0-7}}$	Port 0	I/O
$\overline{\text{P1-0}}$-$\overline{\text{P1-7}}$	Port 1	I/O

[1]Note: The same microcomputer is manufactured by: FAIRCHILD—F 3870. FAIRCHILD also makes F 3878 which is identical to the F 3870 except for the ROM size which is 4K bytes in F 3878.

PIN NAME	DESCRIPTION	TYPE
$\overline{\text{P4-0}}$–$\overline{\text{P4-7}}$	Port 4	I/O
$\overline{\text{P5-0}}$–$\overline{\text{P5-7}}$	Port 5	I/O
$\overline{\text{STROBE}}$	Ready Strobe	I
$\overline{\text{RESET}}$	Reset	I
EXT INT	External Interrupt	I
XTL1, XTL2	Crystal	I
TEST	Test	I
V_{CC}	Power Supply	
GND	Ground	

Special Features

- 2048 bytes mask programmable ROM.
- 64 bytes scratchpad RAM.
- 32 bits (four ports) TTL compatible I/O.
- Programmable binary timer: interval timer mode; pulse width measurement mode; event counter mode.

PIN CONFIGURATION

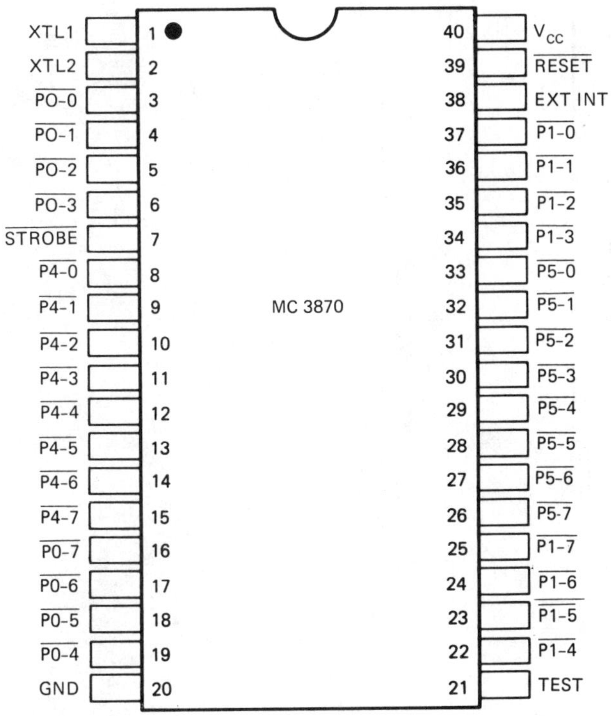

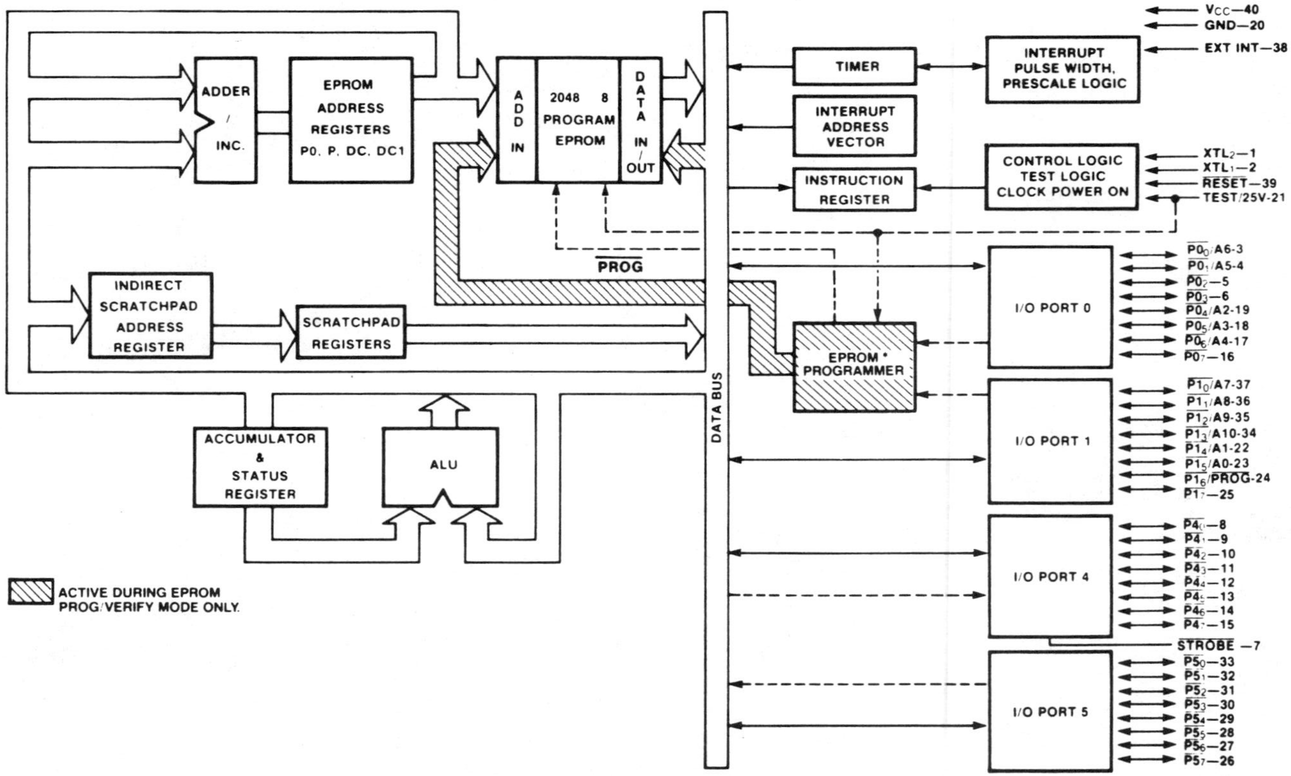

Reprinted by permission of Fairchild Camera and Instrument Corp.

Block Diagram—3870, 38E70, 8-Bit μC
Fig. 9-6

- External interrupt.
- Crystal, LC, RC, external, or internal time base.
- Low Power 275mW typical.
- +5V ± 10% power supply.

IN-CIRCUIT QUICK-TESTS

FOR 75% CONFIDENCE LEVEL:

1. Volt-ohmmeter Measurements:
   a) Make sure PC board has good connnection to pin 20.
   b) Measure power supply voltage or 4.5 to 5.5 volts DC at pin 44.
2. Oscilloscope Measurements:
   a) Observer clock signals at pins 1 and 2. They should be square waves with a frequency of 0.4 to 4.0 MHz.
   b) Observe the signal on pin 7. This signal is the strobe output and is synchronized to the clock.

FOR 90% CONFIDENCE LEVEL:

In addition to the 75% confidence level tests, use a dual-trace oscilloscope to observe the following:

a) Monitor the clock signal on pins 1 or 2 on one trace, while observing the P00 signal on pin 3 on the other.
b) Monitor the clock signal on pins 1 or 2 one trace, while observing the PI0 signal on pin 37 on the other.

EXACT REPLACEMENT ESSENTIAL.

F 3872/F 3876 (FAIRCHILD) 8-Bit MICROCOMPUTER[2]

These devices are two of the expanded memory versions of the F 3870 single chip microcomputer. They are identical to the F 3870 in the following areas: instruction set, architecture, AC and DC characteristics, and pin-out. The differences are in the memory expansion and the appropriate memory address registers.

---

[2]NOTE: The same microprocessor is manufactured by ROCKWELL with the following equivalences:

ROCKWELL	COMMODORE
R6500/1P	MPS6500/1
R6500/1AP	MPS6500/1A
R6500/1C	MCS6500/1
R6500/1AC	MCS6500/1A

(P = plastic; C = ceramic).

PIN NAME	DESCRIPTION	TYPE
$\overline{\text{P02}}$-$\overline{\text{P07}}$	Port 0 (bits 2-7)	I/O
$\overline{\text{P10}}$-$\overline{\text{P17}}$	Port 1	I/O
$\overline{\text{P40}}$-$\overline{\text{P47}}$	Port 4	I/O
$\overline{\text{P50}}$-$\overline{\text{P57}}$	Port 5	I/O
$\overline{\text{STROBE}}$	Ready Strobe	O
EXT INT	External Interrupt	I
$\overline{\text{RESET/RAM PRT}}$	External Reset/RAM Protect	I
TEST	Test Line	I
XTL1, XTL2	Crystal	I
$\overline{\text{P01}}/V_{SB}$	Port 0 bit 1/Standby Power Supply	I/O or I
$\overline{\text{P00}}/V_{BB}$	Port 0 bit 0/Substrate Decoupling	I/O or I
V_{CC}	Power Supply	
GND	Ground	

Special Features

- F 3872 has 4032-Byte mask programmable ROM.
- F 3876 has 2048-Byte mask programmable ROM.

PIN CONFIGURATION

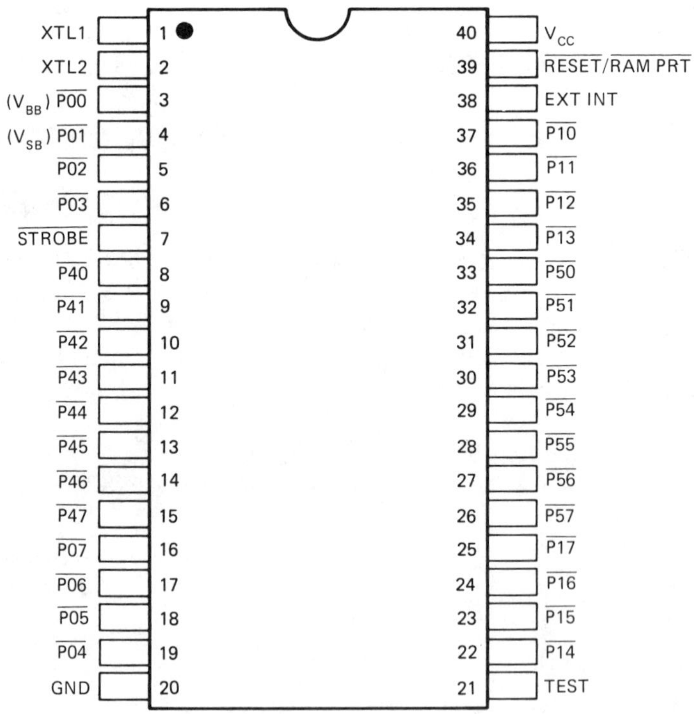

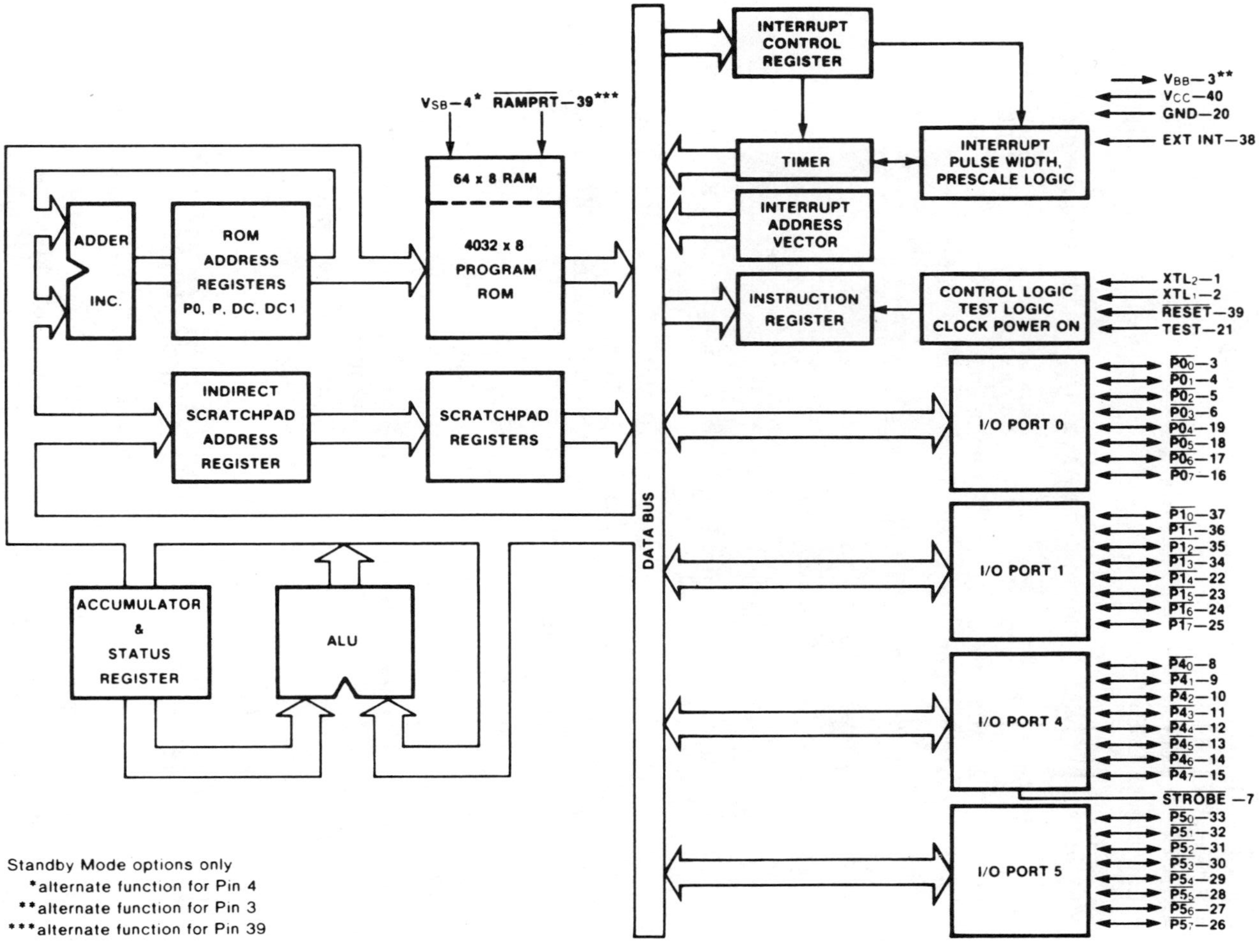

Reprinted by permission of Fairchild Camera and Instrument Corp.

Block Diagram—3872, 3876, 8-Bit μC
Fig. 9-7

- 64-byte scratchpad RAM.
- 32 bits (four ports) TTL compatible I/O.
- Programmable binary timer with an interval timer mode, a pulse width measurement mode, and an event counter mode.
- External interrupt.
- Crystal, LC, RC or External Time Base.
- Low power (285 mW typical).
- Single +5 ± 10% Power supply.
- 64 additional bytes of executable RAM addressable by program or data counter.
- Standby option for executable RAM including low standby power, (8.2mW, 3.2V min. standby supply voltage).
- No external components required to trickle charge battery.

IN-CIRCUIT QUICK-TESTS

For 75% Confidence Level:

1. Volt-ohmmeter Measurements:

   1) Make sure PC board ground has good connection to pins 20 and 21.

   b) Measure power supply voltage of 4.5 to 5.5 volts DC at pin 40.

2. Oscilloscope Measurements:

   a) Observe clock signals at pins 1 and 2. They should be square waves with a frequency of 1.0 to 4.0 MHz.

   b) Observe the signal on pin 7. This signal is the STROBE output and is synchronized to the clock.

For 90% Confidence Level

In addition to the 75% confidence level tests, use a dual-trace oscilloscope to observe the following:

a) Monitor the clock signal on pins 1 or 2 on one trace, while observing the PO2 signal on pin 5 on the other.

b) Monitor the clock signal on pins 1 or 2 on one trace, while observing the P50 signal on pin 33 on the other.

EXACT REPLACEMENT ESSENTIAL.

6500/1 (Commodore Semiconductor Group) Microprocessor

This device is a completely self-contained microcomputer system. Included in the 6500/1 are 2048 bytes of mask-programmable ROM, 64 bytes of RAM, 32 I/O lines, a 16-bit timer/counter and an on-chip clock oscillator. The internal processor architecture is identical to the 6502 to provide software compatibility.

PIN NAME	DESCRIPTION	TYPE
PA0–PA7	Port A	I/O
PB0–PB7	Port B	I/O
PC0–PC7	Port C	I/O
PD0–PD7	Port D	I/O
XTL 1	Crystal, Clock or RC Network	I
XTL 0	Crystal or RC Network	O
$\overline{RES}$	Reset	I
$\overline{NMI}$	Non-maskable Interrupt	I
CNTR	Counter	I/O
V_{CC}	Power Supply	
V_{RR}	Standby Power Supply	
V_{SS}	Ground	

Special Features

- Containing the 6502 CPU, it has software upward/downward compatibility.

PIN CONFIGURATION

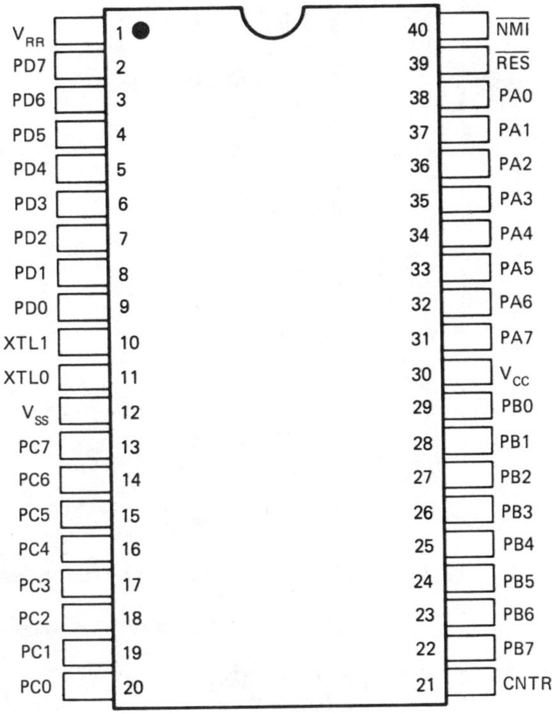

- Decimal or binary arithmetic modes.
- 13 addressing modes.
- True direct and indirect indexing.
- Memory addressable I/O.
- 2048 × 8 mask-programmable ROM.
- 64 × 8 static RAM.
- 32 bidirectional TTL compatible I/O lines (4 ports).
- One bidirectional TTL compatible counter I/O line.
- 16-bit programmable counter/latch with four modes: Interval Timer, Pulse Generator, Event Counter, Pulse Width Measurement.
- Five Interrupts: Reset, Non-maskable, Two external edge sensitive, Counter.
- 1 or 3 frequency references: Crystal, Clock, RC (resistor only).
- 4MHz maximum crystal or clock external frequency.

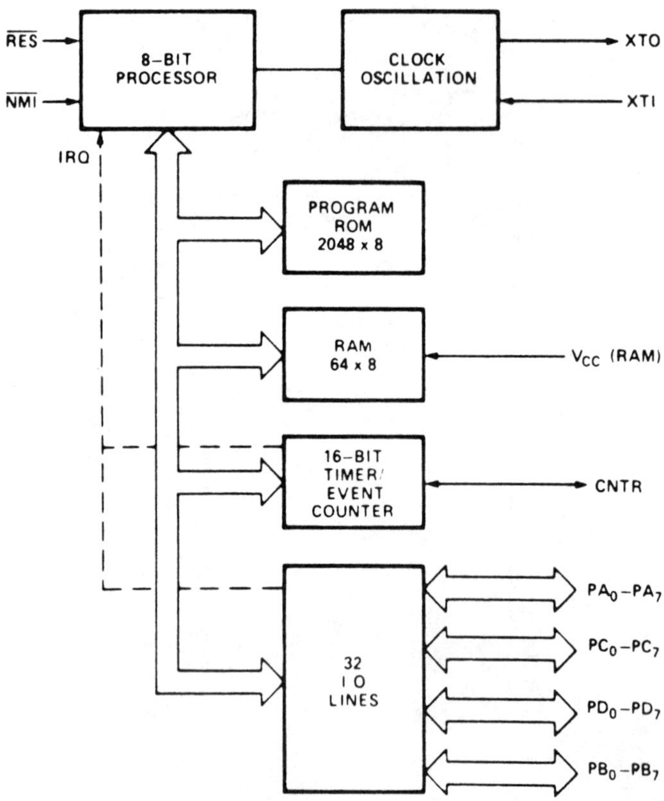

Courtesy of Commodore Business Machines, Inc.

Block Diagram—6500/1, 8-bit μC
Fig. 9-8

- 1MHz (6500/1) or 2MHz (6500/1A) internal clock.
- 1.0 μsec. minimum instruction execution time.
- Single +5V power supply.
- 500 mW operating power.
- Separate power pin for RAM.

IN-CIRCUIT QUICK-TESTS

For 75% Confidence Level:

1. Volt-ohmmeter Measurements:
   a) Make sure PC board ground has good connection to pin 12.
   b) Measure power supply voltage of 4.75 to 5.25 volts DC at pin 30.
2. Oscilloscope Measurements:
   a) Observe clock signals at pins 10 and 11. They should be square waves with a frequency of 2.0 to 4.0 MHz.
   b) Observe the signal on pin 9. This signal is the PORT D, O, output and is synchronized to the clock.

For 90% Confidence Level:

In addition to the 75% confindence level tests, use a dual-trace oscilloscope to observe the following:

a) Monitor the clock signal on pins 10 or 11 on one trace, while observing the PA0 signal on pin 38 on the other.
b) Monitor the clock signal on pins 10 or 11 on one trace, while observing the PB0 signal on pin 29 on the other.

EXACT REPLACEMENT ESSENTIAL

MC 6801/MC 6803/MC 6803NR (Motorola) Microprocessor[3]

This device is a member of the M6800 family and includes an upgraded M6800 microprocessor unit (MPU) with upward source and object-code compatibility. The device can function as a monolithic microcomputer or

---

[3a]Note: The MC 68701 is essentially the same as the MC 6801. The difference is that the MC 68701 has 2048 bytes of UV erasable, user programmable ROM (EPROM). The pin assignment differs at pin 6 which is $\overline{\text{RESET}}/V_{PP}$-Reset/Power supply needed for EPROM programming.
MC 68701—1.0MHz; MC 68701—1.25 MHz
MC68A701—1.5MHz; MC68B701—2.0 MHz

[3b]Note: The same microcomputer is manufactured by AMI—S 6801. Hitachi—HD6801 SO.

8-Bit μC

can be expanded to a 64K byte address space. On-chip resources include 2048 bytes of ROM, 128 bytes of RAM, a serial communications interface (SCI), parallel I/O, and a three function programmable timer.

The MC 6803 can be considered as an MC 6801 operating in modes (2) or (3) (i.e. MULTIPLEXED/RAM and MULTIPLEXED/RAM & ROM).

The MC 6803NR is comparable to MC 6801 operating in mode (3) (i.e. MULTIPLEXED/RAM & ROM).

PIN NAME	DESCRIPTION	TYPE
XTAL 1, EXTAL 2	Crystal or TTL Compatible Clock	I
$\overline{\text{RESET}}$	Reset	I
E	Enable	O
$\overline{\text{NMI}}$	Non-Maskable Interrupt	I
$\overline{\text{IRQ1}}$	Maskable Interrupt Request 1	I
SC1	Strobe Control 1	I
SC2	Strobe Control 2	O
P10-P17	Port 1	I/O
P20-P24	Port 2	I/O
P30-P37	Port 3	I/O
P40-P47	Port 4	I/O
V_{CC} STANDBY	Standby Power Supply	
V_{CC}	Power Supply	
V_{SS}	Ground	

Special Features

- TTL compatible.
- 8 × 8 multiply instruction.
- 64 bytes of RAM retainable during power-down (MC6801, MC6803).
- 29 parallel I/O and two handshake control lines.
- Internal clock generator with divide-by-four output.

IN-CIRCUIT QUICK-TESTS

FOR 75% CONFIDENCE LEVEL:

1. Volt-ohmmeter Measurements:
   a) Make sure PC board ground has good connection to pin 1.
   b) Measure power supply voltage of 4.75 to 5.25 volts DC at pin 7.
2. Oscilloscope Measurements:
   1) Observe clock signals at pins 2 and 3. They should be square waves with a frequency of 0.1 to 4.0 MHz.
   b) Observe the signal on pin 40. This signal is the ENABLE

PIN CONFIGURATION

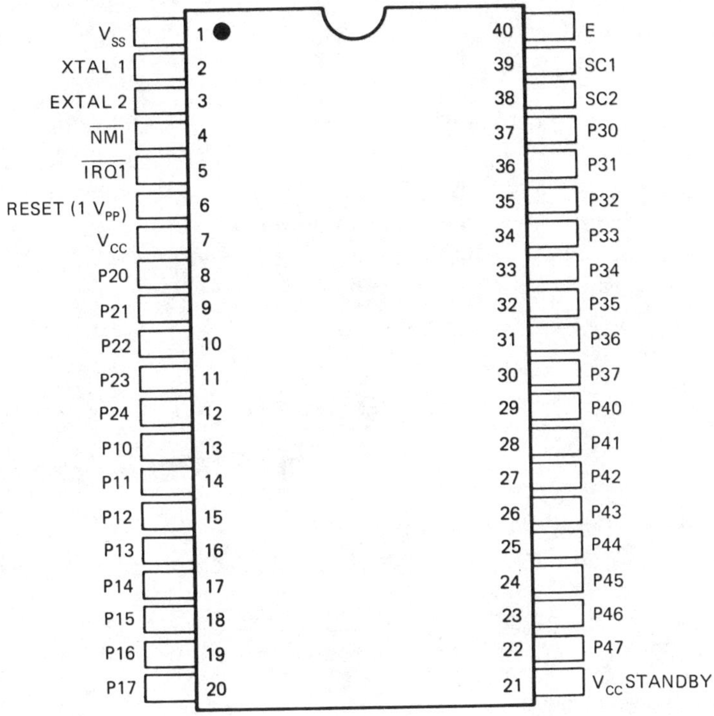

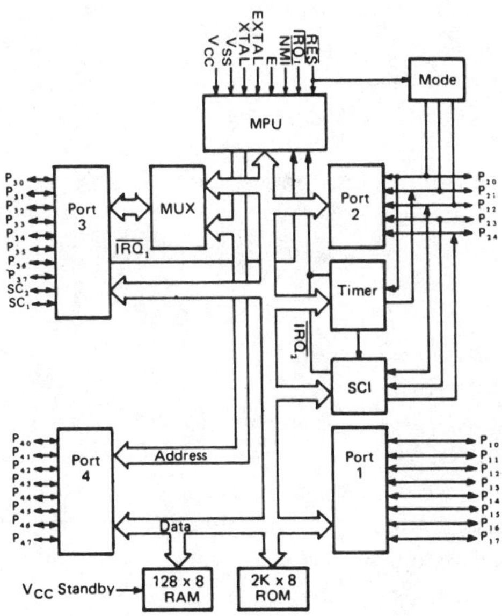

Courtesy Hitachi America, Ltd.

Block Diagram—6801/6803, 8-Bit μC
Fig. 9-9

output and is synchronized to the clock. Its frequency is ¼ of that on pins 2 and 3.

FOR 90% CONFIDENCE LEVEL:

In addition to the 75% confidence level tests, use a dual-trace oscilloscope to observe the following:

a) Monitor the ENABLE signal on pin 40 on one trace, while observing the SC2 signal on pin 38 on the other.
b) Monitor the ENABLE signal on pin 40 on one trace, while observing the SC1 signal on pin 39 on the other.

EXACT REPLACEMENT ESSENTIAL.

M 6805 FAMILY (MOTOROLA) OF MICROCOMPUTERS.[4]

- *M* 6805—A family of microcomputers.
- *MC* 6805 *P2*—A part number; A particular M6805 family version.
- MC 68705 P3—EPROM version.
- MC *146*805 E2—A CMOS M6805 family member.
- MC 6805 P2*L 1*—An evaluation program stored in ROM; a package type.

Hardware Features

- 8-bit architecture.
- Memory mapped I/O.
- On-chip clock generator.
- Zero-crossing detection (see note 4).
- Self-check mode.
- Complete development system support on EXORciser (see note 4).
- Single Power Supply: −0.3V to +7V for MC6805P2/P4/R2/T2/U2; MC68705R3/P3/U3, −0.3V to +8V for MC146805E2/F2/G2.

Software Features

- Byte efficient instruction set.
- True bit manipulation.
- Bit test and branch instructions (see note 4).
- Versatile interrupt handling.
- Versatile index register (see note 4).
- Powerful indexed addressing for tables (see note 4).
- Full set of conditional branches (see note 4).
- Memory usable as registers/flags (see note 4).

[4]Note: Not applicable for MC146805E2/F2/G2.

- Single instruction memory examine/change.
- 10 addressing modes.
- All addressing modes apply to ROM (EPROM), RAM and I/O.

User Selectable Options (where applicable)

- Internal 8-bit timer with selectable clock source (external timer input or internal machine clock).
- Timer prescaler option (7 Bits 2^N).
- 8 bidirectional I/O lines with TTL or TTL/CMOS interface option.
- 4 vectored interrupts: timer, software, and two external.

MC 146805E2

Special Features

- CMOS member of the M6805 family.
- 112 bytes of on-chip RAM.
- Capable of addressing up to 8K bytes of external memory.
- Internal 8-bit timer with software programmable 7-bit prescaler.
- External timer input.
- Full external and timer interrupts.
- Multiplexed address/data bus.
- Master reset and power-on reset.
- Chip-carrier also available.
- Typical full speed operating power of 35mW @ 5V.
- Typical WAIT mode power of 5mW.
- Typical STOP mode power of 25μW.
- Software features similar to the M6800 family's.

PIN NAME	DESCRIPTION	TYPE
PA0-PA7	Port A	I/O
PB0-PB7	Port B	I/O
A8-A12	High Order Address Lines	O
B0-B7	Address/Data Bus	I/O
$\overline{IRQ}$	Maskable Interrupt Request	I
$\overline{RESET}$	Reset	I
TIMER	Timer	I
AS	Address Strobe	O
DS	Data Strobe	O
R/$\overline{W}$	Read/Write	O
OSC1, OSC2	Oscillator	I
LI	Load Instruction	O
V_{DD}	Power supply	
V_{SS}	Ground	

8-Bit μC

Pin Configuration

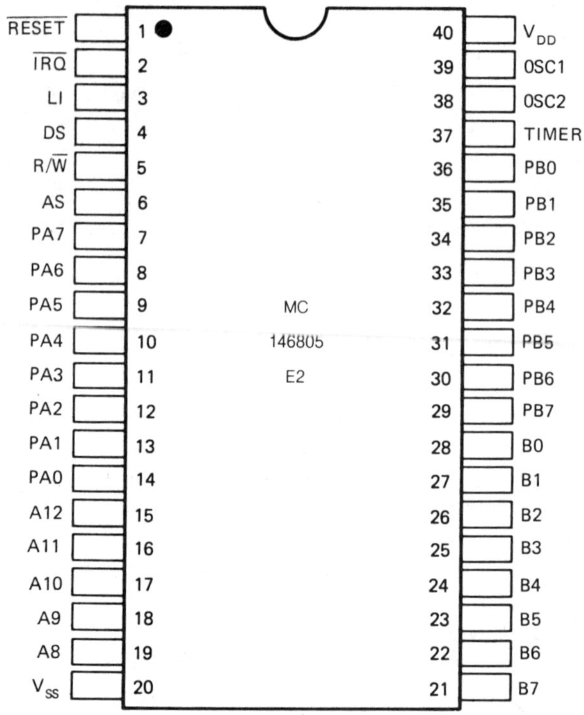

IN-CIRCUIT QUICK-TESTS

For 75% Confidence Level:

1. Volt-ohmmeter Measurements:
   a) Make sure PC board ground has good connection to pin 20.
   b) Measure power supply voltage of 3.0 to 6.0 volts DC at pin 40.
2. Oscilloscope Measurements:
   1) Observe clock signals at pins 38 and 39. They should be square waves with a frequency of 0.03 to 1.0 MHz.
   b) Observe the signal on pin 6. This signal is the ADDRESS STROBE output and is synchronized to the clock.

For 90% Confidence Level:

In addition to the 75% confidence level tests, use a dual-trace oscilloscope to observe the following:

a) Monitor the clock signal on pins 38 or 39 on one trace, while observing the DS signal on pin 4 on the other.

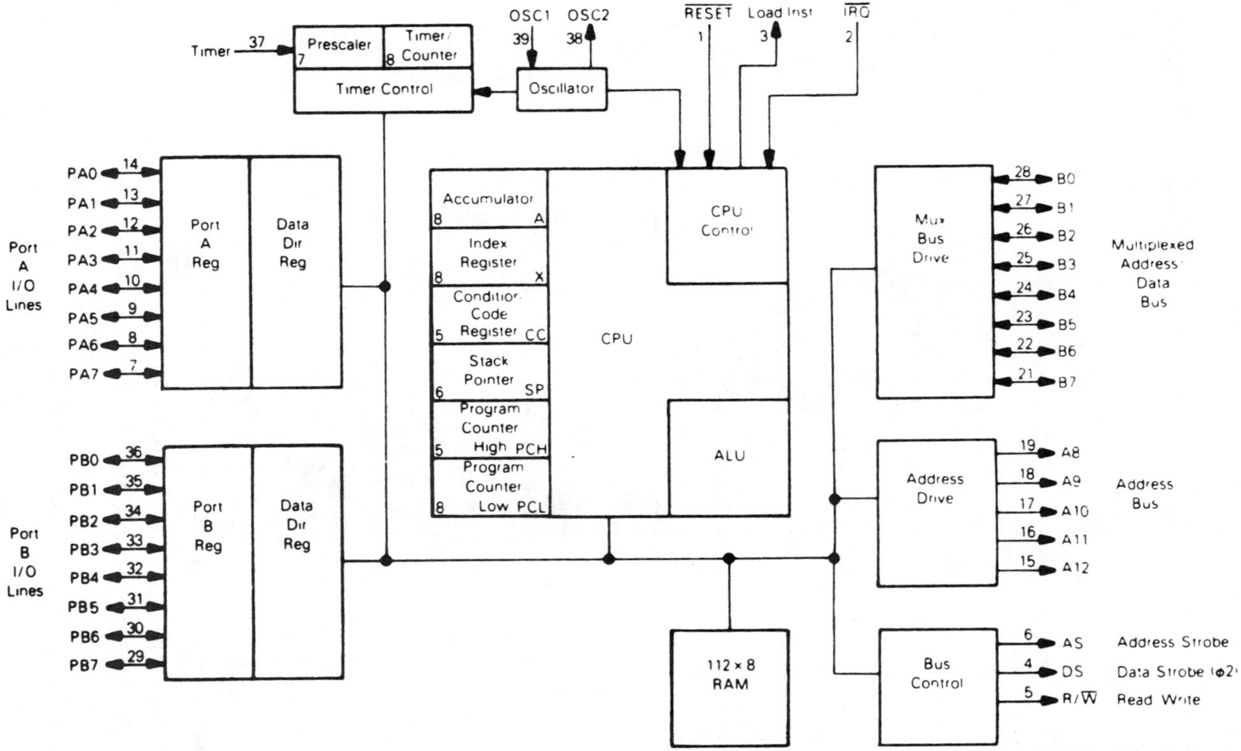

Courtesy Motorola, Inc.

Block Diagram—6805E2, 8-Bit μC
Fig. 9-10

b) Monitor the clock signal on pins 38 or 39 on one trace, while observing the R/W signal on pin 5 on the other.

EXACT REPLACEMENT ESSENTIAL.

MC 146805F2

Special Features

- CMOS member of the M6805 family.
- 1080 bytes of mask programmed user ROM.
- 64 bytes of on-chip RAM.
- 16 bidirectional I/O lines.
- Four input lines.
- Internal 8-bit timer with software programmable 7-bit prescaler.
- Full external and timer interrupts.
- Master reset and power-on reset.
- Chip carrier also available.
- Typical full speed operating power of 20mW.
- Standby power modes to less than 1mW.
- Software features similar to the M6800 family's.

PIN NAME	DESCRIPTION	TYPE
PA0-PA7	Port A	I/O
PB0-PB7	Port B	I/O
PC0-PC3	Port C	I
$\overline{\text{IRQ}}$	Maskable Interrupt Request	I
$\overline{\text{RESET}}$	Reset	I
TIMER	Timer	I
OSC1	Oscillator 1	I
OSC2	Oscillator 2	I
NUM	Non-User Mode	
V_{DD}	Power supply	
V_{SS}	Ground	

IN-CIRCUIT QUICK-TESTS

FOR 75% CONFIDENCE LEVEL:

1. Volt-ohmmeter Measurements:
   a) Make sure PC board ground has good connection to pin 14.
   b) Measure power supply voltage of 3.0 to 6.0 volts DC at pin 28.
2. Oscilloscope Measurements:
   a) Observe clock signals at pins 4 and 5. They should be square waves with a frequency of 0.03 to 1.0 MHz.
   b) Observe the signal on pin 22. This signal is the PBO output and is synchronized to the clock.

PIN CONFIGURATION

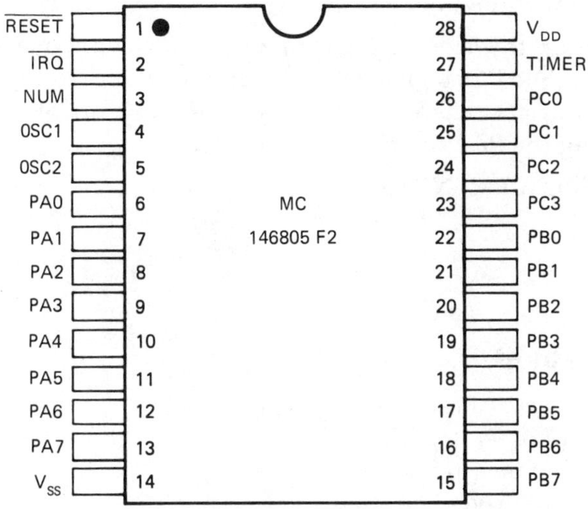

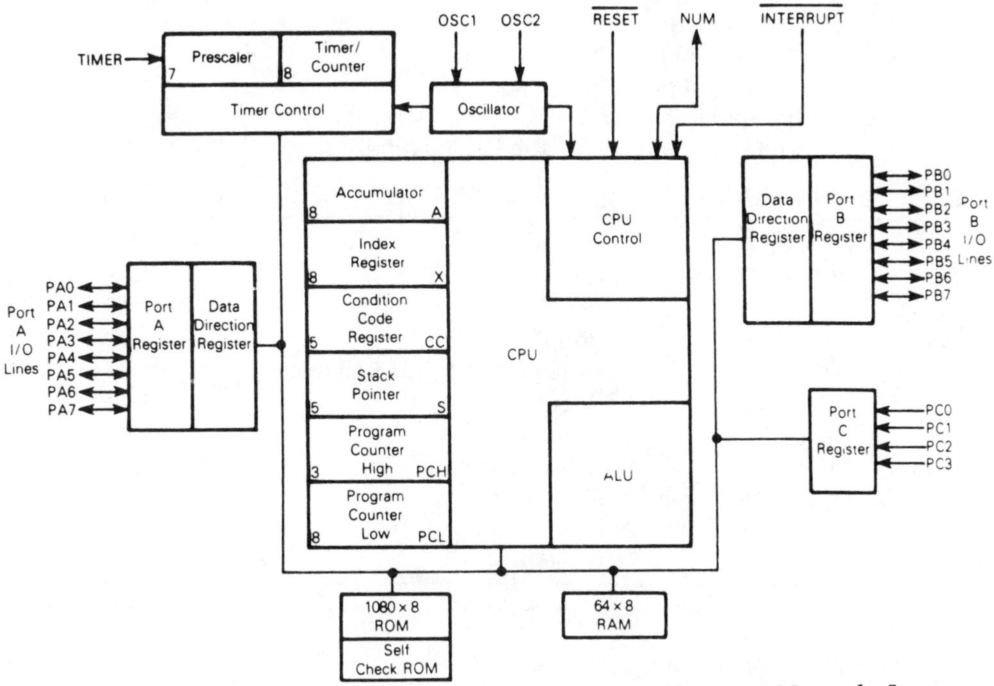

Courtesy Motorola, Inc.

Block Diagram—6805 F2, 8-Bit μC
Fig. 9-11

For 90% Confidence Level:

In addition to the 75% confidence level tests, use a dual-trace oscilloscope to observe the following:

a) Monitor the clock signal on pins 4 or 5 on one trace, while observing the PC0 signal on pin 26 on the other.
b) Monitor the clock signal on pins 4 or 5 on one trace, while observing the PA0 signal on pin 6 on the other.

EXACT REPLACEMENT ESSENTIAL.

MC 146805G2

Special Features

- CMOS member of the M6805 family.
- 112 bytes of on-chip RAM.
- 2106 bytes of on-chip ROM.
- High current drive.
- Internal 8-bit timer with software programmable 7-bit prescaler.
- External timer input.
- External and timer interrupts.
- Master reset and power-on reset.
- On-chip oscillator with RC or crystal mask options.
- Software features similar to the M6800 family's.

PIN NAME	DESCRIPTION	TYPE
PA0-PA7	Port A	I/O
PB0-PB7	Port B	I/O
PC0-PC7	Port C	I/O
PD0-PD7	Port D	I/O
$\overline{IRQ}$	Maskable Interrupt Request	I
$\overline{RESET}$	Reset	I
TIMER	Timer	I
NUM	Non-User Mode	
OSC1, OSC2	Oscillator	I
V_{DD}	Power Supply	
V_{SS}	Ground	

IN-CIRCUIT QUICK-TESTS

For 75% Confidence Level:

1. Volt-ohmmeter Measurements:
   a) Make sure PC board ground has good connection to pin 20.
   b) Measure power supply voltage of 3.0 to 6.0 volts DC at pin 40.

Pin Configuration

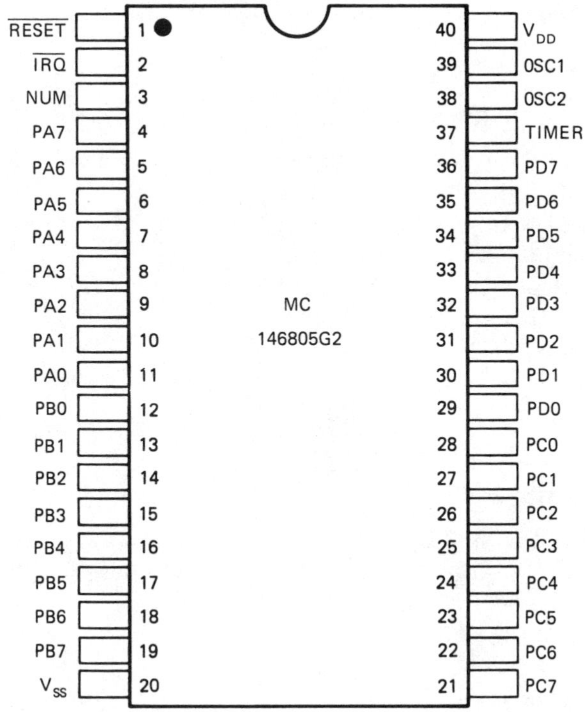

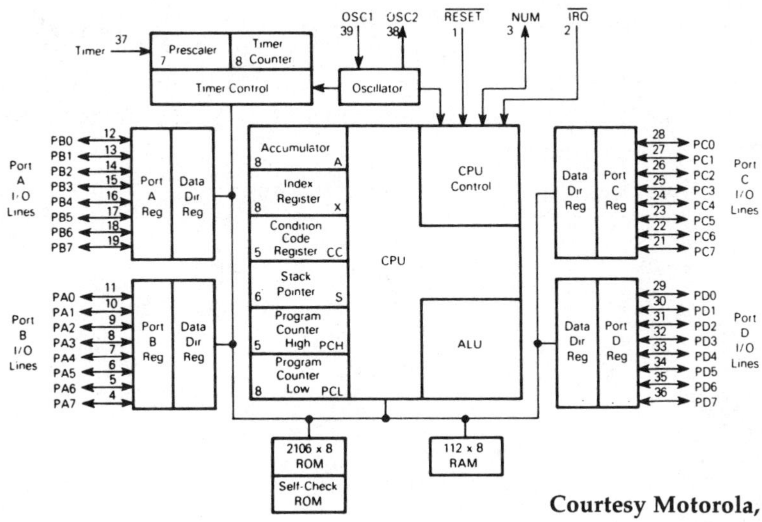

Courtesy Motorola, Inc.

Block Diagram—6805 G2, 8-Bit μC
Fig. 9-12

2. Oscilloscope Measurements:
   a) Observe clock signals at pins 38 and 39. They should be square waves with a frequency of 0.03 to 4.0 MHz.

b) Observe the signal on pin 11. This signal is the PA0 output and is synchronized to the clock.

For 90% Confidence Level:

In addition to the 75% confidence level tests, use a dual-trace oscilloscope to observe the following:
a) Monitor the clock signal on pins 38 or 39 on one trace, while observing the PB0 signal on pin 12 on the other.
b) Monitor the clock signal on pins 38 or 39 on one trace, while observing the PC0 signal on pin 28 on the other.
EXACT REPLACEMENT ESSENTIAL.

MC 6805P2, MC 6805P4[5]

Special Features

- Members of the M6805 family.
- 64 bytes of RAM (MC6805P2), and 112 bytes of standby RAM (MC6805P4).
- 1100 bytes of user ROM.
- 20 TTL/CMOS compatible bidirectional I/O lines (eight lines are LED compatible).
- User selectable options: Internal 8-bit timer with selectable clock source (external timer input or internal machine clock); timer prescaler option (7 Bits 2^N); eight 8 bidirectional I/O lines with TTL or TTL/CMOS interface option; crystal or low cost resistor oscillator option; low voltage inhibit option; four vectored interrupts—timer, software, and two external.

PIN NAME	DESCRIPTION	TYPE
PA0-PA7	Port A	I/O
PB0-PB7	Port B	I/O
PC0-PC3	Port C	I/O
$\overline{\text{INT}}$	Interrupt	I
XTAL, EXTAL	Crystal	I
$\overline{\text{TIMER}}$	Timer	I
$\overline{\text{RESET}}$	Reset	I
NUM	Non-User-Mode	

[5]Note: Pin 6 is NUM for MC6805P2 and V_{SB} for MC6805P4, and Pin 8 is PCO for MC6805P2 and PCO/NUM for MC6805P4.

V_{CC}	Power Supply
V_{SS}	Ground
V_{SB} (MC6805P4 only)	Standby Power Supply

PIN CONFIGURATION

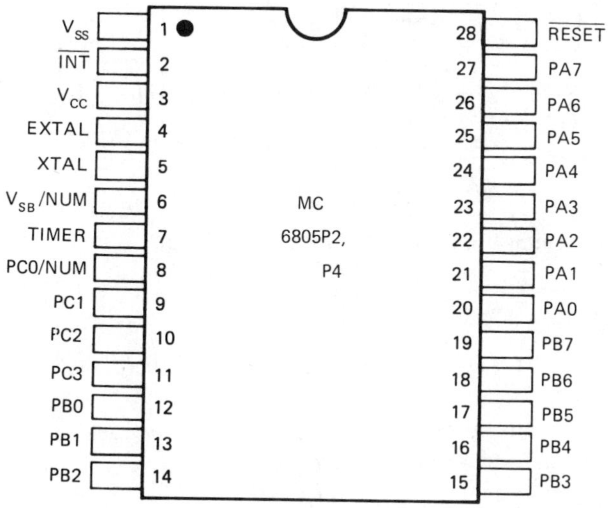

IN-CIRCUIT QUICK-TESTS

FOR 75% CONFIDENCE LEVEL:

1. Volt-ohmmeter Measurements:
   a) Make sure PC board ground has good connection to pin 1.
   b) Measure power supply voltage of 5.0 to 5.5 volts DC at pin 3.
2. Oscilloscope Measurements:
   1) Observe clock signals at pins 4 and 5. They should be square waves with a frequency of 0.4 to 4.2 MHz.
   b) Observe the signal on pin 20. This signal is the PA0 output and is synchronized to the clock.

FOR 90% CONFIDENCE LEVEL:

In addition to the 75% confidence level tests, use a dual-trace oscilloscope to observe the following:

a) Monitor the clock signal on pin 4 on one trace, while observing the PB0 signal on pin 12 on the other.

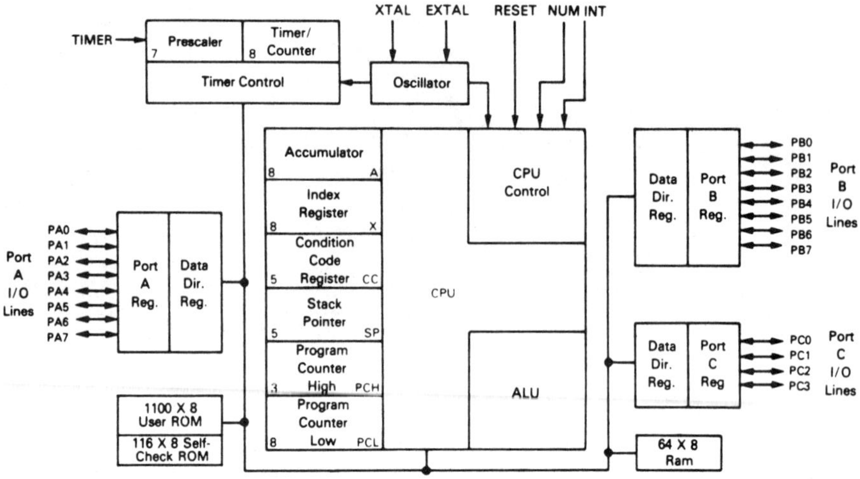

Courtesy Motorola, Inc.

Block Diagram—6805 P2/P4, 8-Bit μC
Fig. 9-13

b) Monitor the clock signal on pin 4 on one trace, while observing the PC0 signal on pin 8 on the other.

EXACT REPLACEMENT ESSENTIAL.

MC 6805R2[6]

Special Features

- Member of the M6805 family.
- 64 bytes of RAM.
- 2048 bytes of user ROM.
- 24 TTL/CMOS compatible bidirectional I/O lines (8 lines are LED compatible).
- Two to five digital input lines.
- A/D Converter: 8-bit conversion, monotonic; 1 to 4 multiplexed analog

[6]Note: The MC 6805U2 microprocessor is essentially the same as the MC 6805R2, the only difference being that port D of the MC 6805U2 is for digital input only. (The pin configuration differs at pin 19, 20, 21, 22, 23, and 24 because the voltages references V_{RH}, V_{RL} and the option AN3–AN0 do not exist).

inputs; ±½ LSB quantizing error; ±½ LSB all other errors; ±1 LSB total error (maximum); ratiometric conversion.

- Software features are identical to the M6800 family's.

PIN NAME	DESCRIPTION	TYPE
PA0–PA7	Port A	I/O
PB0–PB7	Port B	I/O
PC0–PC7	Port C	I/O
PD0/AN0–PD3/AN3, V_{RL}, V_{RH}, PD6/$\overline{\text{INT2}}$, PD7	Port D	I/O or I
$\overline{\text{INT}}$	Interrupt	I
$\overline{\text{RESET}}$	Reset	I
XTAL, EXTAL	Crystal	I
TIMER	Timer	I
NUM	Non-user-mode	
V_{CC}	Power Supply	
V_{SS}	Ground	

PIN CONFIGURATION

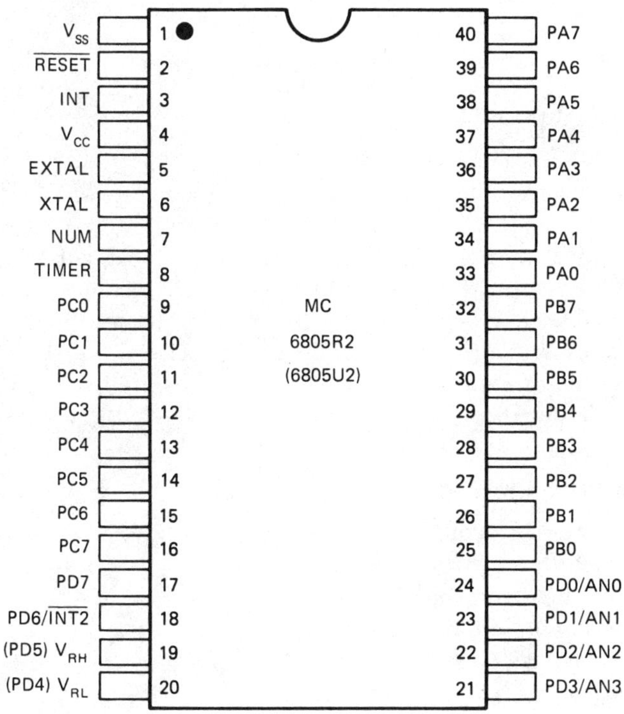

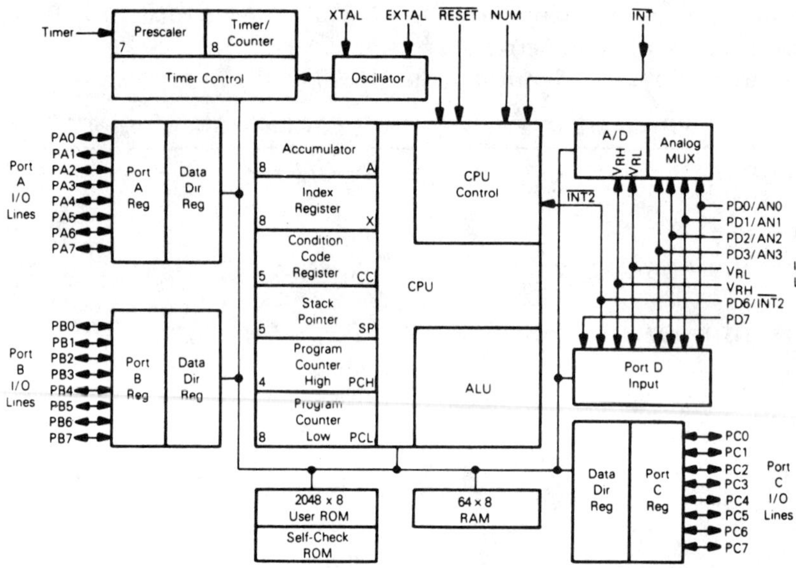

Courtesy Motorola, Inc.

Block Diagram—6805R2, 8-Bit μC
Fig. 9-14

IN-CIRCUIT QUICK-TESTS

For 75% Confidence Level:

1. Volt-ohmmeter Measurements:
   a) Make sure PC board ground has good connection to pin 1 and 7.
   b) Measure power supply voltage of 5.0 to 5.5 volts DC at pin 4.
2. Oscilloscope Measurements:
   a) Observe clock signals at pins 5 and 6. They should be square waves with a frequency of 0.4 to 4.2 MHz.
   b) Observe the signal on pin 33. This signal is the PA0 output and is synchronized to the clock.

For 90% Confidence Level:

In addition to the 75% confidence level tests, use a dual-trace oscilloscope to observe the following:

a) Monitor the clock signal on pin 5 on one trace, while observing the PB0 signal on pin 25 on the other.
b) Monitor the clock signal on pin 5 on one trace, while observing the PC0 signal on pin 9 on the other.

EXACT REPLACEMENT ESSENTIAL.

MC 6805T2

Special Features

- Member of the M6805 family.
- 65 bytes of RAM.
- 2508 bytes of user ROM.
- Timer start/stop and source select.
- 19 TTL/CMOS compatible bidirectional I/O Lines (eight lines are LED compatible).
- 14-bit binary variable divider.
- 10-stage mask-programmable reference divider.
- Three-state phase and frequency comparator.
- Suitable for TV frequency synthesizers.
- Software features similar to the M6800 Family's.

PIN NAME	DESCRIPTION	TYPE
PA0–PA7	Port A	I/O
PB0–PB7	Port B	I/O
PC0–PC2	Port C	I/O
$\overline{\text{INT}}$	Interrupt	I
XTAL, EXTAL	Crystal	I
f_{in}	High Frequency Digital Input	I
ØCOMP	Compared Frequency	O
$\overline{\text{RESET}}$	Reset	I
NUM	Non-user Mode	
V_{CC}	Power Supply	
V_{SS}	Ground	

IN-CIRCUIT QUICK-TESTS

FOR 75% CONFIDENCE LEVEL:

1. Volt-ohmmeter Measurements:
   a) Make sure PC board ground has good connection to pins 1 and 6.
   b) Measure power supply voltage of 5.0 to 5.5 volts DC at pin 3.
2. Oscilloscope Measurements:
   a) Observe clock signals at pins 4 and 5. They should be square waves with a frequency of 0.4 to 4.2 MHz.
   b) Observe the signal on pin 20. This signal is the PA0 output and is synchronized to the clock.

FOR 90% CONFIDENCE LEVEL:

In addition to the 75% confidence level tests, use a dual-trace oscilloscope to observe the following:

PIN CONFIGURATION

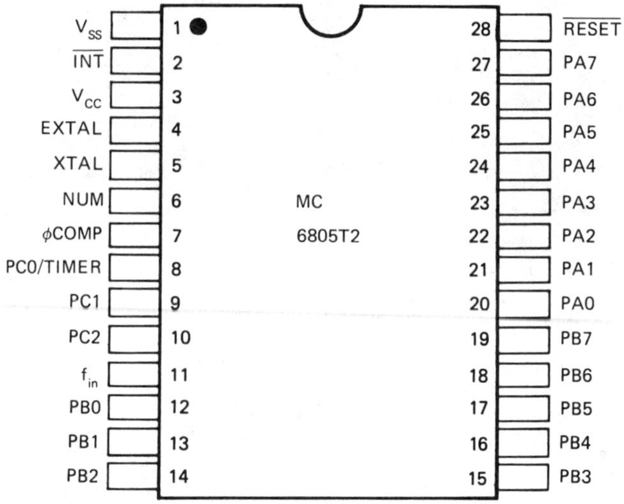

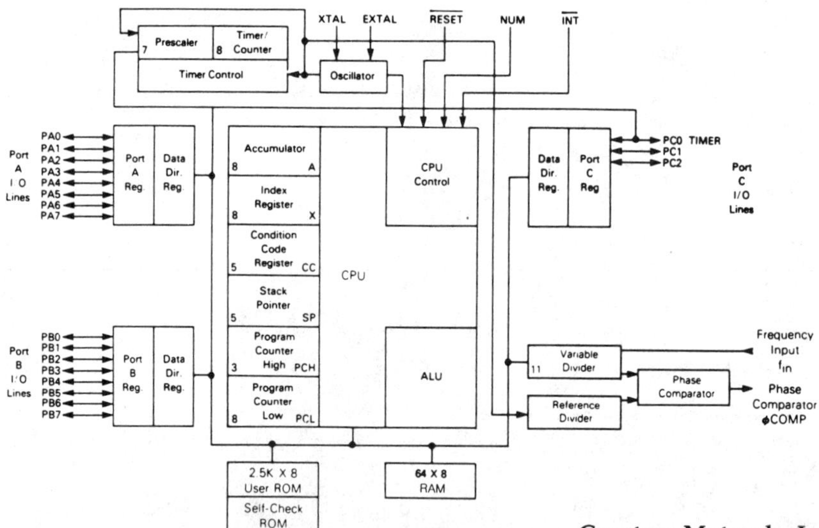

Courtesy Motorola, Inc.

Block Diagram—6805 T2, 8-Bit μC
Fig. 9-15

a) Monitor the clock signal on pin 4 on one trace, while observing the PB0 signal on pin 12 on the other.
b) Monitor the clock signal on pin 4 on one trace, while observing the PB3 signal on pin 15 on the other.

EXACT REPLACEMENT ESSENTIAL.

MC 68705P3

Special Features

- EPROM member of the M6805 family.
- 112 bytes of RAM.
- 1802 bytes of user EPROM.
- Internal 8-bit timer with 7-bit prescaler; programmable prescaler; programmable timer input modes.
- Vectored interrupts: external, timer, and software.
- 20 TTL/CMOS compatible bidirectional I/O lines (eight lines are LED compatible).
- Emulates the MC 6805P2 and MC 6805P4.
- Bootstrap program in ROM simplifies EPROM programming.
- Software features similar to the M6800 family's.

PIN NAME	DESCRIPTION	TYPE
PA0–PA7	Port A	I/O
PB0–PB7	Port B	I/O
PC0–PC3	Port C	I/O
$\overline{\text{INT}}$	Interrupt	I
XTAL, EXTAL	Crystal	I
TIMER/$\overline{\text{BOOT}}$	Timer/Bootstrap	I
$\overline{\text{RESET}}$	Reset	I
V_{PP}	EPROM Power Supply	
V_{CC}	Power Supply	
V_{SS}	Ground	

IN-CIRCUIT QUICK-TESTS

FOR 75% CONFIDENCE LEVEL:

1.) Volt-ohmmeter Measurements:
 a) Make sure PC board ground has good connection to pin 1.
 b) Measure power supply voltage of 5.0 to 5.5 volts DC at pin 3.

2. Oscilloscope Measurements:
 a) Observe clock signals at pins 4 and 5. They should be square waves with a frequency of 0.4 to 4.2 MHz.
 b) Observe the signal on pin 20. This signal is the PA0 output and is synchronized to the clock.

FOR 90% CONFIDENCE LEVEL:

In addition to the 75% confidence level tests, use a dual-trace oscilloscope to observe the following:

a) Monitor the clock signal on pin 4 on one trace, while observing the PB0 signal on pin 12 on the other.

PIN CONFIGURATION

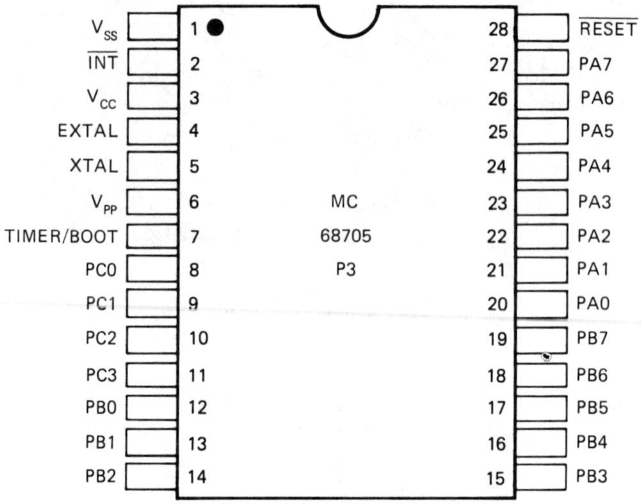

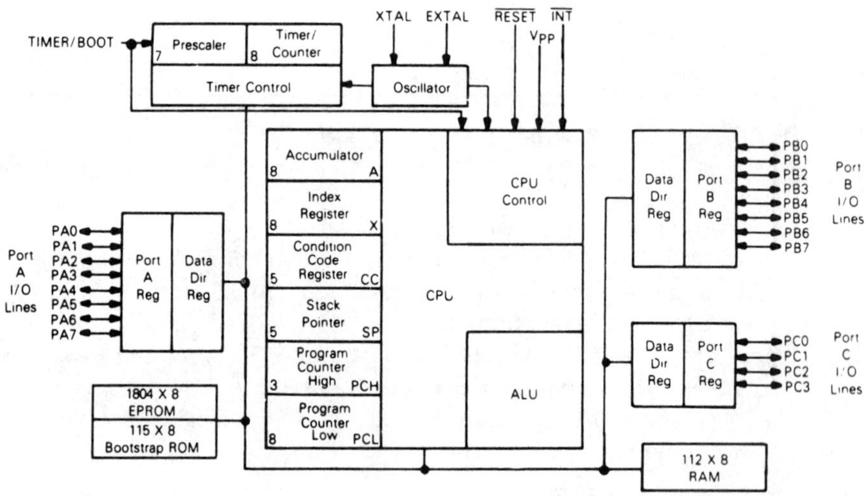

Courtesy Motorola, Inc.

Block Diagram—68705P3, 8-Bit μC
Fig. 9-16

b) Monitor the clock signal on pin 4 on one trace, while observing the PC0 signal on pin 8 on the other.

EXACT REPLACEMENT ESSENTIAL.

MC 68705R3[7]

Special Features

- EPROM member of the M6805 family.
- 112 bytes of RAM.
- 3776 bytes of user EPROM.
- Internal 8-bit timer with 7-bit prescaler; programmable prescaler; programmable timer input modes.
- Four vectored interrupts: external (2), timer (1), and software (1).
- Two to eight digital input lines.
- A/D converter: 8-bit conversion, monotonic; one to four multiplexed analog inputs, ±½ LSB quantizing error; ±½ LSB all other errors; ±1 LSB total error (max.); ratiometric conversion.
- Emulates the MC 6805R2.
- Bootstrap program in ROM simplifies EPROM programming.
- Software features are identical to the M6800 family's.

PIN NAME	DESCRIPTION	TYPE
PA0–PA7	Port A	I/O
PB0–PB7	Port B	I/O
PC0–PC7	Port C	I/O
PD0/AN0–PD3/AN3, PD4/V_{RL}, PD5/V_{RH}	Port D	I/O
PD6/$\overline{INT2}$, PD7 $\overline{INT}$	Interrupt	I
XTAL, EXTAL	Crystal	I
TIMER/BOOT	Timer/Bootstrap	I
$\overline{RESET}$	Reset	I
V_{PP}	EPROM Power Supply	
V_{CC}	Power supply	
V_{SS}	Ground	

[7]Note: the MC 68705U3 is essentially the same as the MC 68705R3, the difference being that port D of the MC 68705U3 is for digital input only. (The features related to the A/D converter do not apply to the MC 68705U3).

8-Bit μC

PIN CONFIGURATION

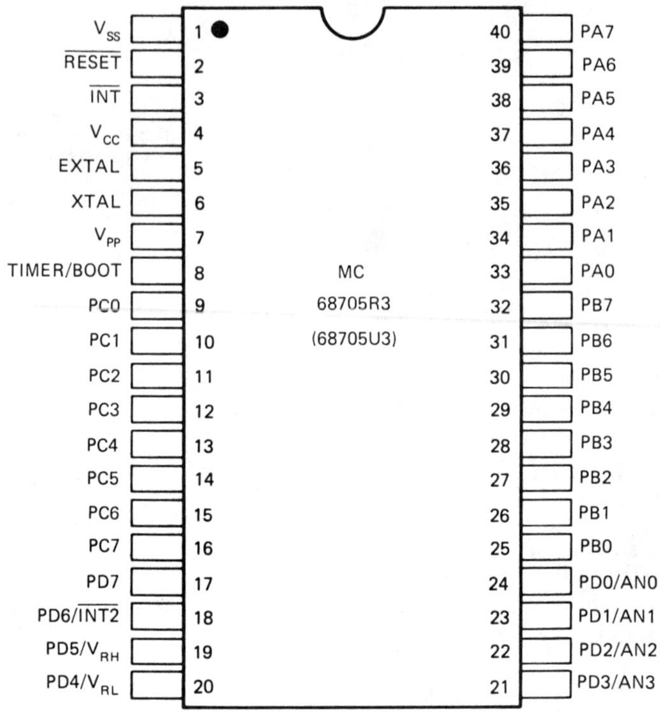

IN-CIRCUIT QUICK-TESTS

FOR 75% CONFIDENCE LEVEL:

1. Volt-ohmmeter Measurements:
   a) Make sure PC board ground has good connection to pin 1.
   b) Measure power supply voltage of 5.0 to 5.5 volts DC at pin 4.
2. Oscilloscope Measurements:
   1) Observe clock signals at pins 5 and 6. They should be square waves with a frequency of 0.4 to 4.2 MHz.
   b) Observe the signal on pin 33. This signal is the PA0 output and is synchronized to the clock.

FOR 90% CONFIDENCE LEVEL:

In addition to the 75% confidence level tests, use a dual-trace oscilloscope to observe the following:

a) Monitor the clock signal on pin 5 on one trace, while observing the PB0 signal on pin 25 on the other.

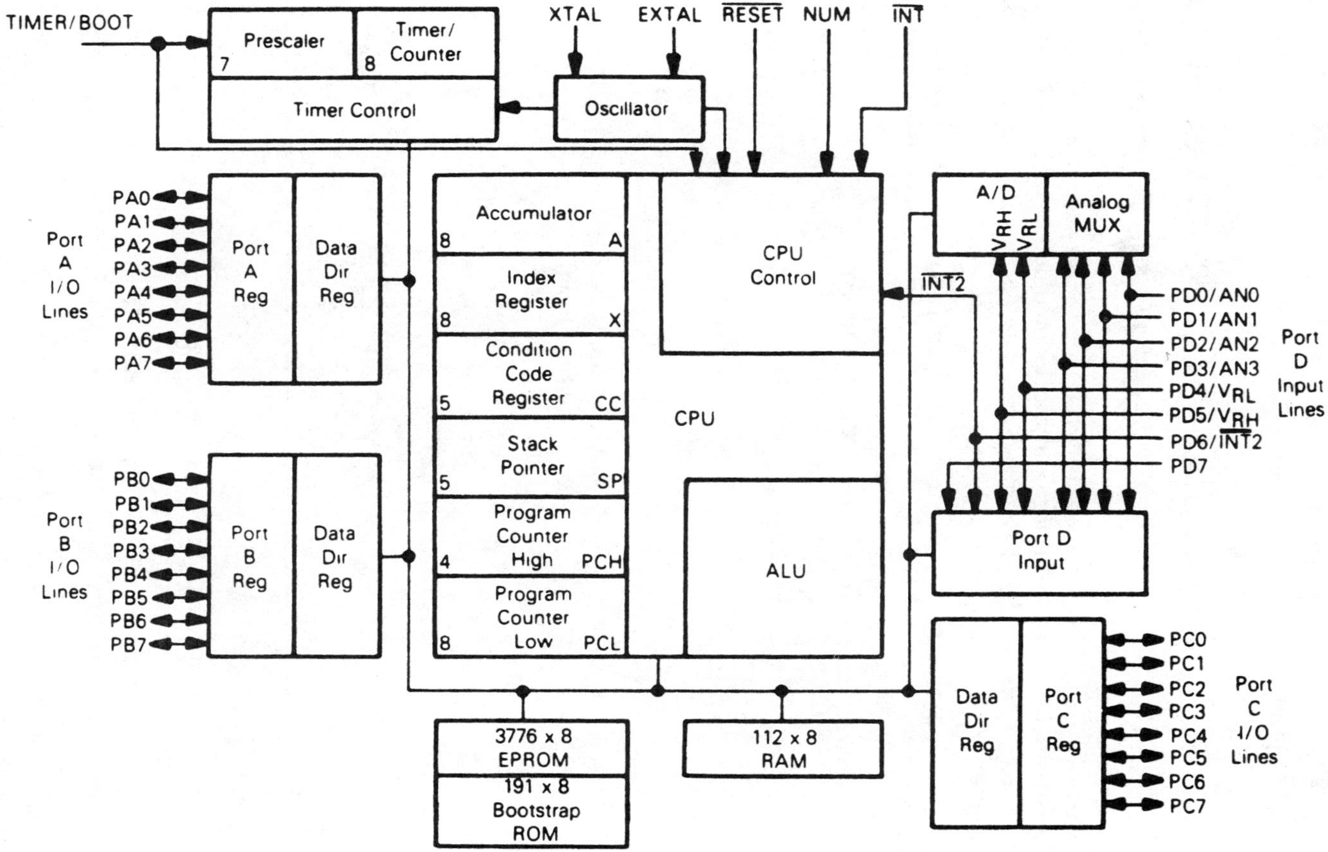

Courtesy Motorola, Inc.

Block Diagram—68705R3, 8-Bit μC
Fig. 9-17

b) Monitor the clock signal on pin 5 on one trace, while observing the PC0 signal on pin 9 on the other.

EXACT REPLACEMENT ESSENTIAL.

μPD 7800 (NEC MICROCOMPUTER)
8-BIT MICROCOMPUTER

This device is fully compatible with the industry standard 8080A bus structure. Basic on-chip functional blocks include 128 bytes of RAM data memory, 8-bit ALU, 32 I/O lines, serial I/O port, and 12-bit timer. Total memory address space is 64K bytes.

PIN NAME	DESCRIPTION	TYPE
AB0-AB15	Address Bus	O
$\overline{EXT}$	External Memory	O
DB0-DB7	Data Bus	I/O
$\overline{INT0}$, INT1, INT2	Interrupts	I
$\overline{WAIT}$	Wait	I
$\overline{M1}$	First State of the Cycle	O
$\overline{WR}$	Write	O
$\overline{RD}$	Read	O
PC0-PC7	Port C	I/O
$\overline{SCK}$	Serial Clock	I/O
SI	Serial Data Input	I
SO	Serial Data Output	O
RESET	Reset	I
STB	Strobe	O
X1	Clock	I
PA0-PA7	Port A	O
PB0-PB7	Port B	I/O
V_{CC}	Power Supply	
V_{SS}	Ground	

Special Features

- NMOS silicon gate technology requiring single +5V power supply.
- On-chip 1MHz serial port.
- Five-level vectored, prioritized interrupt structure; serial port; timer; 3 external interrupts.
- Wait state capability.
- Alternate Z80™ type register set.
- Bus expansion capability: fully 8080A bus compatible; 64K byte memory address range.

- 140 instruction set.
- Eight address modes, including auto-increment/decrement.
- Multi-level stack capabilities.
- Fast 2μs cycle time.
- Bus sharing capabilities.

Pin Configuration

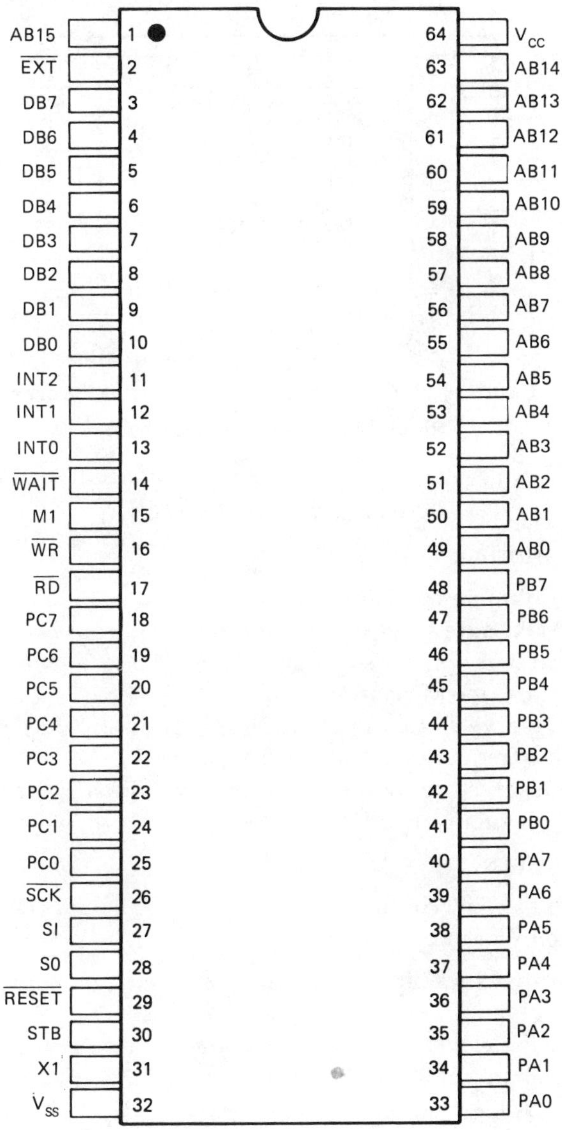

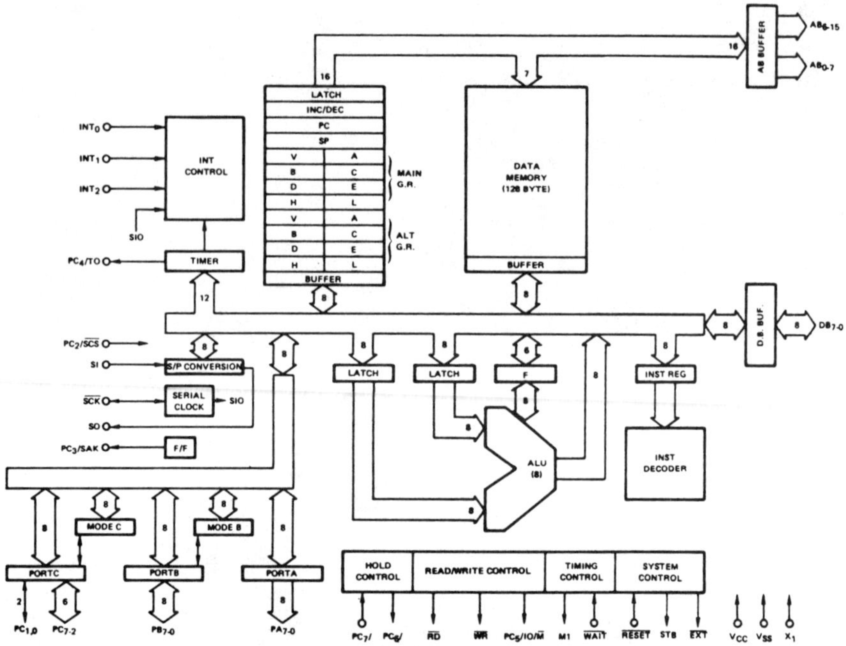

Courtesy NEC Electronics, U.S.A., Inc., Microcomputer Division.

Block Diagram—7800, 8-Bit μC
Fig. 9-18

IN-CIRCUIT QUICK-TESTS

For 75% Confidence Level:

1. Volt-ohmmeter Measurements:
   1) Make sure PC board ground has good connection to pin 32.
   b) Measure power supply voltage of 4.5 to 5.5 volts DC at pin 64.
2. Oscilloscope Measurements:
   a) Observe clock signals at pin 31. They should be square waves with a frequency of 2.0 to 4.0 MHz.
   b) Observe the signal on pin 16. This signal is the WRITE output and is synchronized to the clock.

For 90% Confidence Level:

In addition to the 75% confidence level tests, use a dual-trace oscilloscope to observe the following:

a) Monitor the clock signal on pin 31 on one trace, while observing the RD signal on pin 17 on the other.
b) Monitor the clock signal on pin 31 on one trace, while observing the SO signal on pin 28 on the other.

EXACT REPLACEMENT ABSOLUTELY ESSENTIAL.

μPD 7801, μPD 7802 (NEC MICROCOMPUTERS) 8-BIT MICROCOMPUTER

These devices are fully compatible with the industry standard 8080A bus structure, therefore expanded system operation can be implemented using any of the 8080A/8085A peripherals and memory products. Total memory space can be increased to 64K bytes. Basic on-chip functional blocks include: ROM, RAM, ALU, I/O lines, serial I/O port, timer and clock generator. The instruction set includes 140 instructions.

PIN NAME	DESCRIPTION	TYPE
PE0-PE15	Address Bus	O
0_{OUT}	Prescaled Output Clock	O
DB0-DB7	Data Bus	I/O
INT0, INT1, INT2	Interrupts	I
$\overline{WAIT}$	Wait	I
M1		O
$\overline{WR}$	Write	O
$\overline{RD}$	Read	O
PC0-PC7	Port C	I/O
$\overline{SCK}$	Serial Clock	I/O
SI	Serial Data Input	I
SO	Serial Data Output	O
$\overline{RESET}$	Reset	I
X2	Oscillator	O
X1	Clock	I
PA0-PA7	Port A	O
PB0-PB7	Port B	I/O
V_{CC}	Power Supply	
V_{SS}	Ground	

Special Features

- NMOS silicon gate technology requiring +5V power supply.
- 4K bytes ROM (μPD7801); 6K bytes ROM (μPD7802).
- 128 bytes RAM (μPD7801); 64 bytes RAM (μPD7802).
- 48 I/O lines.
- Internal 12-bit programmable timer.
- On-chip 1MHz serial port.
- Five-level vectored, prioritized interrupt structure; serial port; timer; three external interrupts.
- On-chip clock generator.
- WAIT state capability.
- Alternate Z80™ type register set.

- Eight address modes, including auto-increment/decrement.
- Multi-level stack capabilities.
- Fast 2μsec. cycle time.
- Bus sharing capabilities.

PIN CONFIGURATION

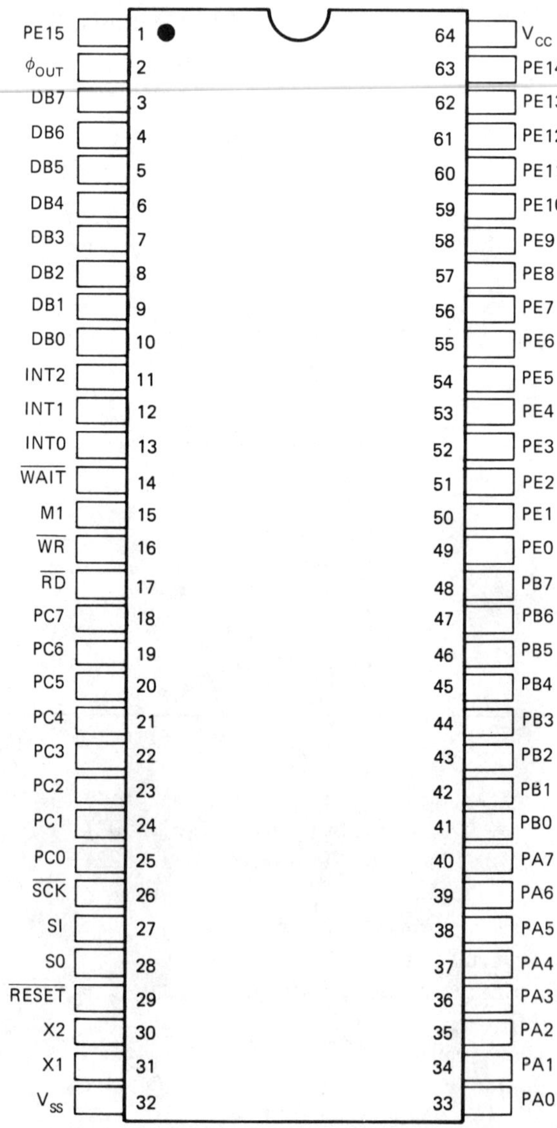

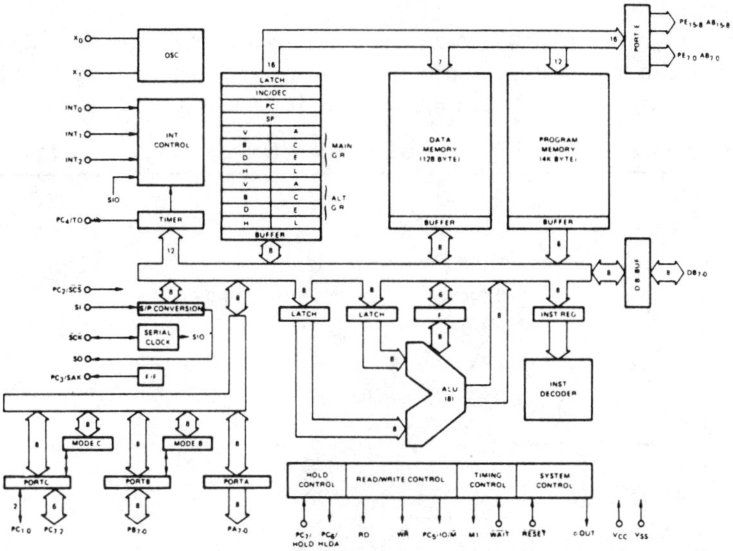

Courtesy NEC Electronics, U.S.A., Inc., Microcomputer Division.
Block Diagram—7801, 7802, 8-Bit μC
Fig. 9-19

IN-CIRCUIT QUICK-TESTS

FOR 75% CONFIDENCE LEVEL:

1. Volt-ohmmeter Measurements:
   a) Make sure PC board ground has good connection to pin 32.
   b) Measure power supply voltage of 4.5 to 5.5 volts DC at pin 64.
2. Oscilloscope Measurements:
   a) Observe clock signals at pins 30 and 31. They should be square waves with a frequency of 2.0 to 4.0 MHz.
   b) Observe the signal on pin 15. This signal indicates the OP CODE FETCH cycle and is synchronized to the clock.

FOR 90% CONFIDENCE LEVEL:

In addition to the 75% confidence level tests, use a dual-trace oscilloscope to observe the following:

a) Monitor the clock signal on pins 30 or 31 on one trace, while observing the WR signal on pin 16 on the other.

b) Monitor the clock signal on pins 30 or 31 on one trace, while observing the RD signal on pin 17 on the other.

EXACT REPLACEMENT ABSOLUTELY ESSENTIAL.

8020H (INTEL) 8-BIT MICROCOMPUTER

This device is fabricated on a single silicon chip using N-channel silicon gate HMOS process. It has instructions and hardware on-board to interface to TTL I/O expansion packages. Its instructions are no longer than 2 bytes, with 70% of the instructions at one byte. For control-oriented applications, arithmetic instructions are supported using binary and BCD operands.

PIN NAME	DESCRIPTION	TYPE
P00-P07	Port 0	I/O
P13-P17	Port 1	I/O
PROG	Port Extender Strobe	O
T1	Test or Timer/Event Counter	I
RESET	Reset	I
XTAL1, XTAL2	Crystal	I
V_{CC}	Power Supply	
V_{SS}	Ground	

Special Features

- 1K × 8 ROM.
- 64 × 8 RAM.
- 13 I/O lines.
- Internal timer counter.
- 8.38μsec cycle with 3.58MHz crystal.
- Instructions—8048 subset.
- 30mA operation @ 25°C.

PIN CONFIGURATION

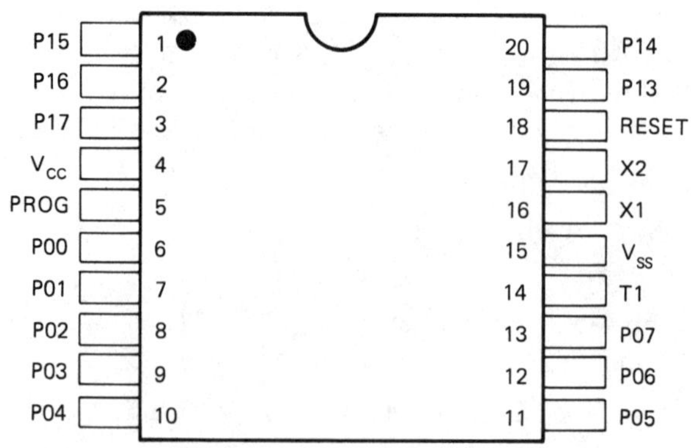

IN-CIRCUIT QUICK-TESTS

FOR 75% CONFIDENCE LEVEL:

1. Volt-ohmmeter Measurements:
   a) Make sure PC board ground has good connection to pin 15.
   b) Measure power supply voltage of 4.5 to 5.6 volts DC at pin 4.

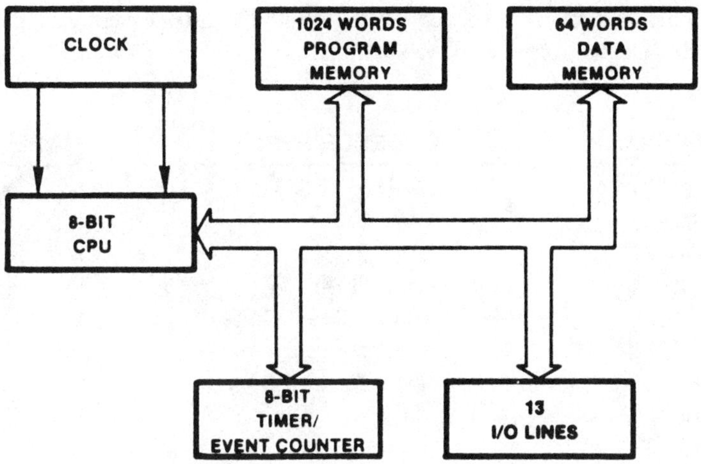

Reprinted by permission of Intel Corporation.

Block Diagram—8020H, 8-Bit μC
Fig. 9-20

2. Oscilloscope Measurements:
   a) Observe clock signals at pins 16 and 17. They should be square waves with a frequency of 2.0 to 4.0 MHz.
   b) Observe the signal on pin 5. This signal is the STROBE output and is synchronized to the clock.

FOR 90% CONFIDENCE LEVEL:

In addition to the 75% confidence level tests, use a dual-trace oscilloscope to observe the following:

a) Monitor the clock signal on pin 16 or 17 on one trace, while observing the PO0 signal on pin 6 on the other.

b) Monitor the clock signal on pin 16 or 17 on one trace, while observing the PO1 signal on pin 7 on the other.

EXACT REPLACEMENT ABSOLUTELY ESSENTIAL.

8021 (INTEL) 8-BIT MICROCOMPUTER[8]

This device is designed to be a controller as well as an arithmetic processor. It has bit handling capability as well as facilities for both binary and BCD arithmetic. The features of the 8021 include a subset of the 8048 optimized for low cost, high volume applications, plus additional I/O flexibility (for

---

[8]Note: The same microprocessor is manufactured by:
NEC Micro: μPD 8021
SIGNETICS: 8021

Note 2: The 8021L is identical to the 8021, but is considered a low power 10mA 8-bit microcomputer (V_{cc}: +4.5V to 8V).

systems that require extra I/O capability the 8021 can be expanding using the 8243 or discrete logic) and power.

PIN NAME	DESCRIPTION	TYPE
PO0-PO7	Port 0	I/O
P10-P17	Port 1	I/O
P20-P23	Port 2	I/O
PROG	Output Strobe	O
TI	Timer/Event Counter	I
RESET	Reset	I
ALE	Address Latch Enable	O
XTAL 1, XTAL2	Crystal	I
V_{CC}	Power Supply	
V_{SS}	Ground	

Special Features

- 8-bit CPU, ROM, RAM, I/O.
- +4.5V to +6.5V single po er supply.
- 8.38μSec. cycle with 3.58MHz crystal, all instructions one or two cycles.
- Instructions—8048 subset.
- High current drive capability—2 pins.
- 1K × 8 ROM, 64 × 8 RAM, 21 I/O lines.

PIN CONFIGURATION

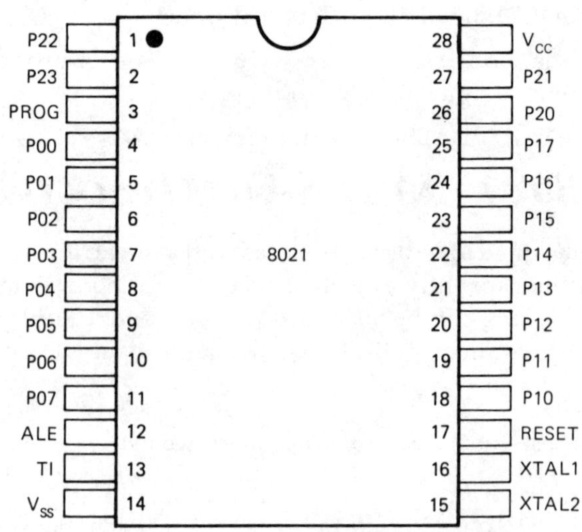

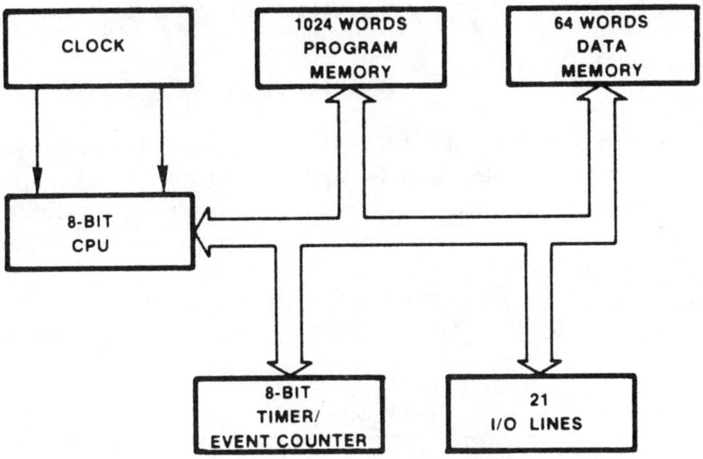

Reprinted by permission of Intel Corporation.

Block Diagram—8021, 8021H, 8-Bit μC
Fig. 9-21

- 8-bit timer event counter, on-board oscillator.
- Clock generated with single inductor or crystal.
- Zero-crossing detection capability.

IN-CIRCUIT QUICK-TESTS

FOR 75% CONFIDENCE LEVEL:

1. Volt-ohmmeter Measurements:
   a) Make sure PC board ground has good connection to pin 14.
   b) Measure power supply voltage of 4.5 to 5.5 volts DC at pin 28.
2. Oscilloscope Measurements:
   a) Observe clock signals at pins 15 and 16. They should be square waves with a frequency of 2.0 to 4.0 MHz.
   b) Observe the signal on pin 3. This signal is the STROBE output and is synchronized to the clock.

FOR 90% CONFIDENCE LEVEL:

In addition to the 75% confidence level tests, use a dual-trace oscilloscope to observe the following:

a) Monitor the clock signal on pin 15 or 16 on one trace, while observing the ALE signal on pin 12 on the other.
b) Monitor the clock signal on pin 15 or 16 on one trace, while observing the PO0 signal on pin 4 on the other.

EXACT REPLACEMENT ABSOLUTELY ESSENTIAL.

8022/I8022/8022H (INTEL) 8-BIT MICROCOMPUTER[9]

This device is a member of the MCS-48™ family. It is designed for applications that involve analog signals, capacitive touch-panel keyboards, and/or large ROM space. The 8022 addresses these applications by integrating functions as A/D conversion, comparator inputs and zero-crossing detection on-chip.

The I8022 is the industrial 8022 and it has longer cycle time.

The 8022H is the high performance 8022 and it has the shortest cycle time.

PIN NAME	DESCRIPTION	TYPE
PO0-PO7	Port 0	I/O
P10-P17	Port 1	I/O
P20-P27	Port 2	I/O
TO	Interrupt	I
T1	Timer/Event Counter	I
PROG	Output Strobe	O
RESET	Reset	I
SUBST	Substrate	I
ANO, AN1	Analog Inputs to A/D Converter	I
ALE	Address Latch Enable	O
XTAL1, XTAL2	Crystal	I
V_{TH}	Port 0 Threshold Reference	
AV_{SS}	A/D Converter GND Potential	
AV_{CC}	A/D Power Supply	
V_{AREF}	A/D Converter Reference Voltage	
V_{CC}	Power Supply	
V_{SS}	Ground	

Special Features

- On-chip 8-bit A/D converter; two input channels
- Eight comparator inputs (Port 0)
- Zero-Crossing Detection Capability
- 4.5V to 6.5V single power supply
- High current drive capability—2 Pins
- Two interrupts—external and timer

[9]Note: The same microcomputer is manufactured by:
NEC Micro: μPD8022
SIGNETICS: 8022.

- 2K × 8 ROM, 64 × 8 RAM, 28 I/O Lines
- 8.38μsec. cycle (8022) all instructions 1 or 2 cycles; 10μsec. cycle (I8022) all instructions 1 or 2 cycles; 5μsec. cycle (8022H) all instructions 1 or 2 cycles (6MHz Clock)
- Instructions—8048 Subset
- Interval timer/event counter
- Clock generated with single inductor or crystal

PIN CONFIGURATION

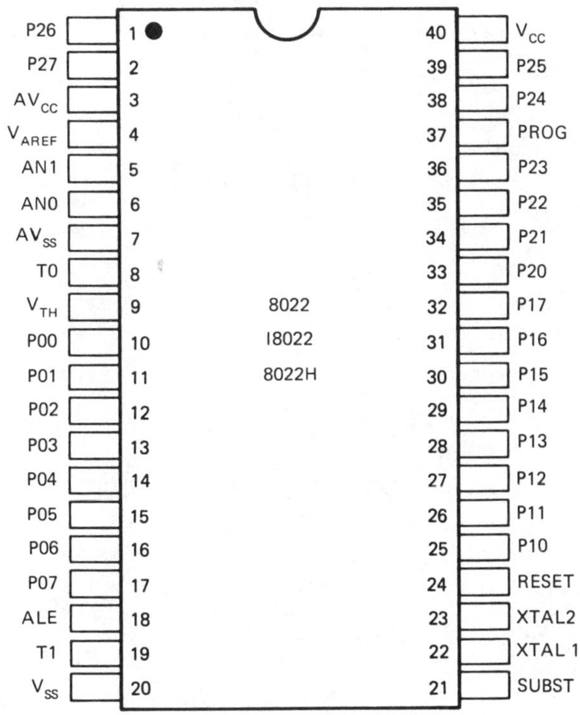

IN-CIRCUIT QUICK-TESTS

FOR 75% CONFIDENCE LEVEL:

1. Volt-ohmmeter Measurements:
   a) Make sure PC board ground has good connection to pin 20.
   b) Measure power supply voltage of 4.5 to 5.5 volts DC at pin 40.
2. Oscilloscope Measurements:
   a) Observe clock signals at pins 22 and 23. They should be square waves with a frequency of 2.0 to 6.0 MHz.

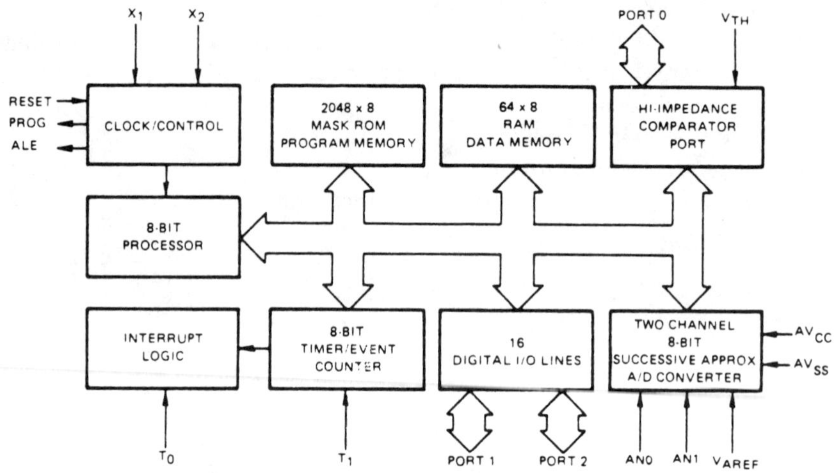

Courtesy NEC Electronics, U.S.A., Inc., Microcomputer Division.

Block Diagram—8022, 8022H, 8-Bit μC

Fig. 9-22

b) Observe the signal on pin 18. This signal is the ALE output and is synchronized to the clock.

FOR 90% CONFIDENCE LEVEL:

In addition to the 75% confidence level tests, use a dual-trace oscilloscope to observe the following:

a) Monitor the clock signal on pin 22 or 23 on one trace, while observing the PO0 signal on pin 10 on the other.
b) Monitor the clock signal on pin 22 or 23 on one trace, while observing the PO1 signal on pin 11 on the other.

EXACT REPLACEMENT ABSOLUTELY ESSENTIAL.

8031/8051/8751 (INTEL)
8-BIT MICROCOMPUTER[10]

8031 Control Oriented CPU wit RAM and I/O
8051 An 8031 with Factory Mask-Programmable ROM
8751 An 8031 with User Programmable/Erasable EPROM

The 8051 is used as a controller and as an arithmetic processor. It has facilities for binary and BCD arithmetic. The instruction set consists of 44%

[10]Note: The I8031/I8051 are the industrial version of the 8031/8051. They are identical, except for the temperature range (−40°C to +85°C for the I8031/I8051).

of one-byte, 41% two-byte, and 15% three-byte instructions. With a 12 MHz crystal, 58% of the instructions execute in 1 μsec., 40% in two μsec. and multiply and divide require only 4 μsec.

The 8051/8751 contains a non-volatile 4K × 8 read only program memory, a volatile 128 × 8 read/write data memory; 32 I/O lines, two 16-bit timer/counters; a five-source, two-priority level, nested interrupt structure; a serial I/O port for either multiprocessor communications, I/O expansion, or full duplex UART; and on-chip oscillator and clock circuits. The 8031 is identical, except that it lacks the program memory. For systems that require extra capability, the 8051 can be expanded using standard TTL compatible memories and the byte oriented MCS-80 and MCS-85 peripherals.

PIN NAME	DESCRIPTION	TYPE
PO0-PO7	Port 0 Address and Data Bus	I/O
P10-P17	Port 1	I/O
P20-P27	Port 2 or Address Bus	I/O or O
P30-P37	Port 3 or	I/O or
RXD/DATA	Receiver Data Input or Data I/O	I
TXD/CLOCK	Transmitter Data Output or Clock Output	O
$\overline{\text{INT0}}$	Interrupt 0 or Gate Control for Counter 0	I
$\overline{\text{INT1}}$	Interrupt 1 or Gate Control for Counter 1	I
T0	Input to Counter 0	I
T1	Input to Counter 1	I
$\overline{\text{WR}}$	Write	O
$\overline{\text{RD}}$	Read	O
RST/VPD	Reset/Standby Power Supply for RAM	I
XTAL 1	Input to the Oscillator or Crystal	I
XTAL 2	Output from the Oscillator or Crystal	O
$\overline{\text{EA}}/V_{DD}$	Internal ROM/EPROM or External Program Memory Select/EPROM Programming Supply Voltage	I
ALE/$\overline{\text{PROG}}$	Address Latch Enable	O
$\overline{\text{PSEN}}$	Program Store Enable	O
V_{CC}	Power Supply	
V_{SS}	Ground	

Special Features

- External memory expandable to 128K.
- Compatible with MCS-80[R]/MCS-85[R] peripherals.
- Boolean processor.
- MCS-48[R] architecture enhanced with: non-paged jumps; direct address-

8-Bit μC

PIN CONFIGURATION 4R

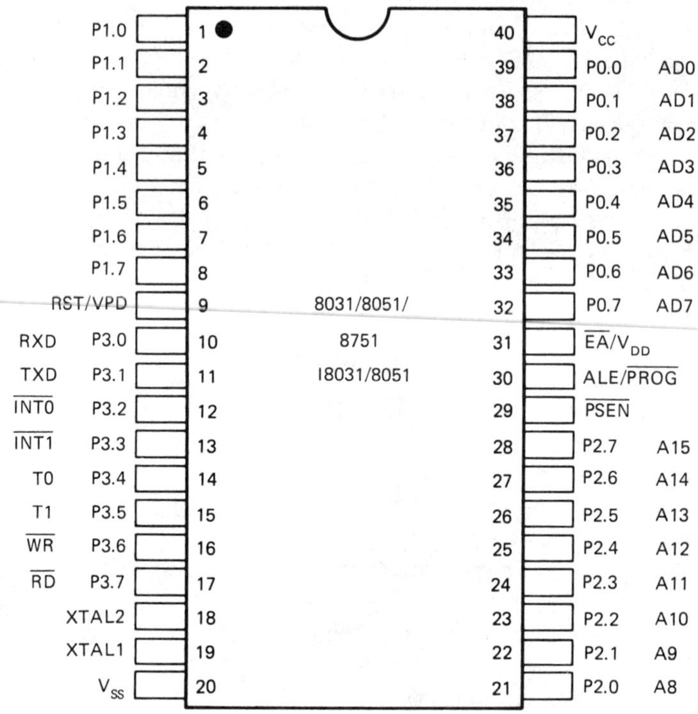

ing; four 8-register banks; stack depths up to 128 bytes; multiply, divide, subtract, and compare.

IN-CIRCUIT QUICK-TESTS

FOR 75% CONFIDENCE LEVEL:

1. Volt-ohmmeter Measurements:
   1) Make sure PC board ground has good connection to pin 20.
   b) Measure power supply voltage of 4.75 to 5.25 volts DC at pin 40.
2. Oscilloscope Measurements:
   a) Observe clock signals at pins 18 and 19. They should be square waves with a frequency of 1.0 to 12.0 MHz.
   b) Observe the signal on pin 30. This signal is the ALE output and is synchronized to the clock.

FOR 90% CONFIDENCE LEVEL:

In addition to the 75% confidence level tests, use a dual-trace oscilloscope to observe the following:

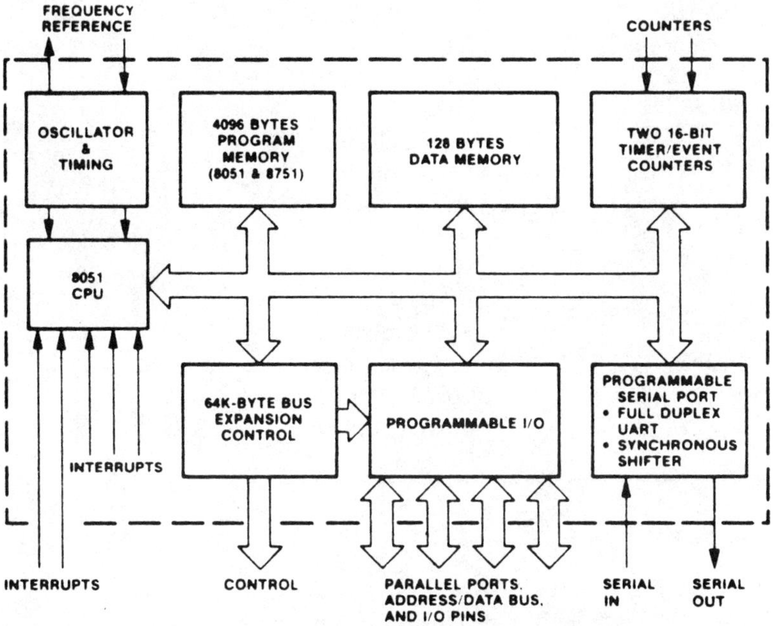

Reprinted by permission of Intel Corporation.

Block Diagram—8031, 8051, 8751, 8-Bit μC
Fig. 9-23

a) Monitor the clock signal on pin 18 or 19 on one trace, while observing the PO0 signal on pin 39 on the other.
b) Monitor the clock signal on pin 18 or 19 on one trace, while observing the P20 signal on pin 21 on the other.

EXACT REPLACEMENT ABSOLUTELY ESSENTIAL.

μPD 8041 (NEC MICROCOMPUTER) 8-BIT MICROCOMPUTER[11]

This device contains an 8-bit CPU, 1K × 8 ROM program memory, 64 × 8 RAM data memory, 18 I/O lines, 8-bit timer/counter and clock generator. The bus structure, data register, and status register enable interface to 8048, 8080A, or 8085A based systems.

PIN NAME	DESCRIPTION	TYPE
P10-P17	Port 1	I/O
P20-P27	Port 2	I/O

D0–D7	Data Bus Buffer	I/O
T0, T1	Test	I
X1, X2	Crystal	I
$\overline{\text{RESET}}$	Reset	I
$\overline{\text{SS}}$	Single Step	I
$\overline{\text{CS}}$	Chip Select	I
EA	External Access	I
$\overline{\text{RD}}$	Read	I
$\overline{\text{WR}}$	Write	I
AO	Address	I
SYNC	Synchronize	O
PROG	Program Pulse	O
V_{DD}	Low Power Standby	
V_{CC}	Power Supply	
V_{SS}	Ground	

Special Features

- Fully compatible with 8048, 8080A, and 8085A bus structure.
- 4-bit status and 8-bit data register for asynchronous slave-to-master interface.
- Interrupt, DMA, or polled operation.
- Expandable I/O.
- Two interrupts.

Note: The μPD 8041A/μPD 8741A are essentially the same as the μPD8041. The difference is that they have 8-bit status and two data registers for asynchronous slave-to-master interface. The pin configuration differs at port 2: P24 and P25 can be used as port lines or can provide interrupt request (IBF-input buffer full flag and OBF-output buffer full flag); P26 and P27 can be used as port lines or can provide DMA handshake lines, (DRQ-DMA request and DACK-DMA acknowledge).

The μPD 8041A's program memory is factory mask programmed while the μPD 8741A's program memory is UV EPROM.

IN-CIRCUIT QUICK-TESTS

For 75% Confidence Level:

1. Volt-ohmmeter Measurements:
   a) Make sure PC board ground has good connection to pin 20.
   b) Measure power supply voltage of 4.5 to 5.5 volts DC at pin 40.

---

[11]Note: the same microcomputer is manufactured by: INTEL—8041A/8641A/8741A (the 8641A is a one-time progammable 8741a).

PIN CONFIGURATION

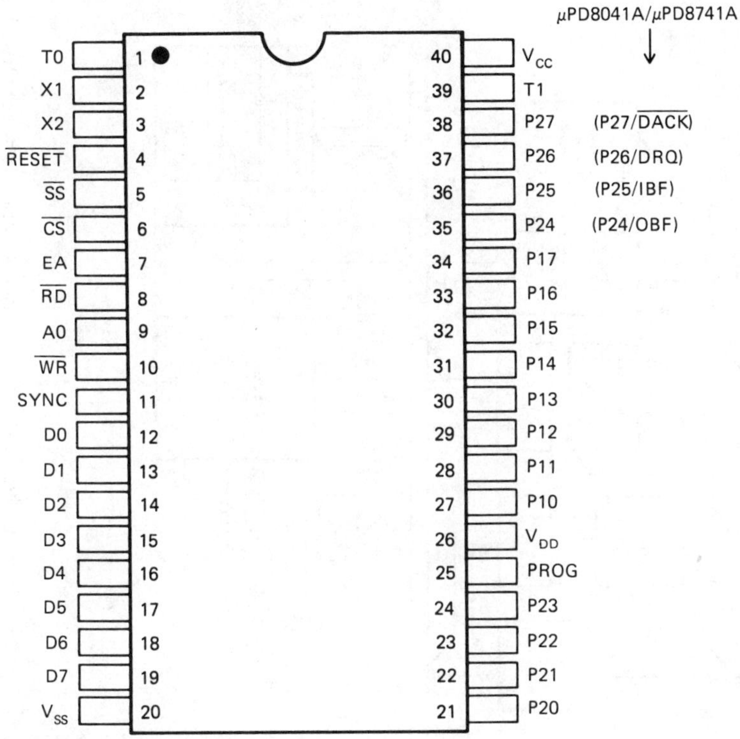

2. Oscilloscope Measurements:
   a) Observe clock signals at pins 2 and 3. They should be square waves with a frequency of 2.0 to 6.0 MHz.
   b) Observe the signal on pin 11. This signal is the SYNC output and is synchronized to the clock.

FOR 90% CONFIDENCE LEVEL:

In addition to the 75% confidence level tests, use a dual-trace oscilloscope to observe the following:

a) Monitor the clock signal on pin 2 or 3 on one trace, while observing the D0 signal on pin 12 on the other.
b) Monitor the clock signal on pin 2 or 3 on one trace, while observing the D1 signal on pin 13 on the other.

EXACT REPLACEMENT ABSOLUTELY ESSENTIAL.

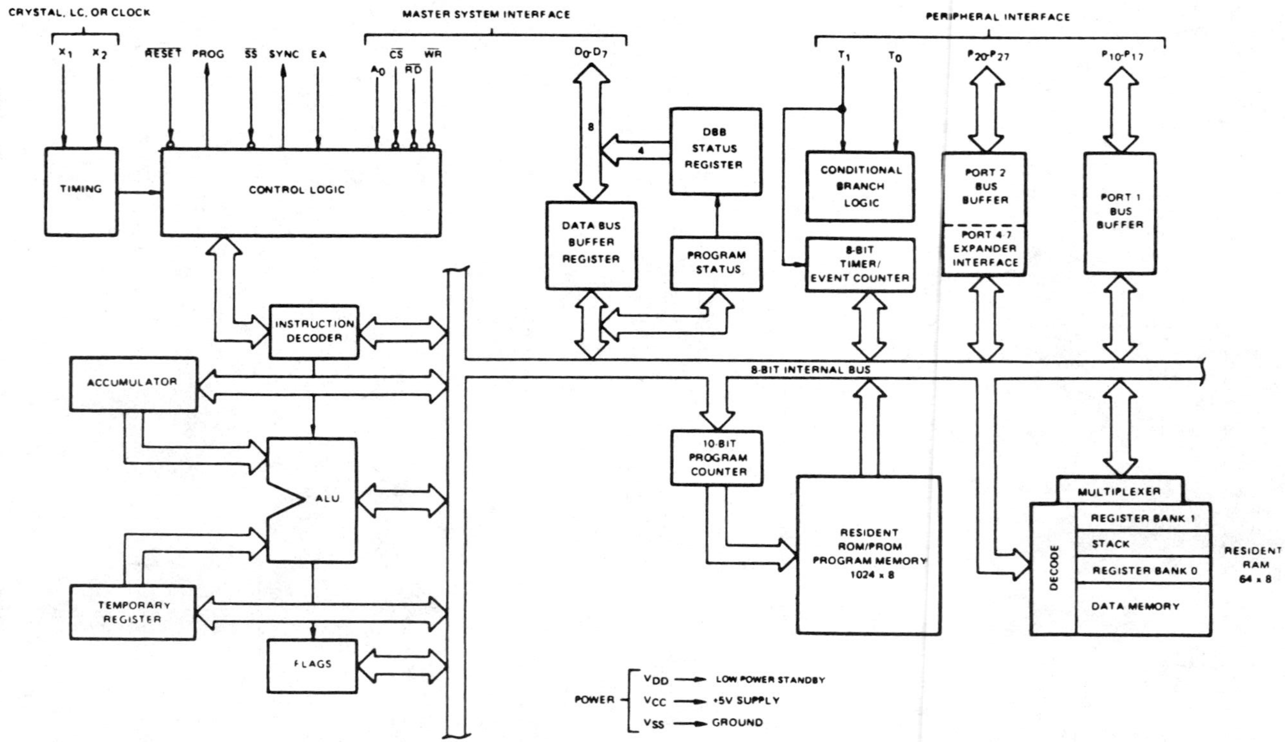

Courtesy NEC Electronics, U.S.A., Inc., Microcomputer Division.

Block Diagram—8041, 8041A, 8-Bit μC
Fig. 9-24

8048H/8048H-1/8748/8035HL/8035HL-1 8049H/8749/8039HL (INTEL) 8-BIT MICROCOMPUTER SERIES

8048H/8048H-1/8049 Mask Programmable ROM
8035HL/8035HL-1/8039HL CPU Only With Power-Down Mode
8748/8749 UV Erasable User-Programmable EPROM[12]

The above devices are designed to be controllers as well as arithmetic processors. They have bit handling capability as well as facilities for both binary and BCD arithmetic. All have the same block diagram and basic pin configuration. The instruction set consists mostly of single byte instructions (70%), and no instruction over two bytes in length. For systems that require extra capability the 8048H and 8049H can be expanded using standard memories and MCS 80[R]/MOS 85[R] peripherals.

The 8035HL (8039HL) is the equivalent of the 8048H (8049H) without program memory and can be used with external ROM and RAM.

The 8748 (8749) will emulate the 8048H (8049H) up to 6MHz (1MHz) clock frequency with minor differences.

PIN NAME	DESCRIPTION	TYPE
P10-P17	Port 1	I/O
P20-P27	Port 2	I/O
DB0-DB7	Data Bus	I/O
T0	Input Pin Testable or Clock Output	I or O
TI	Input Pin Testable or Timer/Counter Input	I
$\overline{\text{PROG}}$	Port Expander Strobe	O
$\overline{\text{INT}}$	Interrupt	I
$\overline{\text{RD}}$	Read	O
$\overline{\text{RESET}}$	Reset	I
$\overline{\text{WR}}$	Write	O
ALE	Address Latch Enable	O
$\overline{\text{PSEN}}$	Program Store Enable	O
$\overline{\text{SS}}$	Single Step	I

[12]Note A: The 8048L is considered the special low power consumption version of the 8048. The pin assignment and the main special features are the same as for the 8048H. The differences are: typical power consumption of 100 mW; typical standby power 10 mW, V_{DD} minimum of 2.2V; and 4.17 μsec. instruction cycle. All instructions are one or two cycles in length.

Note B: National makes the same devices in their INS8048 family.

PIN NAME	DESCRIPTION	TYPE
EA	External Access	I
XTAL1, XTAL2	Crystal	I
V_{DD}	Low Power Supply	
V_{CC}	Power Supply	
V_{SS}	Ground	

Special Features

- HMOS technology.
- 1.4 μsec. and 1.9 μsec per cycle versions. All instructions one or two cycles.
- 1K × 8 ROM, 64 × 8 RAM, 27 I/O lines for 8048H/8035HL.
- 2K × 8 ROM, 128 × 8 RAM, 27 I/O lines for 8049H/8039HL.
- Interval timer/event counter.
- Compatible with 8080/8085 series peripherals.
- Two single level interrupts.

I 8048H (INTEL) INDUSTRIAL 8-BIT MICROCOMPUTER

This device is the industrial version of the 8048H. The pin assignment and the main special features are identical. The different features are listed below.

- RAM power-down mode.
- Interchangeable with 8748.
- 8 MHz operation.
- Reduced power consumption, typically 50mA, 100mA at extended temperature.
- 1.9 μsec. per cycle, all instructions one or two cycles in length.
- −40°C to +85°C temperature range.

I 8049/8039 (INTEL) INDUSTRIAL 8-BIT MICROCOMPUTER

This device is the industrial version of the 8049/8039. The pin assignment and the main special features are identical. The different features are listed below.

- 6MHz operation.
- 2.5 μsec; per cycle, all instructions one or two cycles in length.

- Compatible with MCS[R] memory and I/O.
- Single level interrupt.
- Pin compatible with 8048/8748.
- −40°C to +85°C temperature range.

I 8049H/8039H (Intel) Industrial 8-Bit Microcomputer

This device is the industrial version of the 8049H/8039H. The pin assignment and the main special features are identical. The different features are listed below:

- 11MHz operation.
- 1.36 μsec per cycle, all instructions one or two cycles.
- Single level interrupt.
- Pin compatible with 8048/8748.
- −40°C to +85°C temperature range.

I 8048/8748/8035L (Intel) Industrial 8-Bit Microcomputer

This device is the industrial version of the 8048/8748/8035L. The pin assignment and the main features are identical. The different features are listed below.

- Interchangeable ROM and EPROM versions.
- 2.5 μsec. and 5.0 μsec. per cycle versions. All instructions one or two cycles in length.
- 1K × 8ROM/EPROM, 64 × 8RAM, 27 I/O lines.
- −40°C to +85°C temperature range.
- Single level interrupt.

M 8048/8748/8035L (Intel) Military 8-Bit Microcomputer

This device is the military version of the 8048/8748/8035L. The pin assignment and the main features are identical. The different features are listed below:

- −55°C to + 125°C 6MHz operation for M8048/M8035L
- −55°C to + 125°C 3.6MHz operation for M8748

I 8749 (INTEL) INDUSTRIAL 8-BIT MICROCOMPUTER

This device is the industrial EPROM version of the 8049H. The pin assignment and the main features are identical. The different features are listed below.

- 11MHz operation.
- Interchangeable with 8049.
- Pin compatible with 8048/8748.
- 1.4 μsec per cycle versions. All instructions one or two cycles in length.
- 2K × 8 ROM/EPROM, 128 × 8 RAM, 27 I/O lines.
- Single level interrupt.
- −40°C to +85°C temperature range.

PIN CONFIGURATION

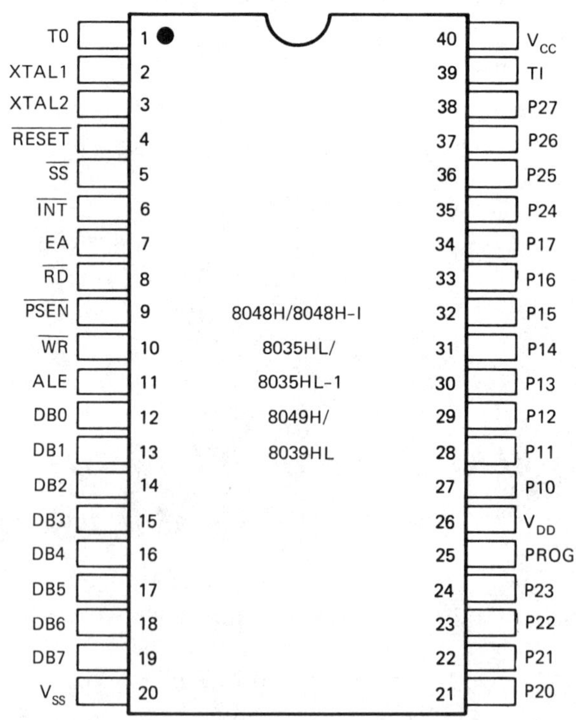

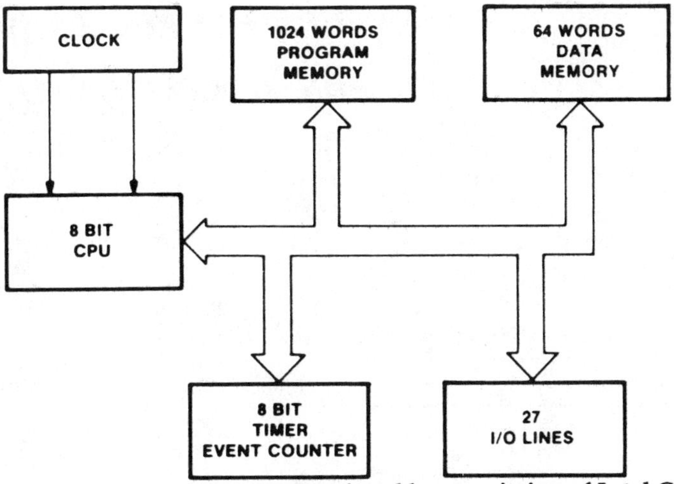

Reprinted by permission of Intel Corporation.

Block Diagram—8048H Series, 8-Bit μC
Fig. 9-25

IN-CIRCUIT QUICK-TESTS

For 75% Confidence Level:

1. Volt-ohmmeter Measurements:
   a) Make sure PC board ground has good connection to pin 20.
   b) Measure power supply voltage of 4.5 to 5.5 volts DC at pin 40.
2. Oscilloscope Measurements:
   a) Observe clock signals at pins 2 and 3. They should be square waves with a frequency of 1.0 to 11.0 MHz.
   b) Observe the signal on pin 11. This signal is the ALE output and is synchronized to the clock.

For 90% Confidence Level:

In addition to the 75% confidence level tests, use a dual-trace oscilloscope to observe the following:

a) Monitor the clock signal on pin 2 or 3 on one trace, while observing the RD signal on pin 8 on the other.
b) Monitor the clock signal on pin 2 or 3 on one trace, while observing the WR signal on pin 10 on the other.

EXACT REPLACEMENT ABSOLUTELY ESSENTIAL.

μPD 80C48/μPD 80C35 (NEC MICROCOMPUTERS) 8-BIT MICROCOMPUTER[13]

The μPD 80C48 contains the following functional blocks: 1K bytes ROM, 64 bytes RAM, 27 I/O lines, on-chip 8-bit timer/event counter, and an on-chip clock generator. For designs requiring extra capability the μPD80C48 can be expanded using industry standard μPD8080A/μPD8085A peripherals and memory products.

The μPD 80C35 differs from the μPD 80C48 only in that the μPD 80C35 contains no internal program memory (ROM).

PIN NAME	DESCRIPTION	TYPE
P10-P17	Port 1	I/O
P20-P27	Port 2	I/O
DB0-DB7	Data Bus	I/O
T0, T1	Test	I
XTAL1, XTAL2	Crystal	I
$\overline{\text{RESET}}$	Reset	I
$\overline{\text{SS}}$	Single Step	I
$\overline{\text{INT}}$	Interrupt	I
EA	External Access	I
$\overline{\text{RD}}$	Read	O
$\overline{\text{PSEN}}$	Program Store Enable	O
$\overline{\text{WR}}$	Write	O
ALE	Address Latch Enable	O
PROG	Strobe (for the μPD8243)	O
V_{CC}	Power Supply	
V_{DD}	ROM Power Supply	
V_{SS}	Ground	

Special Features

- CMOS technology (requiring +5V power supply).
- Hardware/software compatible with industry standard 8048, 8748, 8035 products.
- 2.5μSec. instruction cycle time (6MHz crystal).
- All instructions one or two cycles in length.
- 97 instructions: 70% single byte.
- Two interrupts (external and timer).
- Bus compatible with 8080A/8085A peripherals.

---

[13]Note: The same microcomputer is manufactured by: INTERSIL—IM80C35/IM80C48/IM87C48 (the last has UV EPROM).

- Effective low power standby functions:
  Halt mode: 2mA typical supply current; maintains internal logic values and control status; initiated by HALT instruction; released by external interrupt or reset.
  Stop mode: 20μA maximum supply current; disables internal clock generation and internal logic; maintains RAM; initiated via hardware (V_{DD}); released via reset.

IN-CIRCUIT QUICK-TESTS

For 75% Confidence Level:

1. Volt-ohmmeter Measurements:
   a) Make sure PC board ground has good connection to pin 20.
   b) Measure power supply voltage of 4.5 to 5.5 volts DC at pin 26. Pin 40 should have same voltage when μC is in the RUN mode.
2. Oscilloscope Measurements:
   a) Observe clock signals at pins 2 and 3. They should be square waves with a frequency of 1.0 to 6.0 MHz.
   b) Observe the signal on pin 11. This signal is the ALE output and is synchronized to the clock.

Pin Configuration

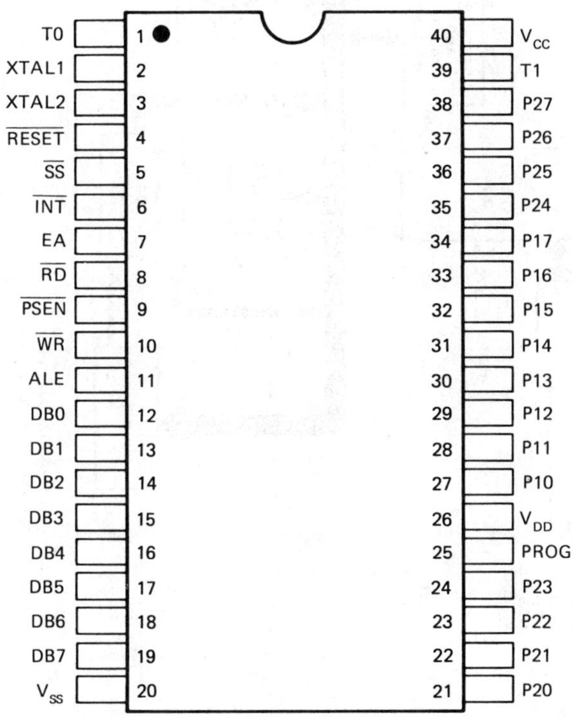

8-Bit μC

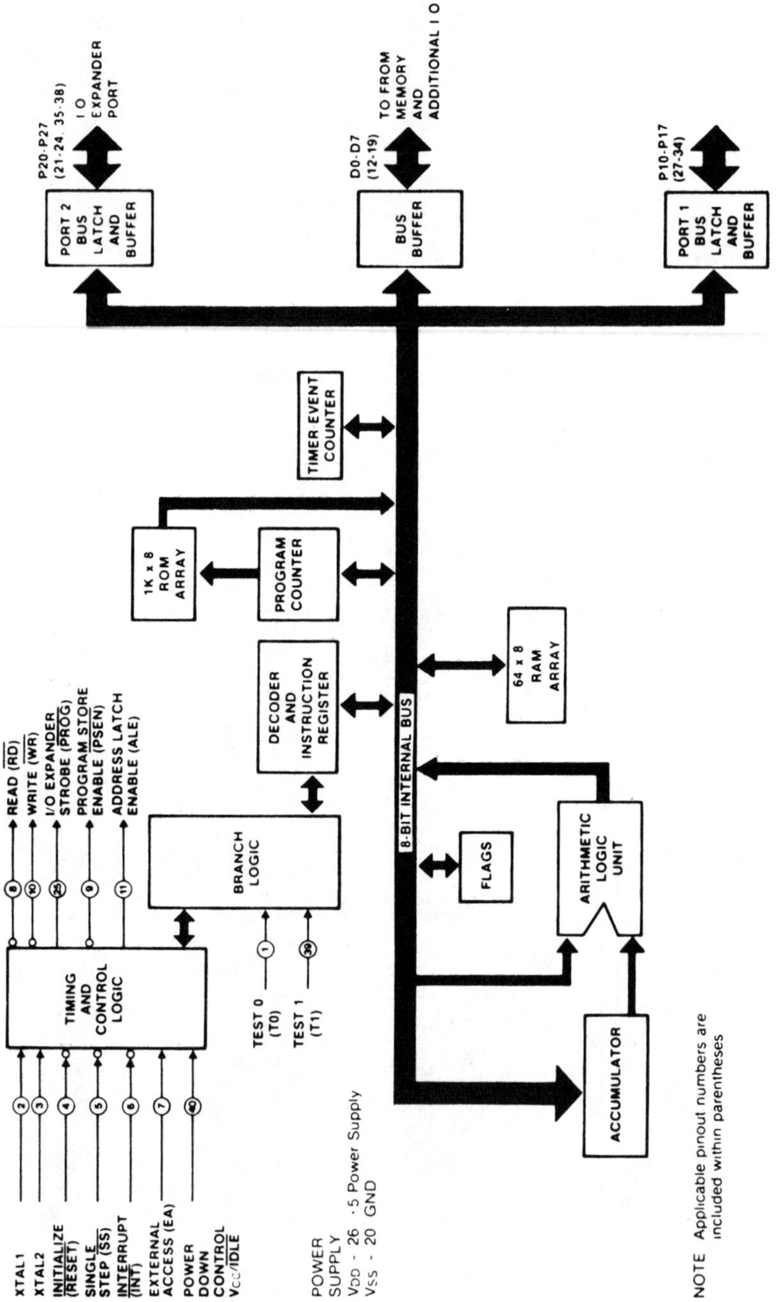

Courtesy of National Semiconductor Corporation.

Block Diagram—80C48, 80C35, 8-Bit μC
Fig. 9-26

For 90% Confidence Level:

In addition to the 75% confidence level test, use a dual-trace oscilloscope to observe the following:

a) Monitor the clock signal on pin 2 or 3 on one trace, while observing the RD signal on pin 8 on the other.
b) Monitor the clock signal on pin 2 or 3 on one trace, while observing the WR signal on pin 10 on the other.

EXACT REPLACEMENT ABSOLUTELY ESSENTIAL.

8050H/8750H (Intel) 8-Bit Microcomputer

This device is fabricated using the N-channel silicon gate HMOS process. It contains a 4K × 8 non-volatile program ROM, a 256 × 8 RAM, 27 I/O lines, and an 8-bit timer/counter in addition to on-board oscillator and clock circuits. It has bit handling capability as well as facilities for both binary and BCD arithmetic.

The 8750H is a logically and functionally pin-compatible version of the 8050H with UV-erasable, user-programmable EPROM program memory available. It emulates the 8050H to 11MHz with minor differences.

PIN NAME	DESCRIPTION	TYPE
P10–P17	Port 1	I/O
P20–P27	Port 2	I/O
DB0–DB7	Data Bus	I/O
T0	Test or Clock Input	I
T1	Test or Timer/Counter	I
$\overline{\text{INT}}$	Interrupt	I
$\overline{\text{RD}}$	Read	O
$\overline{\text{RESET}}$	Reset	I
$\overline{\text{WR}}$	Write	O
ALE	Address Latch Enable	O
$\overline{\text{PSEN}}$	Program Store Enable	O
$\overline{\text{SS}}$	Single Step	I
EA	External Access	I
XTAL1, XTAL2	Crystal	I
PROG	Port Extender Strobe	O
V_{CC}	Power Supply	
V_{DD}	Low Power Standby	
V_{SS}	Ground	

Special Features

- Compatible with 8080/8085 series peripherals.
- Two single level interrupts.
- Interval timer/event counter.
- 1.36 μsec cycle version.
- All instructions one or two cycles in length.
- Over 90 instructions (70% single byte).
- Reduced power consumption.

PIN CONFIGURATION

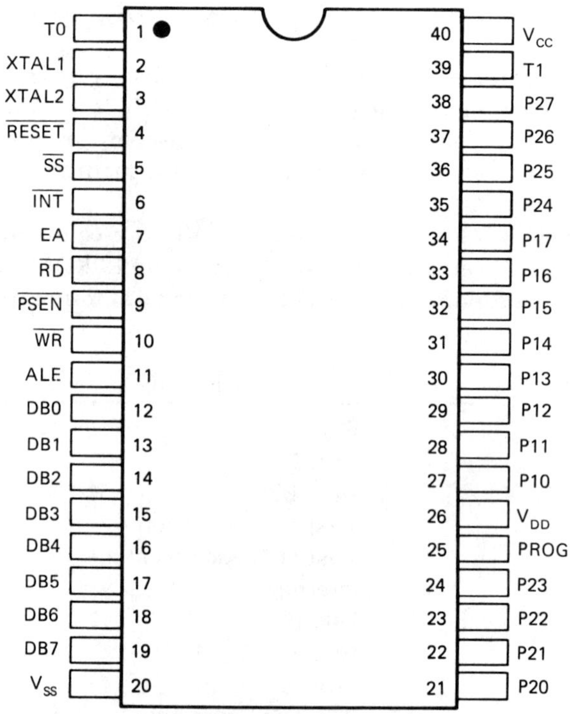

IN-CIRCUIT QUICK-TESTS

FOR 75% CONFIDENCE LEVEL:

1. Volt-ohmmeter Measurements:
   a) Make sure PC board ground has good connection to pin 20.
   b) Measure power supply voltage of 4.5 to 5.5 volts DC at pin 40.

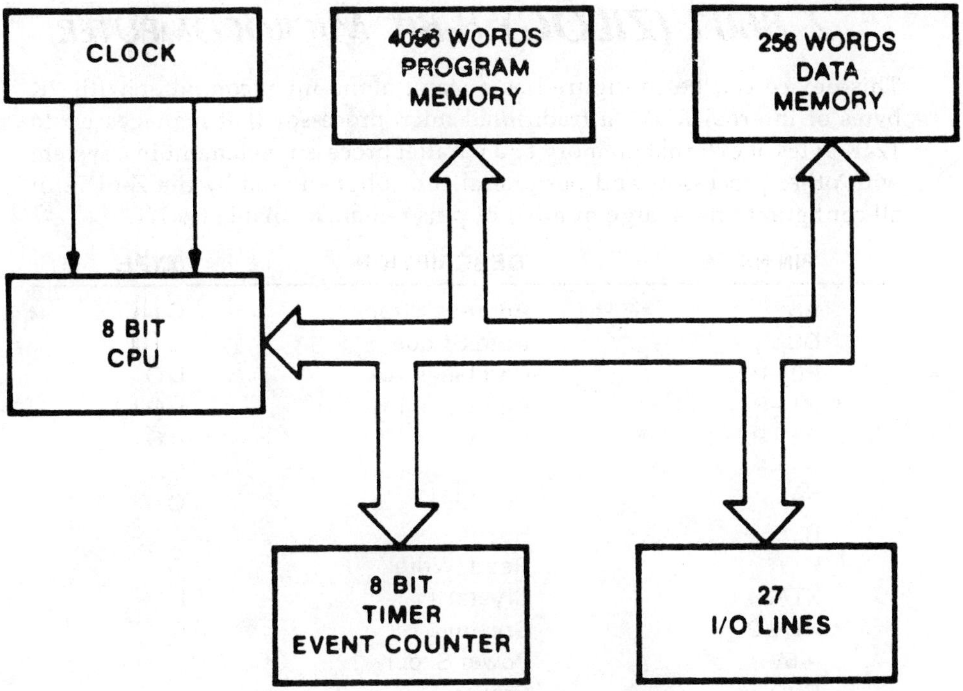

Reprinted by permission of Intel Corporation.

Block Diagram—8050H, 8750H, 8-Bit μC
Fig. 9-27

2. Oscilloscope Measurements:
   a) Observe clock signals at pins 2 and 3. They should be square waves with a frequency of 1.0 to 11.0 MHz.
   b) Observe the signal on pin 11. This signal is the ALE output and is synchronized to the clock.

For 90% Confidence Level:

In addition to the 75% confidence level tests, use a dual-trace oscilloscope to observe the following:

a) Monitor the clock signal on pin 2 or 3 on one trace, while observing the RD signal on pin 8 on the other.
b) Monitor the clock signal on pin 2 or 3 on one trace, while observing the WR signal on pin 10 on the other.

EXACT REPLACEMENT ABSOLUTELY ESSENTIAL.

Z 8601 (ZILOG) 8-BIT MICROCOMPUTER[14]

This device can be configured as a stand alone microcomputer with 2K bytes of internal ROM, a traditional microprocessor that manages up to 124K bytes of external memory or a parallel processing element in a system with other processors and peripheral controllers linked by the Z-BUS. In all configurations, a large number of pins remain available for I/O.

PIN NAME	DESCRIPTION	TYPE
$\overline{AS}$	Address Strobe	O
$\overline{DS}$	Data Strobe	O
$P0_0$-$P0_7$	Port Lines (0)	I/O
$P1_0$-$P1_7$	Port Lines (1)	I/O
$P2_0$-$P2_7$	Port Lines (2)	I/O
$P3_0$-$P3_3$	Port Lines (3)	I
$P3_4$-$P3_7$	Port Lines (3)	O
$\overline{RESET}$	Reset	I
R/$\overline{W}$	Read/Write	O
XTAL1	Crystal 1	I
XTAL2	Crystal 2	O
+5V	Power Supply	
GND	Ground	

Special Features

- Complete microcomputer, 2K bytes of ROM, 128 bytes of RAM, 32 I/O lines, and up to 62K bytes addressable external space each for program and data memory.
- 144-byte register file, including 124 general purpose registers, four I/O port registers, and 16 status and control registers.
- Average instruction execution time of 2.2 μsec., maximum of 4.25 μsec.
- Vectored, priority interrupts for I/O, counter/timers, and UART.
- Full-duplex UART and two programmable 8-bit counter/timers, each with a 6-bit programmable prescaler.
- Register pointer so that short, fast instructions can access any of nine working register groups in 1.5 μsec.
- On-chip oscillator which accepts crystal or external clock drive.
- Low power standby option which retains contents of general purpose registers.
- Single +5V power supply; all pins TTL compatible.

[14]Note: The Z8611 is identical to the 8601, except that the 8611 has 4K bytes of internal ROM and up to 60K bytes addressable external space each for program and data memory.

PIN CONFIGURATION

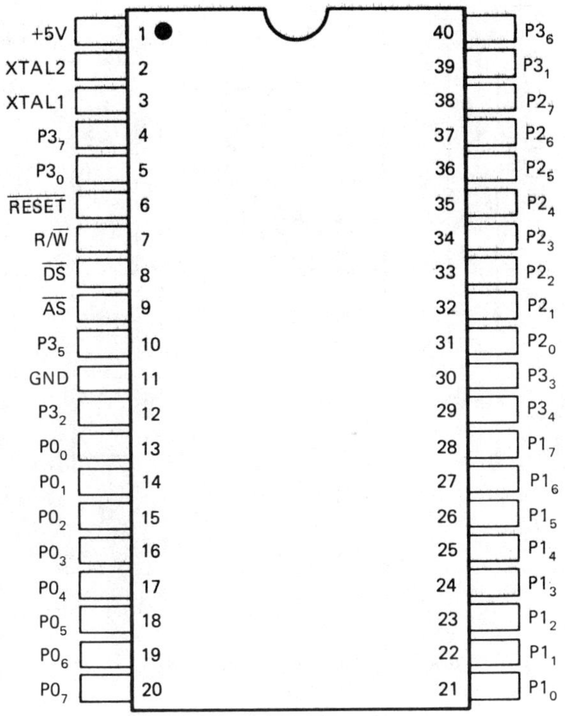

IN-CIRCUIT QUICK-TESTS

FOR 75% CONFIDENCE LEVEL:

1. Volt-ohmmeter Measurements:
   a) Make sure PC board ground has good connection to pin 11.
   b) Measure power supply voltage of 4.75 to 5.25 volts DC at pin 1.
2. Oscilloscope Measurements:
   a) Observe clock signals at pins 2 and 3. They should be square waves with a frequency of 1.0 to 8.0 MHz.
   b) Observe the signal on pin 9. This signal is the AS output and is synchronized to the clock. The strobe indicates the start of each machine cycle.

FOR 90% CONFIDENCE LEVEL:

In addition to the 75% confidence level tests, use a dual-trace oscilloscope to observe the following:

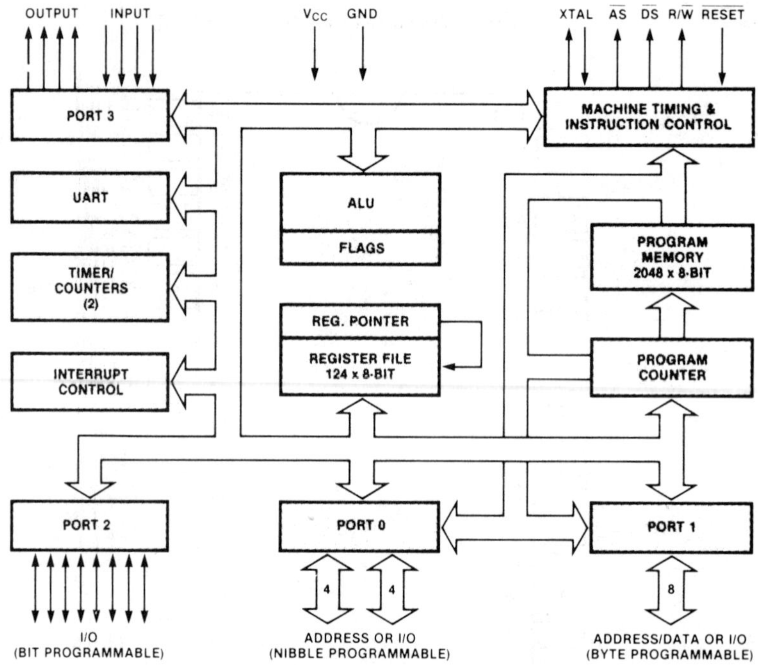

Reproduced by permission of Zilog, Inc.

Block Diagram—8601, 8-Bit μC
Fig. 9-28

a) Monitor the clock signal on pin 2 or 3 on one trace, while observing the DS signal on pin 8 on the other.
b) Monitor the clock signal on pin 2 or 3 on one trace, while observing the R/W wignal on pin 8 on the other.

EXACT REPLACEMENT ABSOULTELY ESSENTIAL.

Z 8602 (ZILOG) MICROPROCESSOR[15]

This 64-pin development version of the 40-pin mask-programmed Z8601 allows the user to prototype the system in hardware with an actual device and to develop the code that is eventually mask-programmed into the on-chip ROM of the Z8601. The Z8602 is identical to the Z8601 with the following exceptions: the internal ROM has been removed, and the ROM address lines and data lines are brought out to external pins and buffered, and control lines for the new memory have been added.

[15]Note: The Z8612 is identical to Z8602.

PIN NAME	DESCRIPTION	TYPE
$\overline{AS}$	Address Strobe	O
$\overline{DS}$	Data Strobe	O
$R/\overline{W}$	Read/Write	O
XTAL 1	Crystal 1	I
XTAL 2	Crystal 2	O
$\overline{RESET}$	Reset	I
$P0_0$–$P0_7$, $P1_0$–$P1_7$	Port Lines	I/O
$P2_0$–$P2_7$	Port Lines	I/O
$P3_0$–$P3_3$	Port Lines	I
$P3_4$–$P3_7$	Port Lines	O
A0–A11	Program Memory Address	O
D0–D7	Program Data	I
IACK	Interrupt Acknowledge	O
$\overline{MDS}$	Program Memory Data Strobe	O
SCLK	System Clock	O
$\overline{SYNC}$	Instruction Sync	O
V_{CC}	Power Supply	
GND	Ground	

IN-CIRCUIT QUICK-TESTS

FOR 75% CONFIDENCE LEVEL:

1. Volt-ohmmeter Measurements:
   a) Make sure PC board ground has good connection to pin 48.
   b) Measure power supply voltage of 4.75 to 5.25 volts DC at pin 64.
2. Oscilloscope Measurements:
   a) Observe clock signals at pins 62 and 63. They should be square waves with a frequency of 1.0 to 8.0 MHz.
   b) Observe the signal on pin 56. This signal is the AS output and is synchronized to the clock. This strobe indicates the start of each machine cycle.

FOR 90% CONFIDENCE LEVEL:

In addition to the 75% confidence level tests, use a dual-trace oscilloscope to observe the following:

a) Monitor the clock signal on pin 62 or 63 on one trace, while observing the DS signal on pin 57 on the other.

b) Monitor the clock signal on pin 62 or 63 on one trace, while observing the R/W signal on pin 58 on the other.

EXACT REPLACEMENT ABSOLUTELY ESSENTIAL.

PIN CONFIGURATION

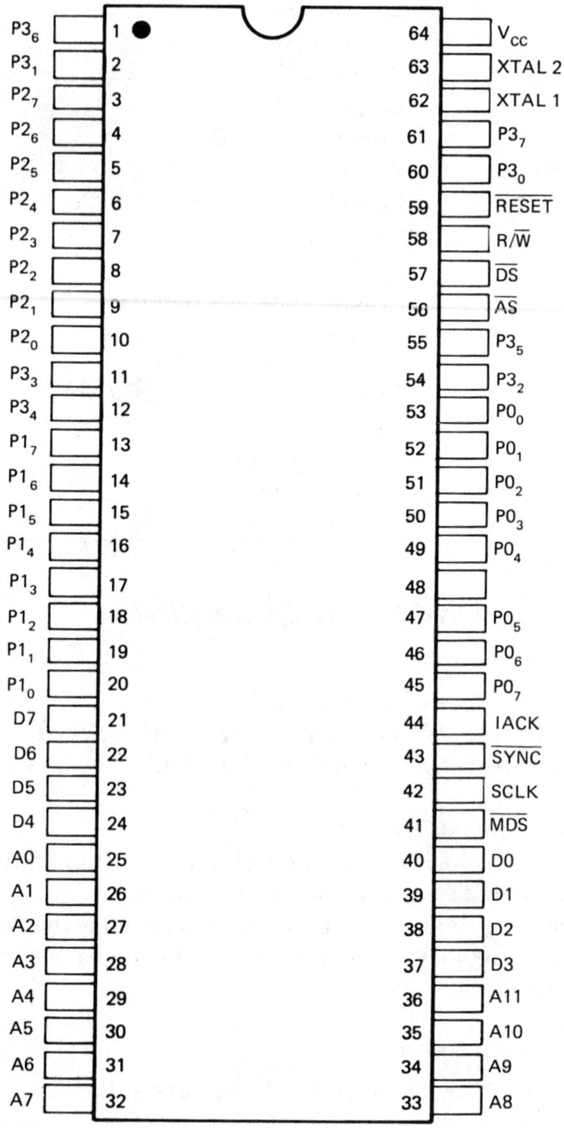

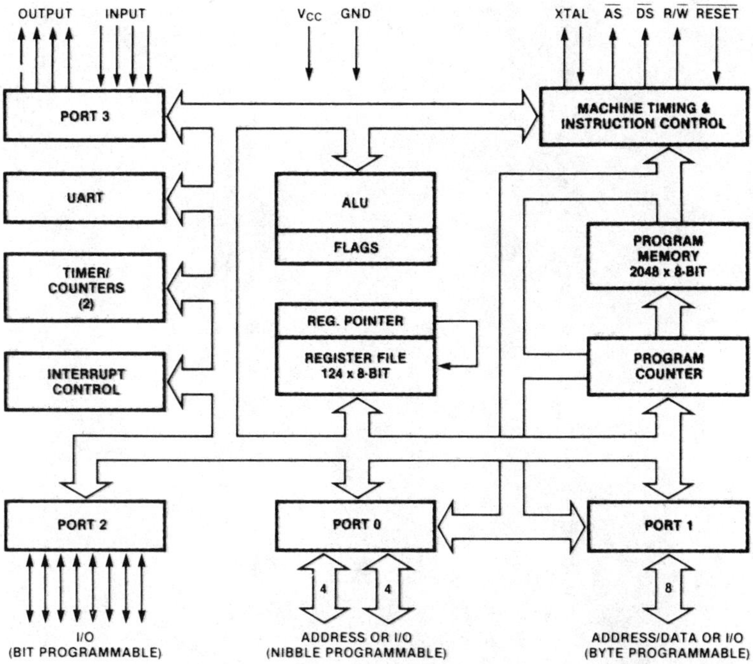

Reproduced by permission of Zilog, Inc.

Block Diagram—8602, 8-Bit μC
Fig. 9-29

CHAPTER 10

16-BIT MICROCOMPUTER (μC)

Z 8 (ZILOG) MICROCOMPUTER 16-BIT μC

This device can be used as 16-bit CPU or it can be configured as a microcomputer with 2K bit of internal ROM, a traditional microprocessor that manages up to 124 K bit of external memory, or as parallel processing element in a system with other processors and peripheral controllers linked by the Z-BUS. In all configurations, a large number of pins remain available for I/O.

PIN NAME	DESCRIPTION	TYPE
$P0_0$–$P0_7$ (or AD_8–AD_{15})	Nibble Programmable Port	I/O
$P1_0$–$P1_7$ (or AD_0–AD_7)	Byte Programmable Port	I/O
$P2_0$–$P2_7$	Bit Programmable Port	I/O
$P3_0$–$P3_3$	Serial and Parallel I/O	I
$P3_4$–$P3_7$	and Control	O
$\overline{RESET}$	Reset	I
$R/\overline{W}$	Read/Write	O
$\overline{DS}$	Data Strobe	O
$\overline{AS}$	Address Strobe	O
XTAL 1	Crystal 1	I
XTAL 2	Crystal 2	O
+5V	Power Supply	
GND	Ground	

PIN CONFIGURATION

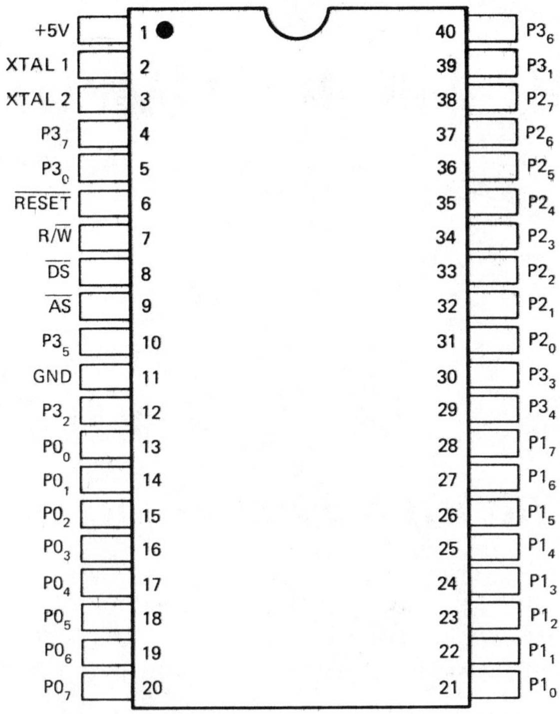

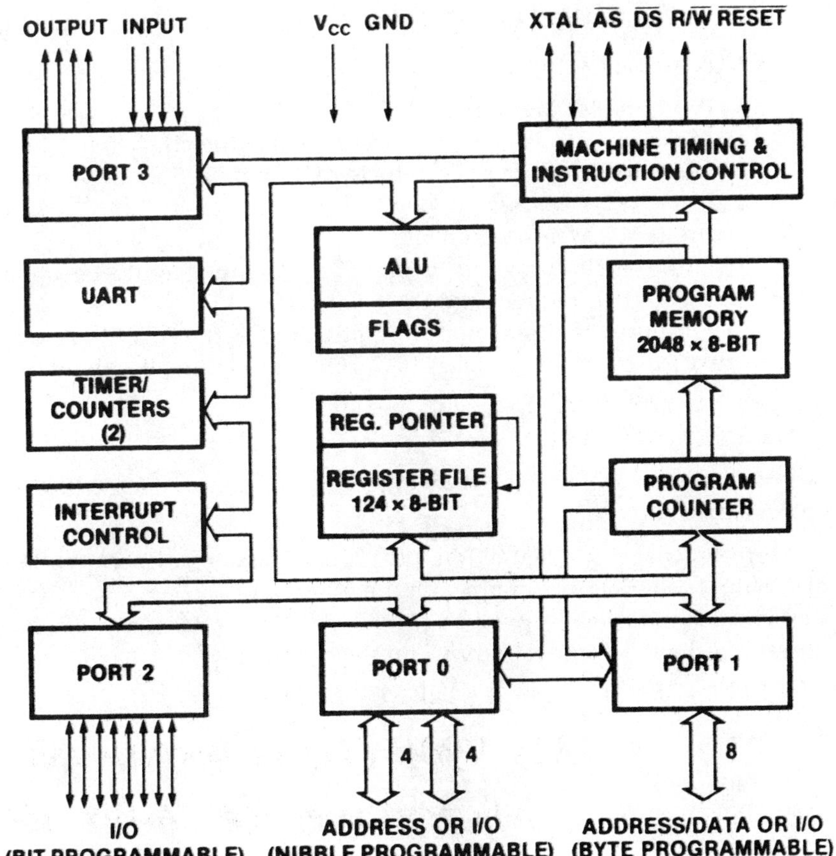

Reproduced by permission of Zilog, Inc.

Block Diagram—8, 16-Bit μC
Fig. 10-1

Special Features

- 144-byte register file, including 124 general purpose registers, four I/O ports registers, and 16 status and control registers.
- Full duplex UART and two programmable 8-bit counter/timers, each with a 6-bit programmable prescaler.
- Register pointer to allow short, fast instructions to access any of nine working register groups in 1.5 μSec.
- Average instruction execution time of 2 μsec., maximum of 4.25 μsec.
- Vectored, priority interrupts for I/O, counter/timers, and UART.
- On-chip oscillator which accepts crystal, RC or LC reference, or external clock drive.
- Low power standby option which retains contents of general purpose registers.

IN-CIRCUIT QUICK-TESTS

For 75% Confidence Level:

1. Volt-ohmmeter Measurements:
   a) Make sure PC board ground has good connection to pin 11.
   b) Measure power supply voltage of 4.75 to 5.25 volts DC at pin 1.
2. Oscilloscope Measurements:
   a) Observe clock signals at pins 2 or 3. They should be square waves with a frequency of 1.0 to 8.0 MHz.
   b) Observe the signal on pin 9. This signal is the AS output and is synchronized to the clock. This strobe signal indicates the start of each machine cycle.

For 90% Confidence Level:

In addition to the 75% confidence level tests, use a dual-trace oscilloscope to observe the following:

a) Monitor the clock signal on pin 2 or 3 on one trace, while observing the DS signal on pin 8 on the other.
b) Monitor the clock signal on pin 2 or 3 on one trace, while observing the R/W signal on pin 7 on the other.

EXACT REPLACEMENT ABSOLUTELY ESSENTIAL.

TMS 9940 (Texas Instruments) Microcomputer 16-Bit μC[1]

This device contains a CPU, memory (128 bytes of RAM and 2048 bytes of EPROM/ROM), and extensive I/O lines. The unique memory to memory architecture features multiple register files, resident in the RAM, which allow faster response to interrupts and increased programming flexibility. The TMS 9940 implements four levels of interrupts including an internal decrementer which can be programmed as a timer or an event counter. All members of the TMS 9900 family of peripheral circuits are compatible with TMS 9940.

PIN NAME	DESCRIPTION	TYPE
XTAL 1	Crystal	I
XTAL 2	Crystal or External Oscillator	I
$\overline{RST}$/PE	Reset/Program Enable	I
INT1/TST	Interrupt 1/Test	I
$\overline{INT2}$/PROG	Interrupt 2/Program Pulse	I

[1]Note: the same microprocessor is manufactured by: AMI—S9940.

PIN NAME	DESCRIPTION	TYPE
P0-P7/A1-A8	General Purpose I/O Lines/Address Bus	I/O
P8/CRUIN	General Purpose I/O Line/CRU in	I/O
P9/CRUOUT	General Purpose I/O Line/CRU out	I/O
P10/CRUCLK	General Purpose I/O Line/CRU Clock	I/O
P11/$\overline{TC}$	General Purpose I/O Line/Transfer Clock	I/O
P12/TD	General Purpose I/O Line/Transfer Data	I/O
P13/$\overline{\emptyset}$	General Purpose I/O Line/Clock Output	I/O
P14/$\overline{HLD}$	General Purpose I/O Line/Hold	I/O
P15/$\overline{HLDA}$	General Purpose I/O Line/Hold Acknowledge	I/O
P16/$\overline{IDLE}$	General Purpose I/O Line/Idle State Indicator	I/O
P17/EC	General Purpose I/O Line/Event Counter	I/O
P18-P31	General Purpose I/O Lines	I/O
V_{CC1}	Standby Power Supply	
V_{CC2}	Normal Power Supply	
V_{SS}	Ground	

Pin Configuration

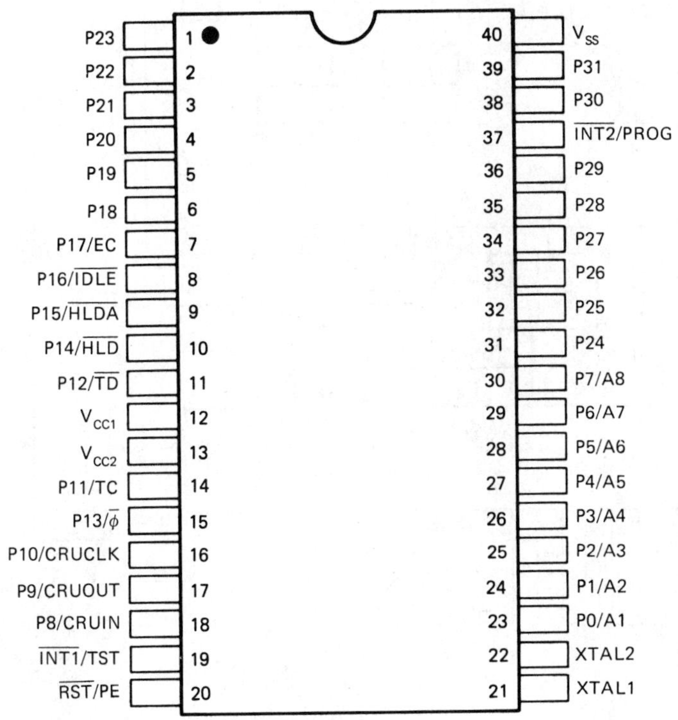

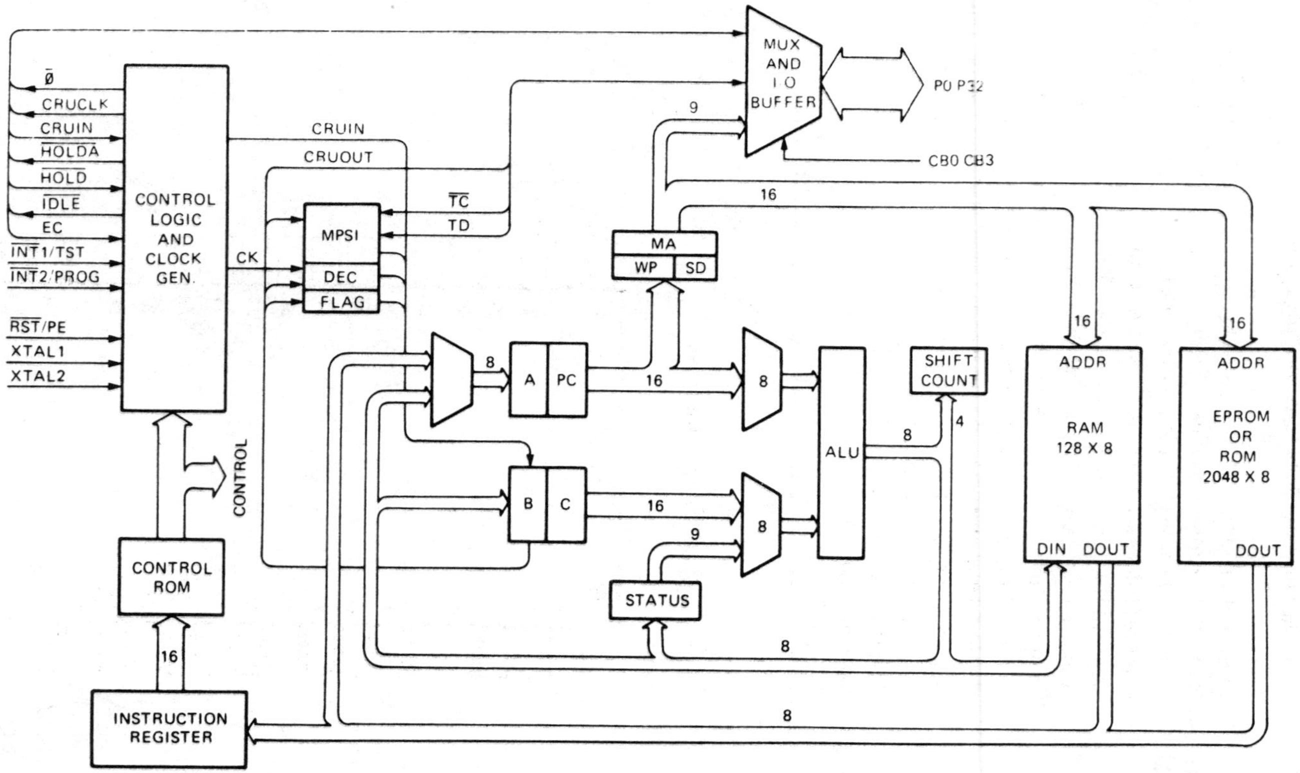

Courtesy Texas Instruments Incorporated.

Block Diagram—9940, 16-Bit μC
Fig. 10-2

Special Features

- Minicomputer instruction set including multiply and divide.
- Four prioritized interrupts.
- On-chip timer/event counter.
- 32-bit general purpose I/O ports.
- 256-bit I/O expansion.
- Multiprocessor system interface.
- Five speed ranges for maximum performance (5, 4, 3, 2, 1 MHz)
- 5V power supply.
- There are two types of the TMS 9940 microprocessor: TMS 9940 E—an EPROM device, and TMS 9940 M—a mask ROM device.

IN-CIRCUIT QUICK-TESTS

FOR 75% CONFIDENCE LEVEL:

1. Volt-ohmmeter Measurements:
   a) Make sure PC board ground has good connection to pin 40.
   b) Measure power supply voltage of 4.5 to 5.5 volts DC at pins 12 and 13.
2. Oscilloscope Measurements:
   a) Observe clock signals at pins 21 and 22. They should be square waves with a frequency of 1.0 to 5.0 MHz.
   b) Observe the signal on pin 23. This signal is the PO/A1 output and is synchronized to the clock.

FOR 90% CONFIDENCE LEVEL:

In addition to the 75% confidence level tests, use a dual-trace oscilloscope to observe the following:

a) Monitor the clock signal on pin 21 or 22 on one trace, while observing the P1/A2 signal on pin 23 on the other.
b) Monitor the clock signal on pin 21 or 22 on one trace, while observing the P18 signal on pin 6 on the other.

EXACT REPLACEMENT ABSOLUTELY ESSENTIAL.

CHAPTER 11

4-BIT MICROCONTROLLER (μ Controller)

WD 4020 (WESTERN DIGITAL) MICROCONTROLLER 4-BIT μCONTROLLER

This device is a ROM-less member of the Control Oriented Processors (COP). It contains CPU, RAM, and I/O, and is identical to a WD4200 device, except that the ROM has been removed; pins have been added to output the ROM address and to input the ROM data. In a system, the WD4020 performs exactly like the WD4200, but is used for development and debugging of a WD4200 program prior to masking the final part.

PIN NAME	DESCRIPTION	TYPE
CKO	System Oscillator Output	O
CKI	System Oscillator Input	I
IP0–IP7	Bidirectional ROM addess and Data Ports	I/O
$\overline{\text{RESET}}$	System Reset	I
L0–L7	Bidirectional I/O Ports	I/O
IN0–IN3	General Purpose Inputs	I
SI	Serial Input (or Counter Input)	I
SO	Serial Output (or General Purpose Output)	O
SK	Logic-controlled Clock (or General Purpose Output)	O
G0–G3	Bidirectional I/O Ports	I/O
SKIP	Instruction Skip	O
AD/$\overline{\text{DATA}}$	Address-out/Data-in Flag	O
P8–P9	ROM Address Outputs	O
D0–D3	General Purpose Lines	O
V_{CC}	Power Supply	
GND	Ground	

PIN CONFIGURATION

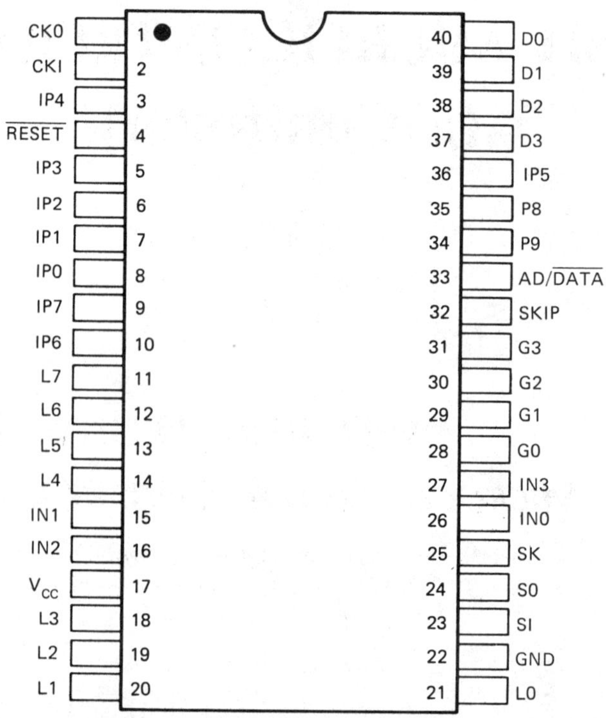

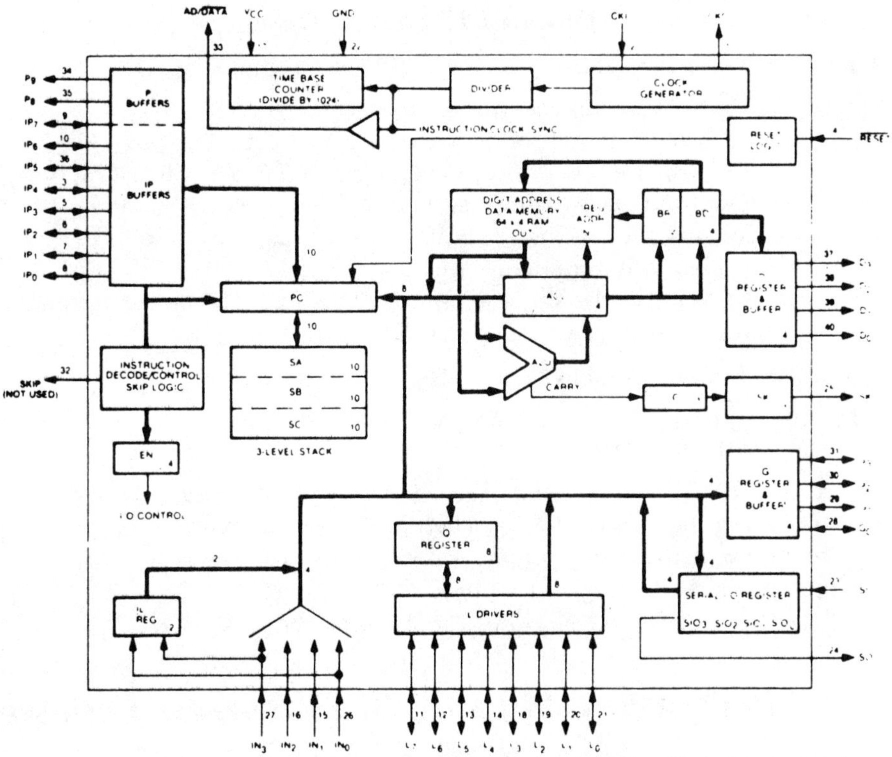

Courtesy of Western Digital Corporation.

Block Diagram – 4020, 4-Bit μController
Fig. 11-1

Special Features

- Exact circuit equivalent of WD4200.
- Interfaces with standard PROM or ROM.
- 64 × 4 RAM, addresses up to 1K × 8 ROM.
- Powerful instruction set.
- True vectored interrupt, plus restart.
- Three-level subroutine stack.
- 4.0 μsec. instruction time.
- Single supply operation (4.5V to 6.3V).
- Internal time base counter for real-time processing.
- Internal binary counter register with serial I/O capability.
- Software/hardware compatible with other members of WD4200 family.

IN-CIRCUIT QUICK-TESTS

FOR 75% CONFIDENCE LEVEL:

1. Volt-ohmmeter Measurements:
   a) Make sure PC board ground has good connection to pin 22.
   b) Measure power supply voltage of 4.5 to 5.5 volts DC at pin 17.
2. Oscilloscope Measurements:
   a) Observe clock signals at pins 1 and 2. They should be square waves with a frequency of 1.6 to 4.0 MHz.
   b) Observe the signal on pin 24. This signal is the SO output and is synchronized to the clock. This a serial output.

FOR 90% CONFIDENCE LEVEL:

In addition to the 75% confidence level tests, use a dual-trace oscilloscope to observe the following:

a) Monitor the clock signal on pin 1 or 2 on one trace, while observing the AD, DATA signal on pin 33 on the other.
b) Monitor the clock signal on pin 1 or 2 on one trace, while observing the DO signal on pin 37 on the other.

EXACT REPLACEMENT ABSOLUTELY ESSENTIAL.

WD 4200/WD 4210 (WESTERN DIGITAL) MICROCONTROLLER 4-BIT μCONTROLLER

This device is a member of the control oriented processor family. It is a complete microcomputer, containing 1K × 8 ROM, 64 × 4 RAM, internal time base counter for real time processing, internal binary counter register with serial I/O capability, and I/O necessary to implement dedicated control functions.

PIN NAME	DESCRIPTION	TYPE
L7-L0	I/O Ports	I/O
G3-G0	I/O Ports	I/O
D3-D0	General Purpose Outputs	O
IN3-IN0	General Purpose Inputs	I
S1	Serial Input (or Counter Input)	I
SO	Serial Output (or General Purpose Output)	O
SK	Logic-controlled Clock (or General Purpose Output)	I or O
CK1	System Oscillator Input	I
CKO	System Oscillator Output (or General Purpose Input or RAM Power Supply)	O or I

PIN NAME	DESCRIPTION	TYPE
$\overline{\text{RESET}}$	Reset	I
V_{CC}	Power Supply	
GND	Ground	

PIN CONFIGURATION

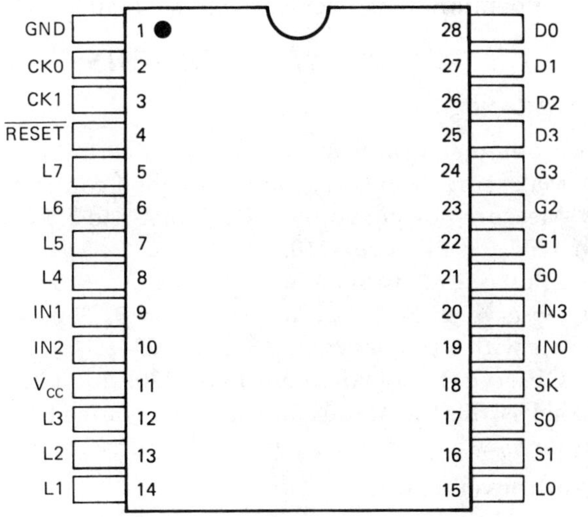

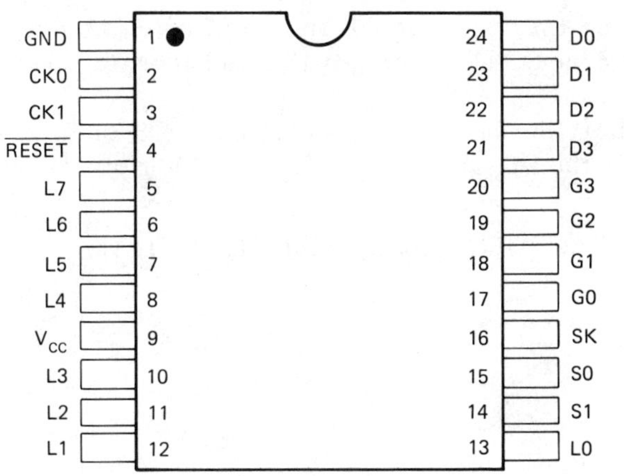

Special Features

- 23 I/O lines (WD 4200), 19 I/O lines (WD 4210).
- True vectored interrupt, plus restart.
- Three-level subroutine stack.
- 4.0 μsec. instruction time.
- Single supply operation (4.5V to 6.3V).
- General purpose and TRI-STATE outputs.
- TTL/CMOS compatible in and out.
- LED direct drive outputs.
- MICROBUS compatible.
- Software/hardware compatible with other members of WD4200 family.
- Extended temperature range device available (−40°C to +85°C)

IN-CIRCUIT QUICK-TESTS

FOR 75% CONFIDENCE LEVEL:

1. Volt-ohmmeter Measurements:
   a) Make sure PC board ground has good connection to pin 1.
   b) Measure power supply voltage of 4.5 to 5.5 volts DC at pin 11 on 4200 and pin 9 on 4210.
2. Oscilloscope Measurements:
   a) Observe clock signals at pins 2 and 3. They should be square waves with a frequency of 0.8 to 4.0 MHz.
   b) Observe the signal on pin 18 on 4200 and pin 16 on 4210. This signal is the SK output and is synchronized to the clock. It is either 1/4, 1/8 or 1/16 of the frequency on pins 2 and 3.

FOR 90% CONFIDENCE LEVEL:

In addition to the 75% confidence level tests, use a dual-trace oscilloscope to observe the following:

a) Monitor the clock signal on pin 2 or 3 on one trace, while observing the SO signal on pin 17 on 4200 or pin 15 on 4210 on the other.
b) Monitor the clock signal on pin 2 or 3 on one trace, while observing the D0 signal on pin 28 on 4200 or pin 24 on 4210 on the other.

EXACT REPLACEMENT ABSOLUTELY ESSENTIAL.

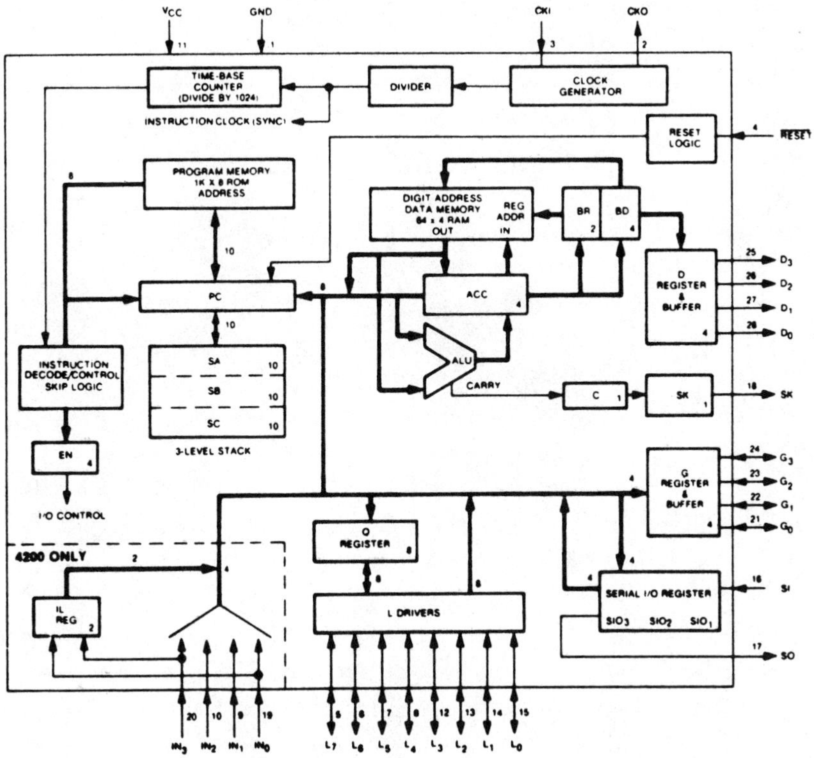

Courtesy of Western Digital Corporation.

Block Diagram—4200, 4210, 4-Bit μController
Fig. 11-2

CHAPTER 12

8-BIT MICROCONTROLLER (μ Controller)

8-Bit μ Controller

8X300 (Signetics) Microcontroller

8-Bit μController

This device is a high-speed bipolar microprocessor implemented with low power Schottky technology. It is designed for industrial control, input/output control, and data communication. The 8X300 uses three separate buses—one for 13-bit instruction addresses, one for 16-bit instructions, and a bidirectional 8-bit input/output data bus; except for the I/O bus, there is no time multiplexing of functions.

PIN NAME	DESCRIPTION	TYPE
A0–A12	Program Address Lines	O
I0–I15	Instruction Lines	I
$\overline{\text{IV0}}$–$\overline{\text{IV7}}$	Input/Output Bus	I/O
X1, X2	Clock	I
MCLK	Master Clock	O
WC	Write Command	O
SC	Select Command	O
$\overline{\text{LB}}$	Left Bank	O
$\overline{\text{RB}}$	Right Bank	O
$\overline{\text{RESET}}$	Reset	I
$\overline{\text{HALT}}$	Halt	I
VR	Reference Output Voltage	O
VCR	Regulated Voltage	I
V_{CC}	Power Supply	
GND	Ground	

Special Features

- Fetch, decode, and execute a 16-bit instruction in a minimum of 250 nanoseconds (nsec. or one machine cycle).
- Bit-oriented instruction set (addressable single- or multiple-bit subfields).
- Separate address, instruction, and I/O buses.
- Source/destination architecture.
- On-chip oscillator and timing generation.
- Eight 8-bit working registers.
- TTL inputs and outputs.
- 3-state I/O bus.

IN-CIRCUIT QUICK-TESTS

FOR 75% CONFIDENCE LEVEL:

1. Volt-ohmmeter Measurements:
   a) Make sure PC board ground has good connection to pin 12.
   b) Measure power supply voltage of 4.5 to 5.5 volts DC at pin 37.
2. Oscilloscope Measurements:
   a) Observe clock signals at pins 10 and 11. They should be square waves with a frequency of 1.0 to 8.0 MHz.

PIN CONFIGURATION

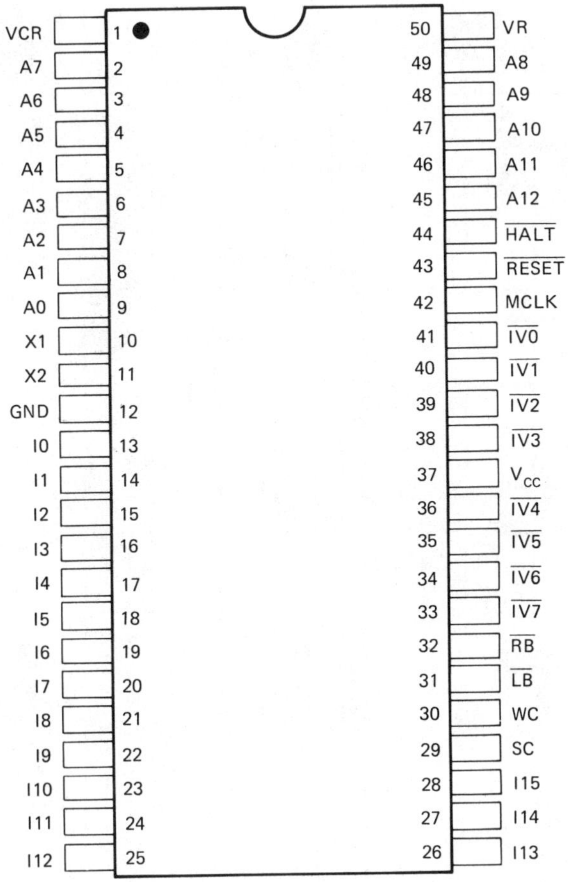

b) Observe the signal on pin 42. This signal is the master clock output and is synchronized to the clock.

FOR 90% CONFIDENCE LEVEL:

In addition to the 75% confidence level tests, use a dual-trace oscilloscope to observe the following:

a) Monitor the clock signal on pin 10 or 11 on one trace, while observing the WC signal on pin 30 on the other.
b) Monitor the clock signal on pin 10 or 11 on one trace, while observing the SC signal on pin 29 on the other.

EXACT REPLACEMENT ABSOLUTELY ESSENTIAL.

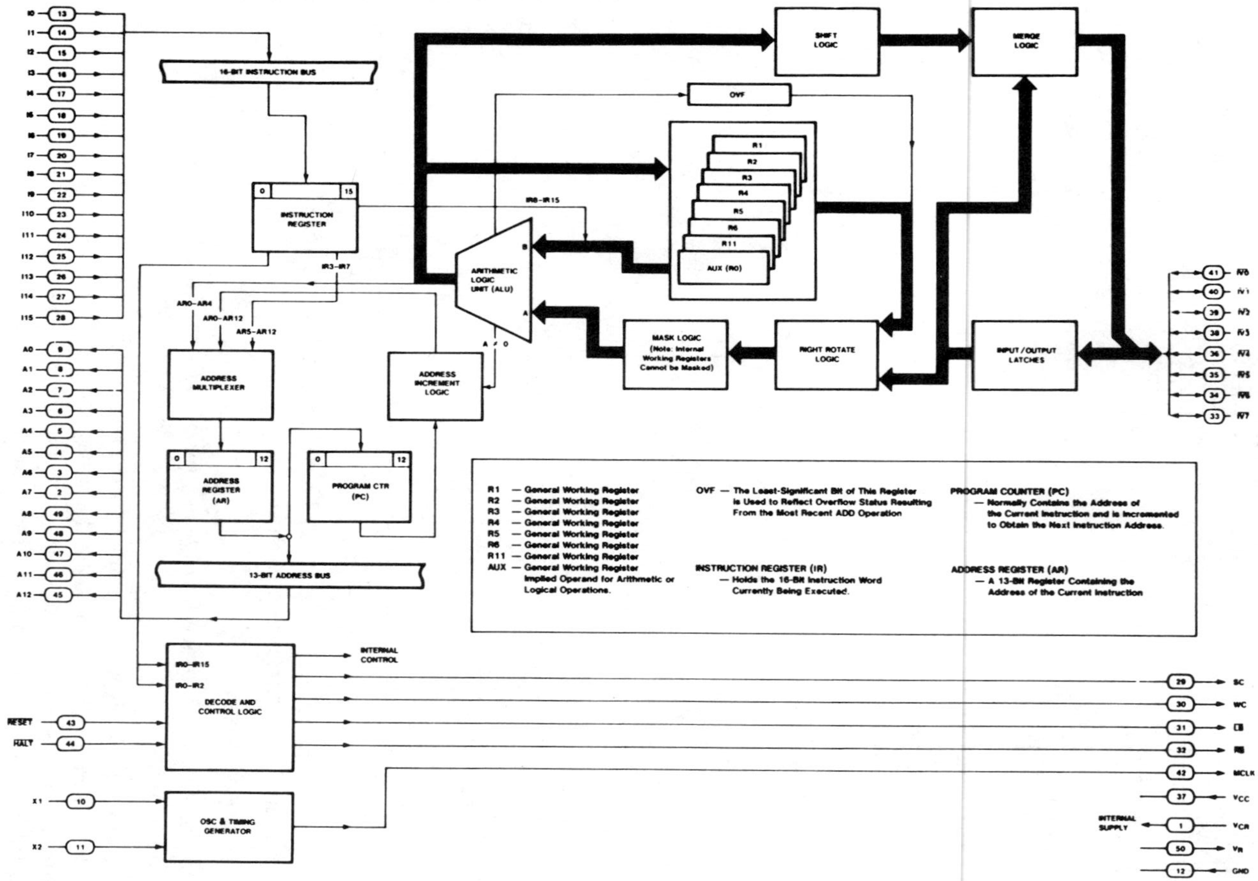

Courtesy of Signetics, 811 East Arques Avenue, Sunnyvale, CA 94086.

Block Diagram—8X300, 8-Bit μController
Fig. 12-1

APPENDIX

Appendix A contains a list of manufacturers of all types of microprocessor ICs, together with the address of their main office in the U.S.
Appendix B contains the mechanical drawings and dimensions of all standard IC packages for the microprocessors described in this book.
Appendix C contains the essential electrical characteristics of each of the major IC families according to the manufacturing process used.

APPENDIX A
MANUFACTURERS OF MICROPROCESSORS

- Adar/Scientific-Atlanta, 154G Middlesex Tpke Burlington MA 01803 .... (617)273-1850
- Advanced Micro Devices, 901G Thompson Pl Sunnyvale CA 94086 .... (408)732-2400
- Altek Corp, 2150G Indl Pkwy Silver Sprg MD 20904 .... (301)622-3906
- American Microsystems Inc, 3800G Homestead Rd Santa Clara CA 95051 . . .. (408)246-0330
- Applied Sys Corp, Computer Sys, 26401G Harper Av St Clair Shores MI 48081 (313)779-8700
- Blakely Assoc, 97G Madison Pl Ridgewood NJ 07452 .... (201)444-8929
- Fairchild Camera & Instru Corp, Semiconductor Prods, 464G Ellis Mtn View CA 94042 .... (415)962-5011
- General Instru Corp, Microelectronics, 600 W John St GB Hicksville NY 11802 .... (516)733-3107
- GTE Prods Corp, GTE Microcircuits, 2000 W 14th St Tempe AZ 85281 .... (602)968-4431
- Hughes Aircraft Co, Solid State Prods, 500G Superior Av Newport Bch CA 92663 .... (714)759-2411
- Integrated Computer Sys, 3304G Pico Blv Santa Monica CA 90405 .... (213)450-2060
- Intersil Inc, Dept G, 10710 N Tantau Av Cupertino CA 95014 .... (408)996-5000
- Levit Electronics Inc, 200G Park Av S NY NY 10003 .... (212)777-5517
- Matsushita Elecs Corp, Dept G, 1-1 Saiwai-cho, Takatsuki-City, Osaka 569, Japan 0726-82-5521
- Mitel Corp, Semiconductor Mktg, 350G Leggett Dr, Kanata, Ont K2K 1X3, Canada .... (613)592-2122
- MOS Technology Inc, 950G Rittenhouse Rd Norristown PA 19401 .... (215)666-7950
- Mostek Corp, Dept G, 1215 W Crosby Rd Carrollton TX 75006 .... (214)323-6000

- Motorola Semiconductor Prod Inc, Dept G, PO Box 20912 Phoenix AZ 85036 .... (602)244-6900
- NEC Microcomputers, Inc, 1 Natisk, Executive Park, Nastik, MA, 01760 .... (617)655-8833
- Raytheon Co, Semiconductor Div, Dept G, 350 Ellis St Mtn View CA 94042 .... (415)968-9211
- RCA Solid State Div, Dept G, Somerville NJ 08876 .... (201)685-6000
- Semiconductor Specialists Inc, Dept G, Box 66125 O'Hare Intl Arpt Chicago IL 60666 .... (312)279-1000
- Signetics Corp, US Philips Corp, Bin 12-27GB, 811 E Arques Av PO Box 409 Sunnyvale CA 94086 .... (408)739-7700
- Standard Microsystems Corp, 35G Marcus Blv Hauppauge NY 11787 .... (516)273-3100
- Synertek Inc, 3001 Stender Way Santa Clara CA 95051 .... (408)988-5600
- Temtron Elecs Ltd, 15G Main St E Rockaway NY 11518 .... (516)599-6400
- Texas Instrus Inc, Semiconductor Grp, Dept G, PO Box 225012 M/S 84 Dallas TX 75265 .... (214)995-6611
- Unitronix Corp, 198G Rte 206 S Somerville NJ 08876 .... (201)725-2560
- Zilog Inc, Components, 10460G Bubb Rd Cupertino CA 95014 .... (408)446-4666

APPENDIX B
IC MECHANICAL DRAWINGS AND DIMENSIONS

24-PIN PACKAGES

CERAMIC PACKAGE
CASE 716

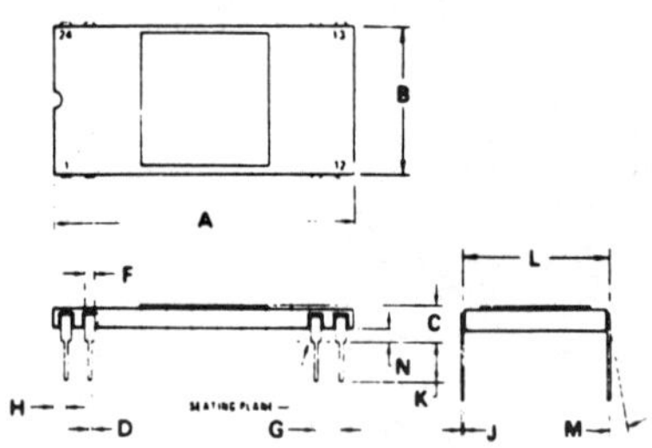

NOTE:
1. LEADS TRUE POSITIONED WITHIN 0.25mm (0.010) DIA (AT SEATING PLANE) AT MAXIMUM MATERIAL CONDITION.
2. DIM "L" TO CENTER OF LEADS WHEN FORMED PARALLEL.

DIM	MILLIMETERS		INCHES	
	MIN	MAX	MIN	MAX
A	27.64	30.99	1.088	1.220
B	14.73	15.34	0.580	0.604
C	2.67	4.32	0.105	0.170
D	0.38	0.53	0.015	0.021
F	0.76	1.40	0.030	0.055
G	2.54 BSC		0.100 BSC	
H	0.76	1.78	0.030	0.070
J	0.20	0.30	0.008	0.012
K	2.54	4.57	0.100	0.180
L	14.99	15.49	0.590	0.610
M	–	10°	–	10°
N	1.02	1.52	0.040	0.060

MECHANICAL DATA (CONTINUED)

24-PIN PACKAGES (CONTINUED)

PLASTIC PACKAGE
CASE 709

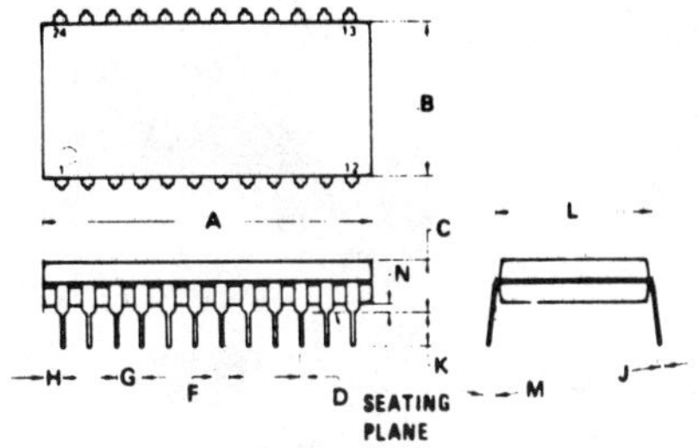

NOTES:
1. POSITIONAL TOLERANCE OF LEADS (D), SHALL BE WITHIN 0.25 mm (0.010) AT MAXIMUM MATERIAL CONDITION, IN RELATION TO SEATING PLANE AND EACH OTHER.
2. DIMENSION L TO CENTER OF LEADS WHEN FORMED PARALLEL.
3. DIMENSION B DOES NOT INCLUDE MOLD FLASH.

DIM	MILLIMETERS		INCHES	
	MIN	MAX	MIN	MAX
A	31.37	32.13	1.235	1.265
B	13.72	14.22	0.540	0:560
C	3.94	5.08	0.155	0.200
D	0.36	0.56	0.014	0.022
F	1.02	1.52	0.040	0.060
G	2.54 BSC		0.100 BSC	
H	1.78	2.03	0.070	0.080
J	0.20	0.38	0.008	0.015
K	2.92	3.43	0.115	0.135
L	15.24 BSC		0.600 BSC	
M	0°	15°	0°	15°
N	0.51	1.02	0.020	0.040

CERDIP PACKAGE
CASE 623

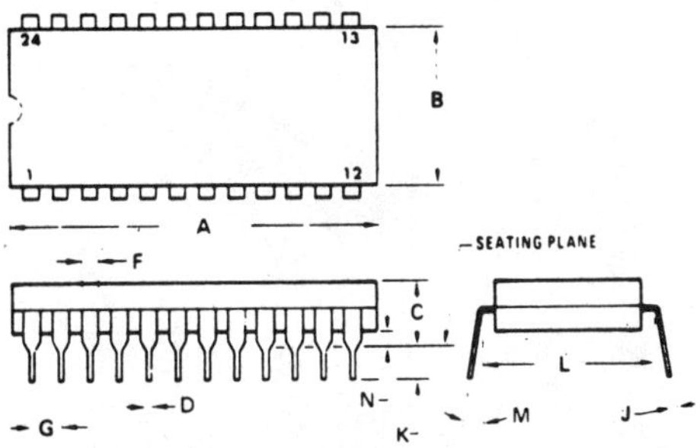

NOTES:
1. DIM "L" TO CENTER OF LEADS WHEN FORMED PARALLEL.
2. LEADS WITHIN 0.13 mm (0.005) RADIUS OF TRUE POSITION AT SEATING PLANE AT MAXIMUM MATERIAL CONDITION. (WHEN FORMED PARALLEL)

DIM	MILLIMETERS		INCHES	
	MIN	MAX	MIN	MAX
A	31.24	32.77	1.230	1.290
B	12.70	15.49	0.500	0.610
C	4.06	5.59	0.160	0.220
D	0.41	0.51	0.016	0.020
F	1.27	1.52	0.050	0.060
G	2.54 BSC		0.100 BSC	
J	0.20	0.30	0.008	0.012
K	2.29	4.06	0.090	0.160
L	15.24 BSC		0.600 BSC	
M	0°	15°	0°	15°
N	0.51	1.27	0.020	0.050

MECHANICAL DATA (CONTINUED)

28-PIN PACKAGES

CERAMIC PACKAGE
CASE 719

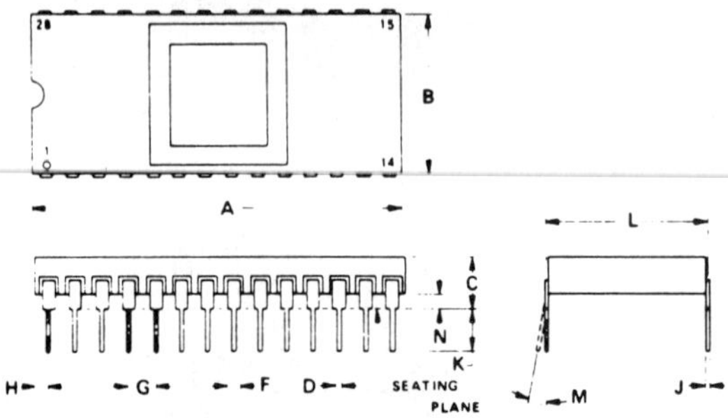

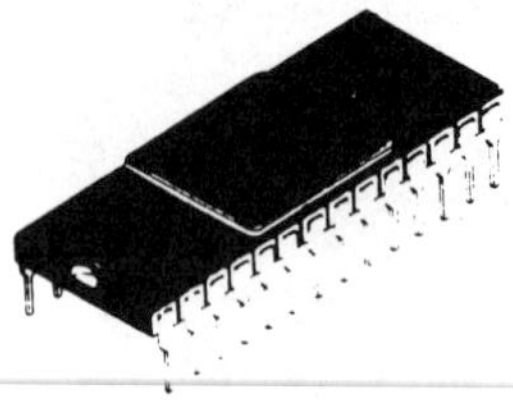

DIM	MILLIMETERS		INCHES	
	MIN	MAX	MIN	MAX
A	35.20	35.92	1.386	1.414
B	14.73	15.34	0.580	0.604
C	3.05	4.19	0.120	0.165
D	0.38	0.53	0.015	0.021
F	0.76	1.40	0.030	0.055
G	2.54 BSC		0.100 BSC	
H	0.76	1.78	0.030	0.070
J	0.20	0.30	0.008	0.012
K	2.54	4.19	0.100	0.165
L	14.99	15.49	0.590	0.610
M	–	10°	–	10°
N	0.51	1.52	0.020	0.060

NOTES:
1. LEADS, TRUE POSITIONED WITHIN 0.25 mm (0.010) DIAMETER (AT SEATING PLANE) AT MAXIMUM MATERIAL CONDITION.
2. DIMENSION "L" TO CENTER OF LEADS WHEN FORMED PARALLEL.

PLASTIC PACKAGE
CASE 710

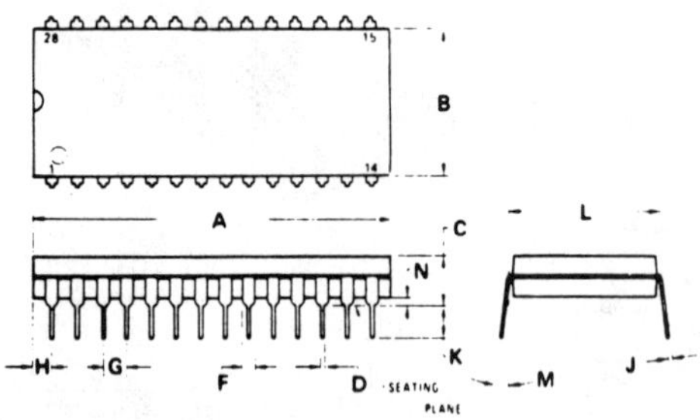

DIM	MILLIMETERS		INCHES	
	MIN	MAX	MIN	MAX
A	36.45	37.21	1.435	1.465
B	13.72	14.22	0.540	0.560
C	3.94	5.08	0.155	0.200
D	0.36	0.56	0.014	0.022
F	1.02	1.52	0.040	0.060
G	2.54 BSC		0.100 BSC	
H	1.65	2.16	0.065	0.085
J	0.20	0.38	0.008	0.015
K	2.92	3.43	0.115	0.135
L	15.24 BSC		0.600 BSC	
M	0°	15°	0°	15°
N	0.51	1.02	0.020	0.040

NOTES:
1. POSITIONAL TOLERANCE OF LEADS (D), SHALL BE WITHIN 0.25mm(0.010) AT MAXIMUM MATERIAL CONDITION, IN RELATION TO SEATING PLANE AND EACH OTHER.
2. DIMENSION L TO CENTER OF LEADS WHEN FORMED PARALLEL.
3. DIMENSION B DOES NOT INCLUDE MOLD FLASH.

28-PIN PACKAGES (CONTINUED)

CERDIP PACKAGE
CASE 733

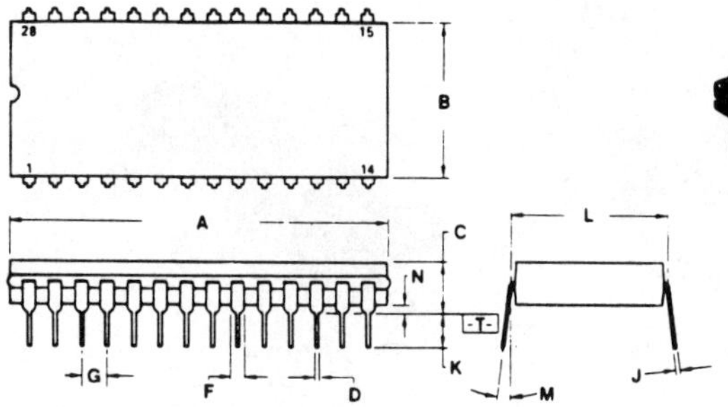

NOTES:
1. DIM -A- IS DATUM.
2. POSITIONAL TOL FOR LEADS:
   ⌖ | Ø 0.25 (0.010) Ⓜ | T | A Ⓜ
3. -T- IS SEATING PLANE.
4. DIM A AND B INCLUDES MENISCUS.
5. DIM -L- TO CENTER OF LEADS WHEN FORMED PARALLEL.
6. DIMENSIONING AND TOLERANCING PER ANSI Y14.5, 1973.

	MILLIMETERS		INCHES	
DIM	MIN	MAX	MIN	MAX
A	36.45	37.85	1.435	1.490
B	12.70	15.37	0.500	0.605
C	4.06	5.84	0.160	0.230
D	0.38	0.56	0.015	0.022
F	1.27	1.65	0.050	0.065
G	2.54 BSC		0.100 BSC	
J	0.20	0.30	0.008	0.012
K	2.54	4.06	0.100	0.160
L	15.24 BSC		0.600 BSC	
M	5°	15°	5°	15°
N	0.51	1.27	0.020	0.050

CHIP CARRIER
CASE 753

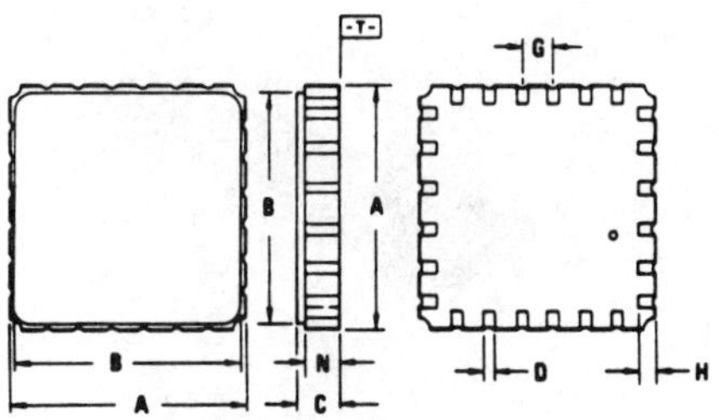

NOTES:
1. DIMENSION A IS DATUM. (2 PLACES)
2. -T- IS GUAGE PLANE.
3. POSITIONAL TOLERANCE FOR TERMINALS (D): 24 PLACES
   ⌖ 0.25 (0.010) Ⓜ | T | A Ⓢ
4. DIMENSIONING AND TOLERANCING PER ANSI Y14.5, 1973.

	MILLIMETERS		INCHES	
DIM	MIN	MAX	MIN	MAX
A	9.91	10.41	0.390	0.410
B	9.78	9.90	0.385	0.390
C	1.63	1.93	0.064	0.076
D	0.39	0.63	0.015	0.025
G	1.27 BSC		0.050 BSC	
H	0.77	1.01	0.030	0.040
N	1.40	1.65	0.055	0.065

MECHANICAL DATA (CONTINUED)

40-PIN PACKAGES

CERAMIC PACKAGE
CASE 715

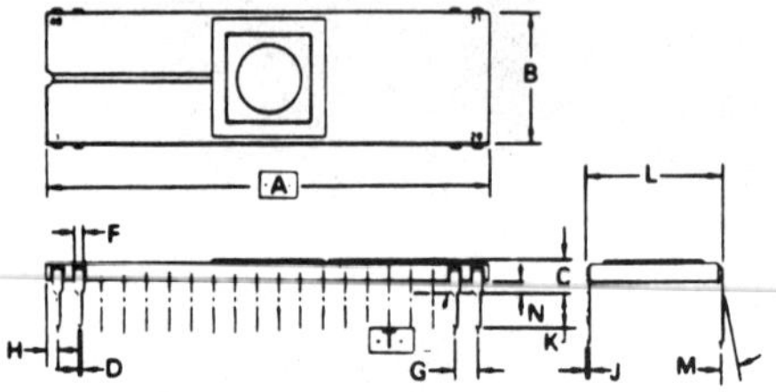

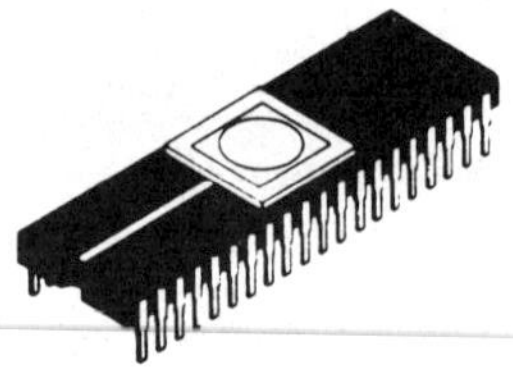

DIM	MILLIMETERS		INCHES	
	MIN	MAX	MIN	MAX
A	50.29	51.31	1.980	2 020
B	14.63	15.49	0.576	0.610
C	3.18	5.08	0.125	0.200
D	0.38	0.53	0.015	0.021
F	0.76	1.52	0.030	0.060
G	254 BSC		0.100 BSC	
J	0.20	0.33	0.008	0.013
K	2.54	4.57	0.100	0.180
L	14.99	15.65	0.590	0.616
M	–	10°	–	10°
N	1.02	1.52	0.040	0.060

NOTES:
1. DIMENSION -A- IS DATUM.
2. POSITIONAL TOLERANCE FOR LEADS:

⊕ 0.25 (0.010) Ⓜ T A Ⓜ

3. -T- IS SEATING PLANE.
4. DIMENSION "L" TO CENTER OF LEADS WHEN FORMED PARALLEL.
5. DIMENSIONING AND TOLERANCING PER ANSI Y14.5, 1973.

PLASTIC PACKAGE
CASE 711

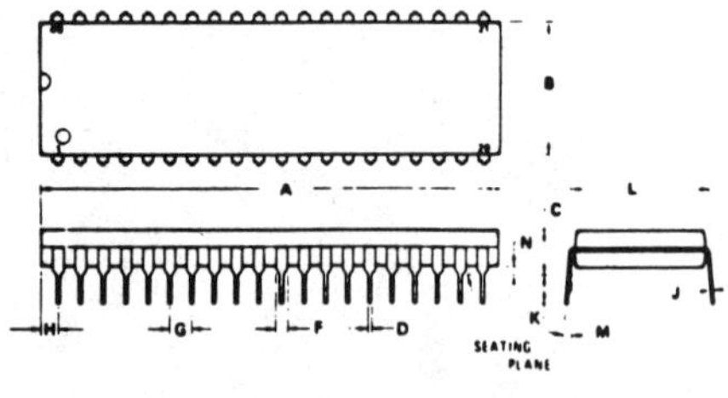

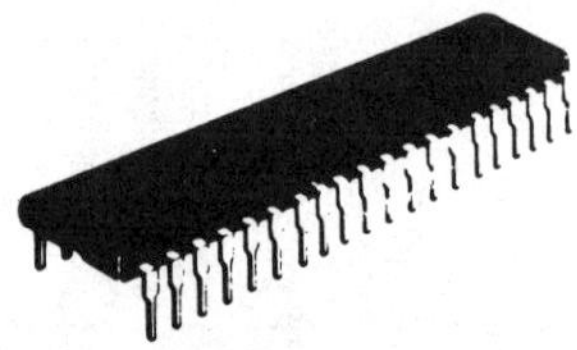

NOTES:
1. POSITIONAL TOLERANCE OF LEADS (D), SHALL BE WITHIN 0.25 mm (0.010) AT MAXIMUM MATERIAL CONDITION, IN RELATION TO SEATING PLANE AND EACH OTHER.
2. DIMENSION L TO CENTER OF LEADS WHEN FORMED PARALLEL.
3. DIMENSION B DOES NOT INCLUDE MOLD FLASH.

DIM	MILLIMETERS		INCHES	
	MIN	MAX	MIN	MAX
A	51.69	52.45	2.035	2.065
B	13.72	14.22	0.540	0.560
C	3.94	5.08	0.155	0.200
D	0.36	0.56	0.014	0.022
F	1.02	1.52	0.040	0.060
G	2.54 BSC		0.100 BSC	
H	1.65	2.16	0.065	0.085
J	0.20	0.38	0.008	0.015
K	2.92	3.43	0.115	0.135
L	15.24 BSC		0.600 BSC	
M	0°	15°	0°	15°
N	0.51	1.02	0.020	0.040

MECHANICAL DATA (CONTINUED)

40-PIN PACKAGES (CONTINUED)

CERDIP PACKAGE
CASE 734

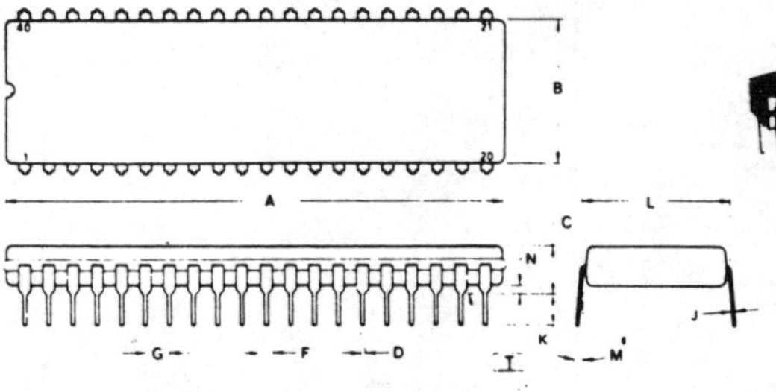

NOTES
1. DIM -A- IS DATUM.
2. POSITIONAL TOLERANCE FOR LEADS. ◆ Ø 0.25(0.010) Ⓜ T A Ⓜ
3. T IS SEATING PLANE.
4. DIM L TO CENTER OF LEADS WHEN FORMED PARALLEL.
5. DIMENSIONS A AND B INCLUDE MENISCUS.
6. DIMENSIONING AND TOLERANCING PER ANSI Y14.5, 1973

DIM	MILLIMETERS MIN	MILLIMETERS MAX	INCHES MIN	INCHES MAX
A	51.31	53.24	2.020	2.096
B	12.70	15.49	0.500	0.610
C	4.06	5.84	0.160	0.230
D	0.38	0.56	0.015	0.022
F	1.27	1.65	0.050	0.065
G	2.54 BSC		0.100 BSC	
J	0.20	0.30	0.008	0.012
K	3.18	4.06	0.125	0.160
L	15.24 BSC		0.600 BSC	
M	5°	15°	5°	15°
N	0.51	1.27	0.020	0.050

MECHANICAL DATA (CONTINUED)

48-PIN PACKAGES

CERAMIC PACKAGE
CASE 740

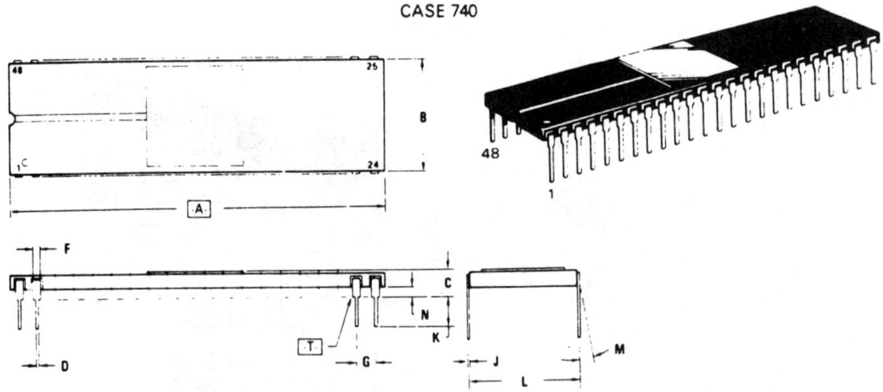

	MILLIMETERS		INCHES	
DIM	MIN	MAX	MIN	MAX
A	60.35	61.57	2.376	2.424
B	14.63	15.34	0.576	0.604
C	3.05	4.32	0.120	0.160
D	0.381	0.533	0.015	0.021
F	0.762	1.397	0.030	0.055
G	2.54 BSC		0.100 BSC	
J	0.203	0.330	0.008	0.013
K	2.54	4.19	0.100	0.165
L	14.99	15.65	0.590	0.616
M	0°	10°	0°	10°
N	1.016	1.524	0.040	0.060

NOTES:
1. DIMENSION -A- IS DATUM.
2. POSTIONAL TOLERANCE FOR LEADS:
   ⌖ Ø 0.25 (0.010) Ⓜ T A Ⓜ
3. -T- IS SEATING PLANE.
4. DIMENSION "L" TO CENTER OF LEADS WHEN FORMED PARALLEL.
5. DIMENSIONING AND TOLERANCING PER ANSI Y14.5, 1973.

MECHANICAL DATA (CONCLUDED)

64-PIN PACKAGES

CERAMIC PACKAGE
CASE 746

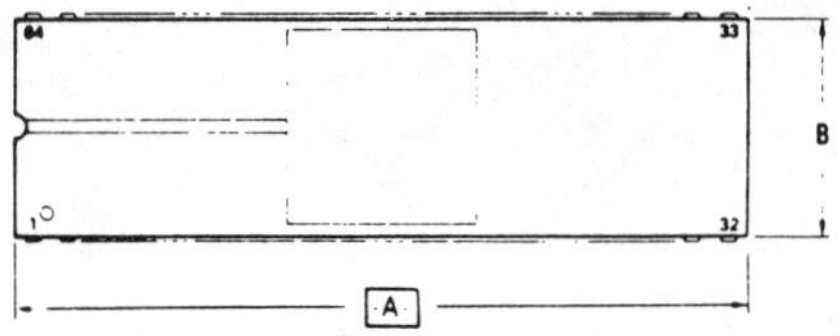

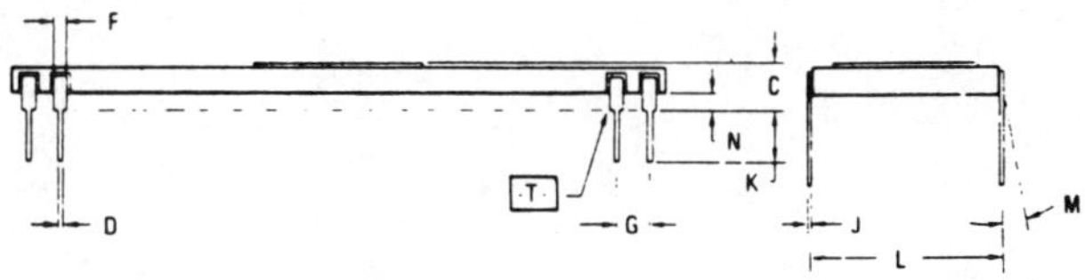

NOTES:
1. DIMENSION -A- IS DATUM.
2. POSITIONAL TOLERANCE FOR LEADS:
   ⊕ 0.25 (0.010) Ⓜ T A Ⓜ
3. -T- IS SEATING PLANE.
4. DIMENSION "L" TO CENTER OF LEADS WHEN FORMED PARALLEL.
5. DIMENSIONING AND TOLERANCING PER ANSI Y14.5, 1973.

DIM	MILLIMETERS MIN	MILLIMETERS MAX	INCHES MIN	INCHES MAX
A	80.52	82.04	3.170	3.230
B	22.25	22.96	0.876	0.904
C	3.05	4.32	0.120	0.170
D	0.38	0.53	0.015	0.021
F	0.76	1.40	0.030	0.055
G	2.54 BSC		0.100 BSC	
J	0.20	0.33	0.008	0.013
K	2.54	4.19	0.100	0.165
L	22.61	23.11	0.890	0.910
M	–	10°	–	10°
N	1.02	1.52	0.040	0.060

APPENDIX C

Essential electrical characteristics of each of the major IC families according to the manufacturing process used. To illustrate these electrical characteristics, the data for a specific microprocessor representative of the IC family are reproduced here.

The TTL (Transistor-Transistor Logic) type microprocessors are designed for a 5 Volt power supply. The power dissipation is within 800–2000 mW, relatively insensitive to operating frequency. The clock frequency is within the 6 to 14 MHz range and the Register to Register add time is 85 to 150 nsec/data word.

The TTL microprocessor electrical characteristics are exemplified by the 2901–4-bit slice.

The CMOS (Complementary Metal-Oxide-Semiconductor) type microprocessors offer the advantage of a wide operating voltage range: 1.4 V to 15 V. They have a very low power dissipation (10 μW for the Texas Instruments 4-bit microcomputer TMS1000C/TMS1200C). The clock frequency is within the 600 kHz–11 MHz range.

The CMOS microprocessor electrical characteristics are exemplified by the MC141000 Family–4-bit microcomputer.

The HMOS (Hybrid Metal-Oxide-Semiconductor) type microprocessors require a 5 V power supply. Their power dissipation is relatively low. The clock frequency is within 3 to 10 MHz and HMOS permits a high density of components on-chip and a relatively high speed.

The HMOS microprocessor electrical characteristics are exemplified by the 8049A–8-bit microcomputer.

The NMOS (Negative Metal-Oxide-Semiconductor) type microprocessors offer the advantage of a wide operating voltage range (from −3 V to 12 V). They have a medium power dissipation, relatively low clock frequency and a relative low speed.

The NMOS microprocessor electrical characteristics are exemplified by the 8080A–8-bit CPU.

The PMOS (Positive Metal-Oxide Semiconductor) type microprocessors offer a very wide range of operating voltages (from −12 V to 17 V). They have a medium power dissipation (generally a few hundred mW), low clock frequency (generally, a few hundred kHz) and very low speed.

The PMOS microprocessor electrical characteristics are exemplified by the μCOM45 Family (except μPD652)–4-bit microcomputer.

The P^2CMOS (Positive Positive Complementary Metal-Oxide-Semiconductor) type microprocessors combine the functional capabilities of NMOS with the low power requirements of CMOS. The required supply voltage is 3 V to 12 V, the average power dissipation is 50 mW and the clock frequency up to 4 MHz.

The P^2CMOS microprocessor electrical characteristics are exemplified by the NSC800–8-bit CPU.

The I^2L (Integrated Injected Logic) type microprocessors have 500 mA supply current requirement and need a current regulator supply. They feature a moderate power dissipation (500 mW), and moderately high speed.

The I^2L microprocessor electrical characteristics are exemplified by the SPB9900A–16-bit CPU.

The I^3L (Isoplanar Integrated Injected Logic) microprocessors require 350 mA supply current. They have a relatively high power dissipation. This technology offers a very high speed (300 ns for one instruction execution time @ 20 MHz clock frequency) and a very high density of on-chip components.

The I^3L microprocessor electrical characteristics are exemplified by the F9445–16-bit CPU.

MAXIMUM RATINGS (Above which the useful life may be impaired)

Storage Temperature	−65°C to +150°C
Temperature (Ambient) Under Bias	−55°C to +125°C
Supply Voltage to Ground Potential	−0.5 V to +7.0 V
DC Voltage Applied to Outputs for HIGH Output State	−0.5 V to +V_{CC} max.
DC Input Voltage	−0.5 V to +5.5 V
DC Output Current, Into Outputs	30 mA
DC Input Current	−30 mA to +5.0 mA

ELECTRICAL CHARACTERISTICS OVER OPERATING RANGE (Unless Otherwise Noted)
(Group A, Subgroups 1, 2, and 3)

Parameters	Description	Test Conditions (Note 1)			Min.	Typ. (Note 2)	Max.	Units
V_{OH}	Output HIGH Voltage	V_{CC} = MIN. V_{IN} = V_{IH} or V_{IL}		I_{OH} = −1.6mA Y_0, Y_1, Y_2, Y_3	2.4			Volts
				I_{OH} = −1.0mA, C_{n+4}	2.4			
				I_{OH} = −800μA, OVR, $\overline{P}$	2.4			
				I_{OH} = −600μA, F_3	2.4			
				I_{OH} = −600μA $RAM_{0,3}$, $Q_{0,3}$	2.4			
				I_{OH} = −1.6mA, $\overline{G}$	2.4			
I_{CEX}	Output Leakage Current for F = 0 Output	V_{CC} = MIN., V_{OH} = 5.5V V_{IN} = V_{IH} or V_{IL}					250	μA
V_{OL}	Output LOW Voltage	V_{CC} = MIN., V_{IN} = V_{IH} or V_{IL}	Y_0, Y_1, Y_2, Y_3	I_{OL} = 20mA (COM'L)			0.5	Volts
				I_{OL} = 16mA (MIL)			0.5	
			$\overline{G}$, F = 0	I_{OL} = 16mA			0.5	
			C_{n+4}	I_{OL} = 10mA			0.5	
			OVR, $\overline{P}$	I_{OL} = 8.0mA			0.5	
			F_3, $RAM_{0,3}$, $Q_{0,3}$	I_{OL} = 6.0mA			0.5	
V_{IH}	Input HIGH Level	Guaranteed input logical HIGH voltage for all inputs (Note 7)			2.0			Volts
V_{IL}	Input LOW Level	Guaranteed input logical LOW voltage for all inputs (Note 7)					0.8	Volts
V_I	Input Clamp Voltage	V_{CC} = MIN., I_{IN} = −18mA					−1.5	Volts
I_{IL}	Input LOW Current	V_{CC} = MAX., V_{IN} = 0.5V		Clock, $\overline{OE}$			−0.36	mA
				A_0, A_1, A_2, A_3			−0.36	
				B_0, B_1, B_2, B_3			−0.36	
				D_0, D_1, D_2, D_3			−0.72	
				I_0, I_1, I_2, I_6, I_8			−0.36	
				I_3, I_4, I_5, I_7			−0.72	
				$RAM_{0,3}$, $Q_{0,3}$ (Note 4)			−0.8	
				C_n			−3.6	
I_{IH}	Input HIGH Current	V_{CC} = MAX., V_{IN} = 2.7V		Clock, $\overline{OE}$			20	μA
				A_0, A_1, A_2, A_3			20	
				B_0, B_1, B_2, B_3			20	
				D_0, D_1, D_2, D_3			40	
				I_0, I_1, I_2, I_6, I_8			20	
				I_3, I_4, I_5, I_7			40	
				$RAM_{0,3}$, $Q_{0,3}$ (Note 4)			100	
				C_n			200	
I_I	Input HIGH Current	V_{CC} = MAX., V_{IN} = 5.5V					1.0	mA
I_{OZH} I_{OZL}	Off State (High Impedance) Output Current	V_{CC} = MAX.	Y_0, Y_1, Y_2, Y_3	V_O = 2.4V			50	μA
				V_O = 0.5V			−50	
			$RAM_{0,3}$ $Q_{0,3}$	V_O = 2.4V (Note 4)			100	
				V_O = 0.5V (Note 4)			−800	
I_{OS}	Output Short Circuit Current (Note 3)	V_{CC} = MAX. + 0.5V, V_O = 0.5V		$Y_0, Y_1, Y_2, Y_3, \overline{G}$	−30		−85	mA
				C_{n+4}	−30		−85	
				OVR, $\overline{P}$	−30		−85	
				F_3	−30		−85	
				$RAM_{0,3}$, $Q_{0,3}$	−30		−85	
I_{CC}	Power Supply Current (Note 6)	V_{CC} = MAX.	COM'L and MIL	T_A = 25°C		160	250	mA
			COM'L Only	T_A = 0°C to +70°C			265	
				T_A = +70°C			220	
			MIL Only	T_C = −55°C to +125°C			280	
				T_C = +125°C			198	

Notes: 1. For conditions shown as MIN. or MAX., use the appropriate value specified under Electrical Characteristics for the applicable device type.
2. Typical limits are at V_{CC} = 5.0V, 25°C ambient and maximum loading.
3. Not more than one output should be shorted at a time. Duration of the short circuit test should not exceed one second.
4. These are three-state outputs internally connected to TTL inputs. Input characteristics are measured with I_{678} in a state such that the three-state output is OFF.
5. "MIL" = Am2901XM, DM, FM. "COM'L" = Am2901XC, PC, DC
6. Worst case I_{CC} is at minimum temperature.
7. These input levels provide zero noise immunity and should only be tested in a static, noise-free environment.

MAXIMUM RATINGS (Voltages referenced to V_{SS})

Rating	Symbol	Value	Unit
DC Supply Voltage	V_{DD}	−0.5 to +6.5	V
Input Voltage, All Inputs	V_{in}	−0.5 to V_{DD}+0.5	V
DC Current Drain per Pin, All Inputs	I	10	mA
DC Current Drain, V_{DD} Pin	I	250	mA
DC Current Drain, V_{SS} Pin	I	20	mA
Operating Temperature Range	T_A	−40 to +85	°C
Storage Temperature Range	T_{stg}	−65 to +150	°C
Total Power Dissipation	P_D	See Figure 1	mW

This device contains circuitry to protect the inputs against damage due to high static voltages or electric fields; however, it is advised that normal precautions be taken to avoid application of any voltage higher than maximum rated voltages to this high-impedance circuit. For proper operation it is recommended that V_{in} and V_{out} be constrianed to the range $V_{SS} \leq (V_{in}$ or $V_{out}) \leq V_{DD}$. Although internal pulldown resistors are used, it is recommended that all unused inputs be tied to an appropriate logic level (e.g., either V_{SS} or V_{DD}).

RECOMMENDED OPERATING CONDITIONS (V_{SS} = 0)

Parameter	Symbol	Vaue	Unit
DC Supply Voltage High Speed Clock Full Range Operation	V_{DD}	+4.75 to +6.0 +3.0 to +6.0	V
Clock Frequency V_{DD} = 5.0 V ±5% V_{DD} = 3.0 V Min.	f_{CLK}	DC to 600 DC to 200	kHz

MC141000/MC141200 ONLY

DC ELECTRICAL CHARACTERISTICS (V_{DD} = +5 Vdc ±5%, V_{SS} = 0 V, unless otherwise noted)

Characteristic	Symbol	T_A = 0 to 70°C			T_A = −40 to 85°C		Unit
		Min	Typ	Max	Min	Max	
Input Current — K Inputs and INIT V_{in} = 5.0 V V_{in} = 0.0 V	I_{in}	35 —	100 −0.005	165 −1.0	30 −0.005	215 −1.0	μA
Input Voltage	V_{IL} V_{IH}	— 3.6	— —	1.4 —	— 3.6	1.4 —	V
Output Drive — R and O Outputs (V_{OL} = 0.4 V, V_{DD} = 4.75 V) (V_{OH} = 2.4 V) — See Figure 1	I_{OL} I_{OH}	— −15	— —	1.6 —	— —	1.5 —	mA
Average Supply Current	I_{DD}	—	—	See Figure 6	—	See Figure 6	mA
Static Supply Current	I_{DD}	—	—	See Figure 2	—	See Figure 2	μA
Oscillator Frequency (V_{DD} = 4.75 V)	f_{CLK}	DC	—	600	DC	600	kHz
Internal Oscillator Frequency for R_{ext} = 25 kΩ	f_{CLK}	400	500	600	400	600	kHz

MC141099 ONLY

DC ELECTRICAL CHARACTERISTICS (V_{DD} = +5.0 Vdc, V_{SS} = 0 V, T_A = 25°C unless otherwise noted)

Characteristic	Symbol	Min	Typ	Max	Unit
Input Current — K Inputs and INIT (V_{in} = 5.0 V) (V_{in} = 0.0 V)	I_{in}	65 —	100 −0.00001	140 −0.3	μA
Input Current — I Inputs (V_{in} = 5.0 V) (V_{in} = 0.0 V)	I_{in}	— —	−0.00001 −0.00001	0.3 −0.3	μA
Input Voltage — I Inputs	V_{IL} V_{IH}	— 2.0	— —	0.8 —	V
Input Voltage — Other Inputs	V_{IL} V_{IH}	— 3.6	— —	1.4 —	V
Output Drive — R and O Outputs (V_{OH} = 2.4 V) (See Figure 1) (V_{OL} = 0.4 V)	I_{OH} I_{OL}	−15 1.6	— —	— —	mA
Output Drive — PA and PC Outputs (V_{OH} = 4.6 V) (V_{OL} = 0.4 V)	I_{OH} I_{OL}	−100 100	— —	— —	μA
Average Supply Current	I_{DD}	—	—	See Figure 6	μA
Static Supply Current	I_{DD}	—	—	See Figure 2	μA
Oscillator Frequency (V_{DD} = 4.75 V)	f_{CLK}	DC	—	600	kHz
Internal Oscillator Frequency for R_{ext} = 25 kΩ	f_{CLK}	400	500	600	kHz
Input Capacitance — K Inputs and INIT	C_{in}	—	—	7.5	pF
Input Capacitance — Clock Input	C_{in}	—	—	30	pF

8049H/8039HL

ABSOLUTE MAXIMUM RATINGS*

Ambient Temperature Under Bias .... 0°C to 70°C
Storage Temperature .... -65°C to + 150°C
Voltage On Any Pin With Respect
to Ground .... -0.5V to +7V
Power Dissipation .... 1.5 Watt

**NOTICE: Stresses above those listed under "Absolute Maximum Ratings" may cause permanent damage to the device. This is a stress rating only and functional operation of device at these or any other conditions above those indicated in the operational sections of this specification is not implied.*

D.C. CHARACTERISTICS (T_A = 0°C to 70°C, V_{CC} = V_{DD} = 5V ± 10%, V_{SS} = 0V)

Symbol	Parameter	Limits			Unit	Test Conditions
		Min	Typ	Max		
V_{IL}	Input Low Voltage (All Except $\overline{RESET}$, X1, X2)	-.5		.8	V	
V_{IL1}	Input Low Voltage ($\overline{RESET}$, X1, X2)	-.5		.6	V	
V_{IH}	Input High Voltage (All Except XTAL1, XTAL2, $\overline{RESET}$)	2.0		V_{CC}	V	
V_{IH1}	Input High Voltage (X1, X2, $\overline{RESET}$)	3.8		V_{CC}	V	
V_{OL}	Output Low Voltage (BUS)			.45	V	I_{OL} = 2.0 mA
V_{OL1}	Output Low Voltage ($\overline{RD}$, $\overline{WR}$, $\overline{PSEN}$, ALE)			.45	V	I_{OL} = 1.8 mA
V_{OL2}	Output Low Voltage (PROG)			.45	V	I_{OL} = 1.0 mA
V_{OL3}	Output Low Voltage (All Other Outputs)			.45	V	I_{OL} = 1.6 mA
V_{OH}	Output High Voltage (BUS)	2.4			V	I_{OH} = -400 μA
V_{OH1}	Output High Voltage ($\overline{RD}$, $\overline{WR}$, $\overline{PSEN}$, ALE)	2.4			V	I_{OH} = -100 μA
V_{OH2}	Output High Voltage (All Other Outputs)	2.4			V	I_{OH} = -40 μA
I_{L1}	Input Leakage Current (T1, $\overline{INT}$)			± 10	μA	$V_{SS} \leq V_{IN} \leq V_{CC}$
I_{LI1}	Input Leakage Current (P10-P17, P20-P27, EA, $\overline{SS}$)			-500	μA	$V_{SS} + .45 \leq V_{IN} \leq V_{CC}$
I_{LO}	Output Leakage Current (BUS, TO) (High Impedance State)			± 10	μA	$V_{SS} + .45 \leq V_{IN} \leq V_{CC}$
I_{DD}	V_{DD} Supply Current		5	10	mA	
I_{DD} + I_{CC}	Total Supply Current		50	100	mA	

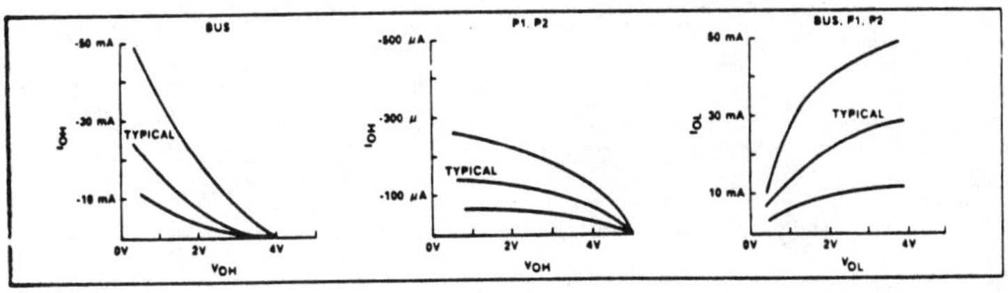

8049H/8039HL

A.C. CHARACTERISTICS (T_A = 0°C to 70°C, V_{CC} = V_{DD} = 5V ± 10%, V_{SS} = 0V)

Symbol	Parameter	f (t_{CY}) (Note 3)	11 MHz Min	11 MHz Max	Unit	Conditions (Note 1)
t_{LL}	ALE Pulse Width	7/30 t_{CY} -170	150		ns	
t_{AL}	Addr Setup to ALE	1/5 t_{CY} -110	160		ns	
t_{LA}	Addr Hold from ALE	1/15 t_{CY} -40	50		ns	
t_{CC1}	Control Pulse Width ($\overline{RD}$, $\overline{WR}$)	1/2 t_{CY} -200	480		ns	
t_{CC2}	Control Pulse Width ($\overline{PSEN}$)	2/5 t_{CY} -200	350		ns	
t_{DW}	Data Setup before $\overline{WR}$	13/30 t_{CY} -200	390		ns	
t_{WD}	Data Hold after $\overline{WR}$	1/15 t_{CY} -50	40		ns	(Note 2)
t_{DR}	Data Hold ($\overline{RD}$, $\overline{PSEN}$)	1/10 t_{CY} -30	0	110	ns	
t_{RD1}	$\overline{RD}$ to Data in	2/5 t_{CY} -200		350	ns	
t_{RD2}	$\overline{PSEN}$ to Data in	3/10 t_{CY} -200		210	ns	
t_{AW}	Addr Setup to $\overline{WR}$	2/5 t_{CY} -150	400		ns	
t_{AD1}	Addr Setup to Data ($\overline{RD}$)	23/30 t_{CY} -250		800	ns	
t_{AD2}	Addr Setup to Data ($\overline{PSEN}$)	3/5 t_{CY} -250		570	ns	
t_{AFC1}	Addr Float to $\overline{RD}$, $\overline{WR}$	2/15 t_{CY} -40	140		ns	
t_{AFC2}	Addr Float to $\overline{PSEN}$	1/30 t_{CY} -40	10		ns	
t_{LAFC1}	ALE to Control ($\overline{RD}$, $\overline{WR}$)	1/5 t_{CY} -75	200		ns	
t_{LAFC2}	ALE to Control ($\overline{PSEN}$)	1/10 t_{CY} -75	60		ns	
t_{CA1}	Control to ALE ($\overline{RD}$, $\overline{WR}$, $\overline{PROG}$)	1/15 t_{CY} -40	50		ns	
t_{CA2}	Control to ALE ($\overline{PSEN}$)	4/15 t_{CY} -40	320		ns	
t_{CP}	Port Control Setup to $\overline{PROG}$	2/15 t_{CY} -80	100		ns	
t_{PC}	Port Control Hold to $\overline{PROG}$	4/15 t_{CY} -200	160		ns	
t_{PR}	$\overline{PROG}$ to P2 Input Valid	6/10 t_{CY} -120		700	ns	
t_{PF}	Input Data Hold from $\overline{PROG}$	1/10 t_{CY}	0	140	ns	
t_{DP}	Output Data Setup	2/5 t_{CY} -150	400		ns	
t_{PD}	Output Data Hold	1/10 t_{CY} -50	90		ns	
t_{PP}	$\overline{PROG}$ Pulse Width	7/10 t_{CY} -250	700		ns	
t_{PL}	Port 2 I/O Setup to ALE	4/15 t_{CY} -200	160		ns	
t_{LP}	Port 2 I/O Hold to ALE	1/10 t_{CY} -100	40		ns	
t_{PV}	Port Output from ALE	3/10 t_{CY} +100		510	ns	
t_{CY}	Cycle Time	1/(f_{XTAL} × 15)	1.36		μs	
t_{OPRR}	T0 Rep Rate	3/15 t_{CY}	270		ns	

Notes:

1. Control Outputs CL = 80 pF
   BUS Outputs CL = 150pF
2. BUS High Impedance Load 20pF
3. Calculated values will be equal to or better than published 8049 values. f(t_{CY}) assumes 50% duty cycle on X1, X2
4. Interrupt pin must remain low for at least 3 t_{CY} to ensure proper operation

8080A/8080A-1/8080A-2

ABSOLUTE MAXIMUM RATINGS*

Temperature Under Bias . . . . 0°C to +70°C
Storage Temperature . . . . -65°C to +150°C
All Input or Output Voltages
With Respect to V_{BB} . . . . -0.3V to +20V
V_{CC}, V_{DD} and V_{SS} With Respect to V_{BB} -0.3V to +20V
Power Dissipation 1.5W

****NOTICE:** Stresses above those listed under "Absolute Maximum Ratings" may cause permanent damage to the device. This is a stress rating only and functional operation of the device at these or any other conditions above those indicated in the operational sections of this specification is not implied. Exposure to absolute maximum rating conditions for extended periods may affect device reliability.*

D.C. CHARACTERISTICS (T_A = 0°C to 70°C, V_{DD} = +12V ±5%, V_{CC} = +5V ±5%, V_{BB} = −5V ±5%, V_{SS} = 0V; unless otherwise noted)

Symbol	Parameter	Min.	Typ.	Max.	Unit	Test Condition
V_{ILC}	Clock Input Low Voltage	$V_{SS}-1$		$V_{SS}+0.8$	V	
V_{IHC}	Clock Input High Voltage	9.0		$V_{DD}+1$	V	
V_{IL}	Input Low Voltage	$V_{SS}-1$		$V_{SS}+0.8$	V	
V_{IH}	Input High Voltage	3.3		$V_{CC}+1$	V	
V_{OL}	Output Low Voltage			0.45	V	I_{OL} = 1.9mA on all outputs,
V_{OH}	Output High Voltage	3.7			V	I_{OH} = -150μA.
$I_{DD(AV)}$	Avg. Power Supply Current (V_{DD})		40	70	mA	Operation
$I_{CC(AV)}$	Avg. Power Supply Current (V_{CC})		60	80	mA	T_{CY} = .48 μsec
$I_{BB(AV)}$	Avg. Power Supply Current (V_{BB})		.01	1	mA	
I_{IL}	Input Leakage			±10	μA	$V_{SS} \leq V_{IN} \leq V_{CC}$
I_{CL}	Clock Leakage			±10	μA	$V_{SS} \leq V_{CLOCK} \leq V_{DD}$
I_{DL} [2]	Data Bus Leakage in Input Mode			-100 -2.0	μA mA	$V_{SS} \leq V_{IN} \leq V_{SS}+0.8V$ $V_{SS}+0.8V \leq V_{IN} \leq V_{CC}$
I_{FL}	Address and Data Bus Leakage During HOLD			+10 -100	μA	$V_{ADDR/DATA} = V_{CC}$ $V_{ADDR/DATA} = V_{SS} + 0.45V$

CAPACITANCE (T_A = 25°C, V_{CC} = V_{DD} = V_{SS} = 0V, V_{BB} = -5V)

Symbol	Parameter	Typ.	Max.	Unit	Test Condition
C_ϕ	Clock Capacitance	17	25	pf	f_c = 1 MHz
C_{IN}	Input Capacitance	6	10	pf	Unmeasured Pins
C_{OUT}	Output Capacitance	10	20	pf	Returned to V_{SS}

NOTES:

1. The RESET signal must be active for a minimum of 3 clock cycles.
2. ΔI supply / ΔT_A = -0.45%/°C.

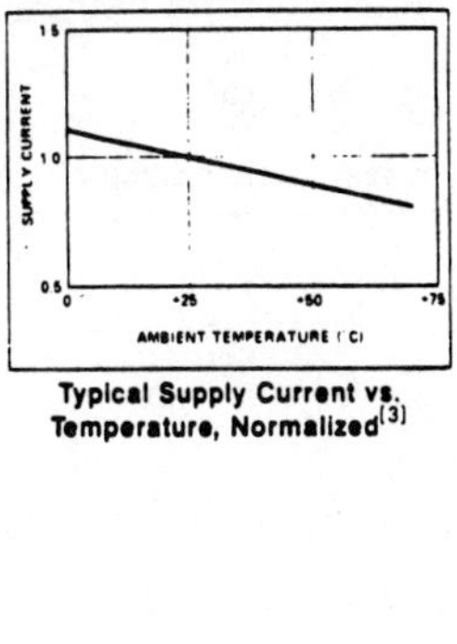

Typical Supply Current vs. Temperature, Normalized[3]

A.C. CHARACTERISTICS (8080A)

(T_A = 0°C to 70°C, V_{DD} = +12V ±5%, V_{CC} = +5V ±5%, V_{BB} = −5V ±5%, V_{SS} = 0V; unless otherwise noted)

Symbol	Parameter	Min.	Max.	-1 Min.	-1 Max.	-2 Min.	-2 Max.	Unit	Test Condition
t_{CY}[3]	Clock Period	0.48	2.0	0.32	2.0	0.38	2.0	μsec	
t_r, t_f	Clock Rise and Fall Time	0	50	0	25	0	50	nsec	
$t_{\phi 1}$	ϕ_1 Pulse Width	60		50		60		nsec	
$t_{\phi 2}$	ϕ_2 Pulse Width	220		145		175		nsec	
t_{D1}	Delay ϕ_1 to ϕ_2	0		0		0		nsec	
t_{D2}	Delay ϕ_2 to ϕ_1	70		60		70		nsec	
t_{D3}	Delay ϕ_1 to ϕ_2 Leading Edges	80		60		70		nsec	
t_{DA}	Address Output Delay From ϕ_2		200		150		175	nsec	C_L = 100 pF
t_{DD}	Data Output Delay From ϕ_2		220		180		200	nsec	
t_{DC}	Signal Output Delay From ϕ_2 or ϕ_2 (SYNC, WR, WAIT, HLDA)		120		110		120	nsec	C_L = 50 pF
t_{DF}	DBIN Delay From ϕ_2	25	140	25	130	25	140	nsec	
t_{DI}[1]	Delay for Input Bus to Enter Input Mode		t_{DF}		t_{DF}		t_{DF}	nsec	
t_{DS1}	Data Setup Time During ϕ_1 and DBIN	30		10		20		nsec	
t_{DS2}	Data Setup Time to ϕ_2 During DBIN	150		120		130		nsec	
t_{DH}[1]	Data Holt time From ϕ_2 During DBIN	[1]		[1]		[1]		nsec	
t_{IE}	INTE Output Delay From ϕ_2		200		200		200	nsec	C_L = 50 pF
t_{RS}	READY Setup Time During ϕ_2	120		90		90		nsec	
t_{HS}	HOLD Setup Time to ϕ_2	140		120		120		nsec	
t_{IS}	INT Setup Time During ϕ_2	120		100		100		nsec	
t_H	Hold Time From ϕ_2 (READY, INT, HOLD)	0		0		0		nsec	
t_{FD}	Delay to Float During Hold (Address and Data Bus)		120		120		120	nsec	
t_{AW}	Address Stable Prior to WR	[5]		[5]		[5]		nsec	C_L = 100 pF: Address, Data C_L = 50 pF: $\overline{WR}$,HLDA,DBIN
t_{DW}	Output Data Stable Prior to WR	[6]		[6]		[6]		nsec	
t_{WD}	Output Data Stable From WR	[7]		[7]		[7]		nsec	
t_{WA}	Address Stable From WR	[7]		[7]		[7]		nsec	
t_{HF}	HLDA to Float Delay	[8]		[8]		[8]		nsec	
t_{WF}	WR to Float Delay	[9]		[9]		[9]		nsec	
t_{AH}	Address Hold Time After DBIN During HLDA	−20		−20		−20		nsec	

A.C. TESTING LOAD CIRCUIT

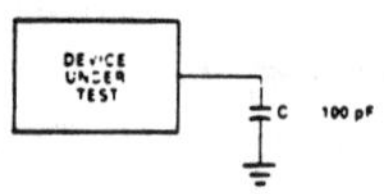

DC CHARACTERISTICS

$T_a = -10°C$ to $+70°C$, $V_{GG} = -8.0V \pm 10\%$

PARAMETER	SYMBOL	LIMITS			UNIT	TEST CONDITIONS
		MIN	TYP	MAX		
Input Voltage High	V_{IH}	0		-1.6	V	Ports A, C, D, $\overline{INT}$, RESET
Input Voltage Low	V_{IL_1}	-4.5		V_{GG}	V	Ports A, $\overline{INT}$, RESET
	V_{IL_2}	-4.5		-35	V	Ports C, D
Clock Voltage High	$V_{\phi H}$	0		-0.6	V	CL_0 Input, External Clock
Clock Voltage Low	$V_{\phi L}$	-5.0		V_{GG}	V	CL_0 Input, External Clock
Input Leakage Current High	I_{LIH}			+10	μA	Ports A, C, D, $\overline{INT}$, RESET $V_I = -1V$
Input Leakage Current Low	I_{LIL_1}			-10	μA	Ports A, C, D, $\overline{INT}$, RESET $V_I = -9V$
	I_{LIL_2}			-30	μA	Ports C, D, $V_I = -35V$
Clock Input Leakage Current High	$I_{L\phi H}$			+200	μA	CL_0 Input, $V_{\phi H} = 0V$
Clock Input Leakage Current Low	$I_{L\phi L}$			-200	μA	CL_0 Input, $V_{\phi L} = -9V$
Output Voltage High	V_{OH_1}			-1.0	V	Ports C, D, $I_{OH} = -2$ mA
	V_{OH_2}			-2.5	V	Ports E, F, G, $I_{OH} = -10$ mA
Output Leakage Current Low	I_{LOL_1}			-10	μA	Ports C through G, $V_O = -9V$
	I_{LOL_2}			-30	μA	Ports C through G, $V_O = -35V$
Supply Current	I_{GG}		-12	-24	mA	

CAPACITANCE

$T_a = 25°C$

PARAMETER	SYMBOL	LIMITS			UNIT	TEST CONDITIONS
		MIN	TYP	MAX		
Input Capacitance	C_I			15	pF	f = 1 MHz
Output Capacitance	C_O			15	pF	
Input/Output Capacitance	C_{IO}			15	pF	

AC CHARACTERISTICS

$T_a = -10°C$ to $+70°C$; $V_{GG} = -8.0V \pm 10\%$

PARAMETER	SYMBOL	LIMITS			UNIT	TEST CONDITIONS
		MIN	TYP	MAX		
Oscillator Frequency	f	100		180	KHz	
Rise and Fall Times	t_r, t_f	0		0.3	μs	External Clock
Clock Pulse Width High	$t_{\phi W_H}$	2.0		8.0	μs	
Clock Pulse Width Low	$t_{\phi W_L}$	2.0		8.0	μs	

CLOCK WAVEFORM

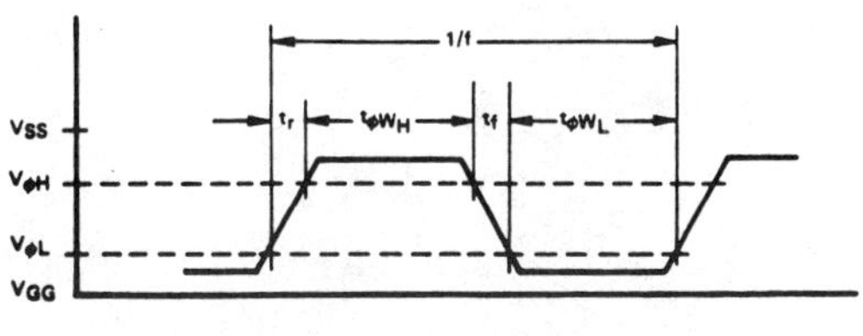

Absolute Maximum Ratings

Storage Temperature .... -65°C to +150°C
Voltage on Any Pin
with Respect to Ground .... -0.3 to V_{CC} + 0.3V
Lead Temperature (Soldering 10 Seconds) .... 300°C
Power Dissipation .... 1 W

DC Electrical Characteristics

T_A = 0 to 70°C, V_{CC} = 5V ± 10%, GND = 0V

Symbol	Parameter	Min	Typ	Max	Unit	Test Conditions
V_{IH}	Logical 1 Input Voltage	0.7 V_{CC}		V_{CC}	V	
V_{IL}	Logical 0 Input Voltage	0		0.3 V_{CC}	V	
V_{HY}	Hysteresis at RESET IN input		0.5		V	V_{CC} = 5V
V_{OH1}	Logical 1 Output Voltage	2.4			V	I_{OUT} = -1.0 mA
V_{OH2}	Logical 1 Output Voltage	V_{CC}-0.5			V	I_{OUT} = -10 μA
V_{OL1}	Logical 0 Output Voltage	0		0.4	V	I_{OL} = 2 mA
V_{OL2}	Logical 0 Output Voltage	0		0.1	V	I_{OUT} = 10 μA
I_{IL}	Input Leakage Current	-1.0		1.0	μA	$0 \le V_{IN} \le V_{CC}$
I_{OL}	Output Leakage Current	-1.0		1.0	μA	$0 \le V_{IN} \le V_{CC}$
I_{CC}	Active Supply Current		10		mA	I_{OUT} = 0, f_{XIN} = 5MHz

AC Electrical Characteristics

T_A = 0 to 70°C, V_{CC} = 5V ± 10%, GND = 0V

Symbol	Parameter	Min	Typ	Max	Unit	Test Conditions (Note 1)
t_X	Period at XIN and XOUT pins		200		ns	
t	Period at "CLK" output (= 2 tx)		400		ns	
$t_{S(AD)}$	Address Set Up Time		$\frac{t}{2} - 75$		ns	
$t_{H(ADL)}$	Address (0-7) Hold Time		$\frac{t}{2} - 75$		ns	
$t_{W(ALE)}$	ALE Width		$\frac{t}{2} - 50$		ns	
t_{DAR}	Falling Edge of ALE to Leading Edge of Read Strobe		$\frac{t}{2} - 50$		ns	
$t_{ACC(RD)}$	Read Access Time (Note 2)		$\frac{3t}{2} - 125$		ns	Add t/2 for Memory Read Cycles
$t_{W(RD)}$	Read Strobe Width During Op-code Fetch. (Note 2)		t - 50		ns	Add t/2 for Memory Read Cycles
$t_{H(ADH)1}$	Address (8-15) Hold Time During Opcode Fetch.		0		ns	
$t_{S(WD)}$	Write Data Setup Time		$\frac{t}{2} - 75$		ns	
$t_{H(WD)}$	Write Data Hold Time		$\frac{t}{2} - 75$		ns	
t_{DAW}	Falling Edge of ALE to Leading Edge of WR		t - 100		ns	
$t_{W(WR)}$	Write Strobe Width (Note 2)		t - 50		ns	
$t_{H(ADH)2}$	Address (8-15) Hold Time during Memory or I-O Read and Write		$\frac{t}{2} - 75$		ns	
$t_{D(RFSH)}$	Falling Edge of ALE to Leading Edge of Refresh Strobe (Note 2)		$\frac{3t}{2} + 50$		ns	
$t_{W(RFSH)}$	Refresh Strobe Width		2t - 75		ns	
$t_{D(WAIT)}$	Falling Edge of ALE to Wait Input Valid		t		ns	
$t_{W(WAIT)}$	Wait Input Width		$\frac{t}{2} + 50$		ns	
$t_{D(I)}$	Falling Edge of ALE to $\overline{INTR}$, $\overline{NMI}$, $\overline{RST}$ A-C, $\overline{PS}$ & $\overline{BREQ}$ Inputs Valid (Note 2)		t			Add t for Opcode Fetch Cycles
$t_{W(I)}$	Width of $\overline{INTR}$, $\overline{NMI}$, $\overline{RST\ A\text{-}C}$, $\overline{PS}$ & $\overline{BREQ}$ Inputs		$\frac{t}{2} + 50$		ns	
t_{DAI}	Falling Edge of ALE to Interrupt Acknowledge Strobe		$\frac{t}{2} - 50$		ns	
$t_{W(INTA)}$	Interrupt Acknowledge Strobe Width (Note 2)		3t - 50		ns	*(Figure 10)*
$t_{D(BACK)1}$	Falling Edge of ALE to Falling Edge of BUS Acknowledge Out-put (Note 2)		$\frac{5t}{2} + 50$		ns	Add t for Opcode Fetch Cycles
$t_{D(BACK)2}$	Rising Edge of Bus Request to Rising Edge of BUS Acknowledge	$\frac{t}{2}$		$\frac{3t}{2} + 50$	ns	*(Figure 6)*
t_{DPA}	Rising Edge of Power Save to Falling Edge of ALE	$\frac{t}{2}$		$\frac{3t}{2} + 50$	ns	*(Figure 12)*
t_S (ALE)	Setup Time		$\frac{t}{2} - 75$		ns	

Notes: 1. Output Capacitive loading = 100pf; 2. Add t for each WAIT state

ELECTRICAL SPECIFICATIONS

SBP 9900A Recommended Operating Conditions, Unless Otherwise Noted I_{CC} = 500 mA

		MIN	NOM	MAX	UNIT
Supply current, I_{CC}		450	500	550	mA
High-level output voltage, V_{OH}				5.5	V
Low-level output current, I_{OL}				20	mA
Clock frequency, f_{clock}		0		2	MHz
Width of clock pulse, t_w	High (67%) (V_{IH} = 2.5 V max)	330			ns
	Low (33%)	170			
Clock rise time, t_r			10		ns
Clock fall time, t_f			10		ns
Setup time, t_{su} (see Figure 24)	$\overline{HOLD}$	210†			ns
	READY	140†			
	D0 – D15	85†			
	CRUIN	65†			
	$\overline{INTREQ}$	25†			
	IC0 – IC3	25†			
Hold time, t_h (see Figure 24)	$\overline{HOLD}$	25†			ns
	READY	65†			
	D0 – D15	65†			
	CRUIN	55†			
	$\overline{INTREQ}$	90†			
	IC0 – IC3	90†			
Operating free-air temperature, T_A	SBP 9900 M/N	−55		125	°C
	SBP 9900E	−40		85	

†Rising edge of clock pulse is reference.

SBP 9900A Electrical Characteristics (Over Recommended Operating Free-Air Temperature Range, Unless Otherwise Noted)

PARAMETER			TEST CONDITIONS†	MIN	TYP‡	MAX	UNIT
V_{IH}	High-level input voltage			2			V
V_{IL}	Low-level input voltage					0.8	V
V_{IK}	Input clamp voltage		I_{CC} = MIN, I_I = −12 mA			−1.5	V
I_{OH}	High-level output current		I_{CC} = 500 mA, V_{IH} = 2 V, V_{IL} = 0.8 V, V_{OH} = 5.5 V			400	µA
V_{OL}	Low-level output voltage		I_{CC} = 500 mA, V_{IH} = 2 V, V_{IL} = 0.8 V, I_{OL} = 20 mA			0.4	V
I_I	Input current	Clock	I_{CC} = 500 mA, V_I = 2.4 V		480	600	µA
		All other inputs			240	300	

†For conditions shown as MAX, use the appropriate value specified under recommended operating conditions.
‡All typical values are at I_{CC} = 500 mA, T_A = 25°C.

SBP 9900A Switching Characteristics, (I_{CC} = NOM, T_A = Recommended Operating Free-Air Temperature Range Unless Otherwise Noted) See *Figures 22* And *23*.

PARAMETER	FROM	TO	TEST CONDITIONS	MIN	TYP‡	MAX	UNIT
f_{max}	MAXIMUM CLOCK FREQUENCY		C_L = 150 pF, R_L = 280 Ω	2			MHz
t_{PLH} or t_{PHL}	CLOCK	ADDRESS BUS (A0 – A14)			170	225	ns
t_{PLH} or t_{PHL}	CLOCK	DATA BUS (D0 – D15)			170	265	ns
t_{PLH} or t_{PHL}	CLOCK	WRITE ENABLE ($\overline{WE}$)			220	295	ns
t_{PLH} or t_{PHL}	CLOCK	CYCLE END ($\overline{CYCEND}$)			170	225	ns
t_{PLH} or t_{PHL}	CLOCK	DATA BUS IN (DBIN)			190	250	ns
t_{PLH} or t_{PHL}	CLOCK	MEMORY ENABLE ($\overline{MEMEN}$)			155	205	ns
t_{PLH} or t_{PHL}	CLOCK	CRU CLOCK (CRUCLK)			187	280	ns
t_{PLH} or t_{PHL}	CLOCK	CRU DATA OUT (CRUOUT)			210	265	ns
t_{PLH} or t_{PHL}	CLOCK	HOLD ACKNOWLEDGE (HLDA)			320	410	ns
t_{PLH} or t_{PHL}	CLOCK	WAIT			155	210	ns
t_{PLH} or t_{PHL}	CLOCK	INSTRUCTION ACQUISITION (IAQ)			155	210	ns

‡All typical values are at 25°C.

Guaranteed Operating Ranges

Part Number	Supply Voltage (V_{CC})			Ambient Temperature
	Min	Typ	Max	
F9445DC	4.75 V	5.0 V	5.25 V	0 to +75°C
F9445DM	4.5 V	5.0 V	5.5 V	−55 to +125°C

DC Characteristics

(Over guaranteed operating ranges unless other wise noted.)
I_{INJ}(min) = 300 mA; I_{INJ}(max) = 400 mA

Symbol	Characteristic	Min	Typ	Max	Unit	Test Conditions
V_{IH}	Input HIGH Voltage	2.0			V	Guaranteed Input HIGH Voltage
V_{IL}	Input LOW Voltage			0.8	V	Guaranteed Input LOW Voltage
V_{CD}	Input Clamp Diode Voltage		−0.9	−1.5	V	V_{CC} = Min, I_{IN} = −18 mA, I_{INJ} = 300 mA
V_{OH}	Output HIGH Voltage; RUN, CARRY, INTON, SYN, $\overline{STRBD}$, $\overline{BUSREQ}$, $\overline{STRBA}$, O_0, O_1, $\overline{M}$	2.4	3.4		V	V_{CC} = Min, I_{OH} = −400 μA, I_{INJ} = 300 mA
V_{OH}	Output HIGH Voltage; $\overline{IB}_{(0\text{-}15)}$, $\overline{W}$	2.4	3.4		V	V_{CC} = Min, I_{OH} = −1.0 mA, I_{INJ} = 300 mA
V_{OL}	Output LOW Voltage		0.25	0.5	V	V_{CC} = Min, I_{OL} = 8.0 mA, I_{INJ} = 300 mA
I_{IH}	Input HIGH Current; $\overline{DCHREQ}$, $\overline{INTREQ}$, CLK, $\overline{MR}$, RDYA, RDYD, $\overline{ABORT}$, $\overline{CONREQ}$, BUSGNT		2.0	40	μA	V_{CC} = Max, V_{IN} = 2.7 V, I_{INJ} = 300 mA
I_{IH}	Input HIGH Current; $\overline{IB}_{(0\text{-}15)}$ (3-state)		5.0	100	μA	V_{CC} = Max, V_{IN} = 2.7 V, I_{INJ} − 300 mA
I_{IH}	Input HIGH Current; All inputs			1.0	mA	V_{CC} = Max, V_{IN} = 5.5 V, I_{INJ} = 300 mA
I_{IL}	Input LOW Current; All Inputs		−0.21	−0.4	mA	V_{CC} = Max, V_{IN} = 0.4 V, I_{INJ} = 300 mA
I_{OZH}	Output OFF State (High Impedance) Current $\overline{IB}_{0\text{-}15}$, W			100	μA	V_{CC} = Max, V_{OUT} = 2.4 V, I_{INJ} = 300 mA
I_{OZL}	Output OFF State (High Impedance) Current $\overline{IB}_{0\text{-}15}$		−210	−400	μA	V_{CC} = Max, V_{OUT} = 0.4 V, I_{INJ} = 300 mA
I_{OZL}	Output OFF State (High Impedance) Current; $\overline{W}$			−100	μA	V_{CC} = Max, V_{OUT} = 0.5 V, I_{INJ} = 300 mA
I_{OSH}	Output Short Circuit Current; All Outputs Except $\overline{BUSLOCK}$	−15		−100	mA	V_{CC} = Max, V_{OUT} = 0.0 V, I_{INJ} = 300 mA*
I_{LOH}	Output Leakage; $\overline{BUSLOCK}$			1.0	mA	V_{CC} = Min, V_{OH} = 5.25 V, I_{INJ} = 300 mA
I_{CC}	Supply Current		160		mA	V_{CC} = Max, I_{INJ} = 300 mA
V_{INJ}	Injector Voltage		1.3		V	I_{INJ} = 400 mA

*Not more than one output to be shorted at a time.

AC Characteristics

T_A = 0 to 75°C; V_{CC} = 4.75 to 5.25 V; I_{INJ} = 300 mA; C_L = 15 pF.
Input conditioning: Rise Time = 6 ns; Fall time = 6 ns; Amplitude = 0 to 3 V

Refer to *Symbol Conventions* at the end of this data sheet for explanation of the timing parameter symbols.

Symbol	Characteristic	Min	Typ	Max	Unit
TC(O)	Propagation delay, CLK to O_0, O_1, $\overline{M}$		60		ns
TC(S)	Propagation delay, CLK to SYN		30		ns
TC(W)	Propagation delay, CLK to $\overline{W}$		70		ns
TC(W)z	Propagation delay, CLK to $\overline{W}$ going 3-state		70		ns
TC(IBA)	Propagation delay, CLK to $\overline{IB}_{(0\text{-}15)}$, address		60		ns
TC(IBA)z	Propagation delay, CLK to $\overline{IB}_{(0\text{-}15)}$, address, going 3-state (read cycle)		35		ns
TC(SA)	Propagation delay, CLK to $\overline{STRBA}$		30		ns
TC(IBD)	Propagation delay, CLK to $\overline{IB}_{(0\text{-}15)}$, data out		75		ns
TC(IBD)z	Propagation delay, CLK to $\overline{IB}_{(0\text{-}15)}$, data out, going three-state		35		ns
TC(SD)	Propagation delay, CLK to $\overline{STRBD}$		25		ns
TRA(C) TC(RA)x	Setup time, RDYA to CLK Hold time, CLK to RDYA		3 10		ns ns
TRD(C) TC(RD)x	Setup time, RDYD to CLK Hold time, CLK to RDYD		2 10		ns ns
TIBD(C)	Setup time, $\overline{IB}_{(0\text{-}15)}$, data in, to CLK (read or fetch cycle)		75		ns
TC(IBD)x	Hold time, $\overline{IB}_{(0\text{-}15)}$, data in, after CLK (read or fetch cycle)		25		ns
TREQ(C)	Setup time, $\overline{INTREQ}$, $\overline{DCHREQ}$, $\overline{CONREQ}$, $\overline{MR}$ to CLK, all are the same timing relative to S5		15		ns
TC(REQ)x	Hold time, $\overline{INTREQ}$, $\overline{DCHREQ}$, $\overline{CONREQ}$, $\overline{MR}$ after CLK, all are the same timing		20		ns
TDRh(C)	Data channel ($\overline{DCHREQ}$) off setup time from CLK (to finish data-channel cycle)		100		ns
TA(C)	Setup time, $\overline{ABORT}$ to CLK		30		ns
TC(BL)1	Propagation delay, CLK to $\overline{BUSLOCK}$ going LOW		35		ns
TBG(C) TC(BG)x	Setup time, BUSGNT to CLK Hold time, CLK after BUSGNT		10 10		ns ns
TC(R)	Propagation delay, CLK to RUN		80		ns
TC(CY)	Propagation delay, CLK to CARRY		50		ns
TC(INT)	Propagation delay, CLK to INTON		50		ns
TC(BR)	Propagation delay, CLK to $\overline{BUSREQ}$		40		ns

NUMERICAL INDEX OF MICROPROCESSORS AND MICROCOMPUTERS